BOUTIQUE
BEER

BOUTIQUE BEER

500 of the World's Finest Craft Brews

jacqui
small

Ben McFarland

First published in 2013 by
Jacqui Small LLP
An imprint of Aurum Press
74–77 White Lion Street
London N1 9PF

Publisher: Jacqui Small
Associate Publisher: Joanna Copestick
Managing Editor: Lydia Halliday
Designer: Ashley Western
Editor: Martyn Cornell
Project Editor: Sian Parkhouse
Picture Researcher: Alexandra Labbe Thompson
Production: Peter Colley

ISBN: 9781906417864

A catalogue record for this book is available from the
British Library.

2015 2014 2013
10 9 8 7 6 5 4 3 2 1

Printed in China

CONTENTS

What is boutique beer?

There are more than 500 boutique beers in this book, each made with the same four key ingredients. But every single one is different.

What declares them distinct is not merely the ingredients used, nor is it the method by which they are brewed. What makes each beer in this book unique is that, behind each and every one is an individual.

Peer into the frothy head of each boutique beer and you will discover that an awful lot is going on in there beyond hops, grain, yeast and water. Beneath the surface there are individual ideas, passions, friendships, problems, desires, disappointments, beliefs and more.

Whether made by an Australian who brews using boiling hot Fijian boulders; a bipolar depressive who picks hops in an Amsterdam garden; or a former underpants model who has breathed life back into a 9,000 year-old brewing recipe; each beer is a liquid legacy of the complicated lives of others.

And just as people's lives are shaped by what and who is around them, so too are the beers that adorn the next 218 pages. These boutique beers are not brewed in a vacuum, they reflect the cultural context of a particular place and the people that live there.

A beer reveals a lot about its native surroundings and there is no better way to get to truly know a beer than experiencing it at source, meeting those that make it and those for whom it is brewed, visiting the pubs and bars where it is drunk and eating the food that it complements.

It is the same with all drink. In my early 20s, I studied in Grenoble, France, when I had lots of time and very little to do or worry about. I spent a lot of time playing pétanque against pensioners. The local speciality was Chartreuse, a potent green liqueur distilled up in the mountains by monks. We all drank it as if it was going out of fashion.

When I returned to London, where Chartreuse had never been in fashion, none of my British buddies, or indeed any pensioners, were willing to drink it with me. For me, Chartreuse conjures up magical memories of carefree days. For others it conjures up mouthwash.

Similarly, I simply did not understand Gueuze until I saw Lambics foaming forth from fusty barrels in Brussels nor did I truly understand the underplayed anarchy of Walloon brewing until I was sat sipping a Silly Saison in a village called Silly

having, just the day before, driven through a small village called Dave with a man called Dave who, rather inconveniently for this anecdote, was very serious and didn't do anything very silly at all.

Similarly, before going to Cologne, I mistakenly thought I knew Kölsch: a light-coloured, easy-drinking hybrid beer served in small glasses, and only brewed in Cologne. But then I discovered Kölsch's true character first-hand, within the city's famous brewpubs.

Roped into endless round buying with strangers, I realised the small 20cl 'stangen' were core to Cologne's famous conviviality and, surrounded by every stratum of stangen-swigging society, it dawned on me why Karl Marx had deemed Cologne immune to revolution: the workers, he said, drank too much beer with the bosses.

It slowly occurred to me that the accessible and easy-going beer was the city's culture in a very small glass; that it's the local dialect and a philosophy: a relaxed way of being, a shoulder-shrugging acceptance that 'Hätte noch immer jot jejange' ('It will be all right in the end').

Back in London, Kölsch actually tastes different now. It tastes better. It's not just a dizzy blonde, there is genuine depth to it. My drinking buddies who have not been to Cologne still tell me I'm wrong. But I keep telling them, like a Vietnam vet, you weren't there man.

Of course, if this was a wine book, this would be the bit where I would begin to pontificate luxuriantly about terroir. But such a dreamy, ethereal concept has never quite taken root with beer. It's a wine term and beer's not going to use it just because wine does. Beer's better than that.

While the provenance of hops, barley, water and yeast is clearly integral to a particular beer's personality, it's only a small part of what makes beer so enticing. Beer is not just geography and geology, its secret is not simply in the soil nor are its interesting bits only in the air.

Beer is more profound. It takes you beyond mere terroir. It's everything. It's geography, art, science, politics, religion, history and nature . . . it's intoxicating liquid life. When you drink a beer, you don't merely drink the ingredients or the methods that make it.

More inspiring and intoxicating is the story; it's the people and personalities that shape it; it's their stories . . . it's the romance; it's the drinking in of a dream.

Enjoy the book.
Cheers,
Ben

THE KNOWLEDGE

EVALUATING AND TASTING BEERS

You can't be a real brewery today unless you have laboratory analysis. It helps if you have a white-coated scientist with spectacles and a clipboard, it's useful if you have a microscope or a few Erlenmeyer flasks and some vacuum pumps, but at the very least you need laboratory analysis.

Most people don't have any of that. All they have is their senses. Instead of prodding beer with pipettes and pouring it into petri dishes, we rely on our individual sensory perception to assess beer's freshness, its fidelity to style, balance, flavour, consistency and complexity.

When evaluating a beer, you should use all your senses apart from touch. If you start putting fingers in your pint, people will think you are weird. And rightly so. So don't do it.

Hearing? Yes, lend beer your ears. The sound of a cork being popped or a beer glugging into a glass is a highly evocative one while the 'pffft' of a bottle being opened reveals much about the beer's carbonation. And if you put a glass of beer to your ear, you can hear the sea. It won't have much to say about beer though. You'll also have a wet ear.

Next, use your eyes. Have a look at it. Evaluate the head. Hold up the glass to the natural light, preferably against a white backdrop, and give it a proper look. It's not just colour and clarity you're looking for here, it's the way it moves and keeps its head.

Now it's time to bring out the big guns; your nose, the most important instrument in your analytical arsenal and not just there to keep your sunglasses centred on your face. Right at the top of your nose is your olfactory epithelium, a centimetre-squared strip of nerve tissue that analyses and identifies particular odours.

Olfactory experts reckon that as much as 95% of what we perceive as taste is actually smell: this is easily demonstrated if you take a swig of a beer while pinching your nostrils.

There are thousands of flavour compounds present in beer that your tongue won't tell you about. Each of beer's four core ingredients creates a wealth of aromas that can contribute to a complex bouquet, never mind any additional ingredients that may bring their own nasal impact to the party.

These aromas can evolve according to everything from the height of the liquid in the glass to the temperature of the beer. To get new smell sensations, place your (clean) hand over the rim of the glass and give the beer a swirl, wake up the aromas and take small sniffs.

As well as detecting all of beer's aromatic delights, the sense of smell is also crucial in recognising faults in a beer, flavours that shouldn't be there – like butterscotch, wet cardboard, skunky sulphurous smells or, perhaps worse, absolutely nothing at all.

Having appreciated beer's aromas, it's now to explore its flavour. Flavour is a combination of aroma and taste and can be discovered if you drink it. Unless you've got such bad muscular co-ordination that you miss your mouth entirely, hold your glass upside down, or you use a fork to do it, then chances are, you know how to drink.

Unlike with wine tasting, you should really swallow rather than spit when tasting beer. Not only is it more enjoyable but many say that because the receptors of bitterness, an essential element in beer, can be found at the back of the tongue (with sweetness at the tip and sourness and saltiness filed on either side), it is only by swallowing that you can get a beer's full flavour.

Mind, today the general consensus is that the entire tongue can sense all of these tastes more or less equally, so when you taste beer, slowly circulate it around the tongue, giving it time to get to know the beer. Take another sip and it will tell you more, not just about the flavours but about the texture too. Does it sit on the tongue? Does it feel oily, thin or sharp? Does it fill the mouth or dissipate quickly?

And don't forget to breathe and open up that retro-nasal passage – essential in assessing flavour. Inside the mouth, at the back of the palate, is an opening to those olfactory receptors first reached during appreciation of the aroma.

This was originally a safety net to warn us about poisonous or rotten food. It now sends another important aromatic message to your brain. So before you swallow, aerate the beer, by puckering the lips and breathing in like a backward whistle.

And then, as with life, there's the finish. How does the beer end? Does it fall off a cliff, or stay longer than the mother-in-law? What are the flavours and the feelings that it leaves you with?

Right: Beer's original flavour wheel, designed by Dr Morten Meilgaard in the 1970s, contained 122 separate flavours. This re-invention of the wheel is less scientific, more style specific . . . and designed to make you thirsty.

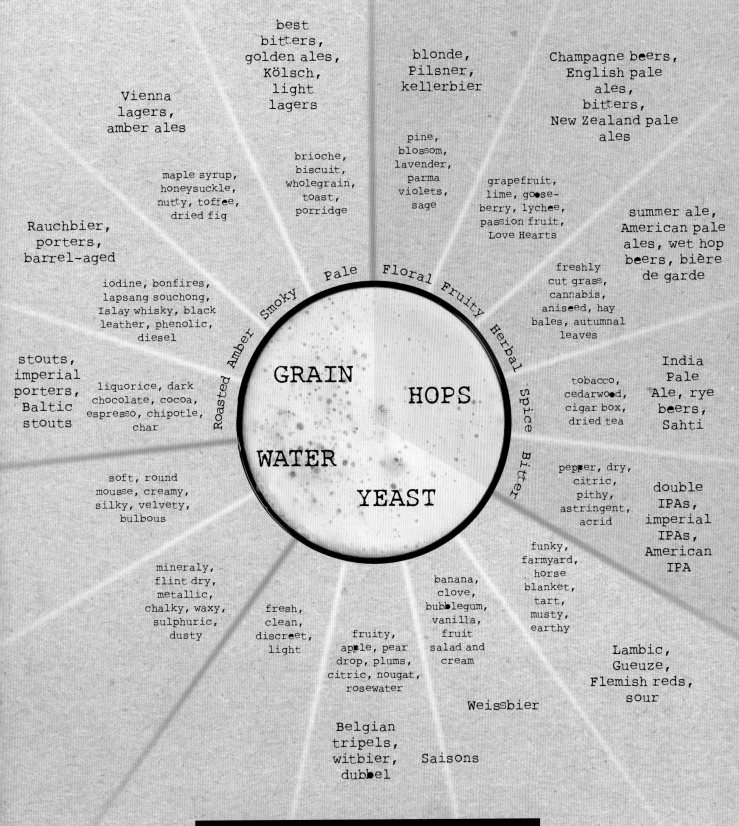

best bitters, golden ales, Kölsch, light lagers

blonde, Pilsner, kellerbier

Champagne beers, English pale ales, bitters, New Zealand pale ales

Vienna lagers, amber ales

pine, blossom, lavender, parma violets, sage

brioche, biscuit, wholegrain, toast, porridge

maple syrup, honeysuckle, nutty, toffee, dried fig

grapefruit, lime, gooseberry, lychee, passion fruit, Love Hearts

summer ale, American pale ales, wet hop beers, bière de garde

Rauchbier, porters, barrel-aged

iodine, bonfires, lapsang souchong, Islay whisky, black leather, phenolic, diesel

freshly cut grass, cannabis, aniseed, hay bales, autumnal leaves

Smoky   Pale   Floral   Fruity

Roasted   Amber   Herbal

Spice

stouts, imperial porters, Baltic stouts

liquorice, dark chocolate, cocoa, espresso, chipotle, char

GRAIN

HOPS

WATER

YEAST

tobacco, cedarwood, cigar box, dried tea

India Pale Ale, rye beers, Sahti

Bitter

pepper, dry, citric, pithy, astringent, acrid

double IPAs, imperial IPAs, American IPA

soft, round mousse, creamy, silky, velvety, bulbous

funky, farmyard, horse blanket, tart, musty, earthy

mineraly, flint dry, metallic, chalky, waxy, sulphuric, dusty

banana, clove, bubblegum, vanilla, fruit salad and cream

Lambic, Gueuze, Flemish reds, sour

fresh, clean, discreet, light

fruity, apple, pear drop, plums, citric, nougat, rosewater

Weissbier

Belgian tripels, witbier, dubbel

Saisons

The Flavour Wheel

OFF-FLAVOURS

If a beer tastes a bit funny, and not in an amusing way, chances are there are some off-flavours in there. Some may be unpleasant while others may be entirely acceptable yet unwelcome in certain styles. Here's an idea of what they may taste like and where they come from:

Skunky/sulphur

Lightstruck beer. Skunky, sulphuric smell created by alpha acids in hops reacting badly to sunlight, like a Gremlin reacting to water. Common in beers bottled in clear and green glass.

Apple/cut grass

This comes from acetaldehyde, a hangover-inducing chemical caused, in most cases, when the yeast hasn't finished fermenting.

Vinegar

Favoured in Flemish Reds and sour beers, this cheek-contorting acetic acid is a funky foe to most brewers, caused by bacterial contamination in the brewhouse or, if you're in a pub, just as likely from infected pipes or lines.

Butter/butterscotch

This is caused by diacetyl, a chemical created just before yeast begins to ferment which, ideally, should be re-absorbed by yeast cells during the full fermentation process. A double-edged sword in brewing, in small quantities it can be beneficial to beer's flavour, especially in ales and stouts. But in lighter tasting beers, such as lagers, it makes a mess of things.

HINDERED FERMENTATION

Barnyard

Earthy, horse-sweat flavour that smells a bit like a damp cellar. Great in spontaneously fermented beers such as Lambics. In other styles? Less so.

Cheesy

If you're getting ripe Brie then it's probably to do with old hops in the beer.

Wet cardboard

The beer may be corked and oxidised. Caused by exposure to oxygen or high temperatures. Also common in beers that peaked some time ago.

Beet/cabbage

Usually killed during kilning or a vigorous boil, dimethyl sulphide (DMS) is liked in lagers but abhorred in ales.

Metal

If drinking your beer is like licking a battery, chances are it is down to old or rusty pipes in the pub/brewery or a by-product of intense malt roasting.

TEMPERATURE

The temperature at which you serve your beer makes a massive difference to the way it tastes and smells.

For this reason brewers are increasingly decorating their bottles with recommended serving temperatures, and there are general guidelines to suit each style.

4–8°C/39–45°F

lagers, helles, Kölsch, wheat Champagne beer, dunkels

8–12°C/39–45°F

pale ales, blondes, cask-conditioned bitters, Saisons, IPAs, Weissbier

12–14°C/54–57°F

Lambics and Gueuze, stouts, porters, milds, tripels, dubbels, Abbey ales

14–17°C/57–63°F

barley wines, imperial stouts, imperial porters, vintage beers

Opposite, clockwise from top left: A man in a hat and dungerees takes a sample from the fermentation tank. This man is pressing buttons and switches to make sure the beer is behaving. Gert Christiaens of Oude Beersel looking pensive. Japanese analysis.
Right: White Labs, San Diego.

HOPS

Hops are truly tremendous plants, giving beer not just its flavour but its bitterness and aroma, too. More crucially, though, they preserve the beer, adding resins that keep bacteria at bay.

While brewing beer without hops is almost inconceivable today, it took centuries for brewers to discover their benefits. Before hops became the seasoning of choice in 14th- and 15th-century Europe, brewers had flavoured their beer with a mix of different herbs known generically as 'gruit', also spelled grout, grut and grutz. Its exact composition differed according to location, but as well as moorland bushes and plants such as juniper, bog myrtle, broom, wormwood and heather, and herbs such as rosemary and sage, other countryside plants such as yarrow, ground-ivy and wild carrot all featured.

We presume, yet cannot be sure, that the Roman author and naturalist Pliny the Elder was the first person to mention hops when he wrote about *Lupus salictarius*, literally 'willow wolf', in his book *Natural History* back in 77–79AD. Many historians have assumed he was talking about hops, but he could equally have been talking about other kinds of shoots and roots.

The earliest evidence of using hops in brewing can be found in 9th-century documents written by Abbot Adalhard of the Benedictine monastery of Corbie, in Picardy, Northern France. Sadly, it does not seem that many took much notice of his texts, as it was around 300 years before hops were hailed as an ingredient in beer.

The first person to write about hops as a preservative was Abbess Hildegard of the Rupertsberg Benedictine convent near Baden, by the German Rhine, who, writing probably some time between 1150 and 1160, suggested hops as a preservative in 'drinks', including beer.

It is thought that the first commercially cultivated hops appeared in Northern Germany in the late 12th and early 13th century, but in Britain, hops were not deliberately grown until the 16th century, and it appears to have been only immigrant brewers from the Low Countries who used them at first.

Having initially been greeted with suspicion by English brewers and drinkers alike, hopped 'beer' took until the 18th century before it completely eradicated the original meaning of 'ale' as an unhopped fermented beverage made from only from water and grain.

While today British hops only make up around 1% of the world's hop production, its varieties are beloved by brewers of traditional cask ale, the earthy Fuggles and zesty Golding being the classic combination.

Hop gardens once quilted much of the English countryside, particularly in Kent, Surrey and Sussex in the south-east, and in Herefordshire and Worcestershire in the Midlands. English hop growing nearly disappeared in the 1960s and 1970s with the decline of cask ale, but now the trade is enjoying a revival, with hop merchants working closely with farmers to cultivate and create new hop varieties to compete with New World versions and to complement a wider spectrum of styles.

Germany is the largest producer of hops in terms of acreage but, since its output consists primarily of low-yielding aroma hops, it is usurped by the United States in terms of hop production. The Bavarian region of Hallertau, fifty miles north of Munich, produces 90% of all German hops, including Opal, Perle, Saphir, Spalter Select and, of course, the eponymous Hallertau varieties. Other German hops come from Tettnang near the Swiss border, Spalt in Franconia and Elbe-Saale in Eastern Germany, the latter renowned for its bittering hops.

The hop heartland of the Czech Republic is Žatec, known in German as Saaz, located 50 miles north-west of Prague, home to the noble Saaz hop, the world's most exalted variety. It classically complements pale Moravian malt and the soft brewing water synonymous with the town of Plsen.

Elsewhere in Europe, France grows Strisselspalt in Alsace; Poland cultivates the Saaz-like Lublin; while Slovenia is strongly associated with Styrian Golding, a hop that, strangely, has closer links to Fuggles than Golding.

In North America, hop cultivation prospered in New England and New York during the early 19th century but it was not long before Wisconsin and the West Coast became the most abundant source of American hops.

Today, the Pacific Northwest states of Oregon and Washington are the core hop hubs with the Willamette and Yakima valleys particularly prolific in the respective provision of aromatic and bittering varieties.

Together, they provide the C-quartet (Chinook, Cascade, Columbus and Centennial) that characterises the classic American IPA. While high-alpha hops have been traditionally more sought after, American growers have begun to steadily shift towards aroma varieties in recent years.

Southern hemisphere hop regions have emerged strongly in recent years. New Zealand is a flourishing font of interesting hops such as the fruity, floral aromatic Nelson Sauvin, Pacific Gem (bittering), Southern Cross (principally aroma) and Green Bullet (bittering).

Next door in Australia, the states of Victoria and Tasmania are the key hop regions with the archetypal, earthy Pride of Ringwood polarising opinion among Australian craft brewers.

Meanwhile, the Japanese Sorachi Ace, developed in the late 1970s, is loved by brewers looking to add lush lemon character to farmhouse ales, IPAs and wheat beers.

BITTERING HOPS VERSUS AROMA HOPS

While there has been a growing buzz about dual-purpose hops and single-hop beers in recent times, hops can still be divided simply into two categories: bittering/kettle hops and aroma hops.

Bittering hops, abundant in alpha acids, are added at the beginning of the boil for bitterness, while aroma hops, oozing with hop oils yet low in alpha acids, tend to be added towards the end of the boil or, sometimes, in the whirlpool.

Aroma hops can also be added to the fermented beer in the cask, a process known as dry-hopping, while fresh-hopping involves adding newly picked 'wet' hops to the beer.

whole leaf hops

pellet hops

HOP TEN FACTS

1 Hops climb clockwise on vines up to 15m

2 At the height of summer, hop vines grow 0.5m every week

3 The hop has male and female flowers but, like the rapper Sir Mix-A-Lot, brewers are only interested in the larger female ones

4 Eating hops can be highly toxic to some breeds of dogs

5 Hops keep their bitter resins and aromatic oils in lupulin, a yellow powder discovered deep within the petals of the hop cone

6 Hops are an aphrodisiac for men yet an inducer of sleep for females, which is rather inconvenient if you think about it

7 Henry VIII banned hops from his own ale but not from his kingdom

8 Hops are mostly picked in the summer, dry-kilned and used predominantly in pellet or whole flower form

9 Hops come from the same botanical family as cannabis

10 Hops help a beer retain its head

YEAST

You wouldn't want to kiss it, even wearing beer goggles. It looks weird and it smells funny. But yeast gives pleasure in a way that no other ingredient in beer is capable of.

Yeast is a unicellular micro-organism, belonging to the fungus family. And it's everywhere. It's on your shoe, it's on your face, it's in the air and it's even over there. There are thousands of different yeasts in the world. Brewers are only really interested in a few, however: the ones that can magically transform a sugary substance into one that is alcoholic.

Yeast devours sugars in the wort and converts them into carbon dioxide and alcohol. It furnishes the beer with an amazingly broad range of flavours, some of which are good and some are less so. An essential part of the brewer's job is to work out when yeast turns from a fermenting friend to a foe.

Yeast doesn't produce beer because it likes you. It really isn't bothered about you or your beer. It does this because it has to: eating sugars, generating energy and, along the way, giving itself all the tools to reproduce is just how yeast rolls.

That the by-product of all this ballyhoo makes the world seem a better place and the people around you appear more attractive is nothing but a bonus. If you suffer a sore head, don't blame the millions of yeast cells present in every sip of your beer. They are just doing their job, living their lives. If you are going to blame any cells for your sorry state, blame your brain cells. After all, it was their idea to go to the pub in the first place.

Brewing yeast has been getting a buzz on since the diplodocuses lived next door. It latched onto sugars present on ripening fruit and excreted alcohol that, millions of years ago, would have wiped out rival micro-organisms.

A powerful weapon in the survival of the fittest fungi, naturally occurring fermentation also got the thumbs up from ancient civilisation, too. They were all over these ripening fruits like a cheap suit: it made them feel good and helped keep them healthy.

As microscopes weren't big in ancient Mesopotamia, everyone attributed the alluring effects of foaming fermentation to the divine. Brewing vessels were set down before shrines and people prayed to pots of grain and water for days, hoping that the life-enhancing lather they dubbed 'Godisgood' would appear.

This was the original spontaneous fermentation: sometimes the good yeast weaved its magic, sometimes other, nastier yeasts thrust an enormous sour spanner in the works. Crucially, however, god's gift had a bit more to give; brewers' yeast was unique in its habit of sticking around on the surface after 'closing time'.

This meant that when a brew went well, ancient brewers could skim the shape-shifting substance from the beer and use it for the next brew. This is why the Anglo-Saxon word for yeast is 'doerst', a derivative of 'dros' meaning dregs; and why one of the Norwegian words for yeast was 'kveik', meaning kindling, which can be used to 'relight the fire' in the wort.

Gradually, through a process of elimination and trial and error, early brewsters worked out when and where, during the brewing procedure, this mysterious manna from heaven was at its happiest.

While they were becoming increasingly familiar with the phenomenon of fermentation, yeast's exact identity and role in the process remained murkier than the foam it produced.

The creators of the Reinheitsgebot, the Bavarian Purity Law of 1516, chose not to put yeast down as one of the only ingredients. They just decided to ignore it. More than 150 years later Anton van Leeuwenhoek, a Dutchman with a microscope, declared he had seen tiny yeast cells but did not quite know what to make of them.

The first person to correctly call yeast a 'sugar fungus' was a German guy called Theodore Schwann in 1837, a year before his fellow countryman, Julius Meyen, gave it its Latin name, *Saccharomyces*.

With Schwann belittled somewhat by fellow chemistry boffins who dismissed his claims, yeast's identity and role in brewing was not unveiled until the second half of the 19th century, courtesy of Louis Pasteur.

In the early 1880s, Emil Christian Hansen, a chemist working at the Carlsberg Laboratory in Copenhagen, set about trying to identify and isolate individual yeast strains that worked best with the beer.

In 1883, Hansen isolated the first pure lager yeast strain, which was named *Saccharomyces carlsbergensis*, for his employer (though today bottom-fermenting lager yeast is better known as *Saccharomyces pastorianus*). Hansen's research meant brewers could suddenly wrestle brewing from the hands of the unknown and command more control of their beer.

BOTTOM VERSUS TOP-FERMENTING YEASTS

Bottom-fermenting yeasts
Lager yeasts like to do their work slowly (up to fourteen days) in cold temperatures (5–10°C/41–50°F) and quietly, leaving very little evidence in terms of flavour. Once they have taken their last bite from the sugary smorgasbord that is the wort, lager yeast tends to drop to the bottom of the fermentation vessel.

Top-fermenting yeasts
The yeast used to brew warm-fermented ales, *Saccharomyces cerevisae*, is much more outspoken than its cold-loving counterpart. With things suitably warm (15°C/59°F and above), it whirlwinds through the wort for two to four days, dispatching fruitiness, spice and, among especially virulent strains, warming fusel alcohols.

A renowned fussy eater, it leaves some residual sugars to add sweetness and texture to the beer. After its work is done, it tends to settle to the top of the fermenting vessel, although some warm fermentation yeasts also fall to the bottom.

Munich malt

Pilsner malt

Maris Otter

GRAIN

BARLEY IS THE SOUL OF BEER

Without it, there would be no fermentable sugars and beer would be bereft of booze, thus rendering it as interesting and intoxicating as a mug of herbal tea.

But barley's role is not merely restricted to fuelling fermentation. No, barley is better than that. It sculpts the body of beer and gives it much of its mouthfeel. It is, often, the sole source of sweetness, and furnishes beer with a wealth of flavours to complement and contrast with the hops.

Carefully choosing the malts that go into the grist, also known as the grain bill, is a fundamental part of the brewer's art. The chosen blend of malted barley forms the foundation of the beer, on which brewers build using water, hops and yeast.

While roasting levels during the malting process have a huge effect on the flavour of the beer, the jury is hovering uneasily around the courtroom door as to whether specific barley varieties deliver tangible taste differences once malted, mashed and brewed.

Many British brewers marvel at the flavour produced by Maris Otter (see page 103) and argue there is a unique biscuity charm to English-grown barley, while Moravian and Bohemian malt is said to add a succulence to Czech Pilsners.

There is, however, a definite difference between two-row and six-row barley – named after the number of kernel rows at the top of the stem. Six-row is synonymous with light lagers and tends to deliver a drier profile than is obtained from the two-row barley used for pretty much everything else.

Barley is, in almost nearly every case, the base grain used in brewing, but other cereals such as rye, wheat and oats can, and increasingly do, play supporting or cameo roles in the mash tuns of creative craft brewers,

Brewing with rice and maize, however, remains the almost exclusive domain of light lager breweries, which use those ingredients to cut costs rather than create any real flavour.

MALTING, KILNING AND MILLING

Malting: Unlike bakers, brewers cannot just take barley and start brewing beer with it. To fulfil its role of fermentation, barley must undergo the malting process which begins with hoodwinking the gullible grain into thinking it is springtime.

The maltster steeps barley in vats of clean water for up to two days, draining the vat and refilling it every eight hours or so. The absorption of water activates enzymes within the barley that kickstart germination.

As the grain germinates, enzymes convert starches within the barley into sugars and nutrients that later, during fermentation, yeast are gobbled up by and turn into carbon dioxide and alcohol. Once the germinating sprout has reached approximately two thirds of the length of the barley grain, the barley is ready to be fully kiln-dried.

Kilning: At temperatures of between 80–90°C/176–194°F, kilning abruptly kills the germination and puts all the delectable sugars and nutrients to sleep in the knowledge that they will be awakened in the mash tun.

The length and intensity of the kilning will create a variety of different styles of malt, varying from very pale to deep black. Exposing barley to very high temperatures will create smoky, roasty characteristics, but will eradicate nearly all the sugars required for fermentation.

Milling: Prior to mashing, the barley is milled to produce a grist. Barley that is crushed finely will release more sugars into the wort while coarser grists will yield less. Too fine a grist and the mash will become sticky and thick, while too coarse a grist will not release enough sugars. Most brewers, therefore, opt for a compromise.

TYPES OF MALT

Malts can be loosely separated into two groups: base malts and speciality. Base malts, often light in colour yet high in fermentable sugars, make up most of the grain bill while speciality malts, ranging from light brown to black, are used in smaller quantities to influence colour and flavour.

Amber malt: Kilned like a pale malt before a second, short and intense blast of heat. Historically used as a base malt, it is now used sparingly in porters, stouts and brown ales as a speciality malt delivering a distinct nutty biscuit flavour.

Black malt: Brings nothing to the fermentation party yet, even when used in small quantities, will render beer darker than your worst nightmare and adorn it with smoky, roasty flavours.

Munich malt: Developed at the Spaten Brewery in Munich and varying in hue from light to dark brown, it can be used as both base and aromatic malts. Delivers biscuit sweetness and a maroon hue. Used in Dunkels, Marzens and Amber ales.

Smoked malt: Two-row barley smoked over beechwood. Doesn't add colour but does add lots of flavour: phenolic, smoky, bacon and leather.

Caramel and crystal malts: Caramel malts (all those pre-fixed with the term Cara) are malted in the same way but instead of being gently kiln-dried, they are taken wet into a drum, where they are robustly roasted at temperatures in excess of 100°C/212°F. This leads to the caramelisation of the sugars. They add copper colour to beer, broaden the body and endow ales and lagers with flavours of caramel, toffee and sweet malt. They also aid foam retention.

Roasted barley: Unmalted barley roasted in a drum to varying degrees. Contributes a broad spectrum of flavours and colours ranging from nuts and chocolate to coffee and toffee.

Pilsner malt: Clean, delicately kilned base malt used in the eponymous lager style, and other bottom-fermented beers.

FLOOR MALTING

Once standard yet now specialist, floor malting is the traditional method of preparing barley for brewing. The barley, after being steeped in water, is spread evenly across a hard stone floor, where it is raked twice a day to ensure it is fully oxygenated and the sprouts are not tangled. The kilning process, meanwhile, uses less heat for longer than more modern methods – up to 48 hours at 50–80°C/122–176°F. The result? A more pungent and intensely aromatic, yet more expensive, malted barley.

GLASSWARE

Far too often, a craft beer finds itself in entirely the wrong receptacle. Visually the proper glass speaks volumes about the beer it holds. The iconic imperial pint or swaying stein is a wide-mouthed clamour for carefree consumption, while a tight-lipped snifter talks of something to savour.

In addition to the emotional, ritual role of glassware, there is the physical element, too. From a sensory perspective, form should follow function. Each glass should be shaped to enhance the olfactory experience of a particular beer style, enhancing aromas and introducing them to one's nose, the sense of smell being the prime perceiver of flavour.

As oenophiles have long argued, the design and thickness of the glass affects the temperature of the liquid within. A stemmed white wine glass will keep a Weissbier chilled while a large red wine goblet, once clutched in one's hands, will slowly warm up a Baltic Porter and coax out its complexity. So opt for the more intelligent imbibing instrument.

PUB PINT GLASS
Fancy a pint? No, not really. Just look at it. It's not very fancy-able, is it? With its fat, bulbous British neck and swollen fairground-fighter lips, it has all the allure of an abandoned greenhouse. It's like pressing your lips against a bankrupt pug. But nothing says 'Back off, Brussels' more vehemently than this imperial icon, otherwise known as the Nonik glass. Ideal for: session-friendly cask-conditioned bitters and mild and bland lagers.

DIMPLED MUG
A classic brought in after World War, II the dimpled mug is making a retro comeback. Olfactory experts may not approve but let's not worry about that. Hard-wearing and ruggedly handsome, with a handle and a kaleidoscopic charisma, they are designed defiantly for drinking. Use with: pale ales, best bitters, other cask conditioned ales.

SNIFTER
More readily associated with whisky and brandy, the lips of this globular glass point inwards, politely ushering aromas towards the nostrils. Cradled in one's palms, you can warm up this after-dinner swirler and cajole out the beer's true character. Use with: strong beers such as barley wines, imperial stouts and porters, quadrupels and so on.

TULIP/THISTLE
Short of stem and wide of mouth, the swirl-friendly tulip has protruding lips which open up the floral aromatics and, on reaching the mouth, launch the liquid to the middle of the tongue. Suits strong and big-smelling beers. Use with: Belgian tripels, Bières de Garde, abbey ales, Scotch ales.

FLUTE
In terms of one's sensory perceptions of beer, this glass is a game-changer. The flute's long, lithe body lends itself classically to beers with lively carbonation and delicate aromas. The inward rim retains the effervescent head and releases the bouquet. Like kittens, chocolate and shoes, ladies love them too. Use with: Lambic and Gueuze, Champagne beers, Kriek, Flemish reds.

PILSNER
Designed to keep its head when glasses all about it are losing theirs, the classic straight-sided slaker gives drinkers the golden glad-eye and heightens the hop character. Use with: Pilsners, Helles, Schwarzbier, light lager, Dunkels.

GOBLET/CHALICE
Beloved of the Belgians and often ecclesiastical in appearance, these short-stemmed, broadly brimmed goblets and larger chalices reach out, arms wide, offering up all the flavours from within. The large surface area keeps your nose close to the aromas of the beer and invites substantial sips. Use with: Trappist beers, Abbey ales, strong and sweet Belgians, quadrupels, tripels, dubbels and winter ales.

WEIZEN
In both looks and taste, a Weiss is twice as nice in this busty Bavarian beauty. As curvy as a dirndl-wearing fraulein, its shape thrusts a frothy white head upwards and unleashes all the big banana and classic clove character you'd expect. Use with: all types of Weissbier, Weizenbock, Hefeweizen, Weizendunkel …

STEIN
Designed for drinking and clinking rather than thinking, the thick-walled stein was originally an earthenware Bavarian beer vessel which, in 19th-century beer gardens, would have sported a thumb-levered tin lid to stop leaves and insects dropping into the beer. Today, solid thick-walled versions made from glass can be seen swaying and sloshing all over Southern Germany. Use with: Oktoberfest lagers, Helles, Dunkel, Marzen.

SMALL IS BEAUTIFUL
Less can be more. In Cologne, Kölsch is always served in straight-sided cylindrical 'stangen', while in nearby Düsseldorf, the city's alt beer comes in a slightly portlier version. For barley wines and strong beers, try a tumbler, an antique 18th-century 'dwarf ale glass' or, if you can't find one, a small sherry glass or a vintage Martini glass works too.

dimpled mug

US pint

Pilsner

Stein

Weizen

flute

tulip

tumbler

wine glass

goblet

CANNED CRAFT BEER

Long considered the badge of the lager-swilling scoundrel, a plebian package synonymous with moribund swill and al fresco drinkers of no fixed abode, the beer can is becoming the sealed container of choice for craft brewers.

'The quality these days is comparable to that of the bottle.'
GARRETT OLIVER
BROOKLYN BREWERY

It was 10 years ago that Oskar Blues became the first microbrewer in America to embrace the can as its principal beer packaging. Since then, another 230 microbreweries have followed suit and, at the last count, more than 725 craft beers are now available in can, covering approximately 80 different styles, ranging from fruit beers and stouts to imperial porters, wheat beers brewed with watermelon and oak-aged Belgian-style abbey ales. Craft brewers in Europe have been slow to adopt the can, with rare exceptions, but Japanese craft brewers are enthusiastic canners.

Brooklyn Brewery puts its beers in cans. Brewmaster Garrett Oliver says: 'Cans are unbreakable and lightweight, block light completely, chill quickly, take up less space, and are less susceptible to oxidisation.

'The same thing has happened in wine with the "stelvin closure", aka the screw cap,' Oliver says. 'There was a lot of resistance to it at first, but now it's perfectly acceptable for restaurants to serve wines this way. Many very good sakes are available in cans in Japan, and it does not seem to be frowned upon. I've yet to see anyone practising "can refermentation"', adds Oliver, 'But it will happen if it hasn't already.'

But how to drink it – from the can or poured into the glass? Shaun O'Sullivan, co-owner of 21st Amendment Brewing, an early adopter of canned craft beer, declares: 'I would never want to drink certain beers directly from the can.

'Canned beers like Oskar Blues Ten Fidy, an imperial stout, or the 21st Amendment's Monk's Blood, a dark Belgian-style strong ale brewed with figs, aged on oak and vanilla beans, deserve to be poured into a glass. I mean, would you ever drink a Cantillon out of the bottle?'

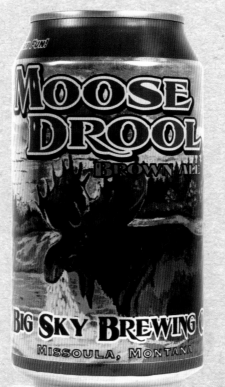

METAL MISCONCEPTION

The most common misconception facing canned craft beer is the idea that the beer will be tainted with a metallic 'off' flavour. It's not. Modern cans are lined with a water-based polymer lining which eliminates metallic contamination or flavours. The beer does not ever touch the metal.

'The quality these days is comparable to that of the bottle,' Oliver says. 'Beer used to pick up a lot of unwanted oxygen during canning, compared to bottling, but that's no longer the case. At the Brooklyn Brewery, we have an internal taste panel, and when we do blind tastings of can versus bottle, people like them equally.'

THE ADVANTAGES OF CANNED BEER

LONGER SHELF LIFE / BETTER BEER

Unlike bottles, cans protect beer from two arch-enemies: sunlight and oxygen. Oxygen reacts with elements in the beer to create stale flavours akin to wet cardboard. Exposure to UV light, meanwhile, will make the beer 'lightstruck'. This gives it an unpleasant 'skunk-like' aroma that brewery boffins call MBT or '3-methyl-2-butene-1-thiol' to its friends.

While clear and green glass bottles offer little protection from light, cans are completely impermeable to ruinous rays. Hermetically sealed, cans also pick up less oxygen in the brewery and are more secure than a bottle cap. Oxygen doesn't get in, carbon dioxide doesn't get out.

MORE ENVIRONMENTALLY FRIENDLY

The can is the most recycled package in the world. Lighter, easier to stack, it uses a fraction of the energy to produce, ship and recycle than glass does.

COST
Cans are cheaper for the brewery and distributor to ship. Cans do not break. They are also cheaper to chill, as they cool down quicker than bottles and take up less space.

PORTABILITY

Cans go where bottles cannot. They can be taken on outdoor adventures: picnics, camping, music festivals, hiking, golf, beaches, fishing trips, trainspotting and so on.

SAFETY

Cans are safer in the brewery, during transport and in the hands of both bartenders and consumers.

GREAT CRAFT BEER BARS AROUND THE WORLD

Best Bars in the US

Bailey's Taproom, Portland, Oregon
www.baileystaproom.com

Brouwer's Café, Seattle, Washington
brouwerscafe.blogspot.co.uk

Churchkey, Washington, DC
www.churchkeydc.com

Deep Ellum, Boston, Massachusetts
www.deepellum-boston.com

Falling Rock, Denver, Colorado
www.fallingrocktaphouse.com

Hamilton's, San Diego, California
www.hamiltonstavern.com

Local Option, Chicago, Illinois
www.localoptionbier.com

Porter Beer Bar, Atlanta, Georgia
www.theporterbeerbar.com

Toronado, San Francisco, California
www.toronado.com

Tørst, New York, New York
www.torstnyc.com

Best Bars in Europe

Akkurat, Stockholm, Sweden
www.akkurat.se

Café Abseits, Bamberg, Germany
www.abseits-bamberg.de

La Capsule, Lille, France
www.bar-la-capsule.fr

The Drunk Monk, Barcelona, Spain
www.cervezabelga.com

In De Wildeman, Amsterdam, Netherlands
www.indewildeman.nl

Kulminator, Antwerp, Belgium
no website

Ma Che Siete Venuti a Fa, Rome, Italy
http://www.football-pub.com

Mikkeller, Copenhagen, Denmark
www.mikkeller.dk/the-bar

Olutravintola Pikkulintu, Helsinki, Finland
www.pikkulintu.fi/Olutravintola Pikkulintu

Zlý Casy, Prague, Czech Republic
www.zlycasy.eu

Rest of the World

The Alibi Room, Vancouver, Canada
www.alibi.ca

BarVolo, Toronto, Canada
www.alibi.ca

Bateau de Nuit, Quebec, Canada
www.bateaudenuit.com

Cervecería Nacional, Santiago, Chile
cervecerianacional.cl

Empório Alto dos Pinheiros, Sao Paulo, Brazil
www.altodospinheiros.com.br

The Globe, Hong Kong, China
www.theglobe.com.hk

Local Taphouse, Melbourne, Australia
www.thelocal.com.au

The Malthouse, Wellington, New Zealand
www.themalthouse.co.nz

Popeye, Tokyo, Japan
www.40beersontap.com

The Scratch Bar, Brisbane, Australia
www.scratchbar.com

Best in the UK

The Anderson, Fortrose, Scotland
www.theanderson.co.uk

Craft Beer Company, London
thecraftbeerco.com/location/clerkenwell-london

Evening Star, Brighton
www.darkstarpubs.co.uk/eveningstar

Grove Inn, Huddersfield
www.groveinn.co.uk

North Bar, Leeds
www.northbar.com

Port Street Beer House, Manchester
www.portstreetbeerhouse.co.uk

Sheffield Tap, Sheffield
www.sheffieldtap.com

Southampton Arms, London
www.thesouthamptonarms.co.uk

Union Tavern, London
www.union-tavern.co.uk

White Horse, London
www.whitehorsesw6.com

THE BEERS

* QUENCH

---

* session

* saison

* blonde

* bitter

* kölsch

Not long ago, while in the pub with a good drinking buddy, I found myself at the bar. It was my round and I had been asked to get a couple of pints of Fuller's Chiswick Bitter.

But instead I returned to the table carrying, not two pints of Fuller's superb session beer, but two bottles of Orval.

Enchanted by the idea of top-notch Belgian beers, I smugly thought that it would be a good idea to impress my buddy with my extensive knowledge of Trappist ales, enlighten him as to the magic of Brettanomyces during secondary fermentation, and wax lyrical about the time I visited the brewery and discussed the true and noble art of beer-making with one of the monks.

And that is exactly what I did, as he sat quietly opposite me, slowly sipping the beer, nodding, raising his eyebrows intermittently, twiddling the tenpin-shaped bottle in his hands and peering at the back label. As soon as I had concluded my sermon, he leant forward and gently broke the bad news. 'I don't really like it,' he said. 'Actually, to be honest, mate, sometimes, I just like a nice pint of bitter.'

Asked whether he had even been tempted to stray romantically, Paul Newman famously replied that when he had steak waiting for him at home, why would he go for a hamburger? As my buddy rightly pointed out, sometimes, a burger may actually be all you really want.

Quench gathers together an array of unintimidating beers including Kölsch, mid-strength cask ales, Saison and other styles that workers once rolled across their hot heads on a summer's day; and lawnmower lagers that cut the mustard as well as the grass.

They are quaffable craft ales that won't buckle your knees but may well make your elbows ache. They are the easy drinkers, the thirst-slakers and the session beers; but they don't want for character or complexity. Any brewer will tell you there is no harder task in the art of brewing than delivering depth at modest strength.

The beers that await your perusal over the next 10 pages are not guilty pleasures. They are simple pleasures. And, often, simple pleasures are the best ones.

RESTRAINED IN STRENGTH YET REMARKABLY RICH IN CHARACTER, AND EACH AN EXERCISE IN ELITE ELBOW-BENDING, THESE BEERS ARE CRAFTED BY THEIR MAKERS WITH UNABASHED EVERYDAY IMBIBING ENJOYMENT IN MIND. LESS LEAVES YOU EAGER FOR MORE.

Adnams Brewery
Southwold Bitter 3.7%
Suffolk, England
www.adnams.co.uk

One of Britain's most significant regional brewers, Adnams is by no means monogamous in its love of life-enhancing liquids. As well as a hugely respected wine business, the company has diversified into distilling and is producing some spectacular spirits, including a 'beer de vie' made from its Broadside ale. Divergence has not diluted its brewing brilliance, however, and while it brews a series of sexy seasonals and a host of great historic beers, it is hard to beat Adnams' legendary bitter. Succulent Maris Otter with Fuggles in both the boil and the barrel give bracing spiciness with a soothing sweet floor.

Bathams
Best Bitter 4.3%
West Midlands, England
www.bathams.com

Bathams is a light golden legend in the Black Country, woven deep into the local cask ale drinking fabric. Beyond Bathams' own few defiantly traditional pubs, its availability is restricted to a small selection of skilled cellarmen who know how to handle the beer once it arrives from the Bull & Bladder brewpub in Brierley Hill, family owned for five generations. An upfront malt sweetness is simmered down with earthy, resinous Goldings and Northdown hops. A hidden gem.

Black Sheep
Best Bitter 3.8%
Yorkshire, England
www.blacksheepbrewery.co.uk

A very well-known beer and a very good one, Black Sheep's flagship session sip is an archetypal English ale made in Masham with Maris Otter and hopped using Fuggles, Challenger and Prospect. Fermentation in the brewery's classic Yorkshire Squares seals it with a distinct softness, while the luscious bready body and lively bitterness are characteristics many others aim for yet few manage to achieve.

Castle Rock
Harvest Pale 3.8%
Nottingham, England
www.castlerockbrewery.co.uk

You can't really go wrong with either the pubs or the lovely beers of Castle Rock. Having craftily accumulated a dozen pubs over 20 years, former Camra chairman Chris Holmes began brewing beer in 1997 and, unable to fulfil a rapacious regional following, moved into a bigger brewery in 2010. The timing could not have been better as, two weeks before, this fabulously floral golden ale won the Champion Beer of Britain at the Great British Beer Festival. It is an extremely erudite piece of ale-making, with Chinook and Cascade woven into a rich base of, once again, Maris Otter.

Crouch Vale
Brewers Gold 4%
Essex, England
www.crouch-vale.co.uk

There are a lot of small breweries that have tried to replicate the easy-sipping, aromatic allure of this golden ale from Essex but few get close to its crisp quaffability. One of the more mature micros, founded in 1981, Crouch Vale is the only brewery apart from Timothy Taylor to win the Champion Beer of Britain title in successive years (2005 and 2006).

Dark Star
Saison 4.5%
Sussex, England
www.darkstarbrewing.co.uk

Seriously stylish and one of two beers in the book from this consistently excellent brewer. Rather than muffling its estery accent, cask-conditioning complements the crisp delicate dryness associated with the beers of Wallonia. A bespoke yeast and Goldings are brought from Belgium and segued with Saaz and Styrian hops to create a kind of muscular golden mild more moreish than uncut crack.

Black Sheep Best Bitter Battered Fish and Chips

Serves 4

Ingredients

- 170g/6oz plain flour
- 1 teaspoon bicarbonate of soda
- 1 pint of Black Sheep Best Bitter
- juice of ½ lemon
- good quality vegetable oil
- 450g/1lb potatoes, peeled
- 4 haddock fillets
- salt and pepper

Method

Put the flour, bicarbonate of soda, and seasoning into a bowl then gradually add the Best Bitter: stop when you have a thick coating of batter. Whisk to remove any lumps. Add the lemon juice then mix again.

Heat the fat up in deep fat fryer.

Cut the peeled potatoes into large, thick chips. Then rinse the chips and dry them using kitchen towel.

Fry the chips in the oil until soft but NOT coloured. This should take about 3 minutes.

Take the chips out, draining and shaking them well and then set them to one side.

Put some flour onto a plate and coat the fish fillets thoroughly.

Take one fillet of haddock at a time, holding it by the end, and swirl it around in the batter until it has a good coating, then plunge it into the hot fat immediately.

As soon as the first fillet has started to crisp, add your other fillets one at a time, taking out the first ones as they cook – between 6 to 10 minutes. Place the cooked fish on a baking tray and keep it warm in the oven.

Return your chips to the hot fat and cook until they are crisp and golden.

Serve with tartare sauce, mushy peas and a pint of Best Bitter.

Grain
Best Bitter 4.2%
Norfolk, England
www.grainbrewery.co.uk

Grain has been growing in reputation since opening in an old dairy in 2006. It eschews the extreme and the unusual in favour of the classic beers that traditional breweries have been doing for a long time. Thing is, Grain do it a lot better than most. Brewed with chocolate, pale and caramel malts, this is simple and rather super.

Hopback Brewery
Taiphoon 4.2%
Wiltshire, England
www.hopback.co.uk

Founded in 1986 in Salisbury, Hopback is synonymous with Summer Lightning, regarded as the golden ale that ignited the blonde beer uprising in Britain. Hopback has some other excellent brews, however, including the delightfully drinkable GFB, hopped with East Kent Goldings; the crisp and clean Crop Circle; and Taiphoon, laced with lemongrass and coriander. It's a bit mental, a little oriental and peerless with a Pad Thai.

Ilkley
Mary Jane 3.5%
Yorkshire, England
www.ilkleybrewery.co.uk

Yorkshire folk tend to like things from Yorkshire, be it pudding, tea or beer. After Carlsberg's decision to take Tetley's out of Leeds, local ale enthusiasts are loving the work of Ilkley Brewery, set up in 2009 near the famous moor. Mary Jane, a citrusy session bitter, is an Anglo-American easy drinker bittered with British Northdown and infused with aromatic Amarillo and Cascade hops, rich in lychee, lime and grapefruit flavours.

Kelham Island
Pale Rider 5.2%
Sheffield, England
www.kelhambrewery.co.uk

A legendary, pioneering pale ale first brewed by Dave Wicket, a legend and pioneer of British brewing who, very sadly, died in 2012. An inspirational alemaker, he almost single-handedly started a beer revolution in Sheffield and his influence is interwoven in the history of both Thornbridge and BrewDog. His most famous liquid legacy, however, is this award-winning pale ale, medium-bodied, fragrant, with dashes of sugar-dusted grapefruit. It was Camra's 2004 Champion Beer of Britain and is brewed with British barley and American hops.

Old Dairy
Sun Top Pale Ale 3.6%
Kent, England
www.olddairybrewery.com

Old Dairy is one of the most accomplished breweries to have sprouted up in the 'Garden of England' in recent years. Doing its flavoursome thing out of – surprise – an old dairy, deep in the countryside, it often uses local whole hops and describes its beer, rather nicely, as retro-rustic. But it is the New World hop Amarillo's Seville orange and floral notes that take centre stage here.

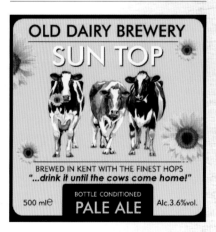

Redemption
Trinity 3%
London, England
www.redemptionbrewery.co.uk

Riding the wave of London's 21st-century craft brewing revival, Redemption, which only started in 2010, turns out some terrific cask ales from its small brewery in Tottenham, North London. While the brewery is entirely powered by renewable resources, its beers are anything but green technically. It is quite incredible how much character that founder Andy Moffat coaxes out of just three grains, three hops and three per cent of alcohol by volume. Late hopping throws peppermint, orange and grapefruit shapes on a succulent malt dancefloor. Trinity is one of the most consistently impressive cask ales to come out of the capital in recent years.

Rooster
Yankee 4.3%
Yorkshire, England
www.roosters.co.uk

Founder Sean Franklin is to hop appreciation what Muhammad Ali was to hitting people very hard in the face. His ales are acutely aromatic, fabulously floral and beautifully balanced. After Franklin's retirement in 2011, this lychee-laced pale ale, with a touch of hibiscus and lemongrass, has maintained its class in the very capable hands of the Fozard family, who have spruced up the range too.

Thornbridge
Wild Swan 3.5%
Derbyshire, England
www.thornbridgebrewery.co.uk

Deep in the Derbyshire Dales, Thornbridge is an immaculate modern brewer who quietly and confidently creates some of the UK's most impressive beers, including Jaipur, Bracia, St Petersburg and the delectable Kill Your Darlings. Like the bass player in a great band, Wild Swan often fails to get the recognition it deserves, especially in cask. Hopped with Chinook, Celeia and Sládek, it's a burst of citrus, grapefruit, spruce and pine sprung from a brioche-like Maris Otter barley base. A sensational session ale.

West Berkshire Brewery
Old Father Thames 3.4%
Berkshire, England
www.wbbrew.co.uk

Along with the malt, the water and the hops, it may be a sprinkle of nostalgia that makes this Berkshire best bitter so special. I was 19 when my Dad bought me a pint at The Bell in Aldworth (see page 123), a remarkable rustic relic whose warped flagstones, bowed by muddy boots, are the only evidence of Old Father Time. I was sat in the beautiful beer garden in July after a long stomp along the Ridgeway, accompanied by a warm brown bread roll filled with ham and pickle, and a packet of dry roasted nuts. Does life often get better than that? No. Not really.

Fyne Ales
Jarl 3.8%
Argyll, Scotland
www.fyneales.com

In a disused dairy on the edge of Loch Fyne, an epicurean outpost famed for its oysters, this small but growing Scottish micro consistently proves that its rather bombastic name is not mere bluster. Hopped solely with Citra, Jarl started as a seasonal: its lychee, lemongrass and kiwi fruit finesse can now be experienced all year round.

Brecon
Bronze Beacons 3.9%
Powys, Wales
www.breconbrewing.co.uk

Justin 'Buster' Grant is a key cog in Wales's well-oiled microbrewing machine. Having previously brewed for Brakspear and the Breconshire Brewery, he opened a new brewhouse in the Brecon Beacons in 2011 'specialising' in consistent cask ale. After a long day of stomping about the beacons or reaching the peak of Pen y Fan, this is what you want: a crisp quencher whose cereal spine is strengthened with the addition of oats. The Sovereign hop delivers a nutty, grassy aroma while Cluster mellows out the middle with touches of dark fruit.

Monty's
Sunshine 4.2%
Montgomery, Wales
www.montysbrewery.co.uk

In 2009, having studied brewing briefly in Sunderland and armed with a fistful of government funding, Pam Honeyman set up this marvellous micro in an old welder's workshop just one mile from the English border. The golden jewel in Monty's crown is this easy-sipping summer slaker: floral, with a dry apricot finish.

Tiny Rebel
Cwtch 4.6%
Newport, Wales
www.tinyrebel.co.uk

The enfant terrible of the Welsh craft brewing crowd comes courtesy of brothers-in-law Bradley Cummings and Gareth Williams. Having homebrewed as a hobby, they set up on an industrial estate where they create slightly off-centre ales. Cwtch, a Welsh word meaning 'snuggle', is a reassuring Irish Red with a gentle blackcurrant undertone, slight sweetness and a dry pine-like send-off.

Tomos Watkin
Cwrw Hâf 4.2%
Swansea, Wales
www.tomoswatkin.com

Tomos Watkin was started in 1995 before being brought under the wing of the Hurns Brewing Company, a soft drink specialist. Pronounced 'Koo-Roo Harv', this summer ale's contempt for vowels is matched only by its downright drinkability. Light, golden and balanced, it does exactly what it says on the label (assuming you can understand it).

Commons
Urban Farmhouse Ale 5.3%
Oregon
www.commonsbrewery.com

A small seven-barrel brewery in a warehouse in southeast Portland is where Commons creates a collection of urban-rustic beers inspired by Belgium yeast, but tweaked with Pacific Northwest hops. Tight and tangy with a hazy copper hue, this is an edgy, acidic aperitif. Flemish Kiss, soured with Brettanomyces, is another one your lips will thank you for.

Jester King
Le Petit Prince 2.9%
Texas
www.jesterkingbrewery.com

From their bucolic barn-like brewery on the outskirts of Austin, brothers Jeff and Michael Stuffings make some phenomenally funky and flavoursome farmhouse beers with distinct yeast profiles. Big on barrel-ageing, wild yeast, Brettanomyces and other bacteria, Jester King creates some extraordinarily ambitious small-batch, limited edition beers. This Texan twist on a traditional Belgian table beer is one of the more obscure ales to come out of the American scene. Hopped heartily with East Kent Goldings and Saaz hops, its light body strengthened with wheat, it's a lip-smacking lesson in low-gravity brewing.

Golden Road
Point The Way IPA 5.2%
Los Angeles
www.goldenroad.la

If Los Angeles's beer scene is to eventually rival that of San Francisco or San Diego, then Golden Road will play an important role in its growth. It's a solid set-up, founded in 2011 by restaurateur Tony Yanow and the young Yale graduate Meg Gill, with former Dogfish Head brewer Jon Carpenter. At just over 5%, Point the Way is more of a pale ale than an IPA, hopped with varieties from New Zealand and the Pacific Northwest. Primed with pine flavour and a kiss of grapefruit, it's a laidback Los Angeles take on West Coast IPA.

Live Oak Brewing
HefeWeizen 5.2%
Texas
www.liveoakbrewing.com

In the town of Austin, two former homebrewers have introduced the European techniques of open fermentation, decoction mashing and lengthy lagering to the locals. When Texas temperatures rise, as they like to do, this Hefeweizen hits the spot with classic clove character, bruised bananas and a terrific tartness.

Mad River Brewing
Steelhead Extra Pale Ale 5.6%
California
www.madriverbrewing.com

Based in the small Northern Californian town of Blue Lake, Mad River has been fashioning some fine ales since 1989, when it inherited the kit on which Ken Grossman, of Sierra Nevada fame, cut his brewing teeth. There is just enough citrus hop here, but reined in on the bitter finish, and a touch of toffee too: very well balanced.

Ommegang
Rare Vos 6.5%
New York
www.ommegang.com

Amber often appears as an afterthought for American craft brewers, a style that pads out a portfolio, a default easy-drinking option when faced with a forest of draught taps. Perhaps this is why this quaffable beer from Cooperstown calls itself a Belgian pale ale? Technicalities aside, this looks like an amber ale yet its soft caramel body is funked up and fructified with Ommegang's Belgian yeast. Spicy, fruity and clean on the finish, from a major East Coast player bought by Belgium's Duvel Moortgat in 2003.

BEER VENUE
Anderson Valley

Boonville, California, home to Anderson Valley brewing, is a countrified cradle of counter-culture and home to left-leaning, lentil-munching locals. It is most famous for its own language, called Boontling, invented in the late 1800s by mischievous kids who did not wish their parents to know what they were talking about.

The labels of Anderson Valley's beers carry the phrase 'It's bahl hornin', meaning 'It's good drinkin'. Each May, Anderson Valley hosts the legendary Boonville Beer Festival, 'the bahlest steinber hornin', chiggrul gormin' tiddrick in the heelch of the Boont Region'.

That's not all. You can also drink and drive, have a foursome and build up a thirst on the brewery's beautiful, bucolic 18-hole disc-golf* course. With its blend of undulating, extensive open fairways, tricky dog-legs, water hazards and tightly-packed oak groves, this is a perfect place to build up a rasping thirst.

More than a dozen fresh Anderson Valley beers pour in the 19th hole or, alternatively, you can grab a six pack of craft beer cans before you tee off. The copper-coloured Summer Solstice is a brow-wiping wheat beer, its hoppy Hop Ottin IPA feeds the regional demand for all things 'herbal' and the Amber Ale is a beautifully balanced drop.

*Disc-golf, for those unsure, is just like golf but with frisbee-like discs instead of balls, hands instead of clubs, baskets rather than holes and no archaic membership rituals or silly clothes.

Anderson Valley Brewing Company
17700 Hwy 253
Boonville, CA 95415-0505

Saint Arnold
Fancy Lawnmower Ale 4.9%
Texas
www.saintarnold.com

This first-class thirst-slaker brewed in Houston using Hallertau hops looks like a Kölsch, smells like a Kölsch, tastes like a Kölsch but it can't legally be called a Kölsch, what with not being brewed in Cologne. The power of suggestion aside, it does actually exude a grassy aroma, bright and zesty, flipped from a juicy biscuit base. It makes for a brainy ballgame beer and general go-to gulper when things heat up in Houston.

CANADA

Alley Kat Brewing Company
Full Moon 5%
Alberta
www.alleykatbeer.com

Despite its name, Alley Kat is the kind of brewery you could bring home to meet your parents. Reliable yet creative, its reputation has been built on the simple premise of fresh, flavoursome beers that people like drinking. Full Moon, a perfectly poised West Coast pale ale, is incredibly well put together, using caramel malt and Centennial and Cascade hops. There may be nothing particularly new in its components, but it is very impressive as a sum of its parts.

GERMANY

Bayer Theinheim
Ungespundetes Landbier 4.7%
Bavaria
www.bayer-theinheim.de

An unfiltered, dewy golden Franconian Kellerbier from a very small brewpub and even smaller distillery situated a few miles outside Bamberg and founded back in 1718. Spritzy and soft, fresh baked bread and a curt herbal bitter finish.

Firestone Walker

Firestone Walker
Double Barrel Ale (DBA) 5%
California, United States
www.firestonewalker.com

Making its beers amid the vineyards of Central California, Firestone Walker is one of the most stylish and assured brewers in America. It was founded in 1996 by an Englishman, David Walker, and Adam Firestone, the great-grandson of the tyre titan Harvey Firestone. It endured a stuttering start in 1996, with unsuccessful attempts to age beer in wine barrels at a time when the craft beer revolution was beginning to eat itself after meteoric growth.

But then it introduced a unique adaption of the Burton Union system, made famous by the pale ale brewers of Burton-upon-Trent in England. The Californian version, patented with the name 'Firestone Union', differs from its inspiration in the use of new oak and a variety of different barrels. A series of 60-gallon American oak barrels, toasted to varying degrees, are used for primary fermentation and then, after a period, retired to become part of Firestone's innovative barrel-ageing programme.

Unlike many of its American craft brewing counterparts, Firestone's oak experimentation is thus inspired by England rather than Belgium and is designed to create clean, classic yet complex flavours. The system plumps out the palate and amplifies the hop character while the oak furnishes the ales with vanilla, chocolate and wood flavours.

Brewed on the union, Double Barrel Ale is about as English as American beer gets. Its clean compartmentalisation of ingredients accentuates the East Kent Golding and coaxes out the succulent character of the Maris Otter barley. One fifth of the oak-fermented beer is blended with beer fermented in standard stainless steel to create an 'ordinary' bitter that is anything but ordinary.

A gold medal winner at both the 2011 and 2012 Great American Beer Festivals, commercial success has not diluted its distinction as the best best bitter in America. The unfiltered version, available at Firestone Walker's taproom, is one of several spectacular beers in the brewery's locker, including the Proprietors Reserve range; the beautiful bourbon barrel-aged Velvet Merlin; and Walker's Reserve, a stout stacked with five different malts and Cascade and Goldings hops. Little surprise Firestone Walker was named champion mid-sized brewery for the fourth time in 2012.

Mahr's Brau
Ungespundet Hefetrüb 5.2%
Bavaria
www.mahrs.de

A classic Kellerbier from Bamberg's most discerning drinking destination. In the winter its jolly, comfy Jubelfest pours supreme, but it's in the summer, sipping this hazy unpasteurised, unfiltered brew beneath the chestnut trees, when Mahr's is at its most memorable. Beneath a big feathery head and deeply fragrant aroma lies a dry and zesty bronze beer, its easy-going effervescence allowing summer fruit flavours to fandango all over your tongue. While it travels relatively well, nothing beats a fresh glass from the family-owned brewery tap.

Malzmühle Schwartz
Mühlen Kölsch 4.8%
Cologne
www.muehlenkoelsch.de

Curt Köbessen (the name given to Cologne's notoriously rude beer waiters – they make the Parisian garçon seem the height of Bonifacian affability) keep gruff, gravel-throated locals content at this wood-panelled time-warp bar, which brews on the premises a soft Kölsch that still manages to bear enough bitterness to saw through huge hunks of Rhineland pork knuckle. The Brauerei zur Malzmühle ('Maltmill brewery') is one of the less touristy and at the same time more charismatic Kölsch taverns in Germany's fourth-largest city.

Päffgen
Kölsch 4.8%
Cologne
www.paeffgen-koelsch.de

Cologne's traditional breweries do not come more diminutive than this. The house beer, brewed since 1883 on the west side of the city, is possibly the spiciest version of the city's signature brew. Having been used to sipping blander, exported versions from the bottle in London, drinking this fruity fellow from the barrel confirmed my Kölsch conversion.

BELGIUM

Brasserie de la Senne
Taras Boulba 4.5%
Brussels
www.brasseriedelasenne.be

Yvan De Baets and Bernard Leboucq, finally based in Brussels after years of itinerant ale-making, are rebels of restraint, bringing balance where some of their countrymen flail on a seesaw of spice and cloying sweetness.

Taras Boulba is hopped in all the right places with a soft citrus bitterness alongside delicate peardrop esters, gentle carbonation and a crisp citrus finish akin to old-fashioned lemonade. This should be the quality control for all budding Belgian pale ales.

Table beer

Historically, table beer was regarded as a refresher, a quick quencher during meals or a break from hard harvest work.

In British brewing tomes, talk of table beer peters out as milds and bitters become more popular. There seems to be more mention of it in countries where monastic brewing has been maintained, especially Belgium where it's known as tafelbier or bière de table.

Given the potency of many Abbey and Trappist beers, it would not have been wise for monks to drink them as regular tipples. So, instead, during meals and as a safer alternative to water, they would take table beer, or patersbier ('father's beer') that is brewed using the weaker wort and only available at the monastery.

Brewed for both Lent and for lunch, examples of patersbier include Petit Orval, Chimay Doree and a 4% beer brewed by Westvleteren until the 1990s. In secular circles, table beer grew in the late 1800s as breweries attempted to appease a growing temperance movement.

Table beer is low in alcohol (typically 1 to 3% ABV), traditionally sweet and varying in colour from light blonde to dark black. Regarded as an L-plate libation, it was the beer that Belgians were traditionally brought up on. Until the 1970s, it was served in schools and, as sugar-riddled soft drinks increasingly undermine modern-day attention spans, there have been calls for its return as a nutrient-rich alternative.

At home in Belgium, table beer was traditionally introduced to the family dinner table, with deliberate insouciance, as an introductory beer that children can sip under parental supervision.

Usurped by soft drinks, bottled water and others, table beer is seldom served with meals anymore but, as part of the on-going exploration of old beer styles, a number of brewers outside Belgium, such as Kernel and Jester King, have begun brewing them again. Although quite where table beers stop and session beers start remains unclear.

De Cazeau
Saison Cazeau 5%
Hainault
www.brasseriedecazeau.be

In 2004, on a site dating back to 1753, civil engineer Laurent Agache reawoke Cazeau from a 35-year slumber. A second-hand brew-kit hauled across the English Channel from Hull was installed in a red-brick farm building near Tournai and put to work making some cunning, well-constructed craft beer. Wonderfully effervescent and underpinned with clean Pilsner malt, this delicate and drinkable drop is gently hopped and enhanced with freshly blossomed elderflower. Light hints of lemon, melon and honeysuckle.

De Hoevebrouwers
Toria 6.5%
East Flanders
www.dehoevebrouwers.be

Subtlety rather than sweetness and strength is what this husband and wife duo do splendidly well. Having honed their skills as home-brewers, they have borrowed other breweries to brew with a rapier rather than a bludgeon. Toria nimbly bridges the gap between a traditional blonde beer and hoppy Belgian pale ales, with esters adding fresh hints of fruit salad to a delicate hop bitterness. A superb summer slaker with a crisp, curt-lipped climax.

Jandrain Jandrenouille
IV Saison 6.5%
Brabant
www.brasseriedejandrainjandrenouille.be

Seldom is a Saison made in Belgium without the addition of spices or special brewing sugars, but both are absent from IV, a sublime, sprightly-scented slaker that derives all its delicate lychee, lemon and grapefruit character from American hops. Discreetly brewed in a stone barn in Wallonian Brabant by Stéphane Meulemans and Alexandre Dumont who, in the interests of conjuring up greatness out of their comparatively small brewkit, import citrusy Yakima Chief hops from half way round the world in Washington State. The hop shines brightly here.

De Ryck
Special de Ryck 5.5%
East Flanders
www.brouwerijderyck.be

About half way between Brussels and Ghent, on the way to Oudenaarde, is a farmhouse brewery overseen by Anne De Ryck, great-granddaughter of the founder, Gustave, who began the business in 1886 after studying brewing in Germany. De Ryck's devotion to the Purity Law, meaning no sugar or spices in the beer, did not even waver when invading Germans purloined its brewing equipment. The Special remains its cleanest, most classic beer, brewed with Saaz and Hallertau hops and matured for a month. Its golden, delicate sweetness, with a lively bitterness, is best matched with a chaser of Bierblomme, De Ryck's 40% ABV hop-infused spirit, distilled next door.

NETHERLANDS

Lindeboom
Gouverneur special 140 5.5%
Limburg
www.lindeboom.nl/en

Limburg, sandwiched between Belgium and Germany, is where Lindeboom has been living since 1870. The family-owned brewery pays homage to both its neighbours with a well-known, hoppy North German style Pilsner, an Alt, a Belgian wit and a trio of Abbey-style ales that come together under the Gouverneur label. First brewed to commemorate the 140-year anniversary, this golden ale is better when bottle-conditioned, like a more charismatic version of the Pilsner.

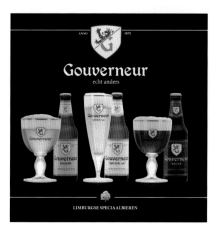

Low and non-alcoholic beer

It is easy to dismiss drinking low and non-alcohol beer as an ultimately futile exercise, like buying a thoroughbred racehorse with erectile dysfunction.

But sometimes alcohol is neither the answer nor even an option. So, if you are pregnant, driving, watching your weight, a recovering alcoholic or operating heavy machinery (heck, you may be all of those things) then here are some brews that leave you sober yet satisfied.

Schneider Weisse Alkoholfrei 0.5%
Hailed as the hefeweisse for the health-conscious connoisseur, it has cleverly kept its clove-like character, with wonderful wort sweetness.

Erdinger Weissbier Alkoholfrei 0.4%
Marketed in Germany as a vitamin-rich, post-exercise isotonic refresher that will replenish lost nutrients and slake your thirst with Teutonic efficiency.

Harvey's John Hop 1%
A lovely light ale from Lewes in Sussex that would have quenched the thirst of those picking hops in the summer.

Super Bock Stout 0.5%
A sensible drinker's stout from Portugal. Scored with a nutty sweetness and a touch of camp coffee, it is dark, drinkable and a little different.

Veltins Alkoholfrei 0.5%
Another German but a bitter Pilsner-style, a lot hoppier than the weissbiers above. Minerally in the mouth, nicely carbonated.

CZECH REPUBLIC

Cerná Hora
Moravské Sklepní unfiltered 4%
Moravia
www.pivovarcernahora.cz

Czech talk of Cerná Hora tends to be accompanied by a knowing nod of recognition. Hailing from the east of the country and with a name that means 'Black Mountain', the brewery has been making beer since 1530, and its brews can be found in Prague's better beer bars. '1530',

an anniversary beer conditioned for three months, is a great beer but if you are settling in for a session then look no further than this bitter-sweet unfiltered blonde, brewed using only Moravian hops and Moravian malt, matured in the cellars ('sklepní' is Czech for 'cellar'), unfiltered to keep as much character as possible, smooth on the tongue, with a barley character that tastes a bit like buttered crumpets.

ITALY

Extraomnes
Zest 5.3%
Lombardy
www.extraomnes.com

Expense and an inclination to over-experiment are two criticisms you could fairly lay at the door of the Italian craft brewing scene. But while its peers indulge in esoteric ingredients, elaborate 75cl bottles and beers designed to sit smugly with the Slow Food movement, Extraomnes, from outside Milan, opts for deftly-brewed, very drinkable beers packaged in 33cl bottles. Zest is a piquant Belgian-style pale ale, with tart lemon, vanilla, peach and basil all noticeable when you pay attention.

FRANCE

Mont Salève
Special Bitter 4.2%
Haute-Savoie
www.labrasseriedumontsaleve.com

This small operation set up by Michaël Novo in Neydens, just over the Swiss border south of Geneva, quickly built a reputation for crisp, clean, hoppy and bitter beers. The Special Bitter, a Chinook single varietal, is a splendid quenching, dry, citrusy and slightly earthy golden ale.

Thiriez
Étoile du Nord 4.5%
Nord-Pas-de-Calais
www.brasseriethiriez.com

In his brewery at Esquelbecq, Daniel Thiriez is widely recognised in French beer circles as much for his pioneering role in the country's microbrewing scene as his liberal use and love of the hop in a brewing nation whose beers are normally synonymous with malt sweetness. Perhaps it's the influence of the hop gardens of Kent, just a short hop across the English Channel. Étoile du Nord (sold in the United States as Thiriez Extra) is an enchanting, quenching blonde ale with a spicy-peppery hop character.

Tri Martolod
Blonde 4.6%
Brittany
www.trimartolod.fr

Organised as a co-operative with An'Alarch and based in Concarneau, Brittany, the specificity of Tri Martolod ('Three Sailors' in Breton) is that it brews only lagers and focuses on local customers. Tri Martolod Blonde is an unpasteurised, dry yet malt-accented pale lager, best sampled on draught, when it rivals local low-gravity ciders for sheer sinkability.

SWITZERLAND

Sudwerk
Gold Miner 4.8%
Zürich
www.sudwerk.ch

A Swiss-born beer (brewed in Pfäffikon, east of Zurich) brewed by a Californian expat called Gerry Farrell yet incredibly English in style. Closer to a quintessentially British bitter than a California copy, it is brewed on an English rather than German brew system using half a dozen malts, to give a blonde, dry, easy-drinking ale with a moderate spicy, piquant hop character.

DENMARK

Det Lille Bryggeri
Sommerbryg 4%
Zealand
www.detlillebryggeri.dk

The 'Little Brewery' is a pioneering, prolific microbrewery with a strong foreign following. While it dabbles in the extreme, with a smashing smoked beer and a rare example of a chocolate-chilli beer, this unfiltered golden drop is liquid proof that it can master clean, uncomplicated quaffable sundowners too. It may rarely register on the beer geek's radar but that doesn't mean it is not an accomplished bit of ale-making.

COSTA RICA

Costa Rica's Craft Brewing Company
Libertas 4.7%
Cartago
www.beer.cr

Flying the flavour flag in Central America since 2010, Costa Rica's Craft Brewing Company was founded by Americans Peter Gilman and Brandon Nappy, with Christopher Derrick, formerly of Flying Dog in the US, at the brewing helm. Surrounded by rainforests and volcanoes, with a strong surfer following, it has created this tropical, tawny-coloured pale ale positioned to coax Costa Ricans away from lacklustre liquids.

AUSTRALIA

Little Creatures
Pale Ale 5.2%
Western Australia
www.littlecreatures.com.au

From a fantastic Freemantle micro, now in the clutches of Japan's Kirin Brewery, this is a cracking copper-coloured, bottle-conditioned pale ale with more hops than a restless 'roo, a lovely refresher after a hard day under the hot Outback sun. Bonza with anything off the barbie: shrimps, seafood, koalas, dingoes, Bouncer from *Neighbours* … Lychees, grapefruit and peppery pine make this Australia's answer to Sierra Nevada Pale Ale, a beer that announced Down Under boutique brewing had arrived. Time will tell if it can match the Californians' commitment to quality on a bigger scale.

Lord Nelson
Three Sheets 4.9%
Sydney
www.lordnelson.com.au

Occupying the city's oldest licensed hotel (1841), the Lord Nelson is an upstanding pillar of British pubbery whose authenticity would set even the stiffest expat's upper lip all a-quiver. They have been brewing with a British accent here since 1985, yet there is definitely a Down Under dimension to Three Sheets, a sparkling balanced Australian pale ale more suited to a pint glass than a schooner.

JAPAN

Kiuchi
Hitachino Nest White Ale 5%
Ibaraki
www.kodawari.cc

Primarily an esteemed producer of Sake and Sochu, Kiuchi dates back to 1823. It began brewing beer in 1996 and, while guilty of some over-eager bottle-conditioning, it's not afraid to experiment with alternative approaches (a Red Rice beer and an impressive Eisbock) or ingredients. As well as nutmeg, orange peel and coriander, a little orange juice is added to this citrusy Belgian wit, giving it a slightly acidic edge.

Shiga Kogen
Miyama Blonde 7%
Nagano
www.tamamura-honten.co.jp

A Nagano-based Sake producer for two centuries, Shiga Kogen only branched off into brewing back in 2004 but stays just the right side of youthful exuberance. Busting the myth that rice must be a cheapener, Miyama Nishiki rice gives this Japanese Saison a leaner sweetness, balanced out with bittering hops sourced from the brewery's own bines.

SOUTH AFRICA

Mitchell's
Bosun's Bitter 3.6%
Western Cape
www.mitchellsbrewery.com

Otherwise known for oysters and its very own elephant, the port of Knysna is also home to the second largest brewery in South Africa. Started in 1983, it has been passed around various owners like a plate of biscuits but this English bitter, the first beer it brewed, is a welcome respite from South Africa's taste-a-like lagers: floral, with a faint hop aroma of melon and lychee followed by a dry finish.

Brian Hunt
Moonlight Brewing
Northern California

Laid-back and legendary among California's craft brewing scene, Brian Hunt brews 1000 barrels a year from his 'abbey brewery' in the woods of Santa Rosa.

✳ **Saison Dupont**
So heavenly, so lofty and delicate yet grainy. The balance of Saison yeast is my gold standard.

✳ **De Ranke XX and De la Senne Taras Boulba**
I've sneaked two into one here. These two both so artfully walk a fine tight wire between obnoxious hop bitterness and teasingly, tantalisingly dry.

✳ **Deschutes Abyss**
It tastes like an abyss: the name is so apt. The character has such depth and complexity, one sip will never tell you everything that's going on in the beer.

✳ **Augustiner Hell**
Flat-out outstanding and uncompromising. Any other pale lager can only dream of being this firm, balanced and subtle.

✳ **Czech beer**
The Czech make delicate beers, the polar opposite of the current trends of brute-force hopping or extreme anything. The beers here are like provocative whispers: intensely hopped while subtle and delicate; ironic by West Coast standards.

BARBECUE BEERS

At the beginning, there were no televisions, no radiators and no microwaves. There was only fire. Man gawped at fire, he heated himself with fire and, having scampered after them and killed them with a spear or some-such, he cooked animals (and maybe a few vegetables that didn't require running after) using fire.

Without fire, man would have been in a whole lot of trouble. That is why man loves fire. Today, man still loves fire but doesn't see as much of it as he would like to. Fire only makes fleeting, cameo appearances: romantic candles, Olympic torches, hippy jugglers, that kind of thing.

But man's inherent love of fire burns bright. Man still loves eating animals (and maybe a few vegetables) and loves to barbecue. Deep down, man is a natural born griller. He's a grill sergeant. He's born with a licence to grill. He kills beasts. He makes fire. He dons 'comedy' apron.

Then the magic begins.

Superb with sausages (St Austell's trbute)

Brilliant with burgers (Oakham Ales' Citra)

Remarkable with sticky ribs (Alaskan Brewing's Smoked Porter)

Lovely with lamb or Merguez (Anchor Brewing's Liberty Ale)

Cracking With Cumberland sausages (Timothy Taylor's Landlord)

Fruit Beers are a friend to flame-grilled food (Lindemans' Cuvée René)

HAMBURGER

As every coal-cajoling connoisseur knows, it begins with a burger. For budget bovine knuckle in a bun, any lacklustre lager will do. But for a freshly baked brioche clutching choice chunk and shin, minced and marinated with an array of exploratory toppings (sweet gherkins, jalapenos, relish)? Something with fresh fruit flavours, a touch of sweetness and a rapier of bitterness to carve through the grease.

Armed with all three is Anchor Liberty Ale, the cult Cascade-clad classic from the West Coast. Or, from England, there's the single-hopped yet multi-layered Oakham Citra, a refreshing whizzbang that opens with light zesty summer fruit and finishes with a dry, gently bitter finish.

STEAK

Skirt or sirloin, T-bone or tenderloin, and be they butter-soft or with a bit of a chew, steaks do not suffer delicate drops gladly. Beers with pronounced malt character complement the crisscross of caramelised sweetness while any savoury crust of seasoning calls for a clean bite of bitterness. William Brothers' Profanity Stout from Scotland stands its ground but doesn't dominate while Victory's Storm King Stout is superb when slightly chilled. In lieu of a rich Argentinian Malbec try a Belgian Dubbel while Flemish Reds are the big Burgundies of the beer world: both raise steaks to another level.

STICKY BARBECUED RIBS

No other flame-grilled food exposes a dearth of grill skills more brutally than barbequed ribs. Get it wrong, leave it too long, and you'll be chewing on nothing but char and bone, a culinary catastrophe that not even beer can salvage. But if you prepare properly, get the basting right, the sauce all gooey and the spices on song, then ribs are a revelation, especially with sweet, smoky rauchbiers. The rare Alaskan Smoked Porter is simply sublime while Rogue's Smoke Ale is a little more subtle. Manchester Star Ale from JW Lees, a resuscitated recipe dating back to 1884, also frees the fatty textures from the tongue.

SAUSAGES

To be a simple sausage these days just isn't enough.

Take the British banger: for so long comfortable in its own collagen casing, the amalgamation of unidentified pork products has now been pimped up with everything from apple and apricots to pepper, sage, onion, chilli, thyme, ginger and parsley. Though your sausages may be highly herbed and spiced, if they're British you needn't look beyond a British bitter, the tangy Timothy Taylor Landlord works well, as does Tribute, a mouthfiller made with Maris Otter by St Austell in Cornwall.

For something spicier like North African merguez, a strong pale ale, high in hop bitterness and with rapier-like refreshment, will have you happier than a pig in the proverbial.

But it is, of course, the Germans who lead the world in beer and sausage matching. In fact, it's a national pastime. Probably. Bavarian beers work best with the wurst, a decent Dunkel with big bratwurst; a smoky Bamberg beer with knackwurst; while a clean, crisp Helles can handle frankfurters and sauerkraut.

CHICKEN

Chicken provides a tabla rasa on which talented tongsmen can express themselves via the medium of marinades. For dry-rubbed drumsticks or ample breasts spangled with herbs and spices, a modern Saison should step up to the plate. Dry, herbal and hoppy, Fantome's Saison from Wallonia is a classic, wonderfully refreshing example while Saison Cazeau is a little lighter.

Staying in Wallonia, Troublette, a bracing Belgian wit from the lovely rustic Caracole brewery deals deftly with a delicate, lighter lemon-led, herbal marinade. Skewered satay chicken is cracking with a Kölsch: the quenching Captain Lawrence version is great if you can't get hold of one from Cologne. Fiery Jamaican Jerk calls for a pale ale with plenty of fruity hops.

But for the ultimate chicken and beer experience, simply stick a can up its behind. Unless you want to be arrested or assaulted by angry poultry, make sure it's dead before you try though.

KING PRAWNS & FISH

Ignore that bit in the Bible where it says you shouldn't eat seafood, and pair seared scallops or king prawns brushed with garlic butter with an Abbey-style Tripel. St Feuillen, Affligem, Karmeliet and Allagash all brew beautiful versions.

For delicate tuna and salmon steaks crying out for fresh, fruit flavours, order Stone & Wood's Pale Ale or Little Creatures from Australia, a nation for whom BBQing is a religion.

Friesian lagers like Jever or Leavenworth Friesian Lager from the aptly-named Fish Brewing cut wonderfully through oily, richly flavoured fish such as lightly smoked mackerel or sardines while, for fleshy flatfish, why not head for a healthily hopped Czech Pilsner . . . just for the halibut?

LAMB CHOPS

Lamb is a fatty fellow. It coats the roof of the mouth, greases the palate and calls for the carbonation and texture-lifting bitterness only found in an American-style IPA, all hoppy and spicy. Daring drinkers can replicate the sweetness of redcurrant jelly with a funky, fruity Lambic kriek.

Right: Walloon witbier works well with lemon chicken marinade.

Far right: Abbey-style ales pair perfectly with prawns.

SAISON STYLE

A hazy shimmer above sheaves of wheat, heat beating down on aching backs and surging up through sore feet; a wipe of the bronzing brow; an eyes-closed-shut tilt of the head against a tree-trunk; a stolen fumble among the hay bales: it was hot and it was hard work.

Above: The quilted countryside of Wallonia.

Left: Gavroche, a classy Bière de Garde from Brasserie St Sylvestre in Northern France.

Right: Saison Pipaix is brewed on a steam-powered brewery.

Looking back, it's enough to moisten the eyes and quiver the lip with nostalgia: the countryside of Northern France and Wallonia, quilted with small fields and farmhouses, a pastoral patchwork dotted with itinerant agricultural workers toiling over the soil.

At the end of each day, the grasping, rasping thirst of these 'saisonniers' was quenched with Saison, meaning 'season' in French. Boiled and spiced, the beer was safer than water and the main source of replacement liquid for the hot, sweating harvesters; a bucolic beer brewed during the colder months and then stored to be drunk throughout the summer.

The reasons for this were threefold. There was no refrigeration and brewing went bad in the hotter months, when the warm air was inundated with irksome, air-borne bacteria intent on ruining fermentation.

Farmers were also simply too busy gathering grain to be able to brew beer during the summer. Brewing in the winter not only ensured itinerant agricultural workers employment during lean labour periods but also produced spent grain – free feed for hungry livestock.

Only the larger farms had their own brewery. Sometimes, smaller farmholders would borrow the brewery of a bigger one and brew communal farmhouse ale that would be divided among them and stored in individual cellars, ready to provide their respective labourers with liquid refreshment in summer.

Each farmer had his own recipe but, seldom burdened with the commercial concern of selling it, they brewed with little care for consistency. From farm to farm and year to year, the constituents and the quality would vary considerably, depending entirely on which ingredients were close at hand; be it barley, rye, wheat and spelt; hops, herbs or spices.

The key requirements, however, were refreshment, energy and relatively low alcohol. As such, Saisons were light of body and pale in colour, with plenty of sweetness. Dry-hopped with a mixture of old and young hops, for keeping ability and bitterness respectively, they were often, but not always, sparingly spiced with star anise and ginger as well as coriander, cumin, honey, orange peel and peppercorns.

A certain sourness and Lambic-like dryness came from open fermentation fuelled by several different yeast strains, some of which would obviously have been wild. An iron-like metallic bitterness is said to have underpinned these low-strength slakers and many have attributed this to the Hainault water, harder than a concrete-covered diamond. Others, however, have blamed it on rusty pipes and old tanks in rustic breweries. Either way, it's not essential now.

By the 1920s, men had been widely usurped by machines, other beer styles had turned drinkers' heads and by the outbreak of Wold War II, farmhouse breweries had all but faded away from Belgium's brewing landscape.

The stronger Saisons survived, and it is these that find themselves at the forefront of a remarkable renaissance on both sides of the Atlantic. They seldom bear much resemblance to their farmhouse forebears, however. At 6.5% ABV, they are neither sessionable nor suitable for an afternoon of swinging a sharp scythe in the sun.

Saison does not have a discernible style. Modern Saisons can be easy drinking and accessible blondes, sweet and dark, highly hopped spicy bitter beers or flint dry with a faint funkiness, a little like 'Lambic lite' if you will. But all tend to be bottle-conditioned, quenching and dry.

Some lower strength 'authentic' Saisons can still be found in Wallonia while Yvan de Baets, a Saison expert and as part of a revival of historical Belgian beers, has re-created a 4.5% version at Brasserie De La Senne in Brussels (see overleaf).

While the likes of Fantome, Lefebvre (Saison 1900) and Vapeur (Saison Pipaix) are all synonymous with the Saison 'style', it has been Saison Dupont from Brasserie Dupont that opened up America and, regardless of whether Wallonia keep brewing it, ensured Saison's survival. Americans have eagerly embraced Saison, picking up the ball and running with it, occasionally kicking it in different directions and seeing where it lands. Hill Farmstead in Vermont specialise in Saisons, Jolly Pumpkin brews a light 'authentic' Saison in Bam Bière while Pretty Little Things' 'Jack d'Or' is one of the more elegant interpretations.

Bière de Garde

There is no other beer style more unambiguously French than 'Bière de Garde', meaning 'Keeping Beer' or 'Beer for Storing' (and which, you might notice, is the same meaning as German 'Lager Bier' and English 'stock ale').

While similar to Saison in that it was originally brewed in winter and aged for summer supping, Bière de Garde tended to be the slightly sweeter sibling in the farmhouse ale family. French farmers would have brewed a low-strength refresher to be drunk during the hot harvest days while a stronger version (Bière de Mars, 'March beer') would have been set aside for drinking at the end of the season once all the work had been done.

Brewed at the northernmost point of L'Hexagon, Bière de Garde is characterised in its classic guise by svelte caramelised sweetness and a touch of liquorice. It is more malt-driven than its Belgian counterpart and, perhaps reflective of France's attitude to work-life balance, better designed for dining than mere eating.

In the 1970s, with the behemoth French brewers flooding the market with lager, French brewers in Bière de Garde land became the retro cause célèbre among young discerning beer drinkers looking for something different and a French alternative to the niche Belgian beer.

Spearheading the revival was Jenlain from Brasserie Duyck who, like the second wave of Saison brewers, raised the alcohol, making it more like the more prestigious and potent 'Bière de Mars', once saved for special occasions.

Several smaller French brewers (St Sylvestre, Choulette and Castelain) catalysed Bière de Garde's comeback in the 1980s, and today it has regained a firm foothold in French beer culture. These days, however, it is a far cry from the fruity and slightly funky farmhouse beers once drunk in the fields, bearing a closer resemblance to the cleaner, crisp Bock and Alt beers across the border in Germany.

BRASSERIE DE LA SENNE

Molenbeek, Brussels   www.brasseriedelasenne.be

Brasserie de la Senne takes its name from the river that once sludged slowly through Brussels, meandering its way from Flanders to Wallonia. You can't see it anymore. As the city swelled with heavy industry in the 19th century, the Senne, thickened with effluent, flooded frequently and caused havoc with the health of the city's poorer 'quartiers'.

In the 1860s, in a move contaminated by controversy and corruption, the decision was taken to cover the river up. Bourgeois boulevards and grandiose buildings were built on top of it in a shift that made Brussels prettier yet pushed the poor out. As the Senne was buried beneath concrete, it pulled a veil over Brussels' proletariat past and, for many, the city's soul was sold down the river.

'It's down there somewhere,' says Bernard Leboucq, one half of Brasserie de la Senne. 'You can't see it but the old Brussels is flowing beneath us.' Sat at a small table in De la Senne's vast brewhouse, Bernard and I debate whether Belgian beer, in its original form, is equally obscured.

'The Belgians persuade themselves that they live in beer paradise, but Belgium is the lost paradise,' he says, sipping a bulbous glass filled with Taras Boulba at 10am in the morning. 'Belgian beers are too sugary, too strong and too spicy. C'est la maladie de la bière Belge,' Leboucq says.

Belgians, he says, are brainwashed into thinking that they have the best beer in the world. 'People are proud of beer but they're blinded by the pride. They just drink the same things – Leffe and Duvel. They never sit down with a Drie Fonteinen, a Cantillon or a Dupont.'

Leboucq, a talented jazz trumpeter with no brewing background, began homebrewing while living in a squat

It's here where Yvan and Bernard engineer their gentle iconoclasm, not so much breaking the Belgian beer mould as gently re-sculpting it with a chisel.

where he and a budding chef together held illicit pop-up gastronomic experiences. 'I wasn't a brewer but I had a love for gastronomy,' Leboucq says. 'People were coming and enjoying my homebrews.'

An amber ale called Zinnebier was his first beer, brewed specifically for the Zinneke Parade, a biennial bohemian bridge-building ballyhoo designed to bring Brussels's diverse cultural districts together.

Yvan de Baets was one of many people who liked it. A former social worker, Yvan was working at De Ranke and liked Leboucq's beers. Reared on table beer from the age of three, Yvan had cut his teeth on the Belgian classics during the 1980s before a coming of age during a visit to Cantillon.

The two had a chat about beer, exchanged numbers and, before long, teamed up with a clear mission in mind: to brew a true beer from Brussels. 'We're from this city and our beer is Brussels beer,' Leboucq says. 'Brussels has urban terroir and being a Brussels brewer was very important for us.'

Brussels used to be a major brewing metropolis. At its peak in the 1880s, it boasted more than a hundred working breweries, but a combination of conflict, consolidation and complacency had left only one: Cantillon, the legendary Lambic producer located in the city's Anderlecht district.

De Baets and Leboucq set out to be the second. They had started in a small place in the Sint-Pieters-Leeuw suburb, but it wasn't 'le vrai Brussels'. The pursuit for new premises was both prolonged and problematic: four years of kicking tyres, being messed about by banks and encountering more red tape than at a Communist Christmas party.

During their search, they had borrowed brewing space at both De Ranke in Wallonia and Thiriez over the border in Northern France. 'It was really difficult,' Leboucq says. 'When you don't have much money, it's hard. Brewing elsewhere was frustrating, especially when people tell you they love the beers.'

But finally, in 2010, Brasserie de la Senne began brewing in Brussels, moving into a huge hangar in Molenbeek, an edgy industrial enclave in the northwest of the city. 'It's a beast of a place and we took it as soon as we saw it. But there was nothing here. No electricity, no gas, no drains. Nothing,' Leboucq says, his words drowned out by his dad who's stood behind him, hunkered over a hinge, visor down, welder in hand, muttering and sending sparks soaring into the sky like a Roman candle.

The brewery occupies an enormous space, the size of three football pitches with stacks of steel kegs and sacks of barley in the far wing, a scattering of tables and chairs next to a mobile bar in the other. Oak barrels are bundled together beneath a makeshift mezzanine office with a direct sightline to the German-made brewery.

All second-hand, the 20-hectolitre set-up is endowed with particularly wide fermentation tanks. 'We purposely went for fatter vessels,' Leboucq says, giving them an affectionate pat.

'It's like a Jacuzzi for the wort. We don't want to stress it out. We want to give it space.'

De Baets and Leboucq produce clean, classic beers that are old-style Belgian: unfussy, unpasteurised, unfiltered and uninterested in cloying sugar, spice, strength and intense fruity esters. 'Bitterness is our calling card but we're not doing what the Americans do,' Leboucq said. 'We like their beers and hops, and we love new ideas, but we don't want flavour trends here. Some flavours are good, but not just because they're new.'

Brewed with the thirsty working man in mind and against the backdrop of big Belgian brewery hegemony, the beers' retro labels celebrate the unlikely uprising of the underdog. Taras Boulba, a sensational slaking modern Saison fermented with two yeast strains, shows an oppressor dropping a barrel onto the head of an idealistic everyman, while Jambe De Bois (Peg Leg), subtitled Belgian Revolution Triple, pays tribute to a French buccaneer whose prosthetic disadvantage did nothing to dim his derring-do.

The dark and drinkable Stouterijk, meaning 'naughty boy', is a rejuvenation of a long-lost local black Irish stout brewed, like all the beers, exclusively with European hops. Zinnebir, the beer where it all began, is a strong, gently hopped golden deceiver that drops down effortlessly.

'We want to strip back to the roots of Belgian beer,' Leboucq said. 'We offer new interpretations of the beers that people in Brussels would have drunk a hundred years ago.

'They're the Belgian beers that people have forgotten about: well-balanced beers and session ales that we want to drink,' he says. 'But most of all they're Brussels beers. They embody real Brussels.'

Above left : Bernard Leboucq.

Left and above: De la Senne's kegs and German-made brewery.

KEY BEERS

Zinnebir 6%
Taras Boulba 4.5%
Stouterik 4.5%
Jambe de Bois 8%
Equinox 8%
Saison de la Senne 4.3%

* LAGER

---

* pilsner

* dunkel

* amber

* helles

* bock

Lager may be the greatest pillar of the modern world of brewing, but no other stylistic term has been more abused.

Around 90% of all the beer drunk in the world is lager. And, in some countries, it seems that familiarity has bred a certain level of contempt. Maligned and much misunderstood, 'lager' has become synonymous with all that can be bad about beer.

At the hands of the accountant rather than those of the brewers, conditioning times have been cut, adjuncts and extracts have been added, and the importance of ingredients and integrity all too often overlooked.

At the behest of the big brewers, lager has been commoditised, stacked high and sold low; it has become the fizzy yellow opium of the masses, the lout's preferred social lubricant, the small-minded substance celebrated in adolescence that you eventually grow out of just as soon as 'real' beer starts to give you the glad-eye. Lager. Just saying the word makes you sound like a bit of a dufus.

But that's just a whole load of stuff and nonsense. Just because a lot of lousy beers are lagers certainly does not mean that all lager is lousy. Lager is deserving of as much unbridled reverence and exploration as ale, that other overarching umbrella term that defines beer.

Meaning 'to store' in German, lager represents a broad brood of different beer styles. Many of which merge yet all are united by low-temperature bottom-fermentation and cold conditioning. Spanning a spectrum of different hues and furnished with a wealth of grain and hop-driven flavours, lager's family includes beers of every colour from palest straw through gold to nut-brown to black. It covers Pilsners, Helles, Marzens and Rauchbier; it brings in Bocks, Doppelbocks, Maibocks, Schwarzbier and more.

Lager. Let it into your life.

STAND UP AND SALUTE SACCHAROMYCES PASTORIANUS, OTHERWISE KNOWN AS BOTTOM-FERMENTING LAGER YEAST, FOR CREATING THE PHENOMENAL BEERS LAGERED IN THIS CHAPTER; EACH AND EVERY ONE, LIQUID PROOF THAT LAGER NEED NOT BE A BYWORD FOR BIG, BLAND AND BORING.

UK

Camden Town Brewing
USA Hells 4.6%
London, England
www.camdentownbrewing.com

It may be housed beneath an array of arches in North London, but Camden Town is no botched-together bucket and barrel endeavour. A shimmering stainless steel set-up fashioning bottom and top fermenting beers, it has cold-shouldered crazy extreme brewing and cask in favour of quality, consistent keg beer that rarely tastes better than from the brewery tap. This American twist on a Bavarian elbow-bender hails citrusy, snappy Stateside hops without overdoing it on the IBUs.

Meantime Brewing
Friesian Pilsner 5.2%
London, England
www.meantimebrewing.com

The snappy, assertive bitterness of Northern German pilsners is replicated courtesy of three German noble hops. Clean, crisp and quenching, it is bright and bracing, carving effortlessly through oily fish, pork belly and other fatty food. This is a superb seasonal from a brewer that kept the capital's craft brewing scene going long before it was trendy to do so.

Gower Brewery
Lighthouse Lager 4.5%
Llanrhidian, Wales
www.gowerbrewery.com

Born in 2011 at the Greyhound Pub in Gower is one of 50 or so microbreweries to have mushroomed all over Wales in recent years. Few lend their name to a lager as lovely as this, however; quenching and crisp with a dusting of dry hop bitterness. Tidy.

IRELAND

Dingle Brewing Company
Tom Crean's 4.6%
Dingle
www.dinglebrewingcompany.com

One of a number new micros emerging on the Emerald Isle in recent years, this six-barrel brewhouse was squeezed into an old creamery on the windy, wild western edge of Ireland. Well-travelled brewmaster Xavier Baker only brews this one beer, a bracing, mineral-rich lager named after the Irish explorer who accompanied Shackleton and Scott to the Antarctic. Surely, a beer that's ripe for an 'extra cold' version.

US

Boston Beer Company
Doppelbock 9.5%
Boston
www.bostonbeer.com

A rich and robust maroon, malt-driven mouthfiller taken from the first runnings of a mighty mash. Each bottle claims to contain half a pound of malt, mostly pale but with a considerable amount of caramel too. Aged for four weeks, it's soothing sweet and honeyed with a balmy boozy body. Not only that, it's also got a goat on the label.

Caldera Brewing
Ashland Amber 5.4%
Oregon
www.calderabrewing.com

In 2005, Caldera, which brewed only draught beer for the first eight years of its existence, became the first Oregonian craft brewer to put its beers into cans. This copper-coloured, effortless-drinking amber is seasoned with a sprinkle of Cascade and Galena fresh whole flower hops. Look out for its Lawnmower Lager, too, a low-gravity lipsmacker, 3.9%, ideal for those wanting to drink beer while driving*.

*Disclaimer: do not drink beer and drive. Don't even putt.

Grand Teton Brewing
5 O'Clock Shadow 7.6%
Idaho
www.grandtetonbrewing.com

Unsurprisingly sought-after, and seldom seen outside of Idaho, this limited edition 'double black lager' is made from a magnified malt bill containing crystal, a little bit of roast and chocolate. Dusted with German noble hops and cold-conditioned for four months, it's roasty and rich, black-ink in colour, lacing the glass and furnishing the palate with espresso, liquorice and a smidgeon of smoke.

Moonlight Brewing
Death & Taxes 5%
California
www.moonlightbrewing.com

Amid the vineyards of Northern California outside Santa Rosa and well off any beaten track, brewer Brian Hunt is a one-man, wide-eyed whirlwind of brewing creativity who began brewing at the once-upon-a-time Milwaukee beer giant Schlitz before an ale-drinking epiphany in England saw him go solo. As well as growing his own hops and delivering the beer himself, he refuses to bottle the beer, declaring it cruel, and works on a rustic and remote ramshackle brewery shoehorned into a shed that Hunt hails as an 'abbey'. Death & Taxes, a stylish roasty Schwartzbier, is the most famous Moonlight brew and can be found scattered around the better beer bars of San Francisco and Sonoma County. Sip it on sight, it's downright delicious.

Shmaltz Brewing Company
Coney Island Lager 5.5%
California
www.shmaltzbrewing.com

Shmaltz's genesis dates back 16 years, when Jewish founder Jeremy Cowan and friends squeezed the juice out of eight crates of pomegranates and gave it, along with $1,500, to a local brewer who transformed it into 100 cases of He'Brew, a kosher craft beer with a picture of a dancing green rabbi on the front. Thanks to Cowan's marketing schtick and the stainless steel skills of Olde Saratoga Brewing, Shmaltz's now sells 16 beers in 31 US states and also abroad. A sideshow to Shmaltz, Coney Island Craft Brewing, began in 2009 when Cowan created 'a pitcher beer for beer geeks' named after the alternative amusement park in New York. It is a great, grassy Pilsner, brewed with eight malts and half-a-dozen hop varieties, which give it a burlesque body and a citrus Cascade kick.

Sly Fox Brewing
Pikeland Pils 4.9%
Pennsylvania
www.slyfoxbeer.com

Sly Fox was championing craft beer in a can long before it became fashionable, and its Pikeland Pils, lively with lychee notes and a grainy foundation, was the first metal-clad micro to win gold at the Great American Beer Festival. On the first weekend of May, the

brewery races goats in the parking lot for its Bock festival. The fastest goat around the lot is honoured by having that year's Maibock named after it.

Sudwerk
Lager Münchener Helles 5.3%
California
www.sudwerk.com

The town of Davis in California is where budding brewers flock to study the art, the science and the magic of beer making. The Master Brewers programme, part of the University of California curriculum and headed by the brilliant Charlie Bamforth, is the oldest in the US and its alumni are crammed with cunning craft brewmasters, including Sudwerk's master brewer, Jay Prahl. In downtown Davis, Sudwerk hews a host of German-style lager beers, of which this heavenly, flawless Helles is the simplest yet the most sublime.

CANADA

King Brewery
Dark Lager 4.8%
Ontario
www.kingbrewery.ca

Short of slapping its lederhosen more often, scoffing on even more unfeasibly enormous sausages or squeezing an oompah band into each bottle, it is difficult to see how King's beers could be more Germanic, except maybe if brewer Phil DiFonzo changed his surname to Von Fontz. Ruthless Teutonic efficiency runs through the brewhouse, which opened little more than a decade ago in the little settlement of Nobleton, part of King Township, north of Toronto, where double-decoction adds depth and body to the beers. This is a gorgeous, grainy, dark copper Dunkel that delivers nuts, toffee and coffee and cuts no corners.

Klosterbrauerei Andechs
Bergbock Hell 7%
Andechs
www.andechs.de/kloster-
andechs/die-klosterbrauerei

Andechs has it all. It's
got history dating back
to the 12th century; a
Benedictine monastery
with real monks; a
handsome church; an
enormous bucolic beer
garden with spectacular
views of the snow-capped
Alps and, of course,
beautifully-made beer.
Others may do the darker,
more famous doppelbock
or the seasonal Spezial
but I prefer this honeyed,
delicately-hopped hybrid.
Difficult to pigeonhole,
easy to drink.

Augustiner Brau
Maximator 7.5%
Munich
www.augustiner-brau.de

Augustiner is the real deal and my favourite
of the six Munich breweries. Fidelity to
yesteryear stretches to its own floor maltings
and dispensing from wooden casks, while the
Augustiner tent is where you'll find locals and
families during Oktoberfest. In the summer,
reach for the Helles, but this deep copper
Doppelbock, dense with dark fruit flavours
and dry in its finish, is wonderful in the winter.

Bayerischer Bahnhof
Schaffner 5%
Leipzig
www.bayerischer-bahnhof.de

While most go for the legendary Gose, the
Bahnhof brewpub in Leipzig also produces
an unfiltered and slightly unusual Pilsner
which translates as 'Conductor'. Hazy with
fruity yeast flavours, it punches a hole in
Pilsner expectations and is just the ticket if
you like the esters of Weissbier yet yearn for
bigger bitterness.

Einbecker
Dunkel 4.9%
Einbeck
www.einbecker.de

It is claimed that the town of Einbeck in
Lower Saxony has had a brewer since as
far back as 1351. I don't know whether
this is true, as, well, I
wasn't there then. This
particular brewery has
been doing its thing
since 1378 and is
renowned throughout
beerdom for brewing
its terrific trio of Bock
beers, the style that
first brought Einbeck
fame, though the
brewery's popular Pils
is what pays the bills.
Beyond the bocks, this
moody, malty mocha-
tinted Dunkel, known
as a Schwartzbier in
the United States, is
delicious and dense, a
fine sipping brew for
chats over chocolate
cake.

Hummel
Raucherator Doppelbock 8.1%
Merkendorf
www.brauerei-hummel.de

This seasonal beer, brewed for Lent, looks
like it is going to smoke you out and make
your eyes water. It doesn't, though. It is more
subtle, smooth and soft than that, like a
bonfire the morning after. It is one of several
Franconian beers furnished by this family-
run brewery and pub, well worth a bus trip
beyond Bamberg. If smoke doesn't do it for
you, the kellerbier drops down like a baggy
pair of lederhosen.

Klosterbrauerei Ettal
Kloster Dunkel 9%
Ettal
www.original-ettaler.de

The Benedictine monks have been knocking
about in Ettal since 1330 and brewing since
1609 and, you'll be pleased to hear, it has
become a bit of a habit. As well as continuing
to meddle in the mash-tun, they also dabble
in distillation too, making lovely liqueurs and
herbal elixirs using hops and herbs from a
herbarium. This does-as-it-says-on-the-bottle
Dunkel is a stand-up example of the style –
deep and drinkable with a dark fruity finish.

Rothaus
Tannenzäpfle 5.1%
Baden-Württemburg
www.rothaus.de

The smiling maiden on
the bottle is called Birgit
Kraft, her name a play
on words meaning 'beer
gives strength' in the
local dialect. Her face
has adorned the label
of this quaint and quirky
cult classic, whose name
means 'little fir cones',
since 1972. Set in the
bucolic hills of the Black
Forest, surrounded by
shimmering lakes, fir
trees and chocolate-
box villages, Rothaus is
the highest brewery in
Germany, founded as
part of the St Blasien
monastery in 1791.
Secularisation in the early
1800s saw it transferred
to the Grand Duchy of
Baden and it still remains 100 per cent
owned by the state of Baden-Württemberg.
Its best-selling Pilsner is wonderfully vibrant,
using water drawn from local springs, with a
crisp pine aroma and a lively fresh bitterness.

Spezial
Marzen 5.3%
Bamberg
www.brauerei-spezial.de

One of Bamberg's big guns, Spezial has been rocking rauchbiers longer than anyone else in town, and smoking its own malt over beechwood behind the terrific, traditional pub. Unlike nearby Schlenkerla, its traditional takes on smoked beers rarely venture beyond Bavaria. They make them mellower here, too, with a subdued, softer smokiness. In single malt whisky terms, it is more like a Lagavulin than a peaty Laphroaig.

Klosterbrauerei Weissenohe
Monk's Fest 5%
Weissenohe
www.klosterbrauerei-weissenohe.de

Housed in a former monastery, Klosterbrauerei Weissenohe is one of hundreds of small breweries scattered around Franconia. Dating back to 1052, it slipped into the hands of the Winkler family in 1803. This dark lager, deepened in flavour from double-decoction, brings nutty notes, a smidgeon of spice and a clean-cut finish.

Zehendner
Ungespundetes Lagerbier 5.5%
Mönchsambach
www.moenchsambacher.de

Tired of tourists? Sick of smoky brews? Bored with relentlessly beautiful Baroque architecture? Then venture beyond Bamberg to this basic brewpub. Within its wooden-clad walls, Franconian folk play cards, devour enormous dumplings and drink this lovely grainy, bready, unfiltered lager. No one speaks English and there is a stork who lives on the roof.

BEER VENUE Zly Casy

With the vast majority of Prague's bars in the pockets of the country's big brewers, the city can be a little disappointing in terms of beer drinking diversity. The likes of Pilsner Urquell, Budweiser Budvar and Gambrinus are decent enough drops, but their ubiquity can become a little one-dimensional after a day or so and only a few venues have enthusiastically embraced the 'fourth pipe', the term given to a tap dedicated to independent breweries.

To get a better flavour of the wider Czech beer scene, take a taxi or tram (11, 8, 7 or 24) from the city centre to the Nusle neighbourhood. Then steal yourself away down to Zlý Casy, a small and cosy bare-brick basement bar whose name means Bad Times.

Ever since Zlý Casy thumbed its nose at the corporate Koruna, it has commanded cult status among Prague's more discerning pivo drinkers looking for well-kept beers seldom seen elsewhere in the city.

The majority of the 25 draught taps are dedicated to the Czech Republic's most impressive independents, including Matuška, Otakar, Chyse, Breznák and Rychtár, alongside a number of lesser-known German offerings.

The continually rotating draught range, scrawled on a board above the bar, is supplemented by an enormous fridge brimming with beers from the Netherlands, Belgium and the US, all overseen by knowledgeable staff with a spooky sixth sense for an empty glass.
Zlý Casy
Cestmírova 5, Prague 4-Nusle
tel +420 723 339 995
www.zlycasy.eu

Antoš
Unfiltered Pilsner 4.7%
Slaný
www.pivovarantos.cz

Having made beer in Mexico, Moldova, South Korea and Iceland, brewmaster David Masa returned to his hometown of Slaný in 2010 to set up a brewpub alongside fellow native Josef Paulik. Slotted sympathetically into the vaulted vestiges of a 16th-century brewery, it is a smooth-looking set-up clad in stone and copper with a great little beer garden. While segueing Saaz hop with Moravian malt is not a new idea, this cloudy gold Pilsner does it better than most. One of several impressive brews, including a dark lager, a wheat beer and an amber ale. The Jesuit historian Bohuslav Balbin apparently wrote in 1681 that 'Beer from Slaný used to be recommended as the number one in Bohemia', and those old-time Bohemians would probably be impressed once again if they could somehow return.

Bernard
Svátecní Ležák, 5%
Humpolec
www.bernard.cz/en

Stanislav Bernard bought the bankrupt, tumbledown Humpolec brewery in 1991, dragged it into the modern day, and ten years later joined forces with the Belgian brewer Duvel-Moorgat. The beers are open-fermented, unpasteurised and bottle-conditioned: Bernard pairs principles with professionalism and is not ashamed to grow. Its marquee lager is full of fruity ester flavours balanced by floor-malted biscuit malt and the citrus snap of Saaz hops.

Budweiser Budvar
Kroužkovaný Ležák 5%
Ceské Budejovice
www.original-budweiser.cz

Rich in texture, munificent in its malt character and boasting a pronounced Saaz sharpness this cloudy cult beer from Ceske Budejovice is, unlike its more famous flagship sibling, neither filtered nor pasteurised but still benefits from 90 days of lagering.

Hastrman
Svetlý Ležák 12° 4.4%
Velky Rybník
www.pivohastrman.cz

Four doses of hopping hand this hazy, hay-coloured effort its richer, resinous Saaz character and bitter bite. This minute micro, only around since 2005, is a bit mental and has ventured into international styles with varying success, while a beer brewed using aloe vera is one of the more off-centre efforts.

Kout Na Šumave
Svetlý Ležák 5%
Kout na Šumave
www.pivovarkout.eu

Any pilgrimage to Pilsen is far from complete without a south-westerly 45km sneak down to the tiny (pop. 1,200) village of Kout Na Šumave, home to what many craft beer cognoscenti consider the Czech Republic's, and thus the world's, finest lager. Built in 1736, owned for many years by the Stadion family, closed in 1969 during Communism and woken from its slumber in 2006, this is a small-batch set-up within the vast remains of the old brewery. Svetlý Ležák is simply the Czech for 'pale lager', but this is very far from a simple beer. Rarely seen outside the Pilsen region, it is a glorious golden drop, alive with effervescence, with a fragrant Saaz finish. Please stand for a proper Pilsner.

Pernštejn
Pardubický Porter 8%
Pardubice
www.pernstejn.cz

A Czech classic, this bottom-fermented beer in the style called Baltic Porter in the West, is an incongruous landmark in Czech brewing's lager-dominated landscape. Less bitter than its Baltic brethren brewed further north, it dances close to a Doppelbock and is laced with liquorice, cinnamon and a coffee-two-sugars sweetness. The Pernštejn brewery has been brewing it since 1890 in the town of Pardubice where, nearly 100km east of Prague, they run a famous horse race, make Semtex and hold annual chess and Rubik's Cube championships. Thankfully, not all at the same time.

Pilsner Urquell
Kvasnicový 4.4%
Pilsen
www.pilsnerurquell.com

Unfiltered, unpasteurised with further yeast added after fermentation and a rare insight into what proper Pilsner can be. Hazy, golden with a soft bitter sparkle, it's spruced with a sensational Saaz hop aroma and laid down on a fresh brioche base of Moravian barley. Unfortunately, it's rarely available beyond the brewery and the bars that surround it but, fresh from the brewery, it's stunning.

Rychtár
Natur kvasnicový 4.9%
Hlinsko v Cechách
www.rychtar.cz

Hlinsko, smack in the centre of the Czech Republic, has had a brewery since 1913. After a tumultuous time under Nazi and Communist rule, it was privatised in 2008. From a solid if not spectacular stable, this glowing hazy yeast beer, grassy hop notes with honeyed toast, can perform alongside the best of Bohemian Pilsners.

Balling Scale

When you go drinking beer in the Czech Republic, often you will see on the bottle label a declaration of degrees: 10°, 12° or 14°.

They are not an exact indicator of alcoholic strength, but alcoholic potential – the equivalent of OG, or original gravity – and they refer to the Balling scale, invented in Prague by a brewing boffin named Carl Josef Napoleon Balling in 1843.

The Balling Scale is a measurement of how much dissolved sugar is in the wort, before fermentation turns it into beer. The brewer will take a sample of the wort, cool it down to 17.5°C/63.5°F, and then drop in the hydrometer, a device looking like a thermometer with a vastly overgrown bulb, which bobs up and down in the beer like a buoy in the ocean.

The height that the hydrometer rises out of the wort reveals the concentration of dissolved sugars in the liquid. It gives an accurate indicator of the possible alcoholic strength of the beer. However, not all the sugars in wort are always turned into alcohol. Fermentation may be stopped before the yeast is full, or the yeast cells may simply not have the appetite for it.

Those sugars that are not turned to alcohol provide the sweetness in the beer, the ying to the crisp, hoppy yang so characteristic in classic Czech Pilsners. Residual sugars also bulk the beer's body, furnishing it with the kind of fuller malty flavours that have, traditionally, distinguished Czech Pilsners and ležáks from less impressive imported lagers. No surprise then that Czech beer drinkers became concerned when, in 1997, the Balling Scale stopped being a legal requirement. With fewer legal checks and balances, brewers were potentially free to minimise the amount of malt they use while maintaining the same strength, the result being a thinner, cost-cutting beer.

The Balling scale has been all but usurped by the similar Plato Scale but the historical habits die hard and the names and numbers of the Czech beers remain. However, while you can say that, eg, a 10° beer will be approximately 4% ABV, a 12° one approximately 5%, the relationship between final strength and original gravity in Czech beer is now as murky as an unfiltered wheat beer.

Strahov Monastery Brewery
Tmavy (dark lager) 5.5%
Prague
www.klasterni-pivovar.cz

The pivos may be pricy and, high up on the hills close to Prague Castle, it is not a place that lures in locals, but Strahov is certainly one of the most scenic spots to sip in the city, especially if you can drink in the cobbled beer garden. A cosy copper brewhouse creates half-a-dozen beers, all named after Norbert, the patron saint of Bohemia, that straddle both old and new worlds. While lupulin lovers will lean towards the strong Golden Ale, hopped ten times with Saaz, American and Kiwi hops, a more orthodox option is this deliciously dry, dreamy, unfiltered dark beer.

Svijany
Svijanský Rytír 5%
Svijany
www.pivovarsvijany.cz

A lovely light Pilsner, from a much-admired micro situated between Prague and the Polish border, which sometimes pops its soft, fruity head up in some of the better-drinking beer bars in Prague. If you see it, introduce your laughing gear to it immediately. They will get on handsomely. If they don't, it's your fault and not the beer's.

U rytíre Lochoty
Kvasnicove 11 4.5%
Pilsen
www.lochota.cz/pivovar.php

It may not be much to look at, it may be quite a distance from Pilsen city centre and the food menu may be a bit 'meh' but, for the beers alone, do yourself a favour and make your way to this minipivovar. On offer are two equally impressive unfiltered, soft and sparkling 'yeast' beers, the less potent of which gets the nod purely on the basis that one can treat oneself to more of it.

Únetický
Únetické Pivo 12° 4.9%
Prague-West
www.unetickypivovar.cz

Closed by the Communists for being too little in the 1940s, Únetický was resurrected with new brew kit in 2011 by a former employee of Staropramen. While other new Czech breweries dabble in the brave new world of IPA, Únetický remain staunchly loyal to traditional Czech brewing. The beers are exceptional, especially this outstanding Bohemian Pilsner which puts the class into classic: softly carbonated with a delicate mineral mouthfeel, a fresh brioche base and a dry, spicy signature Saaz hop finish.

Žatec
Dark Lager 5.7%
Zatec
www.zateckypivovar.cz

Located in the heart of the world's most revered hop country and one of the longest-running breweries in Czech, Žatec remains unwavering in its fidelity to longstanding lagering techniques. Built into the walls

of the Žatec castle back in 1801, it was resuscitated 201 years later by an Englishman, Rolf Munding, who spent what he had to and maintained what mattered: double decoction mashing; three stages of Saaz hopping in copper kettles; open fermentation 'squares' and horizontal lagering tanks, sunk deep beneath the brewery back in 1835. As well as this rich and robust burnished black lager, the Saaz hop shines in the brewery's flagship lager, while Baronka is an awesome amber that stylistically veers towards Vienna.

Felsenau
Junkerbier 5.2%
Berne
www.felsenau.ch

Since taking up the reins of the Felsenau family brewers in Berne back in 1993, Martin Simon and Stephan Thierstein have successfully cleaned up the quality of the beers, showing the brewery's former trademark sickly-buttery diacetyl note the door. They have also unleashed a number of new beers, including this delicate, unpasteurised, crisp, flowery and rounded take on a Pilsner, sealed in a stylish swing-top bottle.

Heineken Switzerland
Coop Helvetia 4.8%
Chur
www.heinekenswitzerland.ch

Dirt-cheap but with more depth than the other stack-'em-high beers brewed by Heineken Switzerland, this Co-op own label lager has a harmonious pale malt body and a moderate yet clearly perceivable floral hop character. A guilty pleasure at a great price.

Locher
Schwarzer Kristall 6.3%
Appenzell
www.appenzellerbier.ch

Locher is the largest of the Swiss independent breweries and by far the most left-field. As well as a biodynamic beer

brewed under a full moon, beer shampoo and the hedonistic hemp lager – not to mention a whiskey distillery – Locher's locker also contains some notable 'normal' beers. This Schwarzer Kristall is an intense, silky-smooth, roasty, smoky, meaty, almost salty black lager, and a far cry from the pedestrian Schwarzbier one might have expected from the land whose only major contribution to civilisation, as Orson Welles once declared, was the cuckoo clock. Must be the effect of drinking Swiss whiskey.

Öufi
Öufi Dunkel Orbi 5%
Solothurn, Switzerland
www.oeufi-bier.ch

This smooth, chocolatey Swiss dark lager twiddles the toffee-flavour knob all the way to öufi ('eleven' in the local dialect). One of half a dozen German-leaning brews plus a 'whimsical' seasonal range from a brewpub established in Solothurn, in the Swiss north-west, by Alex Künzle.

Unser Bier
Amber 5%
Basel
www.unser-bier.ch

Since 2000, there has been an onslaught of amber beers unleashed by breweries based in German-speaking Switzerland. Caramel, toffee, you know the drill. Not many of them are overly inspirational, yet this triple-malted toasty lager, from the Basel-based boutique brewer with a name that simply means 'our beer' in German that first introduced the term to Switzerland, is true to style, with just the right amount of moderate bitterness and hop character.

ITALY

Birrificio Italiano
Tipopils 5.2%
Lurago Marinone
www.birrificio.it

Partial to a proper Pilsner? Then may I recommend you get all over this phenomenal, fragrant Italian beauty like a cheap suit. Each year, to ensure his perfect Pilsner maintains its panache, Agostino Arioli takes a hop-picking trip to the gardens of Tettnang, Germany, and returns to his brewpub in Lurago Marinone, north of Milan, to make this melodious, minerally masterpiece. Gentle, drawn-out fermentation combines with a clipped two-week lagering to produce a beautifully rounded beer, sprightly and with a gorgeous, grassy finish. This is the beer people point to as an example of Italy's best.

FRANCE

Karlsbräu
Licorne Elsass 5.5%
Saverne
www.karlsbrau.com

Exclusive to Alsace, the bit of France that likes to think of itself as Germany sometimes, and still made using only local ingredients, this malty, slightly spicy lager has maintained its character despite being part of a big stable of beers owned by Karlsbräu. One of the better readily available Alsatian lagers, it belies its big-brand looks.

DENMARK

Mikkeller
Draft Bear 8%
Copenhagen
www.mikkeller.dk

Mikkel Borg Bjergsø, a great globe-trotting Dane and the most notorious of the new breed of nomadic brewers, laid the foundations for gypsy brewing. Collaborating with the likes of Nøgne Ø, Three Floyds and De Proef in Belgium, and a freethinking advocate of the unique and the abstract, his stylistic scattergun seldom misses. A reliable regular among an array of one-off esoteric efforts is this lively, punchy, American-hopped 'imperial Pilsner', grainy malt base with marmalade sweetness and a hop prickle of lemon peel bitterness.

Casunziei with Hops and Pils

Serves 4

Ingredients
- 120g/4oz hops (fresh or frozen)
- 10ml cream
- 30cl Pils beer
- 60 pieces casunziei*

Method
In a pan, mix the hop with cream and a little bit of broth. Cook for 10 minutes and add beer.

Cook the casunziei for 5 to 7 minutes.

Combine and mix well. Serve hot and immediately with a hoppy Pilsner.

*Casunziei is fresh pasta with red turnip filling, typical of the culinary tradition of the Trentino mountain area in Northern Italy.

Courtesy of the Beer House, a pub and restaurant in Padua, Northern Italy.

www.ristorantebeerhouse.it

NORWAY

Aass
Bock 6.5%
Drammen
www.aass.no

A muscular, malty Bock from Norway's oldest independent brewery, dating back to 1834. Sweeter than its German cousins, it is a coming together of caramel, coffee and navy rum. There are some writers out there that would make a cheap schoolboy joke about the brewery name, which is pronounced 'orss', resembling something rather rude. Luckily, I am not one of them.

Bokbier

In 1980, with the Netherlands awash with pale-coloured Pils, a group of right-drinking beer lovers, inspired by the Campaign for Real Ale across the North Sea in Britain, embarked on a craft beer crusade aimed at preserving proper Dutch beer. It was called Vereniging Promotie Informatie Traditioneel Bier (PINT) and bokbier became its beacon of hope.

Every October, in Amsterdam, PINT hosts a big bokbier competition where Dutch, German and Belgian brewers, both new and old, lock horns using their bespoke Bocks. With not many Dutch micros lending themselves to lager beers, the Netherland way with bokbier differs from its German counterpart in its use of either bottom or top fermentation, and the Dutch tend to rock Bocks in a slightly sweeter style.

SWEDEN

Jämtlands Bryggeri
Heaven 5%
Pilgrimstad
www.jamtlandsbryggeri.se

Created when Sweden's microbrewing scene was in its embryonic stages in 1995, Jämtlands brews around a dozen small-batch, well-put-together pale ales and Pilsners. Hell, a golden lager that takes its name from the German for 'light', has rightly brought back the most bling from Sweden's brewing competitions but I would opt for this utopian alternative, a smoky, roasty and toasty Schwartzbier that is superb with rye bread and smoked fish.

FINLAND

Vakka-Suomen Panimo Osakeyhtiö
Prykmestar Savu Kataja 9%
Uusikaupunki
www.vasp.fi

There are two things to do in the coastal town of Uusikaupunki. First, visit the Bonk Museum, a collection of fictional, fanciful machines powered by local anchovy oil. Second, head down to this acutely efficient and imaginative micro, brewing left-field lagers and American-style hoppy ales, the most complex being this claret-coloured Sahti-esque Rauchbier, fuelled by beechwood-smoked barley, lagered for three months and finished with aromatic juniper.

AUSTRALIA

Carlton & United Breweries
Crown Ambassador Reserve 10.2%
Victoria
www.thecrowncompany.com

An excellent antidote to the clichéd image of Antipodean lagers, Ambassador Reserve is the jewel in Crown's range. Ringwood hops and bespoke yeast are enhanced with the addition of whole Galaxy hop flowers, less than 24 hours after they have been picked. Each year, the vintage is given a twist – in 2011 some of the 2010 vintage was aged for three months in French oak barrels before being blended back in and decanted into one of only 5,000 hand-waxed 75cl bottles.

CLARE VALLEY
KNAPPSTEIN
ENTERPRISE WINERY & BREWERY
~ EST. 1878 ~

Knappstein
Reserve Lager 5.6%
Clare Valley
www.knappstein.com.au

Where this Bavarian-style sipper differs from its peers is the use of fruity, aroma-laden Nelson Sauvin hops from New Zealand, which steer into a zestier zone otherwise occupied by pale ales or big blondes, with the clipped, bitter finish of a Kölsch. The New Zealand influence manifests itself in a fusion of summer fruit flavours; lychee, grapefruit and, wincing as I write, kiwi, making this a beery equivalent to Sauvignon Blanc. It comes courtesy of the Knappstein Winery, founded in 1969, and housed in the former home of Clare's Enterprise Brewery, which closed after the First World War. Knappstein began brewing the beer in 2006: this is still the only beer they make, and the only one they need to.

McLaren Vale Beer Company
DRK 4.5%
South Australia
www.mvbeer.com

McLaren Vale, a 40-minute drive south of Adelaide, is viniculture country, with nearly a hundred boutique wineries, and an area renowned for producing superb Shiraz. Australia's wine-makers happily admit to being beer drinkers when off duty, and many

swap grape for grain at this marvellous modern micro, which expanded from brewpub to 35-hectolitre modern brewhouse in 2012, making a quality, clean quartet of stylish-looking beers. DRK is an American-hopped Dunkel, deep bronze in hue with Marmite and a smack of caramel up front. It mellows out with dark chocolate bitterness on the finish to make a superb Australian sunset beer.

NEW ZEALAND

Croucher Brewing
Pilsner 5%
Rotorua
www.croucherbrewing.co.nz

From New Zealand's North Island hails this hoppy Bohemian Pilsner spruced up with Motueka and Riwaka, two classic Kiwi hop varieties packing fresh pine, fennel and floral notes. Body is bolstered by the addition of 10% wheat to the grist and there is a rich resinous flavour running right through it, making it ideal for admirers of IPA. Perfect with fish and chips. Or, as they say in Rotorua, fush and chups.

Emersons
Pilsner 4.9%
Dunedin
www.emersons.co.nz

No one does New World Pilsners better than New Zealand and this is a classic example. Filled with passionfruit, freshness and a flint-dry, snappy Riwaka hop finish, it is superb for a sub-5% Pilsner. Richard Emerson, a key man in New Zealand's craft brewing crusade since the early 1990s, also brews an excellent piney pale ale.

JAPAN

Otaru Beer
Dunkel 5.2%
Otaru
www.otaruotarubeer.com
In Otaru, where the water is softer than a mattress full of sheep, German brewmaster Johannes Braun has been brewing beers from his homeland since 1997. Schooled at Weihenstephan and Edinburgh, he does things the way they should be done; double-decoction for a rounder roast flavour; long two-month lagering times; organic ingredients imported from Germany; and a refusal to filter or pasteurise.

BRAZIL

Cervejaria Bamberg
Rauchbier 5.2%
Sao Paulo
www.cervejariabamberg.com.br

There is a tangible Germanic twang to much of Brazil's craft brewing scene, and Cervejaria Bamberg, set up in Sao Paulo back in 2005, brews with a particularly broad Bavarian accent. Alexandre Bazzo, one of three founding brothers, trained in Germany and the beers, running the gamut of German styles, blend trademark Teutonic efficiency with South American swagger. Given the brewer's love for Bamberg-the-city, this sexy smoked beer, with the smoked half of the malt imported from Bamberg's very own Weyermann malting company, is the obvious choice for barbecued meats on a churrasco, all leather and lardons yet lighter in body and drier in finish than its Franconian counterparts. The weizenbock, aged in French oak barrels, is another of Cervejaria Bamberg's great beers.

BOLIVIA

Cerveceria Boliviana Nacional
Paceña Pico de Oro 5.2%
La Paz
www.cbn.bo

Much better for you than the local marching powder, far more refreshing and without the gurning look, this grainy lip-smacker from La Paz somehow sips a little smoother than other big-batch lager beers that saturate South America. Brewed at nearly 12,000 feet above sea level, it reached even loftier heights when it won a gold medal at the 2012 World Beer Cup. That high up, perhaps it has something to do with water boiling at 88°C/190.4°F. Or perhaps not. Either way, it's the best beer in Bolivia even if it isn't very boutique. And, remember, drugs are for mugs. Mind, beer is for mugs, as well: pewter ones, pottery ones, glass ones, whatever you like. Also those nice tall tulip-shaped glasses, or big old brandy-style balloons, or straight-sided pint glasses.

CHILE

Kross
Maibock 6.5%
Curacavi
www.kross.cl

Kross, firmly at the forefront of Chile's burgeoning craft beer movement, can be found in the Casablanca Valley, deep in white wine country. At the brewery helm is a German called Asbjorn Gerlach who set up Kross in 2003 and makes marvellous, mostly malt-driven, beers. Gerlach employs laidback lagering times, does not pasteurise and experiments with oak-ageing, coriander-infused Abbey ales and blueberry porters. This Maibock, a seasonal beer, is a smooth swirl of honey, rye bread and golden rum.

Szot
Rubia al Vapor 5%
Talagante
www.szot.cl

Given that Anchor Steam kick-started the craft brewing revolution in California, the former home of banker-turned-brewer Kevin Szot, it is no surprise that Szot began brewing the cult San Franciscan steam beer style in Santiago. Conditioned like an ale yet brewed with a California lager yeast that likes things a bit more … chilly, it dovetails in darker malts to suit the slightly sweeter Chilean palate.

MY TOP 5 CRAFT BEERS

Mikkel Borg Bjergsø
Mikkeller
Copenhagen, Denmark

Mikkel Borg Bjergsø , the founder of Mikkeller beer and the world's most famous 'gypsy brewer', is a former maths and physics teacher whose unfettered experimentation and audacious approach to brewing has adorned his beers with cult status on both sides of the Pond.

When he's not at his home in Copenhagen, the former home-brewer trots the world like a hedonistic hobo, collaborating with the cream of global craft brewing and borrowing both their brains and their breweries to create his unique beers.

Mikkeller designs drinks that celebrate, and often amplify, the stylistic strengths of each craft brewer he collaborates with. Unshackled by overheads, he has joined forces with an array of highly upstanding new and old world brewers including Cantillon, Struise, Stone, Alesmith, De Molen and Nogne Ø, to name just a few.

While responsible for more than 600 unique beers, the one for which he is most renowned is, arguably, Beer Geek Breakfast Weasel; brewed using kopi luwak coffee, which is produced using beans that have been passed through the digestive tract of a nocturnal weasel.

✴ Orval
This might be the most complete beer in the world: great hops, crispy funkiness from the Brettanomyces and an amazing balance. I can drink this all day, every day and never get tired of it. One to 1½ years old is preferred.

✴ De Dolle Brouwers Stille Nacht
Maybe the most unique element in the universe of brewing is De Dolle's house yeast. No other brewery has a house character like this. The yeast comes together perfectly in Stille Nacht and balances the hops perfectly. The best beer in the world to age. 1982 is still amazing when kept well.

✴ Three Floyds Zombie Dust
Two years ago, the perfect pale ale, in my opinion, was Three Floyds Alpha King. The boys from Chicago outbrewed themselves and created the most amazing pale ale in the world. No other beer comes better straight out of the bottle on a hot summer day.

✴ Cigar City Hunahpuh
So many big bad imperial stouts and, since I can't name my own, Hunaphuh from Cigar City stands out like no other. It's liquid cake, a malty goddess and a hoppy sprinter, all put together in one big amazing beer.

✴ Drie Fonteinen Geuze
The best Lambic brewery in the world. So many amazing beers, it's impossible to name a favourite. But the regular Gueuze is one I can drink every day and never get bored. When aged, it brings out so many unique flavours, it's impossible to find anything like it.

THE SCIENCE OF LAGER

The greatest irony of lager is that this broadly defined style of beer is only known as 'lager' outside of its brewing homeland. The simple reason for this is that storing a beer to mature before serving it, or 'lagering', from the German word meaning 'store', is a standard practice by German brewers, and has been since time began. Given all beer in Germany is 'lagered' what would be the point in referring to it as lager?

The division of the products of brewing into 'top-fermented beers' and 'bottom-fermented beers', calling them ales and lagers for short, may appeal to the taxonomist, but it is as flawed in its technological use as it would be if you divided the gastronomic world into 'food' and 'drink'. What is soup? What do you call a beer made with top-fermenting yeast like an ale, that is then cold-stored like a lager?

Putting aside these philosophical considerations, the reason we are even having this debate is essentially down to one man, Gabriel Sedlmayr, of the Spaten Brewery in Munich, Bavaria. Sedlmayr visited Britain in 1833, aged 22, as part of a 'study tour' designed to uncover the best brewing practices in Europe. At that time Britain led the rest of Europe in many areas of brewing technology, and Sedlmayr was deeply impressed with British malting methods, with the efficiency with which British brewers extracted as much fermentable material as possible from their mash tuns, and, in particular, the use of the saccharometer to measure the strength of the wort run off from the malted barley before it was brewed into beer.

He returned to Munich, filled with this new knowledge, which Sedlmayr said later was 'like the light of the rising sun',

and with a saccharometer made by the highly recommended maker Joseph Long of London. On 6 May 1834 he used his new tool to brew a Scottish-style ale at the Spaten brewery, using malt 'auf die Schottische Art bereitetes', 'made in the Scottish style' – the first time a saccharometer had ever been used in a German brewery.

Sedlmayr soon used his new saccharometer, and knowledge gleaned from brewers in England and Scotland, to make beers in the Bavarian style: cool-brewed, and 'lagered', that is, stored at low temperatures for weeks or months to mature. This Anglo-German meeting of technologies secured the scientific basis for the commercial delivery of lager worldwide.

Beer brewed at cold temperatures for long periods using the special 'cold-loving' yeasts first used by Sedlmayr, and later isolated by Jacobsen at Carlsberg, was found to be highly resistant to spoilage. Beer stored at cold temperatures had a greater propensity to hold and absorb carbonation, like Champagne. Beer stored for long periods would drop perfectly clear and the kilning and mashing technologies founded during Britain's period of world domination as the first industrial brewing power completed the picture.

To this the Bavarian techniques of biological acidification, decoction brewing, the marvellously citric Germanic hops, and above all the use of time, all combined to produce a subtle, gentle beer, which, depending on where it was brewed, had flavours and variants to stimulate the most anaemic of taste-buds. The soft waters of Pilsen, the more moderately soft waters of Vienna and the hard waters of Munich led to an affinity in those cities' breweries for light, amber and dark malts respectively and this geographic 'holy trinity' found its place in brewing history.

Ironically, the impact that Sedlmayr's visit to Britain had on the world of beer went unnoticed in Britain itself until approximately 130 years later, when the industrial conglomerates that had come to monopolise British brewing foisted a pale imitation of 'lager' on an unsuspecting audience, tarnishing lager's name for decades. This was also at a time that the derogatory named 'keg beers' arrived on the scene. The irony here of course was that the somewhat late emergence of these inferior, but ubiquitous beers entailed the

use of cold conditioning, pressurised tanks, filtration and the use of extraneous CO_2; techniques first applied in mainland Europe in the late 19th century. The greater irony was that they were quick-brewed beers that were not 'stored' or 'lagered' for any period of time.

A great lager is not defined by its colour, the use of different malts or hops define their character. Variation on alcoholic strength gave rise to Bock and Dopplebock beers. But in a nutshell the local lager beer brewed and served in the Germanic brewing regions was an expression of the local water, local malt and local hops. These three variants were the mainstay of the Purity Laws that 'protected' the consumer from the injudicious use of 'inferior' ingredients. Given the use of very cold process temperatures, yeast has never had a major impact on the flavour of lager beer, certainly not in the way that many 'expressive' yeasts used in Belgium and England, at warm temperatures, have.

Left: Alastair Hook, brewmaster and founder at Meantime Brewery Company.

Above: Unlike other British micros, Meantime Brewing initially cold shouldered cask ale in favour of bottom-fermented lager styles.

All of my favourite lagers have a defining characteristic, and all are patiently made beers that run in contrast to the helter-skelter brewing practices of the great industrial conglomerates. They have a clarity and preciseness of flavour, and are approachable but never dull. They are not demonstrative and loud, but should be enjoyed, slowly, in good company, in precisely the way they were painstakingly made. Whether a beer is a lager or ale, it is my contention that all great beer needs time to perfect, and I am yet to find a contradiction to that.

Alastair Hook
Brewmaster and Founder
Meantime Brewing Company

BUDWEISER BUDVAR

Ceské Budejovice, Czech Republic   www.budvar.cz

No other type of beer has lined the pockets of the world's lawyers more than 'Budweiser'. A trademark tug-of-war has endured for more than a century between the American Budweiser, currently owned by Anheuser-Busch InBev, and the Czech version, called Budweiser Budvar. Both brewers claim they are the original Budweiser, 'king of beers'. The biggest weapon in the Americans' legal arsenal is that they began making a Budweiser in St Louis some 20 years before Budejovicky Pivovar fired up its kettles in 1895 in the town German speakers call Budweis and Czech ones Ceské Budejovice.

Budweiser Budvar, however, sees Anheuser-Busch's history and raises it with a bit of geography, claiming that Budweiser beer had been brewed in the town since the 15th century and, furthermore, a neighbouring brewery called the Budweiser Burgerbrau had been exporting its 'Budweiser' beers to America before Mr Busch brought out his own version. Hundreds of global trademark disputes have followed, resulting in both beers adopting aliases in different markets. While the litany of lawsuits have proved costly, Budvar has revelled in its role as the underdog and, for a short period, even adopted Anheuser-Busch's distribution arm in the United States, where the beer is known as Czechvar.

The Czech brewery, anything but a meek micro, is still state-owned. In 1989, when the Communist regime collapsed, it was ramshackle, rundown, bereft of investment and, as such, ripe for takeover and Anheuser-Busch put in a bid for $1.5m. 'There were people in the streets, with protests and demonstrations all over Ceské Budejovice', said Josef Tolar, former head brewer at Budvar. 'The trade unions threatened to strike and barricade the brewery if it was released from state hands and, after much negotiations, we gained our independence.'

While several overseas ventures have come along and kicked Budvar's tyres, successive Czech governments have stood firm and refused to sell it – not that talk of privatisation is ever far away. Any prospective purchasers would do well to preserve Budvar's brewing methods: double decoction, three-month lagering, Moravian malt and whole Saaz hops. Its flagship beer is a great go-to premium lager but connoisseurs gravitate towards its yeast lager, the kroužkovaný ležák, which ferments further in the keg. There is a terrific texture, rich and grainy with a gorgeous grassy finish. While American attorneys may argue that their clients' Budweiser was the first, no court in the world could rule that it tastes better.

Top: The gleaming brewhouse in Ceské Budejovice.
Above: Adam Broz, Budvar's brewmaster, selects some Saaz hops.
Opposite: Plzeňsky Prazdroj and its iconic main gate in Pilsen, as seen on the bottle label.

PILSNER URQUELL

Plzeň, Czech Republic   www.pilsnerurquell.com

In the 1830s, Pilsen was an embarrassment to Bohemian brewing. Its lousy local beers were being made a mockery of by those brewed elsewhere, where new malting techniques and innovations had ushered in a beguiling new breed of bottom-fermented beers.

In 1839, in an attempt to protect their local market, a dozen prominent Pilsen businessmen demanded the construction of a new brewery, the Burghers' Brewery. A highly rated architect, Martin Steltzer, who also built the local synagogue, was brought in to design the brewery. Steltzer visited the breweries of Bavaria, where refrigeration, steam power and modern approaches to malt were being eagerly explored. At the same time the builder František Filaus toured Bohemia's biggest bottom-fermenting breweries. On their return, it took less than three years for them to build the Burghers' Brewery.

The owners of the new concern brought in both a Bavarian bottom-fermenting yeast strain and a Bavarian brewer by the name of Josef Groll. He was a notoriously irritable and anti-social individual, but his demeanour must have improved once he realised the raw ingredients and technological tools he had at his disposal. First, Bohemia's sensational, spicy hops, the envy of European brewing, were close at hand. While Saaz is now Pilsner Urquell's famous signature hop, records suggest that for the first two years, Groll used hops from just outside the Saaz region which would have been similar in style.

The grain was great too. Moist Moravian barley was kilned in the on-site malting house using the latest 'English'

techniques. A combination of low nitrate levels and leisurely decoction mash created very clear beer. The labyrinthine cellars below the brewery provided perfect cold conditions for the bespoke Bavarian yeast to perform and the Pilsen water, softer than a bubblebath of kittens, lent itself superbly to bottom-fermented brewing.

But, as important then as it is today, the final vital ingredient was patience. Less haste meant less haze and lengthy lagering was vital – the first batch of the beer was matured for 37 days, which is pretty much how long the beer is matured in Pilsen today more than 170 years after it was first brewed.

When the first barrels were tapped on 11 November 1842, during the St Martin's Fair in Pilsen, the world's first clear, golden lager poured forth. It must have been an incredible sight. Most drinkers, hitherto, had drunk darkish beer from pewter tankards and never before would they have seen a translucent, twinkling gold lager served in clear glassware, a novelty at the time.

Today, under the stewardship of SAB Miller, which bought the brewery in 2005, Pilsner Urquell remains one of the world's most well-known Pilsners. However Kvasnicový, an unpasteurised, unfiltered and relatively untouched draught version, is the Pilsner Urquell that pricks up the ears of enlightened beer drinkers. Available in and around the brewery, and increasingly in European drinking destinations deemed deserving, Kvasnicový is a genuine elbow-bending epiphany that proves Pilsner can compete in complexity with any other beer style in the world.

OKTOBERFEST

It is as if someone has accidentally left the door open at a German cliché factory, with more lazy national stereotypes on show than you can shake an enormous sausage at.

Fresh-faced Frauleins, bursting from bosom-boosting dirndls, float around carrying massive frothing Maße; big burly Bavarians in goat-hair hats bulge out of their lederhosen; steins sway to oompah bands; there are triumphant displays of whip cracking and complicated folk dances involving elaborate ankle touches and thigh-slapping.

To soak up the steins of Oktoberfest beer, there are huge hunks of ox and fatty chunks of roast duck, while pretzels able to parch a palate from twenty paces are piled high next to artery-clogging slabs of pork knuckle; roast chicken halves are handed out with Teutonic efficiency and, even after all that, the wurst is yet to come: Bratwurst, Knackwurst, Currywurst, Weisswurst and more.

Then there is the fun fair. Once you have had enough of epicurean excess, you call your constitution into question on either rickety rollercoasters, or the legendary Teufelsrad (devil wheel), a fast-spinning disc that sends people sprawling using the combination of centrifugal force and an enormous rubber ball. Medieval madness does not come more meticulously organised than here in Munich, where what was originally a big wedding party for the Crown Prince of Bavaria and his bride in 1810 has been recreated almost every year since then, barring war and cholera outbreaks.

To make the most of Oktoberfest, however, it is best to have a plan, albeit one that will no doubt become obsolete after a stein or two. Before you go, you had better pick a beer tent. There are 14 large tents and around 20 smaller ones, each with its own distinctive character and clientele, and each serving Oktoberfest beers from one of six Munich breweries.

AUGUSTINER FESTHALLE
If you are going to spend the whole day drinking high-strength German beers with your children and/or mother-in-law, then this is definitely the best tent to do so. Friendly and fun, it is not nearly as hedonistic as the other tents and it even holds a kid's day every Tuesday, when prices are low.

FISCHER-VRONI
Pescetarians tired of all the pork products on parade flock here for the fish; fish-on-a-stick to be exact, grilled over hot coals: pike, salmon trout, smoked mackerel. If you absolutely insist on pork, however, they will happily knock out a fresh roast suckling-pig for you.

HACKER-PSCHORR BRÄUROSL
Back in the 1970s, members of the 'Lions Club' booked the Bräurosl's balcony. The owners, expecting a rowdy football team, were surprised when a group of gay men turned up. They were better behaved and better dressed than the average festival-goers, and being big spenders, they were encouraged to come back the next year. Since then, the gay contingent has grown so that, on the first Sunday of the festival, Bräurosl's benches are packed with 8,000 gay beer-swillers, swaying and singing traditional Bavarian songs, and yodelling – for which the Bräurosl tent, rather aptly owned by the Heide family, has become famous.

HACKER-FESTZELT
In the tent known as 'Himmel der Bayern' (Heaven of the Bavarians), beneath the clouds and stars daubed on the canvas ceiling, drinkers dance to a different beat, with a German band knocking out classic rock and roll covers. They will play anything you ask for, as long as it's *Hey Jude* by the Beatles.

PAULANER WINZERER FÄHNDL
The alpha male of the Oktoberfest is the Winzerer Fähndl, which proudly announces itself with an enormous tower on which a giant stein of Paulaner is perched. This is the biggest tent in the park, with more than 8,450 catered for inside and a further 2,450 drinking in its adjoining beer garden. You will find fans and players of Bayern Munich football club here, while music comes courtesy of the famous Nockherberger Band. No, me neither.

BESPATEN HIPPODROM
Frequented by the young, free and single, the Hippodrom is not the biggest of the big tents, but it is certainly the most badly behaved. While insouciant bejewelled pretty boys and minor Munich celebrities drape themselves over the Champagne bar, everyone else comes here to dance, drink and, ultimately, get to know each other more intimately. And why not, that is what weddings are for.

SCHOTTENHAMEL
Dedicated followers of tradition drink here. At noon, on the Oktoberfest's first Saturday, the mayor of Munich fires the starting pistol by tapping the first keg and duly proclaiming: 'O'zapft is!' – 'It is tapped' in the Bavarian dialect.

Then, and only then, can beer drinking begin in the other tents. The Schottenhamel tent, meanwhile, is a popular place for young festival-goers, and big sections of it are reserved for local student fraternities wearing uniforms of varying sartorial ambition.

LÖWENBRÄU
No matter how 'tired and emotional' the Maße have made you, it is easy to recognise this tent, the only one with a massive mechanical Lowenbrau lion

above the entrance, its mouth widening every two minutes to belch out a loud roar. This is the tent where local blue-collar beer drinkers tend to go, and it is also the dedicated drinking destination for the fans of TSV 1860 München – also known as the 'Lions'. So, if you have a Bayern Munich shirt leave it at home.

HOFBRÄU FESTZELT
Much like the Hofbräuhaus in the centre of Munich, the second biggest tent at 'Wiesn' attracts the tourist crowd, with its unabashed Bavarian-ness. Adored by Australians and Americans, it is also the tent that provides the most 'Bierleichen', meaning 'beer corpses', the local German word for lightweights. It is said to be decorated with a field's-worth of hops, although the field's exact dimensions remains unclear.

Opposite: Masses of Masse, the Bavarian beer mugs.

Above: Every year, over 6 million people visit the Oktoberfest, drink 70 million hectolitres of beer, eat 522,000 chickens and 58,500 pork knuckles.

What about the beer?

Strict rules prevent brewers other than those within Munich's city limits to sell beer at the festival. These are: Augustiner-Bräu; Hacker-Pschorr; Hofbräu-München; Löwenbräu; Paulaner; and Spaten-Franziskaner-Bräu.

For the first 50 years or so, it was Dunkel that dominated at Wiesn before bock-style beers became popular. After the World Wars, Marzen stole a march in the meadows until the 1990s when the eponymous Oktoberfest style was introduced across the board.

By no means the best beers in Germany and hardly designed for measured contemplation, Oktoberfest beers (5.8–6.3% ABV) differ in character but are, most commonly, delicately hopped, malt-driven blonde beers underscored with a distinct sweetness.

KOCOUR

Varnsdorf, Czech Republic www.pivovar-kocour.cz

I am not sure how it has happened, but it has. Josef Šusta and I are sat on a bed in a stationary 70-year-old railway carriage, just metres from the German border.

He is laughing a lot, chuckling away in Czech, slapping his thigh, dishing out digs in my ribs and leading Mike, the English interpreter, a merry dance. 'How many breweries own a train?' he chortles. 'It's great isn't it? A hotel was too expensive. But a train? It's a laugh, isn't it?'

Šusta is running around ancient yellow carriages that, during Communism in the 1950s, rode the rails from Prague to Moscow and back again. After the installation of a bar, beds and a new engine – probably in that order – the journey Josef has in mind sounds far jollier.

'It's a beer train!' he ta-dahs, arms out wide. 'We're going to drive this all over Europe, visiting breweries and drinking great beer. We can all sleep on it, too. You should come and get oiled up,' he says, his fixed grin waiting patiently until Mike catches up.

After it has been through translation, it can be difficult to know whether a question is rhetorical or not. There is a rare and awkward silence. Šusta looks at me. I look at him. We both look at Mike. And then, just as I am about to respond, he is off again; pointing at things, cracking jokes and stretching Mike's linguistic skills to the limit.

The tardy translation accentuates the surreal setting. We are in Varnsdorf. This is Wild West Czech, where tumbleweed, never mind tourists, seldom treads; a one-horse town where the horse has left.

The only thing that passes through here, it turns out, is the howling shrill of the wind. 'It ripped the roof right off,' says Josef, casually gesturing to workmen hollering and hitting things atop the brewhouse, a former ceramics factory that once made isolators for electricity pylons. 'It came from nowhere, it went really dark, caused chaos and disappeared again. Like a mini tornado.'

The week before, the doors were almost blown off, too; a riotous rock festival with eight hundred people and copious amounts of Kocour. If no one can hear you scream here, then no one is going to call the council either. 'They wouldn't leave. It was crazy.'

Owner of the largest road haulage firm in the Czech Republic and an unadulterated entrepreneur, Šusta runs one of several new Czech breweries embracing new beer styles. He created Kocour, meaning 'tomcat' and pronounced 'kotsore', in 2008 with the beer writer (and current cuckoo brewer) Honza Kocka.

Honza was the brains behind the brewing. A former Czech Airlines steward, he was heavily involved in the international craft beer scene, and invited his brewing buddies from all over the world to craft collaborative beers in conjunction with Kocour's head brewer.

As such, Kocour's approach is incredibly eclectic and international, introducing domestic drinkers to different hops

KEY BEERS

PIVOVAR KOCOUR
Kocour IPA Samuraj 5.1%
Kocour Catfish Sumecek 4.2%
Kocour 70 Quarterback 8.7%
Kocour V3 Rauchbier 5.9%

ÚNETICKÝ PIVOVAR
Únetické Pivo 12° Nefiltrované
Únetické Pivo 10° Nefiltrované
Únetické Pivo 12°
Únetické Pivo 10°

Above: The Kocour Brewery in Varnsdorf.

Opposite: Inside the brewery and the brewery tap.

and ingredients. It kinks the local linear lager landscape with a range of beers including bold German porters; an IPA named Quarterback brewed in collaboration with Ballast Point Brewing Company; a softly smoked Slovenian Rauchbier called V3; and Samuraj, a Japanese IPA designed by Toshi Ishii from Yo-Ho Brewing in Nagano.

Kocour is one of more than a hundred small microbreweries slowly loosening the grip of the big three (SABMiller's Plzeský Prazdroj, Pivovary Staropramen and Heineken CR) who, after the Velvet Revolution in 1989, seduced bar owners with enormous 20-year exclusivity deals that deprived domestic drinkers of any kind of diversity.

Thankfully, though, a new 'fourth pipe' trend has emerged, where independent outlets have added a fourth keg tap offering craft beers sourced from all over the country. This has helped small brewers, and so too has the introduction of a six-tier duty system, which cuts micros some much-needed financial slack. In 1989, there was just one speciality beer.

By 2004 there were 130, but it has only been in the past few years that there has been a real boom in craft beers. There are now nearly a dozen microbreweries in Prague alone, while membership of the Czech-Moravian Association of Small Breweries, whose members each produce less than 10,000 hectolitres annually, is expanding every year.

One such brewery is Úneticky, situated in the eponymous village of Únetice 15km north of Prague. The brewery, dating back to 1710, was mothballed during the Communist years before being revived in 2011 by two former Staropramen employees. They produce just two pale lagers, both of which are open-fermented, unpasteurised, unfiltered and, drunk fresh from the tank, unlike any lager I have tasted before.

Founder Štpán Tkadlec says: 'Our lagers are hazy and we interfere with them as little as we possibly can. We want to make bottom-fermented beers the way they used to be made, using Czech grains, Czech hops and local water. It's simple, but so many do it badly.'

'Czech-style lager has been abused and undermined in recent years,' Tkadlec says. 'But slowly, thanks to small breweries like ours, it's regaining the respect it deserves.'

BOSTON BEER COMPANY

Boston, Massachusetts, USA www.bostonbeer.com

The year is 1984. America is a beer-drinking dystopia, tyrannised by an Orwellian totalitarian ideology. Big Brother is the brewmaster, numbing the nation's minds with insipid liquid newspeak.

But in Boston, there is a brave new beer, Samuel Adams Boston Lager; a double-decocted copper-coloured thought crime peddled from the back of Jim Koch's station wagon. Twice the price of Budweiser, it tasted nothing like any other lager available, did no advertising and it did not even have its own brewery. Jim has three degrees from Harvard but bar owners and wholesalers in 1984 thought he was daft.

'It was a loony proposition and they treated me like a loony,' says Jim, born in Ohio into the sixth generation of a brewing family. 'Every distributor I approached turned me down. It was expensive, they'd never heard of beer brewed in a kitchen and no one knew how to drink it. We had to recalibrate everyone's minds.'

Doing things differently is what Jim does. In contrast to his craft-brewing compatriots, there was no cobbling together of a rudimentary, romantic brewery back in the 1980s. Instead, he perfected his great-great grandfather's pre-Prohibition lager recipe at the Pittsburgh Brewing in Pennsylvania, a basic blue-collar brewery, but one of very

few able to accommodate Jim's crucial criteria of decoction mashing, krausening and dry-hopping.

'I didn't have enough money to build or buy a brewery but, more importantly, I wasn't prepared to compromise on quality,' says Jim, who in 1984 was swimming against a tide of skunky, stale imports as well as well-meaning yet wildly inconsistent microbrews. 'People were using infected pipes, quality control was appalling,' he says. 'I realised I needed great beer every time, and the only way I was going to do that was by using a brewery with proper equipment, sanitation and quality control.'

Contract brewing also allowed him the financial freedom to bring in the finest brewing brains in the business. 'After Harvard, I'd worked for a manufacturing consultancy for six years, where I learned that if you can find the best people in the world and get them excited in what you're doing, then you've got half a chance.'

Jim hired Dr Joe Owades, a white-coated yeast whisperer who, kind of like Robert Oppenheimer and the atom bomb, was infamous for being the father of 'lite' beer. 'Joe was the

Left: Jim Koch in a dunk tank of stale beer.

Opposite: Jim Koch at the Samuel Adams brewery tap in Jamaica Plain, Boston.

'You have to have control, you have got to get to know the individual quirks and the way a brewery works. In fact, I don't think you can understand your beer until you've made it in another brewery.' JIM KOCH

first, the only and the best,' Jim says. 'He was the first real scientist in brewing. He was a microbiologist, fanatical about fermentation and had a real passion for beer.' It took a while to get Louis Koch's recipe right. 'It wasn't complicated, there's no need for hogsheads of treacle or anything like that but they'd never seen a mash like it,' Jim says.

Jim's business plan was simple: five years to reach 5,000 barrels. Selling his beer on flavour and, crucially, freshness, he hit the target within 12 months and Samuel Adams was named the best beer in America. Within weeks, Jim knew something special was happening. 'You simply couldn't get a reliable fresh glass of good beer anywhere, so I knew that there was an opportunity for world class, flavoursome fresh beer... but I didn't know HOW big.'

In 1996 the Boston Beer Company was floated on the stock market. Before the investors could get their hands on his beer, Jim made sure drinkers had first dibs by putting coupons on six-packs offering shares at $15 rather than $20. 'I wanted drinkers to own our company,' Jim says. 'Today, drinkers still own shares while not a single investment company has held onto them. That says it all. But, man, the banks hated me.'

The big brewers were not too fond of him either. With Samuel Adams's sales popping up on its radar, Anheuser-Busch peppered newspapers, beer mats and radio stations with adverts questioning Koch's craft credentials as a contract brewer: 'Why does Sam Adams pretend to come from New England when the truth is, it's brewed and bottled by contract breweries all around the country?', the Budweiser brewer bitched. A-B was eventually forced to withdraw the advertisements, but not before the damage was done; Sam Adams was, for a while, swept from supermarket shelves, banished from bars and dropped by distributors. 'I wasn't shocked that the Empire struck back,' says Jim with a wry smile. 'I've seen *Star Wars* and know how it works, but I didn't realise that it would be that vicious. But, like my dad says, people don't drink the marketing – they drink the beer.'

With Budweiser today in the hands of the the Brazilians, Boston Brewing Company is now the largest American-owned brewery, with a 1% share of the market. Its enormous array of lagers, ales and speciality beers are made in Cincinnati, where

Jim's father brewed; in Pittsburgh where it all began; and at the former Haffenreffer brewery in Boston where, on a pilot ten barrel brewhouse in the Jamaica Plain district, they trial new ideas and innovate with barrel-ageing. 'Every day for the last 29 years, I've woken up scared s***less,' Jim laughs. 'We live in an industry where the competition with the big guys is really frightening. But, hell, I can make 60 beers now. That's awesome! Growing is good if that improves the beer.'

THE FIGHT FOR FRESHNESS
In 1988, Samuel Adams blew the whistle on the industry's dirty secret: stale beer. Unwilling to adhere to a convoluted coded system that drinkers could not read, Jim opted to put clear, easily understandable freshness dates on his beer labels. Each year Boston Beer Company spends millions of dollars buying back stale beer from distributors and destroying it while, in 2012, it introduced a new system drastically cutting the time its beer spends in warehouses and wholesalers.

JIM ON CONTRACT BREWING:
'If an award-winning chef comes to your kitchen and brews with their ingredients, their pots and pans and their ideas, they can still create something spectacular. It takes us a year to make our beer in a new brewery. You have to have control, you have got to get to know the individual quirks and the way a brewery works. In fact, I don't think you can understand your beer until you've made it in another brewery.'

KEY BEERS
Samuel Adams Boston Lager 4.8%
Samuel Adams OctoberFest 5.3%
Samuel Adams American Kriek 7%
Samuel Adams Kosmic Mother Funk 8%
Utopias 27%
Samuel Adams Merry Mischief Gingerbread Stout 9%

* HOP

---

* pale ale

* india pale ale

* double IPA

* imperial IPA

* barley wine

It is difficult to believe that people once consumed ale brewed without hops. Like smoking on aeroplanes, communicating by carrier pigeon and wearing all-in-one ski suits, it's a peculiarity of the past that doesn't make sense any more.

These days, there is an insatiable, almost crazed, hankering for the hop. It may only grow between approximately 30° and 52° latitude, but the hop is being hailed with unbridled enthusiasm by craft brewers and beer drinkers all over the world.

The United States remains the heartland of hedonistic hopping, the birthplace of aggressively bitter styles. Not content with re-inventing IPA by cranking up the aroma and bitterness, American craft brewers have doubled it, tripled it, made it Imperial and even taken it into the black. The Americanisation of India Pale Ale is probably the most significant event to have shaped beer in the past 30 years.

However, what started primarily on the west coast of the United States more than 200 years after English brewers were exporting heavily hopped ales and porters to India, has become a global phenomenon, embraced by both emerging and well-established brewing nations.

While some European brewers have been baffled by this IBU arms race, the American craft beer scene has undoubtedly broadened hop horizons on the other side of the Pond. In addition to classic European varieties and noble hops, brewers in the Old World are experimenting increasingly with American varieties and working closely with growers to create hops with new aromas.

As brewers release single-hop beers and beers with particular hops at the forefront of the flavour profile, drinkers are becoming increasingly aware that each hop imparts a bespoke bouquet and bitterness to beer, just as Cabernet Sauvignon grapes or Riesling grapes give wine certain characteristics. To this end, each beer in this chapter is appendixed, where known, with the hop(s) used.

This chapter will satiate both the hardened hop head and drinkers looking to discover new varietals.

THESE ARE THE PAGES TO PERUSE IF YOU HANKER AFTER HOPPY BEERS. HAILING HUMULUS LUPULUS FROM AHTANUM TO ZYTHOS, HOP FEATURES BLISTERINGLY BITTER IPAS, ACUTELY AROMATIC PALE ALES, FRAGRANT SINGLE-HOPPED SIPPERS, RESIN-RICH STOUTS AND MORE

Buxton
Axe Edge IPA 6.5%
Derbyshire, England
www.buxtonbrewing.co.uk
Hops: Amarillo, Citra, Nelson Sauvin

Named after a nearby moor on which Britain's second highest pub can be found, Axe Edge is the beer that put Buxton Brewery on the map. Buxton is a great modern micro that creates hugely aromatic ales by hopping late in the boil. Resinous without raking the palate, the hit is dashed with marmalade, pine and grapefruit.

Brodies
Hackney Red IPA 6.5%
London, England
www.brodiesbeers.co.uk
Hops: Citra, Amarillo, Columbus

Set up in 2007, within the walls of the old Sweet William Brewery in Leyton, East London, brews from the easy-drinking and the extreme to the downright unusual (Peanut Butter Imperial Stout?) regularly feature on the Brodies roster. More recognised and regular in both senses of the word is this lush amber-coloured IPA, which gets you muttering about lemongrass, plum and toffee apple.

Curious Brew
IPA 5.6%
Kent, England
www.chapeldown.com
Hops: Goldings, Bramling Cross, Citra

Kent winemaker Chapel Down, headed by an ex-Heineken man, makes some elegant beers too, including this Anglo-American IPA brewed with oh-so English Goldings and the blackcurrant-like Bramling Cross, child of an English mother and an American father, finished with the zesty American hop Citra. One of Jamie Oliver's favourites. Apparently.

Dark Star
Six Hop 6.5%
Sussex, England
www.darkstarbrewing.co.uk
Hops: Cascade, Citra, Centennial, Simcoe, Columbus and Amarillo

An overnight sensation nearly 20 years in the making, the Dark Star Brewing Company began as a home-brew operation in the cellar of a Brighton pub and now stands as one of the UK's most impressive ale-makers. Remorselessly flavoursome, its core ales are supplemented by a series of creative seasonal and monthly specials including a sensational Saison that is celebrated elsewhere in the book. This, however, is a hophead's wet dream: a dark golden drop hopped with half-a-dozen varieties added at six separate stages of the brewing process, four in the kettle, one enormous one in the whirlpool and the final variety flung in dry during fermentation. There is a burst of blood-orange on the nose, the shortbread malt character shines through, but the bitterness draws in your cheeks as if you had seen something saucy in the pantry. Made famous on cask, its big flavours suit the uplifting effervescence of the bottled version.

Kent Brewery
Beyond The Pale 5.4%
Kent, England
www.kentbrewery.com
Hops: Green Bullet, Cascade

Founded in West Malling, in the heart of hopland (the Goldings hop was first grown nearby), this fresh-faced newcomer supplements Kentish hops with those from America and New Zealand. An amplified interpretation of its flagship pale ale, this glinting golden drop is underwritten by rich

Maris Otter and seasoned with the Kiwi hop Green Bullet and Cascade from the US. A puckering fine pale from the Kent countryside. That is not a sentence you should try saying after you've had two or three.

Kernel
Pale Ale (Centennial) 5.4%
London, England
www.thekernelbrewery.com

The hops used in Kernel's clean pale ales are where the beers gets their name. Primed solely with Centennial, this classic Kernel pale ale has been simply sensational every single time; hay, elderflower, limes and lychees, grapefruit and a clean, zesty lemongrass finish.

Moor
JJJ IPA 9.5%
Somerset, England
www.moorbeer.co.uk

Hops: Cascade, Centennial, Chinook, Columbus and Citra

Started in 1996, Moor scooped Camra's Champion Winter Beer of Britain for Old Freddy Walker in 2004. But it was not until 2007, when Justin and Maryann Hawke took the brewery over, that Moor discovered its mojo. Enthused by brewers in his native California, Justin turns the hop knob to 11 with a triple IPA made with three times the amount of everything – hops, malt and attitude. The result was a thoroughly convincing reason to drink Moor beer.

Oakham
Citra 4.5%
Peterborough, England
www.oakhamales.com
Hop: Citra

In a derelict warehouse somewhere in Peterborough sits Citra, its arms strapped behind its back, its feet shackled to a chair built from pale malt and wheat. Surrounding it are Oakham's brewers holding hacksaws and hammers. The Citra squeals gooseberry, greengage and grapefruit.

St Austell
Proper Job 4.5%
www.staustellbrewery.co.uk
Hops: Cascade, Chinook, Willamette

Having lost its way in the 1980s, St Austell's reputation was rebuilt by head brewer Roger Ryman on a foundation of Maris Otter malt and New World nous. During a pilgrimage to Portland, Oregon, Roger was inspired by the fruity finesse of Bridgeport IPA. He recreated it using American hops but British barley. While the Job is delicious on draught, I prefer the uplifting carbonation in the bottle.

Summer Wine
Diablo IPA 5.5%
Yorkshire, England
www.summerwinebrewery.
co.uk
Hop: Citra

This youthful Yorkshire operation gets its name from *Last of the Summer Wine*, a British TV 'comedy' set in the brewery's home town of Holmfirth about a trio of coffin-dodgers. SW's exuberant yet excellently engineered ales perform well in cask, keg and bottle. Citra's signature is chiselled deep thanks to hopping in the fermenter, which creates aromas of peach, apricot and bitter cider apple.

Windsor & Eton
Conqueror 1075 7.4%
Windsor, England
www.webrew.co.uk
Hops: Pacific Jade, Cascade

Experienced brewer Paddy Johnson has been making majestic beers since 2010 on an industrial estate in the middle of Her Majesty's manor, almost under the shadow of Windsor Castle (founded by William the Conqueror in 1075). Guardsman and Knight of the Garter toe the traditional line, but Paddy went off-piste with a Kenyan Diamond Jubilee ale, a nod to the Commonwealth, brewed with African millet, sorghum syrup, vanilla pods and yams. This, a pimped up version of the Conqueror Black IPA, only takes the early and intense runnings of

wort and dry-hops with whole-leaf Cascade. While the dark hue might prove problematic if introduced to Prince Philip, he would marvel at the stewed fruit sweetness and long and leggy Grand Marnier finish.

Kingstone Brewery
Humpty's Fuddle IPA 5.2%
Monmouthshire, Wales
www.kingstonebrewery.co.uk
Hops: Fuggles

The moral of the Humpty Dumpty Nursery rhyme is a) Don't sit on a wall if you're an egg. And b) Don't send all the King's horses to perform a medical procedure on aforementioned egg. They have neither the dexterity nor the thumbs for it. Just two points to ponder as this oaky amber unfiltered India Pale Ale, brewed near Tintern Abbey in the Wye Valley using only one, classic English hop, opens up with those typical Fuggles marmalade on toast aromas and finishes slightly bitter – a bit like an egg after a fall.

Otley
O-4 Columb-O 4%
Glamorgan, Wales
www.otleybrewing.co.uk
Hops: Columbus, Cascade

The Otley clan have been breaking down cask beer drinking barriers in a region renowned for its darker beers since 2005. Otley's are aromatic, accessible ales, easy-drinking and easy on the eye, and they don't hide their hops. This delicate drop is a tribute to the North American floral main copper hop Columbus. Quite how they pack so much tropical fruit into the trunk of this 4% sipper remains a mystery that would befuddle the most irritatingly persistent, dishevelled mac-wearing sleuth. Just one more thing – it's perfect with a ploughman's.

Pixie Spring
Deliverance APA 4.5%
Glamorgan, Wales
www.pixiespring.com
Hops: unstated

Based out of the Wheatsheaf pub in the town of Llantrisant in South Wales, this modest-sized micro names its beers after the fairy-tale Asrai water-sprites that are supposed to live beneath the village, like an olden-day version of the Doozers in the children's TV series Fraggle Rock – but with less of a Protestant work ethic. Anyway, the sneaky little pixies would make potions using the local spring water and, it says here, so does the brewery. That may not be true but, what is fact is that this session-friendly American Pale Ale will make you squeal with delight – wet hay, basil and a touch of juniper.

IRELAND

Eight Degrees
Howling Gale Ale 5%
Cork
www.eightdegrees.ie
Hops: Chinook, Amarillo, Centennial

Starting a microbrewery is a risky idea at the best of times but doing it in Ireland during what was less a recession, more a monumental financial meltdown takes nuts of quite enormous proportions. But that didn't stop two brass-balled brewing Antipodeans, Aussie Cameron Wallace and Kiwi Scott Baigent, starting a micro in Mitchelstown, County Cork and using second-hand kit from Carlow Brewing Company to craft some quality gear. A light, bracing breeze of citrus freshness is packaged, thankfully, with a crown cap. You know what they say; you can take a beer out of Cork but you can't take a cork out …

US

Alpine Beer Company
Alpine Ale 5.5%
California
www.alpinebeerco.com
Hops: Cascade, Centennial

Like a dwarf gaining distinction for his dissertation on Dostoevsky, Alpine isn't particularly big but it's awfully clever. The small brewery, created in 2002, is surrounded by woods and a magnificent mountain-scape where no-one can hear you scream. Maybe that's why Alpine doesn't shout more about its stylish, small-batch and rather self-effacing beers. Pure Hoppiness and Exponential Hoppiness are the intense IPAs yet its house beer, a perfectly considered pale ale, is a liquid lesson in balance. If I lived in California, it'd be in my fridge every day. And another thing, I was first introduced to Alpine's beers by an enormous man from Hawaii called the 'Polynesian Powerhouse', who sank six pints of Captain Stout in 30 seconds at the Liar's Club in San Diego, the best bar I've ever been to (sadly no longer with us, probably because it allowed naughty things like that).

Wet-Hopped Beers

Most hops are dried in a kiln before being used in brewing. But in their unswerving pursuit for flavour, an increasing number of committed craft brewers are bringing 'wet' hops straight from the bine to the brewhouse.

It is crucial that the hops are plucked at their prime. Brewers put their hop farmers on speed-dial, brewing kettles are on stand-by, and extra-special heed is paid to traffic and weather reports. As soon as the farmer declares the hop crop is at its peak, it is all systems go.

The brewer has to be quick, really quick. The window of opportunity slams shut around 12 hours after picking as, once broken from the bine, the freshly plucked female flowers endure a fast fall from fecundity to oxidised old age. Fresh wet hops are loosely packed and taken immediately to the brewhouse. Given that wet hops contain approximately 70% more moisture than dry hops, brewers have to at least quadruple the amount used.

Just like dry hops, wet hops can be used at different stages in the boil, while 'wet dry-hopping', when wet hops are added to the finished beer, really accentuates the effect of a hop's aroma oils.

Wet-hop beers, also known as 'fresh-hop', 'green-hop' and 'harvest' beers, tend to be pale ales with a clean, pale malt canvas on which the natural, nuanced hops can be displayed. Flavours are very distinct from dry-hop beers: there is almost an over-exuberance to the aromas, with fresh-cut grass, early morning dew and a green chlorophyll character too.

These are beers at their most naturally hoppy. It takes the notion of terroir in brewing to another level, while vividly showcasing the individual characteristic of a particular hop.

A pioneer of fresh hop beers was Ken Grossman at the Sierra Nevada brewery in California, who rushed hops from the Yakima Valley in Washington down to Chico in 1996. Many brewers followed suit and in 2008, 'Fresh Hop Ales' became a new category at the Great American Beer Festival: in 2012 there were 34 fresh-hopped beers entered.

While the United States has pioneered the process, wet-hopped beers have become increasingly popular among British brewers and each year in Kent, England's heartland of hops, more than a dozen small brewers take part in an annual Fresh Hop Beer Festival.

Ballast Point
Sculpin IPA 7%
San Diego
www.ballastpoint.com

Hops: Warrior, Northern Brewer, Columbus, Magnum, Crystal, Centennial, Simcoe, Amarillo

Ballast Point was the first Californian brewery we visited on our 'research' trip for 'Good Beer Guide West Coast USA' and suitably for a brewer which names its beers after salt-water game fish, it got us hooked (geddit?) on the heady hop aromas of the West Coast pale ale style. Leaner and lighter of body than other American IPAs, Sculpin is barbed with sharp bitterness and soothed with citrus notes. It has won awards and everything.

Bear Republic
Racer IPA 7%
California
www.bearrepublic.com

Hops: Cascade, Columbus, Chinook, Centennial

This archetypal West Coast American IPA does absolutely nothing to dispel my theory that some of the greatest hoppy beers hail from wine country. When they are not spitting at each other and using unnecessary adjectives, oenophiles will no doubt get a Semillon for the Gewürztraminer-esque cacophony of citrus aromas that come courtesy of the classic West Coast C-hop quartet. Indisputably one of America's great beers.

Bell's
Hopslam 10%
Michigan
www.bellsbeer.com

Hops: Hallertau Hersbrucker, Centennial, Glacier, Vanguard, Crystal, Simcoe

While famed for its Kalamazoo Stout and an admirable dedication to the dark stuff, Bell's can also go against the grain with some lovely lupulin-leaning liquids including the well-regarded single-hop (Centennial) Two Hearted Ale. Bigger still is this mammoth made-in-Kalamazoo Double IPA that weaves six different hops from the Pacific Northwest on a base of barley malt infused with a generous drop of honey. As it warms up, grapefruit grows, lychee gets louder and the honey sweetness softens the bitterness.

Brooklyn Brewery
Sorachi Ace 7.6%
New York
www.brooklynbrewery.com

Hop: Sorachi Ace

When the Brewer's Gold hop from England and the Continental Saaz hop got it on in a Japanese hop garden back in the 1970s, Sorachi Ace was the potent progeny they produced. Designed by a chap called Dr Yoshitada Mori of Sapporo Breweries, the new hop was adopted by growers across the Pacific in Oregon in 1994, yet is rarely reached for by the big brewers. It is loaded with lashings of lemon character and, dry hopped post-fermentation, suits the Saison style superbly, bringing zest and zing to a fresh fruit-bowl of flavour that you can thank the Belgian yeast for. As used here by New York's own Brooklyn Brewery, best known for a very American lager and a thumping chocolate stout, Sorachi Ace comes out crisp, clipped and clean with touches of shortbread, lemon curd and coriander. It's all over the heat of summer like a cool, refreshing face flannel.

Single-Hopped beers

Historically, winemakers have worked wonders in enlightening drinkers as to the characteristics of particular grape varieties. You do not have to be an expert oenophile to know your Malbec from your Merlot or your Syrah from your Zinfandel.

But how many people really recognise hops? Or, indeed, even know their names? Not many. Hops have not been hailed in the same hallowed terms by brewers.

That is slowly changing due, in no small way, to the increasing emergence of single-hopped beers.

Rather than using different hop varieties for bitterness and aroma, single-hopped beer uses just one, with the brewer adding it at both the beginning and the end of the boil. While some hops are naturally better multi-taskers than others, each has its own aromatic individuality that, unencumbered by other varieties, is allowed to shine through when it is used on its own.

Mikkeller, the dynamic Danish gypsy brewer, has released more than 20 single-hop IPAs (all 6.9% ABV) as part of his Hop Series, from 'noble' German varieties such as Tettnanger to venerable American hops such as Willamette, to newcomers such as Sorachi Ace from Japan and Nelson Sauvin from New Zealand, while Marston's, the Burton-based brewer, has done something similar with a range of 4% pale ales.

Dogfish Head
90 Minute Imperial IPA 9%
Delaware
www.dogfish.com

Hops: Amarillo, Simcoe, Warrior, Magnum

Instead of staggering the addition of hops at different points during the brew like most brewers, Sam Calagione, who isn't like most brewers, adds a staggering amount of hops continuously over 90 minutes. Originally the brewery used a converted vibrating football game board to shake the hops into the brewery copper during the boil, but today the hops are fired in with a pneumatic cannon, the firing sequence controlled by computer. Dogfish refuses to differentiate between bittering hops and aroma hops, and 90 Minute is also dry hopped, post-fermentation, using another bespoke device called 'Me So Hoppy', to create a piquant, powerful citrus flavour that grabs you by the cheeks and gives them a sharp, awakening wriggle. At 'just' 90 IBUs, it avoids the intense, astringent bitterness that is so irksome in other imperial IPAs. I like this. I like it a lot. And if you find it too much yourself, the brewery does also do a 75-Minute IPA. Or there is always the 120-Minute IPA, if you think you can take it …

Fat Heads
Head Hunter IPA 7.5%
Ohio
www.fatheadsbrewing.com

Hops: Columbus, Simcoe, Centennial

Since 2009 the brewery has grown in both size and reputation, from a small brewpub to a proper brewery, sweeping up medals wherever it goes, including silver medal at the 2012 World Beer Cup for this all-American IPA. It's an in-yer-face aggressive blast of summer fruit and a chewing tobacco finish.

Fort George
Vortex IPA 7.7%
Oregon, United States
www.fortgeorgebrewery.com

Hops: Amarillo, Simcoe, Centennial

In 2007, brewers Jack Harris and Chris Nemlowill transported a small 8-barrel brewery cross-country to the arty town of Astoria and began serving beers in jam jars

at their historic site. The business having expanded into a bigger 30-barrel brewery, this serious citrus sensation is available in cool-looking 16oz cans. It's a premium Pacific Northwest IPA that tucks its talons right into your tongue, and the best thing to come out of Astoria since the Goonies. The Spank Stout is a superb spicy drop, too.

GoodLife
Descender IPA 7%
Oregon, United States
www.goodlifebrewing.com

Hops: Centennial, Chinook, Cascade, Galaxy, Warrior

The people of Bend are fearless folk who eyeball the great outdoors whilst grabbing it by the nuts. It's gnarly, it's radical, it's other words like that. Overseen by Curt Plants, a brewer whose name sounds like a rock climbing manoeuvre, formerly of Rogue Brewing, GoodLife provides post-reckless recreation refreshment from its brewery and tap, installed in an industrial hangar. This is a fresh, fruity fusion of five American hops, though the bitterness is soft and subdued.

Green Flash
West Coast IPA 7.3%
San Diego
www.greenflashbrew.com

Hops: Cascade, Simcoe, Columbus, Centennial

It is what it is, an unashamed, archetypal West Coast IPA from a brilliant brewery that has been central to the San Diegan beer scene since 2002. Rather than chuck all the hops in simultaneously, it tastes as if the brewer has licked his fingers and individually peeled off each one, like a single dollar note from a wad of greenbacks, and layered them gently throughout the golden beer.

The classic grapefruit aroma of Cascade is followed by the peach tones of Simcoe, then the woody lip-smacker Columbus kicks in and finally a soothing Centennial balm combining pine and lemongrass, signs off on the whole, hugely memorable, deeply happy-making experience.

Ithaca
Flower Power IPA 7.5%
New York
www.ithacabeer.com

Hops: Simcoe, Cascade, Ahtanum, Centennial, Amarillo, Chinook

This microbrewery from upstate New York was founded by Dan Mitchell in 1998 and has grown sensibly. A New York bartender hailed Cascazilla, a grapefruit-edged enamel eliminator, as Ithaca's best IPA but I preferred the soothing mix of honey malt and dry-hopped Simcoe, Amarillo and Chinook.

Maine Beer
Zoe 7.2%
Maine
www.mainebeercompany.com

Hops: Simcoe, Centennial, Columbus

From the 'other' Portland on the East Coast, this small brewery set up by two brothers, David and Daniel Kleban, is 100% wind powered and donates 1% of its profits to environmental not-for-profit charities. Even if a kitten was knee-capped every time I took a swig, I would still reach for this hard-to-find resinous, ripe fruity and rounded amber ale, best drunk as fresh as possible. The brewery was due to move to nearby Freeport, doubling production.

Ninkasi
Tricerahops Double IPA 8.8%
Oregon
www.ninkasibrewing.com

Hops: Summit, Amarillo, Centennial, Palisade

In Oregon's capital of counterculture and cannabis, Jamie Floyd is equally liberal with his use of cannabis's less controversial cousin, no more so than in this mammoth medley of four hops that smashes through the 100 IBU barrier with its forehead. If you are in Eugene, they often have a dry-hopped version pouring at the brewery tap.

Odells
IPA 7%
Colorado
www.odells.com

Hops: Cascade, Centennial, Amarillo, Simcoe, Chinook, Perle, Horizon

Odells was brewing beer when most of Colorado's craft breweries were a mere twinkle in the eye of a home-brewer. On the fringes of Fort Collins since 1989, when it opened as only the state's second brewer, Odells sculpts its core beers with impeccable ingredients and mature restraint, eschewing the unnecessarily extreme in favour of balance and fidelity to style. It does stoke the fire of experimentation using its oak-aged 'Woodcut' series and 'Single Serve' beers, primed on the pilot system, yet I always return to this unabashed American IPA, which flexes its malt muscle and whose medley of hops only speaks when it has something to say.

Russian River
Pliny the Elder 8.5%
California
www.russianriverbrewing.com

Hops: Amarillo, Centennial, Columbus, Simcoe

Russian River's Vinnie Cilurzo is widely credited with inventing America's first Double IPA when he brewed Blind Pig in 1994, a beer that slipped a little blue pill into the West Coast's smouldering love affair with heavily-hopped beers. Five years later, Pliny The Elder was born, named after the Roman clever clogs who supposedly came up with the botanical name for hops in the 1st century (although in fact he didn't). It is brewed with four hops on a core of crystal malt and, over a decade later, it continues to command an enormous cult following. This is the ultimate Double IPA, peppering the palate with pine sap, pot pourri, lemongrass and the bittersweet tones of toffee apple. Don't believe a word the label tells you about the Latin name of the hop meaning 'wolf among the scrubs', though. That's doodleflap.

7 Seas Brewing
Ballz Deep Double IPA 8.4%
Washington State
www.7seasbrewing.com

Hops: Magnum, Centennial, Cascade

Initial attempts to launch 7 Seas were reduced to embers after a fire in the original brewhouse in Gig Harbour, Washington. The venture rose from the ashes and, now situated in a rather swanky setting by the sea, 7 Seas is causing ripples among Washington's craft beer community with its unpretentious, quality canned beers. Ballz Deep is the biggest hop-hitter, walking a plank of comfy crystal malt before plunging into a rolling swell of Yakima Valley hops, giving grass, grapefruit and a resiny finish. Also check out the Wheelchair Barleywine.

Stone
Stone Ruination Ten Year Anniversary IPA 10.5%
San Diego
www.stonebrew.com

Hops: Centennial, Columbus, Citra

When Stone set-up in the San Diegan suburbs back in 1996, many were claiming that craft beer was a West Coast whim on the wane. But Greg Koch and Steve Wagner, who had met in Los Angeles while working in the music industry, recognised that the late-blossoming San Diego was perfectly-placed to survive the shake-out. While others would have played it safe, Stone shook things up and unleashed an array of unashamedly aggressive and uncompromising beers. Defiantly disobedient and colossal in character, they hailed the hop with unprecedented audacity, their brazen bitterness big even by West Coast standards and, epitomised by Arrogant Bastard ale, the marketing and tone of voice was equally antagonistic. Crucially, the liquids live up to their brash and bold billing. Beyond keeping hopheads deliriously happy, Stone brews with intelligence and a lot of integrity; its smoked porter and pale ale are deftly made drops. But it is big beers that you turn to Stone for and its year-round Ruination IPA is one of its biggest, a brash bitter hop bomb that coats the palate with pine and rosemary. In 2002, to celebrate its advance into double digits, Stone ramped up the Ruination by making more of

the malt bill and not just heaping even more hops into the boil – but getting more out of them. Each barrel boasts five pounds of the little green fellows; two pounds of which are dry-hopped Citra and Centennial. Strangely, it is less acerbic than the original and more rounded in its bitterness. Hay, tobacco and grass on the nose; lime marmalade on rye in the middle with pine, peach and tart pineapple on the finish. It's a limited-edition 'liquid poem to the hop', and every beer drinker should try one bottle at least.

Surly
Furious 9%
Minnesota
www.surlybrewing.com

Hops: Warrior, Ahtanum, Simcoe, Amarillo

Made in Minnesota using Golden Promise floor-malted barley from Scotland, Furious is an on-the-warpath IPA embittered with four American hops by a brewery which, quite literally, re-wrote the rule book. In 2011, after much campaigning and quarrelling, and helped by pressure from its fan club, the Surly Nation, it successfully persuaded the state of Minnesota to pass the 'Surly Bill', which dismantled the three-tier system and allow breweries to sell their own beer directly to drinkers. This enabled it to open a $20 million restaurant and beer garden at the brewery premises. Surly, founded by Omar Ansari, who began home-brewing in 1994, was a pioneer of putting craft beer into cans, and in 2012 *Esquire* magazine named its CynicAle as one of the 'Best Canned Beers to Drink Now'.

Hop Shoots with Garlic and Pan-fried Scallops

This is an incredibly easy-to-cook dish that, if you've got a portable gas hob, you can cook on the side of the hop field just moments after you've picked the fresh hop shoots.

Ingredients
• 2 tablespoon olive oil
• 1 garlic clove, finely chopped
• 350g/12oz freshly picked hop shoots
• 8 large or 12 small scallops removed from shells, cleaned and halved
• freshly squeezed jouce of 1 lemon
• Salt and pepper

Method
Heat a frying pan with olive oil and add the chopped garlic.
Add the hop shoots and fry gently for 3 to 4 minutes before removing.
In a separate pan, heat the olive oil and add the scallops to the pan and cook until almost opaque (3–5 minutes).
Plate up, drizzle with lemon juice, season to taste with sea salt and freshly ground black pepper, and serve immediately

Tröegs
Nugget Nectar Ale 7.5%
Pennsylvania
www.troegs.com

Hops: Nugget, Warrior, Tomahawk, Simcoe,
  Palisade

Bottles of this excellent Imperial Amber do
not hang about when it's released every
year in February. Rarely seen beyond the
East Coast US, it is an extreme hop version
of Tröegs' HopBack Amber Ale that initially
holds its hops together before firing off fruits
on the finish: satsumas, lychees, ripe plums
and apricots. Hop junkies unable to get hold
of Nugget should seek out Tröegs' Perpetual
IPA, dry hopped with Cascade and Citra.

Upright Brewing
Five 5.5%
Oregon
www.uprightbrewing.com

Hops: Perle, Willamette, Liberty

A synonym for
principled and
honourable, Upright
also refers here to the
double bass played
by Charles Mingus,
the 'angry man of jazz',
who fused tradition
with avant-garde
experimentation.
There is method to
the moniker of a micro
that, like a hipster
wearing a beret, mixes
classic European
(mostly Belgian and
French) styles with
Portland's progressive craft beer scene.
Avoiding aggressive hoppy beers, Upright
releases numbered rustic beers made from
local grain, local hops and a signature Saison
yeast. This is a delicate, fragrant farmhouse
ale, all grainy, grassy and grapefruity, from an
acutely impressive ale-maker.

Victory
HopDevil 6.7%
Pennsylvania
www.victorybeer.com

Hops: Cascade, Centennial

Having risen from a
brewpub in 1996 to
America's 27th biggest
craft brewing company
(by volume sales) in 2011,
Victory cannot really be
considered one of the small
guys anymore. But that
doesn't matter, as they still
make thoroughly decent
beer. Inspired by the pale
ales of the late 1980s,
Hop Devil was first brewed
in 1996, though, with
imperial and double IPAs
an increasingly influence, it
is now brewed with 15 per
cent more hops. Like Clint
Eastwood in *Gran Torino*,
it's a bitter veteran still
capable of opening a can
of whupass on more youthful rivals.

CANADA

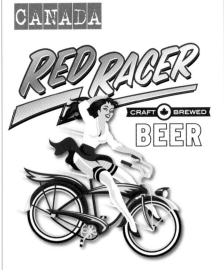

Central City Brewing
Red Racer ESB 5.5%
British Columbia
www.centralcitybrewing.com

Hops: German Magnum, Horizon, Centennial, Cascade

With a roster replete with a whole host of
lupulin-laced liquids, and hopheads heading
for the zealously bitter Red Racer IPA, the
brewpub's ESB citrusy charms are often
overlooked. Sticklers for style guidelines
may question its ESB title but, if you called it
Debbie and put a dress on it, this beer would
still be a marvellous meeting of hop and malt.

Half Pints
Humulus Ludicrous 8%
Winnipeg
www.halfpintsbrewing.com

Hops: Cascade, Centennial

Hoppier than a one-
legged bunny rabbit who
has just stubbed his toe,
this borderline barley
wine breaks the 100 IBU
barrier courtesy of copious
amounts of Cascade and
Centennial. It squeezes
the sweet wort through
a hopback heaving with
hops and then, prior to
conditioning, it is dry hopped
once more. Standing on
broad barley shoulders, the
sweetness softens the spiky bitterness: a deft
touch for a big man.

Russell
Russell IP'eh! 6.5%
British Columbia
www.russellbeer.com

Hop: Cascade

Do you see what those
crazy Canadians have done
there, eh! But a cunning
play on words is not all the
judges at the 2012 World
Beer Cup liked about this
silver-medal winner. The
brewery, although based
in Greater Vancouver and
barely 10 miles from the
US border, eschews its
American neighbours in
favour of an English-style
IPA whose anglicised malt
bill delivers a delicious,
doughy and nutty mouthfeel that is sparked
up by Cascade hops. Citrusy with a snappy,
slam-shut finish.

BELGIUM

Contreras
Valeir Extra 6.5%
East Flanders
www.contreras.be

Hops: Sterling, Amarillo

A fabulous farmhouse brewery dating
back nearly 200 years that is, quite literally,
outstanding in its field. The operation, in
the small town of Gavere just southwest
of Ghent, previously went by the name of
Brouwerij Latte and was in Contreras family

hands until 2004, when Willy Contreras handed over control to son-in-law Frederik de Vrieze, who pointed the beers in a new direction. Valeir Extra, named after a local 15th-century warrior, is a gently spoken, grassy IPA with lovely rustic rough edges and a whole load of estery apricot and peach.

Van Eecke
Hommelbier 7.5%
West Flanders
www.brouwerijvaneecke.be/en
Hops: Brewer's Gold, Challenger, Hallertau

Twinned with Zatec in the Czech Republic and home to the National Hop Museum, the town of Poperinge is hailed as the Humulus lupulus capital of Belgium. Its local 'hop beer', first brewed in 1981, is a liquid lesson in subtlety and strength. A biscuit body made up of three malts is flowered freely with locally grown Brewer's Gold and Challenger and bittered with Hallertau. Vibrant and full-bodied, it sways with grass and touches of honey, pine and cumin. Gung-ho hoppy American pale ales take note.

De Ranke
XX Bitter 6.2%
Hainault
www.deranke.be
Hops: Brewers Gold, Hallertau

Along with Alvinne and Ellezelles, De Ranke is one corner of a remarkable, alternative brewing triangle where humdrum Belgian brewing traditions tend to disappear. Brewers Nino Bacelle and Guido Devos are extremely talented chaps brimming with creativity, whose signature slight sourness comes from yeast sourced from Rodenbach. Every Friday and Saturday, they take over the Deca Brewery in Woesten-Vleteren to make their own brews. Brett plays a cheek-drawing cameo in its glorious Cuvée de Ranke yet is more subdued here where it's all about the hop – Brewers Gold and Hallertau to be precise. The beer has been described as 'Orval with everything turned up to 11', and the hoppiest beer in Belgium. Certainly XX brought bitterness back to Belgium, opening the country's brewers up to the whole idea. The brewery also makes a dark beer, Noir de Dottignies, a Kriek and an Abbey-style triple.

La Rulles
Tripel 8.4%
Luxembourg,
www.larulles.be
Hops: Amarillo, Warrior

If you see one of La Rulles' lovely-looking labels then, rest assured, the ensuing imbibing experience is going to be, at the very least, an interesting one. Ordained with the distinctive Orval yeast and hopped using Amarillo and Warrior by beer headbrewer Gregory Verhelst, here is an immensely aromatic, amber-blond Triple.

Sainte Hélène
Black Mamba Stout 4.5%
Luxembourg
www.sainte-helene.be
Hops: Citra, Simcoe

Not to be confused with the battery-operated neck massager, this sensual stout is sexed up, citrus-style, using Citra and Simcoe. Black Mamba is a big mocha mouthful, dry and dark, anchored by a chunk of chilli chocolate and a slightly sour, long liquorice finish.

Schelde
Hop Ruiter 8%
Antwerp
www.scheldebrouwerij.be
Hops: Cascade and Styrian. Dry-hopped with Nelson Sauvin

American-accented, strong, muscular, golden and Belgian, hopping back and forth on its tip-toes and ready to roundhouse your palate into next week, this is the Jean Claude Van Damme of Belgian strong beers, from the town of Meer, in Belgium's north-east. A transatlantic tripel teeming with tropical fruit, it's a hop punch padded in a velvet glove. Hop Ruiter finishes with a soothing, anaesthetising word in one's ear.

Urthel
Hop-it 9.5%
West Flanders
www.urthel.com
Hops: Magnum, Spalt, Saaz

The first person to write about hops as a preservative in beer was a 12th-century nun called Hildegard of Bingen – who was also the first person to write about the female orgasm. Little surprise, then, that namesake

Hildegard van Ostaden, who founded Urthel in 2000 with husband Bas, was so taken with the hop-heavy beers during an epiphany at the Anchorage Barley Wine Festival in Alaska. Brewed for Urthel at the Koningshoeven brewery in the Netherlands, this is a vibrantly effervescent IPA that borders on a barley wine and highly hopped with three noble European hops. White pepper, green apples and a light lemongrass finish.

Viven
Imperial IPA 8%
West Flanders
www.viven.be
Hops: Columbus/Tomahawk, Simcoe

Yet another immaculate alumnus of the peerless Proefbrouwerij in East Flanders, Viven ventures beyond its Flemish surroundings in search of flavour – here veering sharply and unabashedly into West Coast territory to produce a resinous riot of tobacco, Angostura bitters and grapefruit dusted with brown sugar. Watch out, too, for a smoky, bitter porter, an ale made with English Goldings and a blonde hopped with local Poperinge hops from the same stable.

GERMANY

Schönram
Bavarias Best IPA 8.2%
Bavaria
www.brauerei-schoenram.de
Hops: unrevealed

Not far from the Austrian border, Eric Toft, the only American running a German brewery, remains blissfully unrestricted by the reins of the Reinheistegebot. He happily wanders off the Germanic path by using foreign hops, different barley varieties and yeast strains from Belgium, Britain and beyond. While the brewery also makes a run of excellent traditional Bavarian brews, here Toft has produced an assertively hopped, citrusy IPA, bringing a different kind of bitterness to Bavaria. Unfortunately his iconoclasm seems to be appreciated more abroad than it does at home, but it makes his point that the Reinheitsgebot does not limit German brewers to the safe and the samey. It will be fascinating to see how many others follow his path.

Hildegard von Bingen

Hildegard von Bingen, a very impressive nun and the ultimate multi-tasker, certainly kept herself busy at her convent on the lower Rhine near Bingen.

Not merely a nun, she was a 12th-century prophet and a poet, she composed music and penned highly influential theological and botanical treatises. She was also an adviser and physician to the German Emperor and was the first person to write about the female orgasm.

Hildegard was also the first person to record in writing the preservative powers of hops in brewing. In *Physica*, the second vast volume of her famous medical work 'Liber Subtilitatum Diversarum Naturarum Creaturarum', she dedicated Chapter 61 to the hop.

In 'De Hoppho', or 'Concerning the hop', she wrote: 'It is warm and dry, and has a moderate moisture, and is not very useful in benefiting man, because it makes melancholy grow in man and makes the soul of man sad, and weighs down his inner organs. But yet as a result of its own bitterness it keeps some putrefactions from drinks, to which it may be added, so that they may last so much longer.'

Drinks, however, did not necessarily mean beer and could have referred to elixirs or herbal remedies popular at the time. Direct reference to beer does not arrive until later in the book, in a chapter about the ash tree. There Hildegard wrote: 'If you also wish to make beer from oats without hops, but just with grusz, you should boil it after adding a very large number of ash leaves. That type of beer purges the stomach of the drinker, and renders his heart light and joyous.'

Her writings reveal her to be an accomplished brewster and she probably enjoyed a daily ration of heartily hopped beer until she died aged 81 in 1179.

NETHERLANDS

Rooie Dop
Chica Americana IPA 7.1%
Utrecht
www.rooiedop.nl
Hops: Amarillo, Cascade, Chinook, Columbus

Meaning 'Red Cap' (ie bottlecap), Rooie Dop is a quasi-cuckoo brewer created by three Dutch homebrewers, Cees, Mark and Jos, who make ale out of a cellar in Utrecht and also at the awfully well-respected De Molen. This is an American IPA in all but origin, with Chinook and Cascade doing a fruity fandango on a doughy base fleshed out by flaked oats. Keep an eye out for its ever-changing rota of small-batch experimental brews. One to watch.

SNAB
Pale Ale 6.3%
North Holland
www.snab.nl
Hop: Cascade

SNAB (the North Holland Alternative Brewers' Society) is a group of four men who develop their eclectic range of recipes in their own microbrewery, then commission bigger brewers (mostly De Proef in Belgium) to produce those beers on a commercial scale. In a land of lagers, this signature citrus pale ale using hops and yeast from the Pacific Northwest, was a massive departure for Dutch drinkers. Well-made, well balanced and beautiful with bitterballen.

De Witte Leeuw
Amarillo Sun 6%
Overijssel
www.brouwerijdewitteleeuw.nl
Hop: Amarillo

I first drank this fresh from De Wildeman, a lively old beer drinking den in Amsterdam, and it slaked my rasping thirst almost before I had even walked through the door. Hopped entirely with Amarillo by former home-brewer Rowan Huigen, it is absurdly aromatic, with plenty of peach and a lot of apricot going on.

CZECH REPUBLIC

Kocour
Catfish Sumecek 4.2%
Bohemia
www.pivovar-kocour.cz
Hops: unrevealed

In the far north of Bohemia, close to the borders of Germany and Poland, Kocour brings in brewers from all around the world to chip away at perceptions of Czech brewing. Its international outlook stretches beyond the Saaz hop and embraces an array of ale styles as well as more familiar lager-conditioned beers. This is a fresh and exceptionally fruity pale ale brewed in cahoots with Ballast Point Brewing of San Diego, California, using caramalt and American hops.

Matuška
Raptor IPA 6.2%
Central Bohemia
hwww.pivovarmatuska.cz
Hops: Premiant, Cascade, Amarillo

In a departure from the Czech Republic's traditional ale and dark lagers of admittedly generally excellent character, this growing brewery founded by Martin Matuška and his son in 2009, majors in American-influenced India Pale Ales, Weizenbocks, Weissbiers and Belgian Saisons. It also turns out traditional Czech styles with aplomb, yet it's this engaging IPA, made with one Czech hop and two from the US and with lavender notes anchored by sweet malt, which stands out.

Vyškov
Jubiler Amber IPA 6%
South Moravia
www.pivovyskov.cz

Hops: Kazbek, Cascade, Chinook, Premiant

Hopped not once, not twice but five times, including in the conditioning tank, Jubiler Amber IPA is a strong bitter beer from South Moravia, an area blessed with rich barley and home to the Vyškov brewery since 1680 when it was founded by the Bishop of Olomouc. State-owned from 1945, it had its tyres kicked by several prospective buyers before being privatised in 2011. So far the beer has not suffered, with this brisk IPA still sparking off a pillow-soft palate with a dry and long, lovely mineral finish.

SWEDEN

Nils Oscar
Barley Wine 10.4%
Södermanland
www.nilsoscar.se

Hops: English Fuggles, American Cascade, German Magnum.

A distiller of much distinction and a very conscientious craft brewer, Nils Oscar pretty much does everything itself, from grain to glass. While Nils Oscar's northern location renders it too cold to grow its own hops; it sources oat, barley and wheat from its own Tarno Manor Farm and prepares it in its own malting house. Barley calls the shots here, a burnished bronze snifter-dweller first brewed in 1994 on brewmaster Patrick Holmqvist's home cooker when he was a member of Stockholm's 'Fermentation Army' homebrew club. Do not drink if trying to put together flatpack furniture.

NORWAY

Kinn
Vestkyst 4.7%
Florø
www.kinnbryggeri.no

Hops: Columbus, Simcoe and Centennial in the boil; those plus Amarillo for dry-hopping

It makes sense that a craft brewer on the most western point of all of Scandinavia would make a west coast IPA called, in

Norwegian, 'West Coast'. Kinn, named after a local island, and meaning 'cheek', certainly makes some bold beers inspired by both Belgium and Britain, and demand has been so great that a bigger brewery was due to open in 2013. Brewmaster Espen Lothe uses open fermentation tanks and there is a clinical cleanliness to the copper-coloured canvas here. On it, Lothe has layered grapefruit, red apple skin and pine sap, with three American hops in the boil, and the same three, plus Amarillo, used for dry-hopping. The label also has a hop wearing a turban and sunglasses. That's funny.

Lervig
Reserve Rye IPA 8.5%
Stavanger
www.lervig.no

Hops: Simcoe, Chinook, Amarillo

A native of Philadelphia, Mike Murphy started homebrewing in 1991 and was the man who helped make Mikkeller's legendary 'Beer Geek Breakfast'. After stints in Italy with Birra Del Borgo, he stoked the fire of innovation in Denmark with GourmetBryggeriet before landing in Lervig in Stavanger, Norway. With an annual capacity of 3.5m litres, it was founded by wealthy investors after Carlsberg acquired their local brewery and uprooted it to Oslo. After Mike was put in charge of the mashfork, a bourbon barrel-aged barley wine, Flemish Reds, Saisons and a Belgian wit have all been released. Lervig is also the only Norwegian brewer to package its craft in cans. This chewy Rye IPA really steams up the ironic eyewear of the Scandinavian beer geek community. A whole host of hops hang seamlessly on a muscular mash of rye and oats; there's pine and peach, grass and grain and a touch of sesame seed.

SWITZERLAND

Rappi
XXA Strong Ale 6.7 %
St Gallen
www.bierfactory.ch

Hops: Meridian, Cascade, Hersbrucker, Spalt

Tucked away in Rapperswil, at the southern tip of Lake Zurich, Rappi Bier Factory is overseen by expat Englishman Stephen Hart, who has added British beers to orthodox Germanic brews. XXA is a stylish, fresh and floral Swiss IPA hopped with English, American and German hops, which pepper the palate with marmalade, pine and grapefruit.

Storm and Anchor
India Pale Ale 6.9%
Zurich
www.stormandanchor.com/wordpress

Hops: Columbus, Cascade, Centennial, Simcoe

Tom Strickler runs this great brewery in the Töss valley, near Zurich. In this eastern part of Switzerland, extremely hoppy beers simply aren't the done thing. But Tom doesn't give a Töss: he's done one anyway with no pretence of trying to pander to local palates. It's a very well-made west coast style IPA with the fruity, citrusy, resiny bits in all the right places. He also makes an IPA jam, apparently …

POLAND

Ale Browar
Rowing Jack 6.2%
Pomerania
www.alebrowar.pl/en/idea/

Hops: Simcoe, Chinook, Citra, Cascade, Palisade

On seeing this gipsy brewer's deeply wacky labels, featuring a bearded lady, a man dressed as a cow and a pirate with a paddle

among others, it is easy to suspect the dark arts of marketing are at work. The brewery has just started producing a pumpkin ale called Naked Mummy … possibly the first NSFW beer label. There's no smoke and no mirrors here, however, just a fresh, piney, gently puckering, rare example of a Polish IPA, powered by five different hops.

Del Borgo
ReAle 6.4%
Lazio
www.birradelborgo.it
Hop: Cascade

As behoves a brewer who sounds like a Renaissance artist, Leonardo di Vincenzo awakens old styles from their slumber using plenty of New World nous. Bringing the balance of an English session ale with the maniacal endeavour of an American micro, this pale ale melds mellow Maris Otter malt with foot-to-the-floor Cascade hops. Lime marmalade on wholemeal toast? A little bit, yes.

Brewfist
Spaceman 7%
Lombardy
www.brewfist.com
Hops: Simcoe, Citra, Columbus

A youthful brewery set up in 2010, Brewfist may sound like a repetitive strain complaint but as you repeatedly bring it from tabletop to lips, Spaceman is more likely to make your arm strong (Do you get it? Armstrong? Neil? Spaceman? Oh, never mind). A well-made West Coast IPA that sings all the right citrus notes from the Citra and Simcoe songsheet.

Maltovivo
Noscia IPA 6%
Campania
www.maltovivo.it
Hops: Cascade, Amarillo, Centennial

A dry, dapper IPA from a brewery 25 miles or so inland from Naples, whose smouldering air of sophistication comes courtesy of smoked barley. Like Keyser Söze in the Hollywood thriller *The Usual Suspects*, the hops don't fully reveal themselves until the end and then, just like that, poof, they're gone.

Craig Allan
Agent Provocateur
6.5%
Picardy
www.craigallan.fr
Hops: Amarillo, Cascade

Some writers would make a smutty joke about an eponymous knicker and bra emporium but I'm better than that. The phenomenon of gipsy brewing has got its knockers but it is a growing trend in French brewing and one of the leading lights is Scottish expat brewer Craig Allan. He aspires to open his own brewery in early 2013, somewhere in the Nord-Pas-de-Calais region, but for now this spicy, citrusy, pepper-prodding pale ale is expertly brewed at De Proef in Belgium.

Fleurac
Triple Brune IPA 8%
Auvergne
www.brasserie-fleurac.com
Hops: Cascade, Brewer's Gold, Amarillo

Gregory Murer, a Belgian expatriate in Ydes, deep in the Cantal, has created a smooth fusion of a strong Belgian dark ale and an IPA. While it initially befuddled the locals, it has become the brewery's flagship brew and a beguiling take on a black IPA or, if you're old school, a hoppy porter. Cascade and Brewer's Gold go in the boil and the fermented fresh beer is then dry-hopped with Amarillo all the way to the finish. The effect is like breakfasting on grapefruit with a strong Americano coffee.

La Franche
XXYZ Bitter 6%
Franche-Comté
www.lafranche.net
Hops: Galena, Simcoe, Amarillo

For a brewery that proudly boasts that its beer is 'brewed at the back of the barn' in La Ferté, Jura, it is only apt that this terrific blonde tribute to De Ranke XX (see page 83), is blessed with a distinct barnyard brogue. One of many clever craft beers by Régis Barth and Jean-Yves Nauroy.

Garrigues
Frappadingue 7%
Garrigues
www.brasseriedesgarrigues.fr
Hops: Nelson Sauvin, Amarillo

Surrounded by wineries, this little brewery in a medieval town in Languedoc-Roussillon, named after a type of local scrubland, goes with the grain, sourcing much of its malted barley from the fields around it. Founders Gwenaël Samotyj, Emmanuel Pierre-Auguste and Eric Varray are particularly proud of this gently carbonated, phenomenally fragrant piny IPA bolstered by a strong scaffold of sweet malt.

Matten
Red Fox IPA 7.7%
Alsace
www.matten.fr
Hops: Strisselspalt, Magnum, Halltertau

Brewed in Matzenheim, south of Strasbourg by Anne and Jacek Korczak in a converted barn next to their home, Matten majors on ales imbued with local Alsatian ingredients. Red Fox is an atypical French IPA whose hot peppery prickle only peaks on the palate once the warm fruity notes have faded away.

Le Paradis
Sylvie'cious 5.5%
Lorraine
www.brasserieleparadis.com

Hops: East Kent Golding, Cascade, Summit

Brewing from her violet-shuttered family home in Blainville-sur-L'Eau, east of Nancy, Marjorie Jacobi is a brewer petite in stature yet considerable in character. Sylvie'cious is both a sublimely silly pun and a lower-gravity derivate of Marjorie's flagship La P'tite Sylvie, which clones its big sister's massive yet subtle spicy and citrusy hop kick. 'Houblonnage sérieux', as they say in France.

Pays Flamand
Anosteké 8%
Nord-Pas-de-Calais
www.bracine.com

Hops: Simcoe, Cascade, Strisselspalt

Olivier Duthoit and Mathieu Lesenne, based in Blaringhem, are among the foremost representatives of Nord-Pas-De-Calais's new generation of micro-breweries, revisiting the Bière de Garde tradition with a new approach. Their Bracine is hoppier than most Bières de Garde, yet Anosteké, an astonishingly even-handed spicy, resin-soaked strong blonde, pushes the bitter hop boundaries that little bit further with American varieties combined with Strisselspalt from Alsace, usually found in lagers.

Pleine Lune
Aubeloun 7%
Drôme
www.brasserie-pleinelune.fr

Hops: Citra, Green Bullet, Simcoe, Centennial, Pacific Gem

Another artisanal Alsatian, Benoît Ritzenthaler has made his microbrewing mark in Chabeuil, east of Valence, after working seven years at another brewery in the area. He makes a lovely light lawnmower lager, but his flagship beer, Aubeloun IPA ('aubeloun' means 'hops' in the local Dauphinois patois), is a strong floral US-influenced IPA that pitter-patters the palate rather than pounding it.

St Germain
Réserve Sainte-Hildegarde Blonde 6.9%
Nord-Pas-De-Calais
www.page24.fr

Hops: Brewer's Gold, Strisselspalt

Of all the Nord-Pas-De-Calais's new generation of brewers, Page 24 is the one that you are most likely to stumble across.

Brewed by Stéphane Bogaert and Hervé Descamps in Aix Noulette, the unpasteurised, bottle-conditioned beers only use hops from the region and, occasionally, make a stylistic break for the bizarre – seen its chicory and rhubarb beers, anyone? The most enchanting encounter, however, is Réserve Sainte-Hildegarde Blonde, an impressive study in balance and drinkability named after the lupulin-loving abbess. Sprightly, peppery Brewer's Gold and Strisselspalt perform tricks on a toffee base.

AUSTRIA

Hofstetten
Heller Bock Saphir 7.4%
Gmünd
www.hofstetten.at

Hops: Aurora, Tradition, Magnum, Saphir

Hofstetten, in the hands of the Kramer family since 1847 and a keen exporter to America (where I encountered it), is a small brewery in the town of St Martin in Lower Austria which rocks the bock style incredibly well. This deep amber, bottom-fermented beer hails Hallertau hop varieties with no small amount of gusto, bittering it with Aurora, Tradition and Magnum before dry-hopping it with freshly picked, whole Hallertau Saphir hop flowers grown locally. A two-month infusion adorns the unfiltered caramel core with a finery of apricot, plums and peach. Look out for a version aged in Calvados barrels.

AUSTRALIA

Feral
BFH (Barrel Fermented Hog) 5.8%
Swan Valley
www.feralbrewing.com.au

Hops: Warrior, Chinook, Centennial, Amarillo, Cascade

Hop Hog, Feral's flagship IPA, is a fair dinkum citrussy classic Down Under. Brewed by the highly accomplished Brendan Varis and regularly rewarded with shiny medals, it is one of Western Australia's best beers. Rarer, and gifted with added depth edge through initial fermentation in French oak, is its barrel-blessed brother, teeming from that initiation in wood with tones of pine, cigar box, vanilla and prunes.

Stone & Wood
Stone & Wood Pacific Ale 4.4%
Byron Bay
www.stoneandwood.com.au

A sharp refresher primed with Galaxy, a fruity dual-purpose high alpha hop from Tasmania. Damn drinkable, deftly balanced and intensely aromatic with crisp notes of passion fruit, mango, kiwi and lemongrass. So much more than a simple sundowner.

NEW ZEALAND

Epic
Barrel Aged IPA 7.25%
Auckland
www.epicbeer.com

Hops: Cascade, Centennial, Columbus, Simcoe

Epic is about right, an aggressive oaked IPA from an unashamedly audacious brewery inspired by America's West Coast hop bombs and the journey IPAs endure from Britain to India. Wonderful aromas of toffee, vanilla, wood and sauvignon blanc with a pitter-patter of initial white grape and kiwi on the palate are closely followed by a Gueuze-like sourness that precedes a big hop bitter smack. Mellow wood and vanilla comes with a long drying bitter finish. Amazing.

Tuatara
India Pale Ale 7%
North Island
www.tuatarabrewing.co.nz

Hops: Pacific Jade, Chinook, Styrian Goldings

Emboldened by a trip to England more than ten years ago, Carl Vasta has enthusiastically broadened the horizons of New Zealand beer drinkers for more than a decade from a base in Paraparaumu, 30 miles north of Wellington, taking for his operation the name of a rare and unique New Zealand reptile. A huge hop wallop bursts forth from the white-capped bronze body, peppery bitterness from Pacific Jade tickles the nose, while a long sweet caramel middle ends with an earthy climax. It's good.

SOUTH AFRICA

Porcupine Quill
Karoo Red 5.5%
Kwazulu-Natal
www.craftbrewers.co.za

Hop: Willamette

An ambitious, impassioned epicurean and skilled spear fisherman, John Little founded an esteemed chef's school eight years ago before buying a six-barrel brewkit from Britain. Inspired by the American craft brewing scene, and Dogfish Head's Sam Calagione in particular, Little uses whole hop flowers, smokes his own malt and ages his beer in oak barrels formerly used for chardonnay. The brewery sits in a complex alongside a cheese-making set-up, bakery and sausage manufactory, making it effectively self-sufficient in pub lunches. Of Little's 11 bottle-conditioned beers, this on-the-money amber, the second beer to be brewed, stands out. Fruity nose, lots of watermelon and dried fruits, Willamette hop all the way through to a long, dry, bitter finish.

Robsons
Durban Pale Ale 5.7%
KwaZulu-Natal
www.shongwenibrewery.com

Hops: Cascade, Challenger

In a nation where 98 per cent of the beer market is owned by just three breweries and nearly everyone drinks the same rather fizzy and forlorn lager, bottle-conditioned beers, especially those infused with fruit, are a distinct departure. Englishman Stuart Robson, who imports hops from Europe and America and plays them against South African barley and local fruit, cold-shoulders kegs in favour of bottle-conditioning. While the fruit beer fluctuates, his Durban Pale Ale is a cloudy, zesty and tangy amber ale with an enduring astringency that loiters long and lovely.

BRAZIL

Colorado
Vixnu Imperial IPA 9.5%
Sao Paulo
www.cervejariacolorado.com.br

Hops: not revealed

Back in the 1990s, the market for characterful craft beer in Sao Paulo was slimmer than a well-trimmed Brazilian. But having initially, along with Dado, ploughed a rather lonesome furrow, Colorado is now a bountiful bush in the artisanal allotment of Brazilian craft brewing creativity. Joining forces with Matt Brynildson of the California-based Firestone Walker, the brewery attached electrodes to Colorado's distinctly dry Índica IPA and gave the knob a firm twist. Engrained with much rich malt and American hops, Vixnu – named after the Indian god Vishnu – is woody with a touch of golden syrup and figs.

Dado
Ilex 7%
Porto Alegre
www.especiaisdadobier.com.br

Hops: not revealed

Instrumental in Brazil's embryonic craft beer scene in the mid-1990s, Dado preceded a number of well-respected micros in the

city of Porto Alegre, such as Coruja and Abadessa. While remaining faithful to the Reinheitsgebot in a lot of its beers, it makes a departure here with a strong sprinkling of the indigenous yerba mate (erva-mate in Portuguese), also known as *Ilex paraguariensis*, and a most Brazilian brew. Spicy and slightly smoky, it's a little woody and herbal, like a teenager's treehouse.

Way Beer
Double American Pale Ale 8.8%
Paraná
www.waybier.com.br

Hops: Cascade, Citra, Amarillo

In 2010, this southern Brazilian micro arrived with a maturity beyond its years. Made with just the right amount of whimsy, its beers include a super-strength lager laid down on amburana wood. This barks out a big herbal bouquet and, while dry-hopped Cascade and Citra bombs speckle the back of the palate, it whispers sweet murmurs of malt upfront.

JAPAN

Baird Brewing
Suruga Bay Imperial IPA 7.5%
Shizuoka
www.bairdbeer.com

Hops: Columbus, Nelson Sauvin, Simcoe, Cascade

Begun in 2001 by the Ohio-born brewmaster Bryan Baird and his Japanese wife Sayuri, this micro creates beers whose distinctive flavours blow the doors off mainstream Japanese lagers. Suruga Bay, an aggressive double dry-hopped Double IPA that is krausened in the bottle with beer from a previous batch, is an immense showcase for American hops: there's pungent pine on the nose, marmalade in the middle and a finish drier than a Sumo wrestler's palms.

MY TOP 5
CRAFT BEERS

Fergus Fitzgerald
Adnams
England

Lists of favourite beers are notoriously fickle and are the cause of much soul searching but at least for this list I'm spared the conundrum of whether to include any beers that I brew.

Some of them may be based more on sentiment and a rose tinted memory and there maybe better tasting beers but these are the beers that I would happily drink for the rest of my days.

✳ Bottle-conditioned Guinness
[no longer available]

This was the beer that laid the foundations for how I think about beer. Craft beer didn't exist as a concept in Ireland when I grew up, thankfully that has changed over the past 10 years, but in the 'wilderness' years a fresh bottle of Guinness provided succour. It had a lovely acidity balanced by the roast and coffee notes that made it a refreshing drink despite its robust demeanour. On the farm where I grew up the workers that came to cut the hay or silage usually had a few bottles of Guinness with lunch as they sat by the side of the field, my brothers and I would help with the cutting and as a reward would get a few sips of the beer. Guinness was also the beer that my Dad drank and that in itself is reason enough to include it.

✳ Orval

I love this beer like an old friend. I might not drink it for years but when I do we take over from where we left off. Earthy, herbal, spicy, fruity notes come together in a perfect unison. The previous head brewer at Adnams received a crate of Orval as a gift. I'd never seen him so happy and after he somewhat reluctantly shared a bottle I could see why.

✳ Rodenbach Classic Flanders Red Ale

I love sour beers and this was probably the beer that showed me that Saccharomyces cerevisiae wasn't the only way to go. I had some of Avery's barrel-aged series a while ago and there were a few beers in there that I thought might just overtake Rodenbach, but for now at least I'm sticking with the original. Its wonderful balance of sweet and sour makes for a complex yet easy drinking experience.

✳ Fullers London Porter

I worked at Fullers for 7 years before moving to Adnams. London Porter was a highlight of the brewing calendar, the wort from the mash tun was beautiful in its own right and the finished beer is great, velvety chocolate and coffee, everything a porter should be.

✳ Firestone Walker Union Jack IPA

I first tasted Firestone's IPA on a trip to Denver for the Great American Beer Festival, it was fantastic but it wasn't until a friend arranged to send me some that I really fell in love with it. Despite its name, it is everything an American IPA should be, it's full of resinous pine, and grapefruit with a solid malt base to build it all from. It's big on flavour but still clean and balanced.

INDIA PALE ALE

Around 12 hours: that's how long it takes to get to India from east London these days. A film or two, catch a few winks, quick flirt with the air hostess, cheeky whisky, maybe even a second packet of nuts – why not, you're on holiday. Before you know it, you're there, in Mumbai. Easy. 'Bish. Bosh. Shoom. Shoom. Done,' as they say in Bow.

Above: Acting as ballast, IPA benefited from the rocky sea voyage.

Above right: The Allsopp Brewery in Burton was an instrumental IPA brewer in the early 19th century.

That same journey took up to six months back in the 18th century. Regardless of what state the disrepair you may find the Piccadilly Line in these days, it was a far more precarious, potentially tempestuous journey then, too.

It didn't start well, with currents and winds forcing ships to head off in the wrong direction, towards America rather than India. After taking a left down past Portugal and the Canary Islands, ships would head south on the open seas, with Africa somewhere on their port side, crossing the equator and down to Rio de Janeiro in Brazil, where, enduring sweltering temperatures, they would stop for food, water and a deep breath before sailing east across the South Atlantic, around the notoriously nefarious Cape of Good Hope, north through the Mozambique Channel, across the equator again, before arriving, finally and fortuitously, in Bombay.

After four to six months of being pounded and battered by the elements, the ships and those that sailed them were weary and in need of a rest. The beer below deck, however, was in fine fettle. Acting as sturdy ballast, the beer benefited from the ships being buffeted and battered, the rocking and rolling in oak casks rounded off the bitter edges and created a beer of mature oak-aged character.

The heat helped, too. As the temperature rose gradually to more than 35°C/95°F or more, it would perform a kind of natural pasteurisation, zapping any residual yeast that may have fallen through the filtering process back in London.

Contrary to what many assume, the IPAs were not cask-conditioned. Had that been the case, they would have exploded and spoiled; a silly idea akin to sending an ice cream to India. No, the IPAs consumed in India, often for breakfast among the upper classes, would have been closer to modern-day keg beers.

The pale ales sent to India were simply brewed with more hops and enough alcohol to give them the swashbuckling sea-legs to endure the journey. Not that much alcohol, though: the evidence is that these beers were only 6 to 7% ABV, about average for the time.

They were not new inventions nor were they designed specifically for export to the burgeoning Indian market. Brewers in Britain had long been aware of the preservative powers of hops and alcohol, having brewed October ales and other beers designed for long maturation in oak. These beers were tweaked for the Indian market, and were called 'pale ale as prepared for India'.

The name India Pale Ale did not become part of brewing parlance, strangely, until long after brewers began exporting highly hopped pale ales to Bombay, Calcutta and the other bases for British trade within the sub-continent.

George Hodgson, a middling-sized brewer from Bow, on the eastern edge of London, is often attributed with both coining the term and inventing the beer. He did neither. Imported pale ale in India dated back to the early 18th century and mentions for pale ale appeared well before Hodgson had exported his first batch.

But he was certainly the first brewer to establish a firm foothold in the Indian market, courtesy of a close relationship with the East India Company, an economic and political powerhouse on the sub-continent. His brewery at Bow was close to where the ships of the East India Company docked, and for decades Hodgson's sold considerable quantities of pale ale and porter to the captains and officers of the East Indiamen ships for their own private trading out east.

By the 1830s, however, Hodgson's grip on the Indian export market had begun to slip under competition from the breweries of Burton-upon-Trent. The likes of Samuel Allsopp, Bass and Worthington had lost their lucrative trade selling sweet, strong ales to the Baltic lands in 1822, courtesy of a Russian embargo and, actively encouraged by the East India Company, they soon turned their attention to brewing the same paler, more bitter beers that Hodgson made, and exploiting the Indian market instead.

Burton's water was ideal for hoppy pale ales; its sulphate hardness softened the harsh bitterness of the hops yet maintained their delicate aromas. Burton's pale ales soon commanded a strong following among British expat drinkers in India.

Back home in Britain, IPAs also found a keen market, but over the decades they lost their strength and bitterness, until, by the time the second half of the 20th century started, the name IPA had become little more than a synonym in Britain for 'bitter'.

In the 1990s, however, when the American craft brewing scene started gathering momentum, enthusiasts picked up the IPA banner, using it to flag up beers that were big in hoppiness, bitterness and alcohol. They might not have been exactly the sort of beer the British were drinking in India in the 1830s, but American IPA, infused with acutely bitter, intensely aromatic indigenous hops, high in strength, became the poster boy of American craft beer, particularly on the IPA-obsessed West Coast, where brewers gradually edged up the IBUs until a new style, Double IPA, emerged in 1994.

Triple and Imperial IPAs have, rather predictably followed, but the Americanisation of IPA only really became complete when British brewers reflected IPA through an American prism, brewing Stateside-style IPA in the country where the beer was first born more than 220 years ago.

Brewers in Britain had long been aware of the preservative powers of hops and alcohol, having brewed October ales and other beers designed for long maturation in oak. These beers were tweaked for the Indian market, and were called 'pale ale as prepared for India'. The name India Pale Ale did not become part of brewing parlance, strangely, until long after brewers began exporting highly hopped pale ales to Bombay, Calcutta and the other bases for British trade with the sub-continent.

PRIVATE LANDBRAUEREI SCHÖNRAM

Schönram, Germany www.brauerei-schoenram.de

Eric Toft, middle-aged, handsome, seldom seen out of lederhosen despite being born in the United States, passionate about beer in all its varieties - is an American with a mission: to drag German brewing kicking and screaming out of the 16th century.

After a career that would be the envy of – well, me, certainly – Toft is currently brewmaster at the 233-year-old Schönram brewery in rural Bavaria, just a few miles from the border with Austria.

There he produces the usual run of beers you would expect from a rural Bavarian brewery owned by the eighth generation of the same family: a Pils, a Hell, a Weissbier, a Dunkel. Alongside that, however, Toft, the first and currently the only American to run a Bavarian brewery, also makes beers in styles you might fear a rural Bavarian beer drinker would never even have heard of: an IPA, an imperial stout, a porter, a Belgian pale ale.

The idea, Toft says, is to show that the Reinheitsgebot, or 'purity law', firmly limiting the ingredients that go into beer, to which all Schönram's output sticks as strictly as any German brewery, need not be a straitjacket forcing brewers into making bland clone-beers.

The Reinheitsgebot, which effectively restricts German brewers to using just malted grain, hops, yeast and water as ingredients for their beer – no brewing sugars, as the Belgians do in, for example Abbey ales, and British brewers do in, say, milds and Burton Ales, no wacky flavourings such as cherries, coriander or sweet gale – started as a regulation imposed on the brewers of Munich in 1487, and later spread to cover the whole of Bavaria. When the Bavarians joined up to the new German Empire in 1871 they did so only on the condition that the Reinheitsgebot became law across the whole of Germany. The European Union in 1988 effectively overturned the Reinheitsgebot, meaning beers imported into Germany no longer had to comply with it. But German brewers have pretty much stuck to Reinheitsgebot-style brewing all the same, basically as a marketing tool to try to impress German beer drinkers with the authenticity of their beers.

Toft's motto, however, is 'Reinheitsgebot, not Einheitsgebot', which doesn't sound quite as good translated into English, 'purity decree, not sameness decree', but you get the idea. 'The Reinheitsgebot should be an inspiration and a motivation to creativity,' Toft says. 'It's blamed for making German beers bland. But the main reason for blandness is

that the purchasing of raw materials has been taken out of the hands of brewers and given to the accountants.'

Born in Colorado, Toft studied at the Colorado School of Mines in Golden, which is next door to Coors' brewery. That proximity helped Toft become interested in home-brewing, and after graduating he decided he was much more keen on a career making beer than spending years in Saudi Arabia prospecting for oil.

Clearly a man who believes that if you're going to do something, do it properly, Toft's next step was to go to Germany, learn German and enrol at the brewing school at Weihenstephan, near Munich, recognised as one of the best places in the world to learn about brewing beer. There he discovered a disdain for the self-imposed shackles of German brewing traditions and a delight in the looser, more innovation-friendly ways of brewers in Belgium.

After Toft graduated from Weihenstephan he launched into a career that took him, among other places, to Lamot, a Belgian brewer that was, at the time, owned by the British brewing giant Bass Charrington. Its flagship product was a not particularly distinguished Pils older readers may remember from the British market. But it also made a number of 'speciality' beers for Belgian drinkers, including Bass Stout. Lamot was sold by Bass to its Belgian rival Piedboeuf, which itself turned into Interbrew soon after, and Toft moved on, ending up at Schönram, where he has been since 1998.

Martyn Cornell

KEY BEERS
Bavarias Best India Pale Ale 8.2%
Bavarias Best Imperial Stout 10%
Saphir Bock 8%
German Pils 5%
Altbayrisch Dunkel 5%

SCRÖNRAM BEERS

It would be an exaggeration to say his ideas have swept South Bavaria like a storm: the brewery's speciality beers find a better market in Italy than they do at home. But if you see them, you should buy them, both the specialities and the 'standard' beers such as the Pils and the Dunkel.

Schönram Gold, for example, is a lovely Maibock-style beer, sweet and appley, Saphir Bock nicely balanced with a touch of tangerine from the Saphir hops. Bavarias Best (sic) IPA is a stonking 8.2% ABV number heavy on the hops. Imperial Stout, at 10%, which the brewery recommends laying down for five years or more, is complex and dangerously easy-drinking. The Conatus, made with Belgian yeasts but German hops and malt and no sugar additions, is an excellent palate-cleansing beer that works very well with fatty food.

Top: A rare picture of Eric Toft not wearing lederhosen.

Above: Eric's immaculate Bavarian brewhouse.

THE KERNEL BREWERY

Bermondsey, London, England   www.thekernelbrewery.com

To the regular roar and rumble of trains above, men wearing wellies and facial hair of varying ambition go about their work beneath two nondescript railway arches in South London.

Every so often, a rattle of the metal shutter reveals another gentrified junkie craving Kernel's cultured bonhomie catalyst. The brown-bottled flavoursome fix comes in just two forms: dark beer and pale beer.

After a quick greet and glad-hand, the thirsty pilgrims get what they are given and, clutching bottles of Evin O'Riordain's mood enhancer to their chests, happily head off into the streets of Bermondsey.

Evin's unfussy, idiosyncratic ales, which pour at some of London's finest restaurants and cutting-edge bars, have been instrumental in cultivating a London craft beer scene now boasting more than 45 brewers. 'It's now a great place to brew beer, it's cosmopolitan and there's an open-mindedness that's very exciting,' he says of London today. 'In general, the standard of brewing is pretty high, there's a good mix of tradition and people doing different things.'

Born in the United States but having been raised in Waterford, Ireland, Evin crossed the Irish Channel in 1999 with a degree in Russian and History gained from Trinity College, Dublin. There is a slight resemblance to Rasputin about this Bermondsey brewer; tall, svelte with long hair and a hirsute goatee regularly caressed during the extended, slightly uncomfortable, periods of contemplation that follow each question.

Such enigmatic silences should be expected from someone who studied for a PhD in Samuel Beckett. 'In typical Beckettian fashion, I failed to finish it,' says Evin, who supplemented his studies by working for Neal's Yard Dairy, an artisan cheese shop in nearby Borough Market, the heart of epicurean London.

Having packed in his PhD, Evin was sent over to his native New York in 2006 to help the gourmet grocer Wholefoods open a cheese shop. There he met Jonah Schulz, an American now brewing beer at Kernel, who introduced him to the Big Apple's burgeoning beer scene. 'We went to DBA in the East Village which is not a particularly dynamic beer bar but, for

Below: Evin working with whole leaf hops.

In 2011, Kernel's Export Stout, based on an 1890 recipe from the former East London brewer Truman's, was hailed as the best bottled beer in the country while, later that year, the Guild of British Beer Writers named Evin as the nation's top brewer. Not bad for a novice on a four-barrel plant.

someone from London, it was really impressive,' says Evin, whose beer-drinking orbit had hitherto revolved around the pubs and bars of Borough Market. 'People talked about beers the way I'd talked about cheese. There was a reason for everything, a level of respect for beer that was sadly missing back in the UK. First I thought, "This is good" and, second, "Why isn't it happening back home?"'

LONDON RENAISSANCE

It was late 2006 and very little was happening back home. Once the biggest brewing metropolis in the world, London's brewing landscape was a wasteland in comparison with its past. When Young's of Wandsworth sold up and shipped out, you could count the capital's breweries on the hand of a careless saw operator; just four local breweries for more than 10m Londoners. And one of those breweries made Budweiser.

'People were being deceived by a lack of diversity,' says Evin, taking an early-morning sip of Table Beer, brewed with Citra, Summit, Apollo and Ahtanhum. 'We'd drink in pubs where there would be 12 beers on the bar but no choice at all, just a dozen replicas of the same beers. There was no genuine diversity, no discernment and no focus on what was important: actual quality.'

Evin began to homebrew using plastic buckets, enamel cans and little or no knowledge. He then set up the London Amateurs Homebrewing Club, which attracted stalwarts from the Durden Park Beer Circle (see page 163). 'They'd come along and whip out some old stouts and porters,' he says. 'They brewed using the old recipes but they weren't slaves to the past. If something made the beer taste bad then they took it out. Simple as that. It was an excellent place to learn quickly. We tasted a lot of beers and talked a lot.'

Others liked Evin's beer, and in 2009 he set up a small brewery with money borrowed from family and friends, sharing an arch with a cheesemaker and importer of Italian meats. 'It was one of those points in life when you are open to new ideas,' he says. 'A bit of ignorance goes a long way in the beer business. It's incredibly helpful if you don't know what you're going into.'

In 2011, Kernel's Export Stout, based on an 1890 recipe from the former East London brewer Truman's, was hailed as the best bottled beer in the country while, later that year, the Guild of British Beer Writers named Evin as the nation's top brewer. Not bad for a novice on a four-barrel plant.

There was, Evin admits, no entrepreneurial vision. 'London seemed to make sense and I just made beers I liked

to drink: porters, stouts and clean pale, hoppy beers,' he says. 'We change the hops but the basic premise of what that beer is trying to achieve remains the same: pale and clean, where the hop flavours shine through.'

He craves cleanliness and clarity in the beer. 'I use London ale yeast for the stouts and porters, which furnishes it with clear lines but with a bit of fruity oomph,' Evin says. 'The dark styles are derived from recipes specifically rooted to London and brewed with British malt. It's something that Americans don't have, that quality, biscuity presence that only British malt brings.'

The pale ales, all named after the hops used, are also given a four-month best-before date on the bottle. 'They're designed to be drunk fresh,' he says. 'All that hop flavour will fade over time. I love hoppy American beers but they're not the same after months on the water.'

Now in his own arch down the road from where he started, after moving to create a slightly bigger brewery, he has begun experimenting with barrel-ageing using wine-soaked wood from Burgundy and whisky barrels from Speyside. An Imperial Brown Stout that has been snoozing in Speyside Glen Garioch casks for two months is oily, viscous and simply sublime.

A Berliner Weisse is being brewed and Evin says there are some other exciting elixirs on their way. But growing big is not the endgame. 'A lot of what we do is visceral and physical and I want to be able to touch and smell what is going on,' he says.

'I need that smell to do the paperwork. I didn't want levels or hierarchies. We're all happy working here and that comes through in the beer.'

KEY BEERS

Export Stout London 1890 7.1%
Imperial Brown Stout London 1856 10.1%
Export India Porter 5.7%
India Pale Ale Centennial 7%
India Pale Citra 7.2%
Pale Ale Nelson Sauvin 4.7%

STONE & WOOD

Byron Bay, Australia   www.stoneandwood.com.au

If you're reading these words, which you are, then chances are you've dreamed the dream. No, not the one where you're not wearing any pants in the school playground. It's the dream of owning your own brewery.

Who, during a stolen moment of quiet reflection, amid the drudgery of real life, hasn't let their imagination drift away on a warm current of sweet malty aroma, to the mystical microbrewery of one's mind?

Here, in the quixotic kettle of one's subconscious, the beer sips like success and smells of rainbows; an enchanted blend of angel's tears and succulent barley picked fresh from the Elysian Fields. Everything's easy and artisan, everyone's attractive and happy, the sun is shining and, hell, you're even looking cool in wellies. And as soon as that clock strikes five, you're off surfing till sunset because, of course, the dream craft brewery is on the coast.

Brad Rogers is living this dream. Three years ago, he and two others, Jamie Cook and Ross Jurisich, jacked in their nine-to-fives and opened a craft brewery in Byron Bay, the idyllic, easternmost tip of Australia.

But before you jack in your job and smash your piggy bank into smithereens, it's worth noting that the firm from which they all fled was Foster's, now known as Carlton & United Breweries, Australia's biggest brewer.

Ross and James were working in sales while Brad, a former winemaker and brewer, was brewing for Foster's all over Australasia, including a stint in Fiji. They met at Matilda Bay Brewing, tasked with administering a much-needed shot in Carlton's 'artisan' arm.

'The brief was really to get out and have some fun with craft beer which we all did,' says Brad. 'Beers like Alpha Pale Ale were great to brew and great to drink. It gave us the opportunity to experiment with different grains and hops, learn about different brewing processes and beer styles.'

With Matilda Bay firmly back on its feet, the trio's thoughts naturally turned to their own brewery. 'It just made a lot of sense that the three of us with our individual skills could pull it off,' says Brad. 'There is a very memorable breakfast the three of us had in Melbourne where we all agreed that we would take the plunge.'

Byron was the obvious choice. There was no brewery there, the trio had all grown up near there and, says Ross, it double ticked the lifestyle box. 'The way we saw it was, well, if it goes wrong then at least we'd be living in one of the most beautiful places in the world.'

On a sophisticated 25-hectolitre brewhouse, tucked away on the outskirts of town, Brad brews two core beers, a couple of seasonals and the occasional one-off. 'We just make clean, flavoursome beer that people would drink when they come off the beach and enjoy so much that they want another. And another,' says Ross. So quenching is its flagship Pacific Ale, it could extinguish a flamin' galah. Brewed with

MEDIEVAL MAGIC

Entirely unlike its easy drinking stable mates, Brad's most bizarre beer defies comparison. Every year, he gets a little medieval on his microbrewery amid much excitement and activity using fire, wood and white hot Fijian stones.

The beer from which Stone & Wood gets its name is brewed using wood and white hot Fijian stones, traditionally used for cooking. A fire is lit under the rocks until they go white hot. The hot rocks then get placed into a basket and lowered into the kettle, rousing the boil and getting smothered in sticky caramelised sugars. The yeast then ferments the sticky stones, creating a hearty, claret-coloured beer that is full of rich toffee flavours and has a bitter, nutty finish.

While it's the kind of beer that Foster's would have frowned upon, the trio's big business background has no doubt played a major role in Stone & Wood rising from zero to more than a million litres per annum in just four years.

Opposite: Brad Rogers (centre), Jamie Cook (left) and Ross Jurisich (right).

Above: The Brewery in Byron Bay.

Australian barley, wheat and Galaxy hops from Tasmania, it's floral, fresh and uniquely Australian. 'It's lightly kettle hopped, to give a bitterness in the low 20s, but highly hopped in the fermenter to give a real tropical fruit aroma,' says Brad. 'Like all our beers, it's effortlessly drinkable with interest.'

In terms of sales, it's swiftly followed by a sparkling, spotless and languidly lagered helles brewed with both German malt and German hops, while the sweet and slightly spicy Jasper Ale, its dark amber hue reflective of the red soil synonymous with its surroundings, sits somewhere between a German Alt, an amber ale and an English best bitter. Over and above the awesome beer, where the trio have truly triumphed is getting the other bits of brewing right. The important yet boring bits like admin and investment, sales and strategies, paperwork, keg collection, margins … all the bits that, thankfully, as we fade to fantasy at our desks, we dare not let disturb the dream.

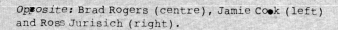

KEY BEERS

Pacific Ale 4.4%
Pale Lager 4.7%
Stone Beer 5.3%
Jasper Ale 4.7%

*GRAIN

---

* weissbier & witbier

* rye

* scotch ale

* stout

* rauchbier

Imagine, if you will, a world without cereal. Futile, hollow and devoid of hope. A world in which Goldilocks and the Three Bears weep silently over empty bowls; where hippies are denied their quinoa and their couscous; where Chinese paddy fields are desolate swathes of nothingness and Uncle Ben is unemployed; a world without cheese or choc-ices; where Belgians can't eat waffles and where cows go hungry, their frowns of displeasure undermined by a lack of eyebrows.

Imagine a world, if you dare, without beer.

As many anthropologists will tell you, and there's a small grain of truth to this, without cereal there would be no civilisation. After millennia of gallivanting, gathering and hunting on the hoof, man awoke to the wonders of an existence based almost entirely on agriculture. He began growing grain, harvested it and made beer and bread with it.

It's worth remembering that. While hops grab all the headlines these days, grain was getting together with water and yeast long before the little green cones clambered on the bandwagon.

Grain is the soul of beer. Without it there would be no sugars for yeast to turn into alcohol and thus, beer would be about as enticing as tap water. But grain is not just beer's engine room. It's better than that.

Depending on how it has been treated, grain gives beer much of its mouthfeel and a cornucopia of textures and flavours including freshly roasted coffee, bitter dark chocolate, spice, smoke and more.

'GRAIN' IS A MULTI-LAYERED MASH CONTAINING A SERIES OF CEREAL THRILLERS; EVERYTHING FROM SPICY RYE ALES AND WONDERFUL WHEAT BEERS TO OATMEAL STOUTS AND BEERS BREWED WITH SMOKED BARLEY, MILLET, QUINOA AND BUCKWHEAT.

UK

Arbor Ales
Oyster Stout 4.6%
Bristol, England
www.arborales.co.uk

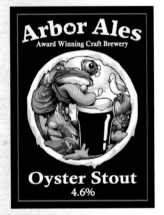

Arbor hauls whole oysters, complete with shells, for the last 15 minutes of a mash that stars a selection of ten different grains, including wheat and mouth-filling oats. Hopped with a trio of English hops, this stout's dark cloak disguises effortless drinkability. Best accompanied by oysters. Obviously.

Beavertown
Smog Rocket 5.4%
London, England
www.beavertownbrewery.co.uk

Brewed out of its bar, Dukes Brew & Que, in the heart of hipster East London,

Beavertown's take on porter, London's original blue collar beer, is deftly done. It spills a dark brown, there is a spiral of smoke on the nose, with chocolate mousse on the mid-palate and a rich tobacco/dry leaves finish.

Bristol Beer Factory
Ultimate Stout 7.7%
Bristol, England
www.bristolbeerfactory.co.uk

Like carbon-fibre on a penny farthing, the Bristol Beer Factory ties together tradition with a modern twist and is among the most impressive small brewers to emerge in recent years. Infusion mash and open fermentation tanks differ it from the vast majority of modern micros and adorn its beers, especially the malt-driven drops, with a terrific, deep texture. This is a creamy, heavyweight stout, with a lovely balance, like chocolate-coated vanilla, and a strong, rich send off.

Kernel
Export Stout 1890 7.8%
London, England
www.thekernelbrewery.com

Part of Kernel's exploration of Britain's

brewing past, this is a remarkable, award-winning resuscitation of a recipe originally brewed by the now long-closed Truman's brewery in East London, once the biggest in the world, in the late 19th century. A phenomenal depth of flavour is deftly coaxed from just three malts, Fuggles hops and a boisterous bottle-conditioning. A smooth, slightly oily and complex sepia-tinted sip, smudged with smoke, old school desks, tar and tannin, and with a nutty, creamy climax.

JW Lees
Manchester Star Ale 6.5%
Manchester, England
www.jwlees.co.uk

This resuscitated recipe dating back to 1884 is a seductive, sparkling squid ink-dyed beer, bordering on Baltic porter in style, and a seriously stellar sip. Rich and roasty with a hint of tart black cherry, it drinks deep and long with a subtle smoky send-off. Try it with smoked ribs or fruity cheesecake.

Williams Bros
Profanity Stout 7%
Alloa, Scotland
www.williamsbrosbrew.com

The Williams Brothers started off in 1992 by bringing age-old Scottish recipes back from the dead. They have found their contemporary voice and now spearhead much of what is great about modern Scottish brewing. They sex up this blacker-than-a-coal-mining-mole stout with Nelson Sauvin hops, deftly clipping the bitterness before it gets too acrid and dry.

IRELAND

Carlow
O'Hara's Stout 4.3%
Carlow
www.carlowbrewing.com

Carlow Brewing, in south-east Ireland, has gradually gained traction in its homeland after initially exporting its quintessentially Irish ales. Its flagship stout is a magnificent mouth-filler with a gorgeous roasted, grainy ground and touches of vanilla, figs and liquorice.

Black Market
Rye IPA 7.5%
California
www.blackmarketbrew.com

Where this wonderful West Coast IPA differs from its fellow Californian counterparts is the addition of rye, which makes up 20% of the grist. A gold medal winner at the 2012 Great American Beer Festival, it comes with a C-hop pine aroma and a spicy tobacco undertow from the rye. One of California's two best rye IPAs.

Evil Twin
Even More Jesus 12%
Brooklyn
www.facebook.com/EvilTwinBrewing

A grainy, globular imperial stout born at the Fanø bryghaus. This is the beer for which Evil Twin is so fondly thought of; smooth and smoky, darker than a mole's shadow, it's a swirling vanillin vortex of fudge, espresso, blackberry, molasses and liquorice. If Jesus had turned water thus, he may not have got himself into so much trouble.

Lagunitas
Little Sumpin' Sumpin' 7.5%
California
www.lagunitas.com

A clutch of different hops, all beginning with the letter 'C', frolic on a fruity fabric woven using three different varieties of wheat, resulting in a sunset-coloured summer drink that is soft and a little spicy, albeit with a strength likely to have you snoozing softly through the long sunny afternoon if you try too many at lunchtime.

Southampton
Double White Ale 6.6%
Long Island
www.publick.com

An excellent East Coast brewpub and brewery that picks up beer awards with the same kind of nonchalance mere mortals pick fluff from their belly buttons. Injecting American audacity into authentically replicated European styles, it does a cracking Kellerbier and a fine Alt. More Belgian than Bavarian is this 'imperial' witbier, locked and loaded with twice as much wheat and primed with curaçao orange peel and coriander: soft of touch, smooth yet not smothering, with spiked notes of clove, lemon drop and vanilla on the finish. If you like those 'fresh banana' yeast flavours, you should be all over this like a spider monkey.

Maris Otter

Maris Otter is considered by many to be the most magnificent malted barley on the market. First produced in 1966 by Dr George Bell, using Proctor and Pioneer barleys as the parents, Maris Otter was named after Maris Lane, Trumpington, just outside Cambridge, then the home of the British Plant Breeding Institute.

It could not be more English if it was a sexually repressed, stiff upper lipped Morris dancer with a cucumber sandwich in one hand and a shiny cricket ball in the other. Like a lot of middle-aged English people, Maris Otter doesn't really like to go abroad; it has tried sunnier continental climes like Australia, Europe and the US but, long term, it couldn't possibly live there.

No, Maris Otter is barley that belongs in Britain, where the maritime climate is made for it. It, meanwhile, is made for British beer. Deliberately designed for the quintessential British beer type, cask ale, Maris Otter allows brewers to make easy-drinking, lightly-effervescent and low-gravity ales with a rich and rounded malt character.

Brewers approve of Maris Otter because it doesn't misbehave in the mash tun. Low in nitrogen, with excellent enzymes, the grain matures quickly after harvest and is easy to mash and easy to malt.

It is not so friendly with farmers though. Maris Otter is susceptible to sickness and disease, and grown far more for flavour than yield, and it fell out of favour in the 1980s. With cask ales on a downward curve, farmers explored other agricultural options, especially the higher-yielding Halcyon barley, and by the early 1990s, Maris Otter was but a fond memory among maltsters.

Thanks to several small and regional brewers, as well as a couple of maltsters, who bought exclusive rights to Maris Otter, the revered barley has made a remarkable return in recent years. While not as widespread as its heyday, Maris Otter is now considered a 'classic' variety by brewers willing to pay a premium for its fuller flavour.

While some have questioned its influence in the finished beer, it is worth noting that since the turn of the century, 10 out of the last 13 winners of the Champion Beer of Britain contest at the Great British Beer Festival have been brewed using Maris Otter barley:

2000	Moorhouse's Black Cat	2001	Oakham Jeffrey Hudson Bitter
2004	Kelham Island Pale Rider	2005	Crouch Vale Brewers Gold
2006	Crouch Vale Brewers Gold	2007	Hobson's Mild
2008	Triple FFF Alton's Pride	2010	Castle Rock Harvest Pale
2011	The Mighty Oak Oscar Wilde	2012	Coniston's No 9 Barley Wine

Sprecher
Shakparo Ale 5.7%
Wisconsin
www.sprecherbrewery.com

This is what occurs when West Africa meets Wisconsin, a sub-Saharan gluten-free beer brewed with sorghum and millet and first made back in 2007. Left-field Lambic sourness lends it a vinous character more similar to a farmhouse cider than a beer. A bit weird, but rather refreshing. And what's more, not only is it gluten-free, it's also certified Kosher by a genuine Rabbi.

Stoudts
Fat Dog Imperial Stout 8%
Pennsylvania
www.stoudtsbeer.com

Bottle-conditioned, with a rather gormless-looking black Labrador adorning the label (they can run to plumpness, Labs), this is a behemoth black beer from an elder statesman of Pennsylvania's beer scene, dating back to the late 1980s (although based at a much older restaurant). Fat Dog is a mellifluous, mouth-filling meeting of two stouts – a rich and rounded oatmeal blended with an astringent, spicy imperial.

Three Floyds
Gumballhead 5.6%
Indiana
www.3floyds.com

Hordes of beer buffs annually flock to Floyds on 'Dark Lord Day' to get their drooling chops around its epic imperial stout, but when the mercury rises in Munster, Indiana, most reach for this perfectly weighted red wheat ale, which gently feeds an entire fruit bowl into your face. Zesty, clean and soft, with lychee, apricot, peach and orange peel, this is a beer that imspires fierce devotion among its lovers.

Rye

No grain polarises opinion among brewers quite like rye.

While celebrated by some for the spice and smoothness it adds to beer, the grain, more belligerent than barley, riles brewers with its lack of husk.

Brewmasters love a husk, as it forms a natural filter in the mash tun and, more importantly, using unhusked grain, the mash quickly turns into a gooey quagmire that is a nightmare to lauter and more suitable for filling cracks in plaster than making beer.

Historically, however, rye's stubborn ability to grow where other grain give up rendered it popular among European brewers of yesteryear. Before the introduction of the Reinheitsgebot in 1516, when barley was declared the only grain allowed, Roggenbier (ryebeer) was a popular beer style in Bavaria.

Rye also cropped up in colder climes. In Finland, rye made up 10% of the grain content in the local ale, sahti, while in Eastern Europe, they fermented rye bread to make Kvass, a low-alcohol beer dating back thousands of years.

More recently, the use of rye has risen in tandem with the rebirth of Roggenbier in both Europe and the United States. While German brewers use as much as 60% rye, American micros tend to keep its role a cameo one, restricting it to around 20%.

Most often fermented with a fruity Weissbier yeast strain, Rye beers tend be hazy and hover around the 5% ABV mark. Rye is a peppery, pugnacious and potent grain which in small quantities will give beer a reddish tint and in larger quantities ride roughshod over other flavours. Flaked rye is said to give off a more minty, grassy character than the malted version.

Esteemed examples of rye beers include Founders Red's Rye PA from Founders Brewing of Michigan; Bruery Rugbrød, brewed with rye bread, from California; Wolznacher Roggenbier from the Hallertau hop growing area in Bavaria, Germany; Thurn und Taxis Roggen from Paulaner in Munich; and Schremser Roggen Bier from Austria. In 2008, Bear Republic brewed the very rare EZ Ryder, thought to be the world's only 100% rye grain beer.

CANADA

Benelux
Ergot Triple Saison au Seigle 9%
Montreal
www.brasseriebenelux.com

One of Montreal's more discerning beer drinking spots, the Benelux brewpub/cafe crafts coherent, quality stuff, including this strong Saison, which spills out golden brown with a kiss of caramel on the nose. Enriched with rye, it is dry and spicy with a glowing hop halo and a finish akin to Demerara-dusted grapefruit.

Brasseurs Sans Gluten
Red Ale 5%
Montreal
www.glutenberg.ca

When I was a young lad, no one really had allergies. There was a guy in my class called Muhammad Abutaleb, from Yemen, who was allergic to both the sun (hence the move from Yemen to West London) and self-raising flour. But that was all. Now everyone has an allergy, ranging from nuts and dairy to soy, sesame and even cute fluffy kittens. The craft ales from this canny Canadian brewer cater for coeliacs (meaning they are gluten-free) and are better than a lot of barley-based brews. Millet, quinoa, chestnut and buckwheat fuel the fermentation in a nutty, fruity amber ale.

McAuslan
St Ambroise Oatmeal Stout 5%
Montreal
www.mcauslan.com

A keystone of the Quebec craft beer scene since 1997, McAuslan has grown substantially yet this sturdy, silken stout, first brewed in 1991, remains its marquee beer. The use of oatmeal, and a substantial amount of it too, thickens the palate with notes of dark rum, praline and hazelnut.

GERMANY

Erdinger
Urweisse 4.9%
Bavaria
www.erdinger.com

Seen by many as the saviours of Weissbier in the 1960s, Erdinger won over what had become an increasingly wheat-intolerant Germany with a softer, less 'fruity' version of its cloudy clove-tastic beer. In 2008, Erdinger revived the original Weissbier, spicier and darker. A really wonderful Weissbier best drunk at the annual Herbstfest held in Erding every year a month prior to Munich's Oktoberfest.

Fässla
Weizla Dunkel 5%
Bamberg
www.faessla.de

Boss little Bamberg brewpub, dating back to 1649, which proudly claims to serve Bamberg's strongest beer – the Bambergator, at 8.5%. Nicer and more nuanced, however, is this deep, dark maroon Weizen, delivering bruised bananas, liquorice and nuts. Proof, if needed, that there is no beer in the world that is not improved by the presence of a gnome on the bottle. Worth noting that locals refer to him as a dwarf. Not sure if that is right.

Hirsch
Hefe Weisse 5.4%
Baden-Württemburg
www.hirschbrauerei.de

All hail this classic hazy Hefeweisse from a southern German brewery based in a village not far from the Black Forest on a site that began brewing in 1657. Family-owned, yet eager adopters of typically Teutonic brewing efficiency, Hirsch boasts a wonderful Zwickelbier, though, in this part of Europe, when the sun is shining, with pretzel in hand, this fruity, morning-fresh wheat beer is simply wonderful.

BELGIUM

Blaugies
Saison d'Epeautre 6%
Hainaul
www.brasseriedeblaugies.com

That the Blaugies Brewery is based in the Walloon municipality of Dour is most misleading because Blaugies is one of the most stylish small breweries in Belgium. Set up in the late 1980s by Pierre-Alex Carlier and his partner Marie-Noelle, it remains in the family hands of their sons Kevin and Cedric, who do down-to-earth and deliciously drinkable bottle-conditioned beers extremely well. They furnish one beer (Darbyste) with fig juice, but the signature sip is a quite sublime saison, floral and fragrant with a rich, rumbling biscuit base enlivened by buckwheat.

Ellezelloise
Hercule Stout 9%
Hainault
www.brasserie-ellezelloise.be

Agatha Christie's Hercule Poirot is the inspiration for this velvet-jacketed stout: he was born in Ellezelles, apparently but, given that he is a fictional detective, you would be right to question that. What is true is that this Irish-leaning, dry-to-desiccated drop may be Belgium's best stout.

NETHERLANDS

Jopen
Jacobus Rye Pale Ale 5.3%
Haarlem
www.jopen.nl

Once a centre of the old Dutch brewing scene, the lovely town of Haarlem was home to several successful breweries and had its very own bespoke spice-laden beer, made from oats as well as barley and wheat. Yet as trends took their toll, Haarlem became entirely bereft of breweries by 1916 and it was not until 1994, with the creation of the Jopen brewing company, that it rediscovered its brewing mojo. After gypsy brewing the beers all over the Netherlands, Jopen built a shrine to Haarlem's brewing history within the walls of a big disused church, in which it loyally resuscitates Haarlem beers. Swathed in stained glass and stainless steel, it is an impressive arena in which to drink. This spicy season, a World Beer Cup medal winner, resembling an American 'Rye PA', is grassy and grainy with a terrific toasty undertow.

De Hemel
Moenen 6%
Nijmegen
www.brouwerijdehemel.nl

The liberal-leaning town of Nijmegen, not far from the German border, is home to De Hemel ('Heaven'), a combination of a small brewery, a distillery, a brewery museum and a restaurant where beers are dovetailed deliciously with the dishes. Its array of artisan ales and elixirs include a distilled beer aged in Limousin oak; a fresh-faced wheat beer liqueur and a lovely, oily jenever. Every winter, they fire up this subtly smoky Rauch replica using smoked malt. It has the aroma of an old leather bar rest mixed with pipe tobacco, sweet caramel on the palate and a touch of crème brûlée.

Ramses
Mamba Porter 6.4%
North Brabant
www.ramsesbier.nl

Five years in Oregon inoculated Ramses Snoeij with the idea of starting his own beer range. In 2008, he began making his beers at the Drie Horne brewery near Breda. Like a Mexican mole sauce, this chewy chocolate porter slithers with liquorice, mellow roast notes and simmering spiciness.

Svaneke
Stout 5.7%
Bornholm
www.svanekebryghus.dk

A daring yet very dependable brewer that has been doing what it does on the island of Bornholm, in the Baltic, since 2000. This is an after-dinner stout porter, broad in body and rich in texture, that seductively drapes a satin scarf of chocolate, espresso and cherry round your palate.

WinterCoat
Vildmoseøl 5.8%
Aarhus
www.wintercoat.dk

In 2003, brewmaster Niels Jom Thomsen rebuilt a second-hand English brewhouse in his barn, in a village not far from Denmark's second city. This beer is inspired by the peat bogs of northern Jutland – 'vildmose' means 'wild bog' – and is brewed using smoked malt, bog myrtle and rowan berries. There is a distinct Islay aroma that drops back on the palate to let the winter spice and dark fruit do its thing.

Einstöck
Toasted Porter 6%
Akureyri
www.einstokbeer.com

Einstöck, meaning 'unique' in Icelandic, was founded in Akureyri, 60 miles south of the Arctic circle, by the learned Baldur Karason, former head brewer at the nearby Viking Brewery. Using water that has percolated through lava fields and glaciers, Karason brews terrific, technically tight ales including this smooth-edged, silky black porter composed using coffee brewed by the neighbouring roaster. Deceptively drinkable.

An Alarc'h
Kerzu Stout 7%
Brittany
yves.bou.pagesperso-orange.fr/brasseries/analarch.htm

The renaissance of brewing in Brittany has many links to British brewing traditions, of which Xavier Leproust's An Alarc'h is a fine example. It is rare among Gallic brewers in that it makes splendid cask ales, including this rich and oily, silky, chocolate-coated imperial stout, perfect to ward off the chilly Breton drizzle.

Brittany

While to many it may be synonymous with cider, Brittany is fast becoming the most creative corner of France's craft beer scene.

The nation's most northwestern nook, nosing out into the North Atlantic, has a bountiful brewing past dating back to the 17th century, when beer competed with cider and a local mead called chouchen, to be the chosen giggle-juice of the local gentry

At the industry's peak there were 75 Breton breweries but, worn down by the rise of wine and sucessive wars, the local brewing scene all but disappeared by the 1950s. While the roots of recovery only appeared in the 1980s, a general return to the region's Celtic roots encouraged a new breed of brewers and, currently, there are approximately two dozen small, independent micros making in Brittany.

Several have breathed life back into the age-old Breton tradition of brewing with buckwheat (blé noir), a local favourite more readily associated with the classic Breton crêpes. Not so much a grain as a cereal/herb hybrid, buckwheat is gluten-free, high in protein but a bit of a sticky mischief-maker in the mash tun.

Buckwheat gives the dark brown beers made from it a noticeable nutty nuance. More like a dunkel-weizen than a porter or a stout, buckwheat beer (bière de blé noir) has a mineral character that drinks handsomely with local oysters and seafood.

Brasserie Lancelot, a romantic brewery situated in an old gold mine in Morbihan, does an especially dapper version with a name meaning Black Harp in Celtic, while the Gwiniz Du (which means 'buckwheat' in Breton), from Brasserie de Britt, is slightly stronger, with more fruit upfront.

Sat with your crêpe in a café, you'll notice that most other Breton beers are colour-coded; Ambré (amber), Rousse (red) and Blanche, the French term for a wheat beer. But delve a little deeper and you'll find some highly esoteric efforts brewed with some slightly left-field local ingredients, such as seaweed, elderberries and honey.

SWITZERLAND

Bière de Neuch
Brune de Neuch 7.5%
Neuchâtel
www.bieresdeneuch.ch

Brewed by David Girardier above Neuchâtel (known locally as 'Neuch', hence the 'Bière de Neuch' moniker), this is more than a mere 'brune'. It's a solid take on a Belgian Dubbel using half-a-dozen malts; rounded, fruity and spicy, yet dry enough with dark chocolate, autumnal fruits and notes of red wine.

Trois Dames
Fraîcheur du Soir 6.8%
Vaude
www.brasserietroisdames.ch

Until a craft beer drinking epiphany in the United States, founder Raphaël Mettler did not much care for beer. On returning home, in 2008 he opened Trois Dames (the three ladies being his wife and two daughters) in Sainte-Croix, north of Lausanne. Surrounded by mountains, he brews a wide range of accomplished ales, all using hops from Yakima Valley in Washington State in the US, including an IPA, an espresso stout, an Indian Brown Ale, and this weighty bottle-conditioned grand cru wit. 'Freshness of the evening', made from half unmalted Jura wheat and half barley, plus bitter oranges and coriander, wears its strength sublimely well. Fruity esters run free on a backdrop of banana, orange and ripe peach.

ITALY

Almond '22
Torbata 8.7%
Abruzzo
www.birraalmond.com

Housed in a former almond-shelling workshop near Pescara on Italy's Adriatic coast, Almond '22 adorns its ales with a whole host of exotic ingredients including pink peppercorns, orange blossom and rose buds. But it is the peat-smoked malt, 5% of the grist, that majors here in this dark mahogany after-dinner snifter sip, hopped with East Kent Goldings. Iodine and leather notes are sweetened and soothed by accompanying orange peel, honey and a dab of cane sugar.

Lambrate
Ghisa 5%
Milan
www.birrificiolambrate.com

Opened in 1996 in an old railway station, this Milanese brewpub was one of the first to get Italian craft brewing on track. A German inflection adorns a lot of its beers: try the cracking Kölsch (Monetstella). Yet this smoked stout talks with a slight Irish brogue: dry yet not acrid, with a black leather jacket bouquet, it conjures up coffee and chipotle.

L'Olmaia
La Cinque 5.5%
Tuscany
www.birrificioolmaia.com

In a region renowned for its vino nobile, this micro from Southern Tuscany makes some equally magnificent beers. Founded in a farmhouse by homebrewer Moreno Ercolani back in 2004, it has moved to a bigger brewhouse in Montepulciano, where its earned a reputation for artisanal yet acutely accessible beers designed for the dining table. A brusque, biscuity blonde bottle-conditioned beer with a lingering honeysuckle finish.

Opperbaco
Bianca Piperita 4.2%
Abruzzo
www.opperbacco.it

From the small town of Notaresco, Opperbaco is highly experimental in its ingredients and oozes cool in everything it does; its website, its glassware and its packaging. Yet with this delicate coriander and orange peel-infused Belgian-style blonde, which includes unmalted wheat and oats alongside Pilsner malt and locally produced honey, plus Styrian Goldings and Saaz hops, the cool comes courtesy of peppermint, 'hopped' late in the boil. That makes for a beer that is a little bit menthol, a little bit mental and a whole load of refreshing.

Burleigh
Hef 5%
Queensland
www.burleighbrewing.com.au

At the 2012 World Beer Cup, this Queensland craft outfit bent the Bavarians over their knee, lowered the lederhosen down to their South German ankles and gave them one hell of a beating on their collective botty. Fruity yeast is flexed to full effect, bashing out bruised bananas, bubblegum and a bushy white head. And there's a moustache drawn on the bottle. What else do you want?

4 Pines
Vostok Stout 5.1%
Sydney
www.4pinesbeer.com.au

Seven different malts make up this manly beer from a Manly brewpub. A solid, silken Sydney stout that spills out squid ink in colour and smells like a double-shot of espresso. Underlying sweetness, some dark chocolate, long caramel and hop bitterness to finish.

Mountain Goat
Surefoot Stout 5%
Melbourne
www.goatbeer.com.au

Founders Cam Hines and Dave Boningham have established this uber-urban micro as one of Australia's most impressive operations. It now turns out more than one million litres of unpasteurised beer a year, including this sultry, sweet seasonal stout earthed by East Kent Golding hops and filled out with four native malts and flaked barley.

Murray's
Dark Knight Porter 4.5%
New South Wales
www.murraysbrewingco.com.au

A perfectly poised porter fashioned by a prolific Port Stephens brewpub perched on the coast north of Sydney. An old-school bottle holds a traditional British dark brown beer hewn from half a dozen malts. Belies its body and strength with a genuine depth of chocolate, caramel flavour.

Van Dieman
Stacks Bluff 5%
Tasmania
www.vandiemanbrewing.com.au

Having cut his brewing teeth at the Milton Brewery in Cambridge, England, Will Tatchell returned home to set up a small brewery in the undulating hills of Evandale in north-eastern Tasmania where, encircled by hundreds of oak trees, he brews British styles with a Tassie twist. Dilated with oatmeal, its mouthfeel is mellowed and roast bitterness broadened with the addition of vanilla.

Duck in Scotch Ale

'During the past 25 years I made so many dishes that sometimes it is hard to dredge them up from the cellars of the mind. Sometimes a little drop of something helps one to remember the taste of an almost forgotten beer. This introduction is being written while enjoying a Hoppin' Frog Outta Kilter Scotch style Red Ale: a good start to a free Sunday afternoon off, a bit sweet and very drinkable.

'It reminded me instantly of De Molen's Boreftse Tien, a beer that was retired some time ago because the yeast strain was so sensitive that there wasn't enough pressure in the bottles. My job was to put a good few bottles to good use. This resulted in the following recipe, a variation on the French way to prepare duck legs. For the hungry ones, allow 1 male duck leg, for the smaller stomachs 1 female leg per person.'

Peter Paul Stil of Eet & Bierlokaal de Molen.

Ingredients
• Enough beer to poach the legs in
• ½ litre/1 pint of orange juice
• Duck legs
• Salt and pepper, bay leaves, a few sprigs of fresh thyme
• Apple (or maple) syrup
• Thickly sliced cured Parma or Serrano ham

Method
Heat the beer with the orange juice until it almost boils.

Add the duck, seasoning, bay leaves and thyme. Simmer for two to three hours. The meat is done when an inch of bone is visible.

Thicken some of the beer/orange and add enough syrup to make the sauce nice and sweet.

Wrap the meat in ham and fry until crisp. Serve immediately.

Good with an Amarillo or similar double IPA

NEW ZEALAND

Renaissance
Stonecutter Scotch Ale 7%
Marlborough
www.renaissancebrewing.co.nz

This rich, rounded Sunday roast beer from a brewery set up in 2005 by a couple of Californians, one a technical whiz, the other a winemaker, as hefty as a muscular Pinot Noir, can name nine malts in its make-up. Cherry, chocolate, blackberry and liquorice are just some of the adjectives worth uttering.

JAPAN

Fujizakura
Rauchbier 5.5%
Yamanashi
www.fujizakura-beer.jp

Replicating a Bamberg Rauchbier using cherry wood rather than beechwood, resulting in a delicious, refreshing dark lager that is both smoky and quite sweet.

Swan Lake
Amber Swan Ale 5%
Niigata
www.swanlake.co.jp

Displaying all the balance and refinement of a ballerina, this glowing copper ale, a regular podium presence at the World Beer Cup, does the simple things well and treads a tightrope between sweet moreish malt and spicy herbal hop.

Yo-Ho
Tokyo Black 5%
Nagano
www.yohobrewing.com

Yo-Ho's head brewer, Toshi Ishi, is formerly of Stone in San Diego, and a bit of a talisman in Japanese craft brewing. His citrus-scented Yona Yona Pale Ale has West Coast US running through it like words through a stick of rock, while his boisterous barley wine is a brilliant British-style brew. This smooth-talking, tuxedo-coloured porter, coming in an über-cool can, is a whirlwind of oak wood, espresso and a smouldering smoky send-off.

SOUTH AFRICA

Darling
Bone Crusher 6%
Western Cape
www.darlingbrew.co.za

Supplier of what it likes to call 'slow beer', its taproom is based in the eponymous village an hour north of Cape Town, though its beers are brewed for it by a brewer in Cape Town itself. Bone Crusher, named after the hyena, is delicious on draught yet just as vibrant in a 550ml bottle. This is an opulent, spicy Belgian witbier with sherbet on the nose and a flurry of fruit in the finish. Almost Weizenbock in style.

MEXICO

Minerva
Stout Imperial 6%
Guadalajara
www.cerveceriaminerva.com

Guadalajara is the gateway to tequila country, and I first tried the native beer after a rather 'tired and emotional' tour of the agave fields and generous distilleries that surround Tequila town. After several days imbibing smoky anejo tequilas and the odd Mezcal, this proved a soothing black balm, whose spicy, chipotle notes went marvellously with mole poblano.

BRAZIL

Eisenbahn
Weizenbock 8%
Santa Catarina
www.eisenbahn.com.br

Founded in 1850 by German immigrants, the southern Brazilian town of Blumenau hosts an annual Oktoberfest and is home to Eisenbahn, the biggest 'craft' brewer in Brazil. Big on bruised bananas, toasty undertones and a touch of toffee and choc-chip on the finish, this is a deep, dark, spicy Dopplebock.

MY TOP 5 CRAFT BEERS

Jean-Francois Gravel
Dieu de Ciel
Quebec

✳ **Cantillon Gueuze**
Back in 1998, this was a revelation. Dry and very sour, more acetic than it is now. I like the complexity of the different organic acid and the fruity, animal character of the Brettanomyces. I like Cantillon because the flavours are intense and complex.

✳ **Schlenkerla Smoked Marzen**
I love smoke flavour and aroma, in beer and food. In the Schlenkerla, the smoke is so intense but the rich malty character makes it silky and not like an ashtray at all.

✳ **Rochefort 10**
A very good example of a quadruple. Rich and complex, the slightly burned caramel mixed with grape and plum makes it almost port-like. When it's aged, it's a perfect beer to sip next to the fireplace after a nice day skiing.

✳ **The Alchemist, Heady Topper**
This is one of my favourite double IPAs. Not too strong in alcohol, so you can have more than just a little glass but potent enough to help to exalt that hop bomb. It is a hop bomb, but it's not a sadomasochist experience.

✳ **Le Trou Du Diable, La Buteuse special reserve**
A nice example of a Belgian-style triple, malty and hoppy with a fruity aroma. However, the version aged in apple brandy barrels and refermented with Brettanomyces is just phenomenal. It evolves a lot with ageing, due to the activity of the Brett.

PORTER

Porter is the beer that made London, for a century or more, the most important brewing city in the world. The capital's craft brewing scene may currently be in fine fettle, but it's a drop in the bucket of significance when compared with London brewing at its most rich and revered 18th-century pomp.

TICKET·PORTER

Success has many fathers, and porter's parentage has been widely and erroneously attributed to Ralph Harwood, an East London brewer who supposedly brewed a beer to replace a mixture called three-threads, knocked up in the pub from a blend of mild (or fresh) beer, stale beer, stout and ale.

Unfortunately the three-threads story has been comprehensively debunked by beer historians. Instead, research has shown, porter was developed by London's brown beer brewers who were beginning to feel the heat from out-of-town pale ale producers and desperately in need of a little innovation. As a rebuttal to their rivals, they launched a hoppier, more aged version of the muggy brown beers that were ubiquitous in London's pubs yet slipping in terms of sales.

The improved version of brown beer was highly hopped, brewed with high-roasted malt, then aged in enormous 108-gallon casks called butts, which gave it a flavour that proved hugely popular with London's porters, the men who moved goods around the city's streets and on and off ships on the River Thames. Almost as importantly, this new beer, which soon took the name of its biggest fans, could be made in huge quantities and crucially, unlike rival brews, it could be brewed for more months of the year: with other beers, brewing had to stop in the summer, when it became too warm.

London's porter brewers became the biggest brewers in the world, and to keep ahead of the competition they introduced technical advances that were decades ahead of brewers elsewhere: steam power, thermometers to record temperatures, saccharometers to test wort strengths. The biggest porter brewers became enormously wealthy, buying country estates, getting themselves elected as Members of Parliament, mixing with and marrying into the aristocracy.

Porter's potential stretched far beyond the geographical limits of London. Its ability to age well made it ideal for travel and, combined with an avaricious British overseas trading ethos, it was to become the world's first truly global beer style. Its unprecedented wanderlust took it to India in quantities that dwarfed those of India Pale Ale; to Australia in 1787 where the First Fleet celebrated their new home with copious glasses of porter; to Russia as a strong version that became known as Russian Stout; and to America, where it became a symbol of imperial oppression before becoming the beer of choice for the colonials including, of course, George Washington, who famously had a weakness for its dark charms.

Back home, porter continued to oil the wheels of industry and swell the coffers of breweries such as Truman's, Barclay Perkins and Whitbread, each of whom were making a

 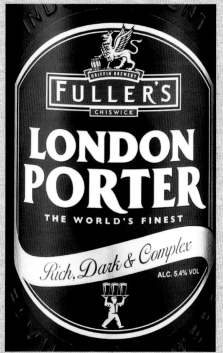 

stronger yet very similar version of their porters they called, rather cleverly, 'Stout Porters'.

Stouts, brewed with more brown malt than the porters, emerged in the late 18th century, but it was not really until the mid-19th century that 'stout' became a distinct style of its own rather than just an alternative name for strong porter.

By that time, porter's party was petering out. The middle classes were drinking bitter pale ale, mild was becoming increasingly popular among the workers and even stout was showing it a clean pair of heels.

The restriction on raw materials during World War I saw brewers reduce porter's strength, often to a level below mild. It was a blow the beer never really recovered from and by the 1950s it had disappeared from the London pubs it had once dominated.

In recent times, London's porter-brewing tradition has been revived by a handful of the city's craft brewers, notably Kernel in Bermondsey, Fuller's in Chiswick and Meantime Brewing in Greenwich who, by tapping their London Porter with the wand of Brettanomyces, adorned it with a stamp of wood authenticity. Whether it is anything like what they drunk in the 18th century remains unclear, but it's the closest thing you'll find to the beer that made London famous.

WHAT IS THE DIFFERENCE BETWEEN STOUT AND PORTER?

If you can't tell the difference between a stout and a porter when you taste them then don't worry too much, because there isn't one.

Traditionally, stout has always just been a stronger version of porter. In the 18th century, 'stout' was merely a term used for something bigger and stronger, a generic prefix that could have been equally applied to other beer styles.

Unfortunately, no one uses the word that way anymore. And in the craft brewing climate, even the 'stronger' distinction no longer holds water.

Scan any beer list or, better still, take a sip of the two different styles and you'll see that porters can be more potent than stouts, and vice versa. Equally, in their ingredients, brewing methods, taste and appearance, stout and porter are, today, indistinguishable.

EVIL TWIN BREWING

Brewed across the world   eviltwin.dk

Jeppe Jarnit-Bjergsø is back home in Brooklyn, fresh from a whistle-stop tour of the US West Coast where, he says, he experienced a minor epiphany in a hot dog joint.

'It was a really cool place, selling kind of hipster hot dogs, loads of different sausages made from alligator, rattlesnake, rabbit, buffalo and stuff,' says Jeppe, his rapid Danish drawl sitting somewhere between Scouse and soft Schwarzenegger. 'I was with Greg Koch from Stone and we were sitting there with this gang member guy behind us, I could hear him talking about guns and girls, all this kind of gangster stuff.

'I'd seen him when we walked in: you know, he was a big guy with tattoos, mean-looking, the kind of guy you wouldn't want to make angry. I turn around to have another look, not for too long, and there he is, stood there holding a fancy dark Belgian beer, like an Abbey beer, swirling it around in a fancy Belgian glass.

'I thought, "Jesus, if guys like that are drinking better beer then we've got something good going on." A year ago, he would have had a Corona.'

Jeppe moved to Brooklyn from Copenhagen in 2011 with his wife, two children and a rapidly growing reputation for great beer. They'd always talked of living Stateside but, he admits, it also made sense to make his hay where the sun shines.

'In Europe, it's still beer geeks and enthusiasts but in the US, it's the normal guys who are into it,' he says. 'Europe still has a lot of growing to do and people are getting into it, but if I go into a bar in Europe and it has ten taps pouring diverse and great beer, it's called a speciality beer bar. Over here, it's just a bar.'

Growing up in Denmark, denial drove a desire for better beer. During his early adulthood in the 1990s, Jeppe got tired of Carlsberg. So, while training to be a teacher, he set up a home-brewing club with 15 friends who felt the same and, before long, they had opened Ølbutikken, a cult boutique beer shop and homebrew store.

'It began with Belgian stuff. We'd all get into a hired van, drive it to Belgium and bring it back full of great beer,' Jeppe says. 'Belgium is where everyone starts.' If Belgium was the gateway drug, a hankering for a harder, different kind of high soon followed.

The crossing of the Rubicon was joining Ratebeer, the beer rating internet site with tens of thousands of members. 'I started getting into the more extreme stuff like Alesmith and the big American beers,' Jeppe says, his words pouring out excitedly, like an addict. 'I just wanted to try different stuff all the time.'

In 2008, Jeppe started 'Drink Kingdom', an import and distribution company, spreading the gospel of good beer beyond Copenhagen. Within two years, he was brewing beer himself.

'I was travelling all over the place, making friends, drinking different beers and talking to a lot of different brewers all around the world,' he says. 'And then I thought, hey, maybe I should try brewing.'

On April Fool's Day in 2010, he unveiled the brewing name Evil Twin, a knowing nod to his identical brother Mikkel, otherwise known as Mikkeller.

Jeppe, like his twin, is a gypsy brewer. He has no brewery of his own or the financial, logistical risks that come with it. Instead, he travels around the world paying for the time, technical expertise and use of the equipment of others to bring his beers to life.

His brewing model is broad and shallow, like a coolship at Cantillon: prolific releases with small production runs. Brewdog in Scotland, De Molen in Holland and Amager in Denmark are just some of the craft breweries with whom he has collaborated. The criteria, Jeppe says, are simple: 'They've got to have capacity and they've got to be great guys who I get on with.'

Pigeon-holing Evil Twin's beer is difficult, like pushing an oyster into a parking meter. On the one hand you have Hipster Ale, an entry-level canned pale beer brewed with different hops for eight different countries; while on the other there is Femme Fatale Brett, a Belgian IPA fermented entirely with Brettanomyces.

'It's the beer I'm most pleased with. I wanted to see how far you could push the Brett, it's extremely fruity and gets funky over time,' he says, before admitting that sour beers scare him.

'I have seen at close hand the likes of Drie Fonteinen and Cantillon and I know for sure that I will never, ever be as good as them. There are a lot of good sour beers in the US, some great ones, but they don't come close to what they're doing in

Jeppe's brewing model is broad and shallow, like a coolship at Cantillon: prolific releases with small production runs. Brewdog in Scotland, De Molen in Holland and Amager in Denmark are just some of the craft breweries with whom he has collaborated. The criteria are simple: 'They've got to have capacity and they've got to be great guys who I get on with.'

EVILTWIN BREWING

DISCO BEER

EVILTWIN BREWING

BISCOTTI BREAK

Belgium. Unless you've been doing it for a hundred years, it's difficult to get it right.'

While 'cuckoo' craft brewers like Evil Twin, Stillwater and Mikkeller have cultivated a strong following, they have faced criticism for being glorified contract brewers, bereft of the balls and the bravery to put their livelihoods on the line.

Jeppe nods in agreement. 'I never say I'm a brewer and I'm totally fine with that,' he says, matter-of-factly. 'Evil Twin is registered as a "beer production company", and while I don't put my hand in the brewing kettle, we still make great beer.'

He even admits to not being present for the brewing process. 'If you have the right ingredients, the right spirit and the correct intentions, then you can make great beer on any brewery,' says Jeppe, for whom brewing is only a part of an Evil Twin empire that includes Tørst, an awesome craft beer bar in New York. 'I like doing different stuff. I like having the bars, selling different beers to new people and keeping every day different,' he says.

His business card reads: 'Jeppe Jarnit-Bjergsø: Beer King'. 'It's not arrogance, it's just a job title,' he says. 'All I'm really interested in is making sure guys have good beer.'

Top: Jeppe Jarnit-Bjergso and a brick wall.

Above left: Disco Beer is an enormous IPA brewed at De Molen.

Above right: Biscotti Break, brewed in South Carolina, is an intense imperial porter.

KEY BEERS

Soft Dookie 10.4%
Yin 10%
Yang 10%
Disco Beer 10.5%
Before, During and After Christmas Beer 8%

BØGEDAL BRYGHUS

Vejile, Syddenmark, Denmark www.boegedal.com

Winemakers have 'terroir'. Bøgedal Bryghus, the most unconventional brewery in Denmark, has 'Fingerspitzengefühl'.

Like schadenfreude, zeitgeist and, to a lesser extent, currywurst, 'Fingerspitzengefühl' is a German term for which there is no exact English equivalent. It is an ethereal descriptor of an instinct, an intuitive awareness, an inherent understanding of one's surroundings.

An expression meaning a kind of tacit tactfulness, Fingerspitzengefühl is the aptitude to approach a situation, however delicate, with 'the sandpapered-fingertip sensitivity of a safecracker'.

'It's about being able to touch it and feel it, a beneath-the-skin feeling at your fingertips,' says Bøgedal's Gitte Holmboe, rubbing her thumbs with her forefingers, doing the worldwide gesture for money – though much gentler. 'But it's also like a gut feeling, it's like a sixth sense that you develop with experience.'

Gitte is gorgeous; her husband, Casper Vorting is cool. They live and work on an idyllic farm. Their brewery is remarkable, their beers exceptional. If they were not such thoroughly decent folk, it would be perfectly understandable to hate them.

Gitte and Casper, a former artist and civil engineer, started brewing in 2004 at the 19th-century courtyard farm where Casper grew up. On the edge of the Vejle river valley, it's a secluded, serene spot that became their home in 1999, after they had spent years living in Copenhagen.

Both were disillusioned with urban life yet, while they were technically and business minded, they were undecided as to how they would make a living. 'We came here and thought, "how can we work and live on the farm?" That was the driving force,' Gitte says. 'Casper had brewed a bit before but brewing isn't the reason we moved here.'

Making traditional Danish beer was an idea that evolved over time. It took more than two years for Casper to acquire all the equipment he needed. Not that there is much of it, just a row of tanks and a brewing copper encased in a huge sculpture shaped like a cow's head. Bøgedal is Denmark's smallest brewery and undoubtedly the sexiest. While other

> Bøgedal is Denmark's smallest brewery and undoubtedly the sexiest. While other breweries boast all the aesthetic appeal of a derelict lift shaft, Bøgedal's brewhouse is rustic, romantic and extraordinarily stylish.

breweries boast all the aesthetic appeal of a derelict lift shaft, Bøgedal's brewhouse is rustic, romantic and extraordinarily stylish. On first sight, you notice something is missing but you are not sure what. It is like meeting someone who has one eyebrow shaved off: eventually you spot the difference. There are no switches and no flashing lights, no temperature control dials. In fact, there is no technology at all.

It is the most primitive and fiercely traditional brewery in Denmark. 'We are the only gravity brewery in all Scandinavia,' Casper says. 'It's a farm, so we're on one level. But we move the beer from tank to tank by hand, using pulleys – to avoid the use of pumps.' Why a such low-tech approach? 'Those centrifugal pumps they use in the breweries are doing the same to the beer as a blender is doing to cream,' he says.

Bøgedal heats its wort over firewood, refuses to chemically manipulate the water drawn from a well and bottles everything by hand. 'There are no computers or man-made controls to keep it consistent,' Gitte says. 'We brew in a truly old-fashioned way: this is the way Danish beer used to be made.'

Bøgedal's beer is a rare re-creation of godtøl, an old fashioned, pre-industrial Danish farmhouse beer made for special, one-off occasions. The idea was not to make the same beer over and over again. Casper does not crave consistency: he just brews the beer and lets the naked, natural process sculpt the style. 'When it comes to cellphones or moon rockets, you need a huge industry to support the development,' he says. 'But the only thing industry has ever done for food is to make it cheap and poor.'

Gitte has created around 20 core brewing recipes, which Casper brings to life in very small, unique batches. No brew is identical and each stretches to around 700 bottles, every one labelled according to the number of the brew, with the only other information being the date it was brewed and bottled, the type of beer and the hops and grain used.

'It's different every time,' Casper says, 'There's a signature flavour to our beer, there's a definite character to our beer, but this is traditional Danish beer, we don't talk endlessly about styles, just ingredients.'

The brewery is at too high a latitude to cultivate its own hops, and barley is the ingredient for which Bøgedal is best-known, barley that is grown on the farm, harvested early by hand, then dried slowly and finished in the brewery's own floor maltings.

'Modern use of combine harvesters demands that the crop stays at the field until you can thresh it, usually in August,' Casper says. 'But at that stage, the quality of the crop has gone down. I harvest it in July with an old machine that binds the barley. Then the crop dries slowly and is separated in November.'

In close conjunction with the Nordic Gene Bank, an enormous library of plants and seeds stored in an abandoned coal mine located at the northern tip of Norway, Bøgedal has single-handedly resuscitated ancient Danish grains that have not been grown for decades.

'This is terroir in that it truly reflects the surroundings where it's brewed,' Casper says. 'There's an old Danish song that encapsulates the spirit of our brewing: "Well hand me then, oh fall, a gravensten [an apple] that tastes of the stream near my father's farm, and the soil of his field."'

At 180 kroner (£22/$30), the premium price reflects the five years it takes to get from field to bottle, not to mention all the pulling, lifting and manual work. All Bødegal's brews are unpasteurised, unfiltered and lauded by Noma in Copenhagen, regarded as the best restaurant in the world, where each batch of beer is matched with bespoke dishes.

While they cannot be pigeon-holed, the beers are united by a lovely, latent sweetness on which hops play charismatic but cameo roles when required. They are not like other contemporary craft beers, but that is probably because they are not brewed like them either.

'We never do extreme beer,' Gitte says. 'Our beers are understated like the English. We admire the English approach, we like the English eccentricity. You have a lot of class but you look scruffy.'

Casper concedes that the couple could expand the brewery, put in a bottling machine and make more beer, but he is not going to do that. 'For us, the way to brew beer is simple: use well-made ingredients in huge amounts, take time doing it and handle with care,' he says.

'It's all in the Fingerspitzengefühl.'

Far left: Bøgedal's cow's head copper.

Left: The brewery entrance in Syddenmark.

Right: Husband and wife brewers Casper Vorting and Gitte Holmboe.

* CLASSIC

---

* trappist

* legend

* pioneer

* original

* iconic

'Classic' (klaesik)' Adjective: 1. a work of art of recognised and established value. 2. judged over a period of time to be of the highest quality and outstanding of its kind.

Old School Classics are the beers that changed the world, the giants on whose shoulders contemporary craft brewers currently stand.

They are the brewing blueprints, the founding fathers, the unwavering upholders of tradition deserving of considered appreciation from every craft beer connoisseur.

Illustrious and inspiring, they are to beer what the Aston Martin is to the automobile; the little black dress is to fashion; and Federico Fellini is to film. These are liquid legends, pioneers of the past, genuine ground-breakers, beers of grand, understated and often undervalued excellence.

Celebrating the sepia-tinted beer drinking of yesteryear, spanning both resurrected styles and individual icons, 'Old School Classic' hails those beer or styles that at some time, somewhere, really made a difference: Belgian Trappist ales; the blue collar beer that oiled the wheels of industry in Germany; Lithuanian farmhouse beers; original English IPAs; and West Coast American brews that fired the first shot across the bow of the big bland brewers.

Liquid legacies of a certain time and place, these are the kind of beers that still, once in a while, turn up quietly, and remind you why they have achieved such greatness.

To fully appreciate the joyous beers of the present, it is essential to understand the beers of the past.

Amid the scampering pomp of the modern beer scene, this may just be the moment to forgive a little faded grandeur and appreciate them a little more.

OLD SCHOOL CLASSICS ARE THE ILLUSTRIOUS ALES AND LEGENDARY LAGER BEERS THAT CHANGED THE WORLD, THE GIANTS ON WHOSE SHOULDERS TODAY'S CRAFT BREWERS STAND, LIVING FOSSILS STILL ABLE TO SHOW YOUNG WHIPPERSNAPPERS HOW IT SHOULD BE DONE.

UK

Fuller Smith & Turner
Gale's Prize Old Ale 9%
London, England
www.fullers.co.uk

Lauded as a now-rare English sour ale, Prize Old Ale (POA) is a little bit weird, a little bit wood-aged and really rather wild. Born in the 1920s at Gale's Horndean Brewery in Hampshire, it became a cult classic among drinkers who enjoyed its signature sour tickle. When Fuller's took over Gale's in 2005, many thought it would be quietly culled. But, thanks to former managing director John Roberts and brewer John Keeling, its legacy has remained, albeit in a slightly altered form. Unable to faithfully recreate the aura of Gale's original vessels, Fuller's use stocks of POA fortified with microflora descended from those found at Horndean, as a starter 'beer' and then blend in a new version brewed in West London every year. There's a frisson of farmyard underneath an earthy layer of fusty wood and dark sour fruit. It's reminiscent of Rodenbach but with a little English eccentricity thrown in.

Old Burton Extra, 7.4%
In 2012, head brewer John Keeling teamed up with the remarkable Ron Pattinson, a meticulous man-manual of ancient British brewing, and unearthed a 1931 recipe for Old Burton Extra (OBE) from Fuller's brewbook. Burton Ale is often erroneously assumed to be an alias for a Burton-style IPA. In fact it's darker, sweeter, and closer to a modern-day 'winter warmer'. Burton brewers exported these beers overseas, particularly to Russia, before IPA became their main focus in the 1820s. It became popular in Britain, too: deceptively strong and vinous, Burton Ale remained remarkably well-liked in London until lager and keg beer swept its legs from beneath it. Slumping sales saw Fullers drop OBE in 1969, replacing it with an embryonic version of ESB, but now it's back, as part of the time-travelling Past Masters series. The original recipe brings together Best Pale Ale malt, crystal malt, maize and a bespoke brewing syrup along with English Fuggles and Goldings in the copper and dry hopping. Fruity and deep, this is a beer for snuggling up with on cold winter nights.

Greene King
Old 5X 12%
Bury St Edmunds, England
www.greeneking.co.uk

Closely guarded by the guys at Greene King, Old 5X is rarely released as a stand-alone beer, blended instead with younger ales to create Strong Suffolk, Winter Ale and the seldom seen St Edmund barley wine. But now and again, Greene King give valued brewery visitors or fortunate beer festival-goers a glimpse of its 18th-century 'country beer', still aged, quietly and contentedly, for more than two years in three vast wooden vats, topped with Suffolk Marl, a mixture of mud and clay. Drunk 'fresh' in Bury St Edmunds, it is an extraordinary experience, a musty, tweed jacket tipple, not far off a fino sherry.

Harvey & Sons
Imperial Russian Stout 9%
Lewes, England
www.harveys.org.uk

The normally quiet Sussex town of Lewes has its dark side, seen every November 5 in its Bonfire Night celebrations, and embodied in this ink-black Imperial Stout, a glutinous drop first brewed in 1998 at Harvey's glorious Victorian tower brewery on the banks of the Ouse. Miles Jenner, Harvey's softly spoken and esteemed head brewer, ignites an almost exact incarnation of the strong stout first brewed more than two centuries ago, using a combination of coloured malts; hopping heavily with Fuggle and Goldings and maturing in tank for more than nine months. A viscous, velvet vortex of pepper, sour liquorice and tobacco-tainted leather.

JW Lees
Harvest Ale 11.5%
Manchester, England
www.jwlees.co.uk

True British Barley Wines rarely get more impressive than this. Brewed every autumn in time for Christmas using newly harvested Maris Otter barley and East Kent Goldings hops, Harvest Ale ages happily in the cellar for years, nay decades. More recently, JW Lees has succumbed to experimentation by maturing the beer in wood influenced by bourbon, Scotch, sherry, port and apple brandy.

Molson Coors
Worthington's White Shield 5.6%
Burton upon Trent, England
www.molsoncoors.co.uk

If you've read Pete Brown's excellent *Hops & Glory*, a riotous retracing of IPA's rocky route from Burton to the Indian sub-continent, you will know all about the wondrous Worthington White Shield. Its Burton-born tale is one of boom, wanderlust, decline, neglect, rebirth and modern day deification. The brainchild of William Worthington, a leading ale-making impresario in the 1800s, White Shield was, alongside IPAs from Allsopp and Bass, refreshing parts of the Raj that the London brewer Hodgson, first of the big exporters of pale ale to India, could no longer reach. When export trade trickled away and the Worthington brewery was absorbed into the Bass empire, White Shield was one of very few bottle-conditioned beers left, somehow surviving even when the 1970s keg craze kicked in. By the 1990s, White Shield was an unwanted, nomadic beer, being passed around regional brewers like an incontinent grandparent at Christmas, ending up at King & Barnes in Sussex. Just as it was due to disappear, a man called Steve Wellington, whose job it was to resuscitate old Bass brewing recipes at the Museum Brewery in Burton, rescued it and returned it to the tower brewhouse, now owned by Molson Coors, where it was first brewed. Under the incongruous auspices of the enormous American brewer, White Shield has enjoyed a remarkable renaissance and, from being one of only five bottle-conditioned beers left in the UK in 1971, it has been instrumental in the resurgence of 'real ale in a bottle'. Brewed with iconic Burton well water (albeit with the minerals dragged out and then thrown back in) and English hops (Challenger, Goldings and Fuggles), it's a marvellous, melodious medley of marmalade, treacle, toffee and peppery spice underwritten by a lovely fresh, bready base. It is to American IPA drinkers what a fossil is to Creationists.

Moorhouse's
Black Cat Mild 3.4%
Lancashire, England
www.moorhouses.co.uk

If one were to send a crack team of quintessentially British beers over to compete against the Americans, like a kind of Ryder Cup of brewers, then this would be one of the first names on the team sheet. Moorhouse's magnificent, fruity mild epitomises British brewers' capability to coax out such complexity from very low gravity beers. First brewed in Burnley, Lancashire, back in 1865, Black Cat won Champion Beer of Britain 135 years later, revived as part of Moorhouse's remarkable reversal of fortunes. A gorgeous gateway Mild that, if you're not careful, will lead to similarly stylish, sensible session beers.

Burton Ale

Before the brewers of Burton-upon-Trent became associated with the export of highly bitter beers to India in the 1820s, they were brewing a legendary liquid by the name of Burton Ale.

Burton Ale was made from pale malt, though the end product wasn't very pale at all and, unlike pale ales of today, it wasn't very bitter or hoppy. In fact, it was often dark and sweet, more like a modern Winter Warmer, and usually very strong, its ABV rising above 10 or 11%.

By the 20th century, at any rate, a typical Burton Ale was made from a mash containing pale ale malts and crystal malts supplemented with bespoke brewing sugars that created colour, flavour and a little extra alcohol.

Burton Ale hit the sweet spot among Baltic beer drinkers, and exports from Burton to Russia via Hull became big business in the latter half of the 18th century. However, the Baltic market was knocked on the head in 1822, when the Russian government brought in new customs regulations that banned the import of ale from Britain. This had two results: the first was that the Burton brewers looked for new markets abroad, including India, where they started exporting a highly hopped beer that eventually became known as India Pale Ale. The second was that they began selling more of a slightly tweaked version of Burton Ale back home in Britain, where it quickly proved popular.

While Burton was synonymous with its birthplace, other British brewers were brewing their own versions and by the late 1880s, Burton Ale, sometimes, confusingly, called Burton Pale Ale, was a style sold by brewers up and down the country, especially in London, where it was a regular part of many brewers' bar-top line-ups: expensive, robust and great at keeping one's cockles from the cold.

It also gained popularity among pre-Prohibition brewers on the East Coast of the United States, including Ballantine & Sons of Newark, New Jersey, whose Burton Ale, it claimed, rivalled that made by Burton-based brewers such as Bass and Allsopp. Ballantine's Burton Ale is reckoned to be the inspiration behind Anchor's Old Foghorn Barley Wine.

Back in Burton, the eponymous ale was being increasingly usurped by pale ale and IPAs; so much so that by the early 1900s, it was somewhat of a speciality in the Staffordshire town. It remained more popular in other parts of Britain and it would still pop up on pumps in pubs until after the Second World War.

But then, just like that, it disappeared. Demand for dark, sweet, strong beers declined as bitter and lager gave drinkers the golden glad-eye. As the term 'Burton Ale' became an old-fashioned idiom only etched on pub mirrors, brewers dropped the term and replaced it with 'winter warmer', selling the beer mostly as a seasonal.

Modern interpretations are often erroneous in being more like an IPA than a proper Burton Ale. The likes of BPA ('Burton Pale Ale') from Greene King (the beer mixed with 5X ale to make Strong Suffolk barley wine), Old Burton Extra from Fullers and the odd unspiced Winter Warmer, such as the one brewed by Young's, are the most reliable modern day replicas.

Ramsgate Brewing
Dogbolter 5.6%
Kent, England
www.ramsgatebrewery.co.uk

In the 1980s, a man called David Bruce placed a ferret down the underpants of big, blasé brewery-owned boozers in London. His new 'Firkin' family of pubs not only brewed their own beer on the premises, unheard of since the 18th century, but also turned the traditional pub formula upside down. Sticky carpets were ripped out and floorboards were bared and covered in sawdust, the only 'theme' being down-to-earth drinking. Bruce launched Dog Bolter in his brewpubs as the result of a mistake: it was meant to be an even stronger brew, but too much water was added to the mash by accident. The 'accident' proved a big hit with customers. I first encountered its potent charms at the age of 11, falling from my inebriated brother's shoulders onto the beer-soaked floor of the Fresher & Firkin in Cambridge. A far more contemporary and refined option is to reach for Ramsgate's reincarnation, brewed by founder Eddie Gadd, formerly of the Firkin parish. It's a juicy, fruity dark porter infused with local Kentish hops.

Robinsons
Old Tom 8.5%
Manchester, England
www.frederic-robinson.co.uk

The story goes that Old Tom was a mice-chasing moggy that lived at Robinson's Brewery in the dying years of the 19th century. Unfortunately for the story, Old Tom was a common name for strong ales in Victoria's time. Never mind: more than a hundred years later, a friendly feline face still adorns a bottle that should sit in the cellar of any right-drinking beer aficionado. It's an oozy, oxblood-coloured eddy of rum-soaked raisins, chocolate and tobacco and tannin. You can thank a whole load of Halcyon pale malt darkened with dollops of Crystal and Chocolate malts for that.

Timothy Taylor
Landlord 4.3%
Yorkshire, England
www.timothy-taylor.co.uk

The flagship brew from this quiet, cloistered brewery from Keighley, a small mill town near Bradford, has been named Champion Beer of Britain more times than any other in the

country since it was first brewed in 1952. Though Landlord was famously named by Madonna as her favourite ale, 'Timmy Taylor's' has never crassly courted publicity, instead preferring to invest in the brewery. Impressive expansion in production has not diluted Landlord's undeniable drinkability, either on draught or in bottle. Rich digestive-like Golden Promise malt pairs up with Pennine water, Fuggles and a trio of Styrian hops to create a swirl of stewed fruit, citrus hops and an earthy bitterness. The beer I give to people who say they don't like bitter.

Theakston
Old Peculier 5.6%
Yorkshire, England
www.theakstons.co.uk

Made in Masham, North Yorkshire, Old Peculier is the strangely spelled, iconic beer on which the famous Theakston legacy is built. Once known to locals as 'lunatic's broth', its name comes from a time when in the Middle Ages, Masham was a 'peculier' parish which meant it was exempt from outside ecclesiastical jurisdiction. While Theakston's has endured a tumultuous time in recent years, leaving and then returning to family ownership, Old Peculier has prevailed as a definitive British 'old' ale which, 100 years ago, would have been a 'stock' ale often blended in with 'newer' beers. But it

is a remarkably reassuring ruby beer on its own. Still brewed using open wooden fermentation vessels, this is a moreish fusion of fruitcake, earthy Fuggles hops and a lingering tannin-like tail.

Mild

Mild is a much misunderstood beer style. The name doesn't help; an inert word with all the pizazz of second-hand bubble wrap. Every year, in the UK, the Campaign for Real Ale declares May to be 'Mild' month, which sees pub-goers drinking a bit more Mild than they did in April or may do in June.

Mild is arguably Britain's most traditional working-class beer and, at its best, it can be magnificent. It got its name originally not from its lack of strength but from its its lack of age: 'mild' beers were always sold new and fresh. Because of that they did not need a lot of hops to preserve them, which meant that 'Mild' became associated with a lack of bitterness.

Today's Milds usually use darker, roasted malts, which tend to give a chocolate, burnt and nutty flavour. It used to be a strong beer, but high taxes during the First World War, malt rationing and the finger-wagging temperance movement saw a reduction in strength. This made it ideal for slaking the thirst of workers, and it was Mild, more than any other beer style, that oiled the wheels of British industry. However, when heavy industry hit the buffers, so did Mild, and sales collapsed like a dodgy smokestack.

Today, Mild is rarer than a sooty-faced chimneysweep, struggling to thrive in a desperately trendy nation where more people work in PR than manufacturing, where the heat of the furnace has been replaced by 'hot desking' and where the only thing people try to hit at work is a meaningless deadline.

But please don't let it disappear. If you see it, order it.

BEER VENUE The Bell

The Bell is rich reward after a ramble on the Ridgeway, an ancient trail that cuts an uplifting swathe through the bucolic Berkshire Downs and beyond.

It is an idyllic pub which dates back at least to the 16th century: some even claim it was an elbow-bending institution as early as 1340. Stepping through the arched doorway is like stepping back in time. There is no music, no fruit machines, not even a till (the landlord tots up the cost of rounds on a notepad) and if you use your mobile phone, locals will consider you a witch and drown you in the old well opposite.

The cosiness knob is cranked up all the way to 11, with low beamed-ceilings, an enormous oak fireplaces and a fabulous flagstone floor, warped and misshapen by generations of contented drinkers.

Beers from Arkell's Brewery, the West Berkshire Brewery and a host of rotating guest breweries are served in immaculate condition and, better still, in dimpled jugs with handles. The food, meanwhile, is restricted to soups and delicious warm crusty rolls stuffed with meat and cheese.

In the summer, the glorious garden makes for a quintessentially English oasis of contentment and calm, the only disturbances being the thwack of cricket balls and the rippled applause from the adjacent village green, and the eeyores and quacks from the resident pub donkeys and geese.

At the Bell Inn, all seems good in the world. It is, quite possibly, the best pub on earth.

The Bell, Ambury Road, Aldworth, Berkshire RG8 9SE Tel: 01635 578272

SA Brains
Brains Dark 4.1%
Cardiff, Wales
www.sabrain.com

This is the beer that SA Brains is built on. First called Red Dragon, it was the blue-collar thirst-quenching beer of Cardiff's working class. In rugby terms, it is more of a number 8 than a full back; more muscular than most Milds, with chocolate roast and burnt toast, stewed Rooibos and an extremely tidy, dry finish. Brain's calls it 'the world's best dark mild ale'. Llanfairpwllgwyngyllgogerychwyrn-drobwllllantysiliogogogoch, as they say in Wales.

US

Anchor Brewing
Anchor Steam 4.9%
San Francisco
www.anchorbrewing.com

Fritz Maytag has always maintained that it was the San Francisco weather that ultimately saved Anchor Brewing. In the 1960s, when the big breweries were tightening the screw on the small guys, other Californian craft brewers crumpled in the sun like a crisp packet in a fire. Yet San Francisco's cooler weather was kinder to Anchor's ales, prolonging their shelf-life and, inadvertently, delaying Anchor's almost certain demise just enough for Maytag to rescue it at the death.

Maytag, a Lucky Lager drinker and an unlikely saviour, had never brewed before, let alone shown interest in beer. But a combination of travel, intensive study and investment, not to mention a return to

traditional brewing techniques, successfully transformed a shambles wrapped up in a farce into America's first successful post-war craft brewer. Maytag's accomplishment owes much to Steam Beer, one of very few indigenous American beer styles, born after the Gold Rush in the mid-1800s. Also known as 'Californian Common', Steam was especially popular in San Francisco where steam rising from the breweries' rooftop fermenters into the cool city air, supposedly earned the beer its name. At its peak, it was brewed in the city by more than two dozen pre-Prohibition breweries.

After the repeal of the 21st Amendment, Anchor resurrected the style in 1933. Thirty-eight years later, in 1971, Anchor began bottling the same beer that was being brewed to the same recipe using the same procedure and ingredients. What makes this hard-nosed hybrid beer distinct is the fermenting of lager yeast at an unusually warm temperature in shallow open fermenters, as well as krausening, the addition of actively fermenting wort to the casks of beer within the brewery. It makes for an all-American historic beer – amber hue, smooth, citrusy and a superb session brew.

Bridgeport Brewery
IPA 5.5%
Oregon
www.bridgeportbrew.com

The Portland metro area is the largest craft brewing market in the United States, with more than 50 breweries, and nearly half of all the beer drunk in the city originating within the state of Oregon. Things were not always this good. In 1984, America's overbearing Big Brother brewers prevailed in Portland. Then came the Company (CBC), opened by the winemaking Ponzi family with UC Davis brewer Karl Ockert in an old rope factory. CBC lured in locals with a solid Scotch Ale called Bridgeporter and, such was its success, they changed the name of the brewery to Bridgeport in 1986. But it is the IPA, first brewed in 1996, on which Bridgeport hangs its bowler hat. It is an elegant English-style IPA that, amid an ocean of assertive American interpretations, will have you coveting Queen, Country and crumpets – even if you've never been to Britain. Those yearning for even more Britishness can ask for it in cask at Bridgeport's very own brewpub.

Russian River
Blind Pig IPA 6.1%
California
www.russianriverbrewing.com

In 1994, young Vinnie Cilurzo created a monster. Not quite on the scale of Albert Einstein and the atom bomb but almost. While a young brewmaster at the Blind Pig Brewing Company in Temecula, Southern California, he unleashed what is widely regarded to be the first ever Double IPA. Unwittingly, he had fired the first shot in a very bitter arms race which, I hope you don't mind me saying, has got a little out of hand of late. Having planted the hoppy seed in San Diego, the sightless Swine made the journey north to Russian River in 1996, where it is now poured next to its Pliny progeny – the Elder, a fellow double IPA, and the Younger, a precocious Triple IPA. Yet it is down in San Diego, the Double IPA mothership, where Blind Pig's influence is most apparent, coiling itself around brewers' consciousness like a hop vine.

Sierra Nevada
Pale Ale 5.6%
California
www.sierranevada.com

In just over 30 years, founder Ken Grossman has grown Sierra Nevada from a tiny former bike shop in Chico to the second biggest 'craft' brewery in the country (only Boston Beer Company is bigger). While it may be no longer boutique in stature, the increase in scale has not, in any way, diluted Grossman's fanatical fidelity to brewing incredibly flavoursome, consistent beer. Environmentally, Sierra Nevada is as green as the hops growing behind the brewery. His Pale Ale, the first beer Ken brewed in 1980 as a chemistry and physics graduate in Chico, was extremely audacious back then. Showcasing the spicy, citrusy Cascada hop long before it was considered a cliché, it fired the starter pistol for many Californian craft brewers and, to this day, it remains incredibly fresh and fulfilling. Not just a pioneering pale ale but liquid proof that principles, progress and profit can be successfully combined.

Brasserie à Vapeur
Saison de Pipaix 6%
Pipaix
www.vapeur.com

Brewed solely on the last Saturday of every month at a steam-powered brewery, this is a most seasoned of Saisons, dating back to 1785, when local Walloons did hard rural jobs and were constantly gasping for a pint. The small brewhouse was rescued from ruin in 1985 by Jean Louis Ditz and his wife, a couple with a passion for Pipaix's brewing past. This, the brewery's classic calling card, undergoes staggered triple fermentation and is spiced with coriander, roast chicory, orange peel, ginger, star anise and pepper. There is an undeniable Lambic lilt running through it like a slightly sour stream, carving kinks and quirks into the permeable biscuit bedrock of malt. Think over-ripe apple, rhubarb and lemon tart, think funky, different and a little bit weird, think the George Clinton of classic beer.

Mussels cooked in St Bernardus Witbeer

Serves 4

Ingredients
• 1 tablespoon olive oil
• 1 garlic clove, chopped
• ½ onion
• 1.25kg/3lb washed mussels
• ½ bottle of St Bernardus Witbeer.
• Zest of 1 lime
• 1 dessertspoon chopped mint
• 2 dessertspoons chopped coriander
• 2 dessertspoons chopped chives
• Salt and pepper

Method
Heat a large pan and add the olive oil.

When the oil is hot, fry the garlic and the onion until softened.

Add the mussels and season with pepper and salt before adding beer

Put a lid on the pan.

When the mussels are open, put in the lime zest and all the herbs.

Serve immediately.

Recipe from the Den Dyver restaurant in Bruges, Belgium

Chimay
Chimay Cinq Cents 8%
Hainault
www.chimay.be

Chided by some for a perceived fading of flavours, Chimay remains a remarkably reliable brewer. Golden and hazy with a snow-white cap of froth, and fuelled by its phenomenally fruity Belgian yeast, this tightly packed, tangy Tripel, (known as Chimay White in the 33cl and draught versions) is dry with a blood orange bitterness, marmalade and shades of sherry.

Orval
Orval 6.2%
Luxembourg
www.orval.be

Enveloped in its iconic tenpin bottle and fashioned for years by tremendously talented Trappist monks, this is a gift from God that keeps on giving. Vibrant and intensely aromatic in its youth, Orval is best left for six months to let its complexity come through. With time, the Brettanomyces yeast begins to funk things up, the floral hops cease straining at the leash and the malt mellows with maturation. Complex doesn't even come close to describing its marvels. A bit like the Chateau Haut-Brion of beer, Orval is very probably the finest pale ale on the planet.

Rochefort
No 10 11.3%
Namur
www.trappistes-rochefort.com

While all three Rochefort beers deserve 'must drink' status, it's the Rochefort 10, especially drawn from the cellar after a few years, that impresses the most. A contemplative and complex brew, slip it into a snifter and swirl up a dark ruby reverie of chocolate, plums, fruit cake and anejo rum. The late great beer writer Michael Jackson suggested this was the beer to pair with strong dark Belgian chocolate.

Rodenbach
Vintage 7%
West Flanders
www.rodenbach.be

Rodenbach is a remarkable beer from a remarkable place. Its hallowed home, in the town of Roeselare, is a Belgian beer basilica where you will find a forest of 300 'foeders' filled with its famous Flemish red ale. Before it is welcomed into the wood, Rodenbach's beer

is brewed using myriad malts, mostly Vienna, and hopped using old hops for preservation purposes rather than bitterness or aroma. Fermentation in cylindro-conical vessels follows, using its bespoke culture of mixed yeast laced with the distinctive lactobacilli.

A month-long secondary fermentation takes place before the beer is decanted into the wooden tuns where, for a period of 18-24 months, critters come out from the cracks, microflora emerge from the oak and Brettanomyces brings something significant to the party. Some of these enormous oak tuns, containing between 120 and 555 barrels each, date back more than 140 years, when they were installed by Eugene Rodenbach, grandson of the founder, Pedro. Eugene lifted Rodenbach to prominence after he returned from an inspirational research trip to England where oak-ageing and blending techniques, particularly in the production of porter, were more advanced than in continental Europe.

Rodenbach Classic, 5%, is a blend of young and old beer (75/25%) while aged beer makes up more than two thirds of the Grand Cru, 6%. Terrifically tart, both have their sharpness rounded with a small dose of sugar. There was a time when a Grand Cru was sourced straight from the foeder but, under Palm's ownership, that particular unblended beer is now called Rodenbach Vintage and it is only available in limited quantities. It is hard to get hold of, but well worth the time once you do. Beneath its Burgundy colour lies a swirl of dark cherry, sherry and balsamic vinegar. It is dry and tart with a faint farmyard funkiness, an ideal aperitif, and great with goose or game.

Westvleteren
12 10.2%
West Flanders
www.sintsixtus.be

It's easy to get swept up in the hysteria and mystique that surround the elusive monastic ales brewed at the St-Sixtus monastery. It is regularly hailed by beer rating sites as the best beer in the world, which some cynics suspect may be more to do with the fact that it is rarely available beyond a small radius around the monastery. The 21 monks who call the monastery home have, inadvertently or otherwise, proved to be masters in the dark arts of marketing, casually whipping up a genteel storm of deification around their beers. Hype and hyperbole aside, however, the top-of-the-range 12 is well worthy of the patience or pilgrimage it takes to find it. Opening with a rich ester, autumnal fruit aroma and a warming pepper prickle on the tongue, there's creamy winter spice, Armagnac-soaked fruit cake, cinnamon and, at 10.2%, a warming tot of navy rum on the finish.

Ayinger
Celebrator Doppelbock 6.7%
Bavaria
www.ayinger.de

When Ayinger first began brewing in 1878, in a small village to the south of Munich, it was a small country concern keeping local Bavarians in good beer. Today, its strapping south German brews are known all over the world. This owes much to current owner Franz Inselkammer's unapologetic expansionist policy and his ability to blend staunchly traditional techniques with uber-advanced brewing technology. By far its most (in)famous offering is its chewy double bock, a strapping bottom-fermented winter beer that sources its intensity from the double-decoction of four malts, a whole lot of Hallertau hops and up to six months of chilly cellar conditioning. Thick of head and body, it conjures up Christmas cake soaked in cognac, dark chocolate and spice. One of the original 'extreme' beers.

Bayerischer Bahnhof
Leipziger Gose 4.3%
Leipzig
www.bayerischer-bahnhof.de

Gose lives in Leipzig, Lower Saxony. It is laced with lactic acid, coriander and salt. It pulls down the pants of the Beer Purity Law and then runs away. It's sharp, it's sour, it's sometimes served with syrup and, just like Keith Richards, it only just survived the 1960s. A rebellious regional speciality, Gose is the weird relative of Berliner Weisse, first born in Goslar in the early 1700s and later adopted by the brewers of nearby Leipzig. In its early years, it was a little like Lambic in its spontaneous fermentation but once science tapped yeast on the shoulder, Gose makers began using both lactic bacteria and ale-yeast. This coming together caused quite a commotion in the cask. In the 1900s, Leipzig was delivered in frothing barrels to more than 90 Gosenschenkes (Gose taverns), where locals would often chase it with a liqueur made with cumin. It was never more than a local niche and it went missing during World War II, slowly re-emerged briefly in the 1950s and then slipped back into the shadows during the 1960s under Communist rule. The 1980s saw it emerge again, mainly thanks to Lothar Goldhahn, a Leipzig pub owner who began brewing it in East Berlin. And then, sure enough, it disappeared again. Now Gose is going great guns (although by the time you read this, it may once again have popped out of fashion). There are currently two Gose breweries in Leipzig, the most famous being the Bayerischer Bahnhof, a railway-themed brewpub. The beer is an off-the-rails, unstrained, almost amber affair that conjures up memories of a margarita, with its lime and salt rim. It is outstandingly refreshing on draught yet more complex when poured from a sitar-shaped bottle with what looks like the chap from Clockwork Orange on the front. After one, you keep on coming back for more. A beer with serious bouncebackability.

Dortmunder Actien Brauerei
DAB Original 4.8%
Dortmund
www.dab-beer.com

Originally launched in 1868 to slake the thirst of those who manned the mines and mills of Rhineland and Westphalia, DAB Original is Germany's blue-collar quencher. Very similar to a Helles but with a bigger bitter bite, the Dortmunder beer style oiled Germany's engine room at a time when Dortmund was Germany's biggest brewing metropolis. World War II wiped evidence of the city's brewing past and now, with industry lighter than it once was and consolidation having kicked in, Dortmund Actien Brauerei is the last large brewery in the city. But the beer remains as a shirt sleeved, elbows on the table, brass tacks beer that you roll across a sweaty, oil-stained brow after doing DIY or changing the fan belt in your car.

Einbecker
Ur-Bock Dunkel 6.5%
Lower Saxony
www.einbecker.de

Einbeck, a small town in Lower Saxony, is the birthplace of Bock, its name a derivation of the 'beck' in Einbeck. Back in the 14th century, almost everyone in Einbeck brewed their own beer. Thing is, Einbeck was not very big and it brewed too much beer. So the burghers began to export it elsewhere and brewed it strong in order to endure long journeys. Einbecker now brews three different Bocks; Ur-Bock Hell, the spring-released Mai-Ur-Bock and the dark Ur-Bock Dunkel, a dry-roasted drop both big of barley and heavy of hop. Oh, and another thing, Bock means 'billy goat' in German which is why you see the hairy-chinned chaps on lots of Bock bottles.

What's up with the Wittelsbachers?

A bit like the Habsburgs but without the absurd chin, the Wittelsbacher family were one of Europe's most influential dynasties. For the best part of 800 years, they climbed into the family tree of pretty much every country on the continent, becoming kings of many of them, including Hungary, Sweden and Greece. The Wittelsbach clan also liked beer, a lot, and were responsible for some of Germany's biggest brewing breakthroughs. In the 13th century, Ludwig Wittelsbach, Duke of Bavaria, set up Munich's first brewery; then Duke Wilhelm IV decreed the Bavarian Beer Purity Law, also known as the Reinheitsgebot, and the family also instituted a Weissbier brewing monopoly for nearly two hundred years, until 1798. What's more, the Hofbrauhaus, the Oktoberfest and the Weihenstephan brewing school may well not have happened without the Wittelsbachers.

Jever
Pilsener 4.9%
Friesland
www.jever.de

This North German Pilsener brings a cold, crisp, bitter bite, like the breeze that blows off the North Sea. Brewed with water as soft as a Pele before his blue pill, and two members of the German hop nobility, Hallertau and Tettnang, in mouth-tightening quantities, Jever gets right in your grill with a distinct grassy hoppiness. Some moan that the edges have been rounded in recent years but its signature snappiness is still significant.

König Ludwig
Schlossbrauerei Kaltenberg
König Ludwig Dunkel 5.1%
Bavaria
www.koenig-ludwig-brauerei.com

In the 1970s, Prince Luitpold of Bavaria, great-grandson of Ludwig III, King of Bavaria, bought a brewery in Fürstenfeldbruck, Bavaria. Unsurprisingly, it came with an enormous castle attached. When he is not organising enormous jousting events, Prince Luitpold lives in the castle alongside a small brewery, which only makes a small proportion of Kaltenberg's beers – the majority are brewed elsewhere in Bavaria. Konig Ludwig Dunkel is the classic Kaltenberg brew, a finely balanced, dark brown lager brewed with myriad malts and dry-hopped, giving notes of toast, chicory and maple syrup.

Köstritzer Schwarzbierbrauerei
Schwarzbier 4.8%
Thuringia
www.koestritzer.de

Köstritzer has been brewing its black bottom-fermented beer in the small spa town of Bad Köstritz since the 16th century. Historically, it would have been drunk mixed with paler beers. Goethe regularly reached for it as part of his recuperation and, no doubt, it improved his accuracy with the wordy gun. Now in the big brewery hands of Bitburger, it is increasingly ubiquitous and accused of not being quite as good as it was. But the roasted malt bitterness still remains, backed by a touch of smoke mixed with aniseed and cherry.

Kulmbacher
Eisbock 9.2%
Kulmbach
www.kulmbacher.de

Not to be confused with the insipid Arctic absurdities invented by misguided marketing monkeys in big brewery boardrooms during the 1990s, this is the original, and altogether more flavoursome ice beer. It was, so the story goes, an erroneous invention that occurred after a wooden barrel of Bockbier was left outside the brewery with nothing but sub-zero temperatures for company. When the brewers brought the splintered barrel in from the cold and chipped away at the frozen beer, they discovered a richer, rounder and more robust version of the original. With the texture of a restorative tincture, it brazenly broadcasts the booze, its potency muffled by mocha, port and burnt chestnuts.

Paulaner
Salvator Doppelbock 7.9%
Munich
www.paulaner.com

Now the biggest brewery in Munich, Paulaner's past dates back to the 17th century when Italian friars from the Order of St Francis of Paula were invited to Munich. by Duke Maximilian I, who loved their good work. While brewing was initially restricted to their own consumption, the Paulaner monks obtained a commercial licence some years later and in 1774 they unleashed what many hail as the world's first doppelbock. It was liquid bread designed to keep the monks going during liquid-only Lent, and the brawny brainchild of one Brother Barnabus. The beer was christened as Sankt Vater Bier (Holy Father Beer), the name morphed into Salvator, meaning 'saviour' in Latin, and since then all other doppelbocks have ended in '-ator'. It's a glorious, nutty, caramel-kissed legend.

St Georgen Bräu
Kellerbier 4.9%
Bavaria
www.georgenbraeu.de

Kellerbier is probably the closest thing German beer gets to British cask ale and it is one of the easiest paths to conversion for cask devotees. Founded in the breweries of Franconia and meaning 'cellar beer', it is lightly effervescent and unfiltered. St Georgen beer is the second most famous thing to come out of the small market town of Buttenheim – the first being Levi Strauss, the man who invented blue jeans. The brewery was founded in 1624 and is still family-owned, the beer is stored in nearby underground rock caverns where it is conditioned, along with live yeast, in oak barrels that are unbunged, allowing the fizz to flee. Beyond Buttenheim and Bamberg, St.Georgen's Kellerbier is served in sexy, swing-top bottles. It is not quite like being in a Bamberg beer garden, but the liquid certainly does not lose its lustre. Delicate, piquant with a bit of fresh brown bread, this is an aromatic aperitif beer, perfect with pretzels.

Schlenkerla 'Heller-Bräu' Trum
Aecht Schlenkerla Rauchbier
Märzen 5.2%
Bamberg
www.schlenkerla.de

The undisputed Big Daddy of Bamberg Rauchbiers. Schlenkerla is something that you should try at least once, ideally while entrenched in the famous brewery tap, an deified drinking den discovered behind the door of number 6 Dominikanerstrasse. Rauchbier has been brewed in Bamberg for more than five centuries. Schlenkerla is a local term for someone with a strange shuffling gait (the name comes from Andreas 'Schlenkerla' Graser, who ran the pub in the late 19th century) and its range of smoke

beers are made by kilning barley over smouldering aged beechwood at its very own maltings. Aecht Schlenkerla Rauchbier Märzen is the brewer's marquee beer, brewed and aged in cellars just down the road from the brewery tap. In it you will find seaweed and iodine, sawdust, bacon and the smoky smoothness of a leather-trousered campfire lothario.

Schneider
Schneider Weisse 5.2%
Bavaria
www.schneider-weisse.de

Halfway through the 19th century, Weissbier was drinking in the last-chance Bavarian beer hall. Disillusioned with what they regarded as a dated drink, locals were clamouring for the clean, clear and contemporary lager-style beers instead. Weissbier had been *the* Bavarian beer since the 16th century and the right to brew it had remained exclusively in the hands of the Bavarian Dukes throughout the 17th and 18th centuries. Yet once the monopoly was repealed, George Schneider leased the Weisses Brauhaus from the ruling Wittelsbach dynasty in 1855 and dragged Weissbier off its deathbed. George is widely seen as the saviour of the Weissbier style. His descendants still make the 'original' beer first brewed at the Weisses Brauhaus, only now it's at the Kelheim brewery, some 70 miles north of Munich, also built by Maximilian I. This is a bottle-conditioned brew with all the banana and bubblegum flavours becoming of a Bavarian Weissbier. Also look out for Schneider Aventinus, a Weizenbock first brewed in 1907 and named after a Bavarian author and philosopher. There is a lot going on here: bruised bananas, figs, dark rum and a bit of spice.

Schumacher Brewery
Latzenbier 5.5%
Düsseldorf
www.schumacher-alt.de

From the oldest altbier brewer in the world, Latzenbier is a stronger version of the dark Dusseldorf drop, only brewed on the third Thursday in March, September and November. Latzen means wooden slats, and refers to the lofty place in the pub where the strong beer was secretly kept while the public were fobbed off with a leaner liquid, commonly known as 'convent beer'. This original 'behind the counter' beer could be bought with a nudge, a wink and a wad of cash, or given by the brewer to friends but it was mostly kept for the brewers themselves. Anyway, it's an Alt with attitude, a muscular malty beer with a huge hop hit on the finish. Tastes a bit like a toffee apple.

Zoigl

Zoigl is esoteric, old-fashioned and, at its most authentic, unique to five towns in the Oberpfälzer Wald, a corner of Bavaria tucked between Franconia and the Czech border. A real rarity now, it's a centuries-old custom, dating back to Medieval times, when only upstanding, land-owning pillars of the community could brew a beer. It started with a mash at a communal brewhouse which would be brought back home, where it was fermented and lagered for a couple of weeks and then sold to locals from what was, in essence, the brewer's living room – known as a Zoiglstube.

That, pretty much, is still what happens today with the brewing rights having been passed down from generation to generation. Each Zoigl house tends to take turns selling the beer so, with each Zoigl supplier open just ten weekends a year, you have to be a tenacious beer tourist with a tight timetable to catch some Zoigl in the right place at the right time. Eagle-eyed imbibers always scan the pub pages of the local newspapers, *Der Neue Tag* or *Oberpfälzer Nachrichten*, or head for Windischeschenbach where, with around a dozen pubs selling the beer, it's easily found.

Always look for the Zoigl brewing sign, a six-pointed star hung from outside the pub that denotes the beer, in fine fettle and fresh as a daisy, is being served – Zoigl is a Franconian word for 'sign'. Similar to the more commonly found Kellerbier, though using slightly darker malt and local Hallertau hops, and generally not lagered as long, Zoigl is unpasteurised and unfiltered.

Spaten-Fraziskaner

Hell 5.2% (Also sold as Premium Lager)
Munich
www.spatenbeer.com

Gabriel Sedlmayr & Son are to Bavarian brewing what The Simpsons are to amusing animated sitcoms. When Gabriel Seldmayr the Elder left his job as brewmaster to the Bavarian Royal Court and bought Spaten, in 1807, the 'Spade' brewery was merely a minnow among Munich's 50 odd breweries. A former brewpub born in 1397, Spaten had been owned by the Spath family (from whom it got its name and logo, 'Spath' being the German for 'spade') for most of the 17th century. But then Gabriel Sedlmayr bought it from the Siesmayr family.

However, Spaten soared under the Sedlmayrs, becoming Munich's most esteemed brewery and the envy of Europe. Both Gabriel Sedmayr and his son, Gabriel the Younger, embraced the knowledge-driven zeitgeist. Gabriel II embarked on a tour of European brewing centres, where he found both instruction and inspiration. In Britain, young Gabriel was especially impressed by the production of pale malt, created using calmer and more controlled kilning techniques. It was here, too, where Gabriel learned how to get more sugars from the mash with the use of cutting-edge scientific equipment: thermometers and saccharometers simply were not widespread back in Bavaria.

It was not an entirely open exchange of ideas, however. While Bass had kindly given Gabriel a saccharometer, other brewers were less forthcoming, and kept their commercial techniques confidential. So, in one of the world's first recorded examples

of industrial espionage, Gabriel helped himself by secretly stuffing a hollow walking stick with brewer's wort and yeast. 'It always surprises me,' wrote Sedlmayr, 'that we can get away with these thefts without being beaten up.'

On returning to Bavaria, Sedlmayr put these new scientific theories into practice and created a new type of Munich malt, paler than the quite dark malts made in Bavaria at the time, before taking over Spaten in 1836 after his father's death. In 1841, a year prior to Pilsner launching in Bohemia, Sedlmayr brought out a new amber-hued lager called Märzen, 'March', before, three years later, making Spaten the first steam-powered brewery outside Britain. Sedlmayr was fascinated by the Bavarian technique of cold fermentation, and his voracious appetite for technological advancement led to a collaboration with Carl Linde, a leading pioneer in artificial cooling. In 1873, Linde installed a refrigeration device in Spaten's cellars, making it the first brewery with the ability to brew and store cold-fermented 'lager' beers all year round.

In 1894, Spaten's status as the biggest brewery in Munich was bolstered by the launch of a straw-coloured lager, called a 'Helles', meaning 'pale' in German, Designed to go toe-to-toe with the golden Bohemian beer from Pilsen, it maddened Munich's brewing families, who felt the new pale lager undermined Märzen, then the mainstay of Bavarian brewing. Eventually, they all saw the light and now Helles and Pilsner represent around half of all beer drunk in Bavaria. But if you find yourself in a Munich beer garden, the sun shining and sizeable sausages on their way, your palate parched with pretzels, then do yourself a favour and hail a Helles. It's the right thing to do.

Zum Uerige

Altbier 4.7%
Düsseldorf
www.uerige.de

As Samuel Johnson famously wrote: 'When a man is tired of Düsseldorf, he's probably just tired of Düsseldorf.' The place is known as 'the office desk of the Ruhr', so it is no surprise that Düsseldorf's very own beer style shares a word with a button on a keyboard. It is a city you might accidentally bump into at a Bilderberg meeting during the Owl Dance, it's shiny of shoe, vast of wallet and all BMW, belts and braces. Cologne, its nearby nemesis, is a complete contrast. Quirky, lefty and counter-culture, Cologne is closer to a collapsible clown car – especially during carnival.

The cities' respective beers are chalk and cheese, too. The only kinship Alt has with the clean and crisp Kölsch is that they are both hybrid beers served in small measures that stood firm in the face of the lager onslaught. Düsseldorf's drop is brewed a bit like an ale (in that it uses top-fermenting yeast), yet it is conditioned cold, like a lager. Alt is darker than its Rhineland rival Kölsch, its copper cloak covering a character that is a little sweeter, smooth and with a big bitter hop bite. Alt is sort of similar to a North American amber ale, but comparisons do not offer much: Altbier is Altbier. The Altbier yeast is a peculiar fellow that quietly, competently does its job without adding much to the flavour, while malt's role is a similarly constrained. If it veers into acrid, burnt barley flavours then something has gone awry. Altbier brewers want a clean interplay between bitter and sweet. Unpasteurised, easy-drinking Altbier is drawn fresh from the cask at Dusseldorf's brewpubs in the Old Town (Altestadt), the best known and bubbliest being the Zum Uerige, all dark oak wainscoting, lead-lined windows and ruthlessly competent apron-clad bar-staff doing their thing since 1862.

Weihenstephan

Hefe Weissbier 5.4%
Bavaria
www.weihenstephaner.de

By all means bow down at this Bavarian beer temple but, whatever you do, don't light a candle. The brewery has been burned down four times since it was founded in the 11th century. It has also endured an earthquake, an array of epidemics and the odd war or three.

While understandably avoided by insurance companies, Weihenstephan is a magnet for budding brewers, who flock to Freising, near Munich, to study at brewing's leading seat of learning. This, the 'Top Gun' of technical Teutonic brewing has a one-in-five pass rate. Its graduates, who come from around the world to study beer in Bavaria, are considered the brewing elite and the facility is home to the biggest bank of yeast strains in the world, which are frequently 'borrowed' by other brewers. Its own Weissbier yeast puts classic clove, bubblegum and banana flavours into a Dunkelweiss, a filtered Kristall and, most notably, the famous unfiltered 'Hefe', made with locally grown barley and wheat, flavoured with Perle and Magnum hops and, once fermentation is over, stored for 30 days before bottling or kegging. Weihenstephan, a mixture of the modern and the monastic, is both one of the most advanced and the oldest brewery in the world, dating back to the 11th century, when Benedictine monks built the abbey and added a brewery to supply beer for themselves.

Kommunbrauhaus Windischeschenbach
Posterer Zoigl 5.1%
Bavaria
www.zum-posterer.de

When you are having a Zoigl here, it is easy to feel like Goldilocks, an intruder with an appetite making oneself comfy in someone else's kitchen. With just a few tables and chairs scattered around, a sideboard here and a dresser there, it feels as if you have stumbled into a domestic idyll rather than a public drinking spot, the sort of experience common 200 years ago when alehouses really *were* someone's house and the purveyance of pints a sideline to something else. Only restored in 2004, Posterer is one of the newest and most popular Zoiglstuben in the village of Windischeschenbach, some 50 or so miles from Nuremburg and less than 10 miles from the Czech border. Its Zoigl, which it sources raw barely half a mile away, is an absurdly easy-drinking, amber-hued problem-solver – ushering cares out the door on a velvet carpet of grain, almonds and sweet malt. Other well-known Windischeschenbacher Zoiglstuben include the Weisser Schwan and Oberpfälzer Hof.

CZECH REPUBLIC

U Fleku
Flekovský tmavý ležák 5.5%
Prague
www.ufleku.cz

In 1499, a maltster by the name of Vit Skremenec began brewing beer in what is today Prague's most legendary brewpub. Dark and smoky, with beerglass iron chandeliers and long wooden tables, it is a must-visit for beer lovers, especially if there is room in the beer garden. Industrious aproned staff, who can spot a thirst or a hunger from a hundred yards, but cannot find a smile for Love nor money, offer just one beer; a 13 degree black lager brewed with four malts, using double-decoction mashing, open fermenters, hopped with Saaz and dispensed from oak vats. With liquorice, dark bitter chocolate and a spicy finish, it's all you need. Tourist taint apart, this bar is a must-see on any enlightened imbiber's Prague itinerary. Unfortunately the constant flow of tourists annoys the local customers but sometimes a drinker has to suffer a little for beer as good as this.

NETHERLANDS

Hertog Jan
Grand Prestige 10%
Limburg
www.hertogjan.nl.

This, dear dedicated drinkers, is a big barley wine of considerable character and clout. There are plums, there is chocolate, there is port and there is an over-riding realisation that if you drink more than one of these, you will do something rather daft or drop off. The brewery is named after John I, Duke of Brabant, a royal who threw big parties with big beers and, who knows, maybe some big ladies. It operates out of premises in the village of Arcen, in the southern province of Limburg, and was instrumental in the defibrillating of a dormant Dutch craft beer scene back in the 1980s. It is now owned by AB-InBev, but it remains one of the Netherlands' most alluring heavyweights.

La Trappe
Quadrupel Oak Aged 10%
Noord-Brabant
www.latrappe.nl

The Koningshoeven abbey was once stripped of its Trappist status as, allegedly, the monks weren't mucking in enough. But once the brothers got more hands-on, the brewery regained its Trappist status in 2005 and four years later began experimenting with oak. A year in wooden barriques curves the corners of a copper-coloured quadrupel which itself undergoes fermentation in oak. The barrels, previously used for whisky, wine or port, are different for every batch but there is a touch of tannin throughout, and a darkening of the estery fruit, morphing from peach to prune.

DENMARK

Carlsberg
Kongens Bryg Morkt Hvidtøl 1.7%
Copenhagen
www.carlsberg.dk

Hvidtøl was historically an ale drunk as a safer alternative to water. Fermentation is cut very short, leading to low alcohol and a seriously sweet beer suitable for children. Sort of this. This dark beer, made with Munich malt, chocolate malt and caramalt, is classically drunk at Christmas Eve as an accompaniment to Danish rice pudding after a traditional Christmas feast of goose and red cabbage.

Ørbæk
Old Danish Beer 10.1%
Nyborg
www.oerbaek-bryggeri.nu

A 'mead beer' dragged back from the 18th century, when Denmark was revelling in its roaring export trade, this is made at the Ørbaek Brewery in Nyborg, on the island of Funen. After years of inaction, brewing was re-started in 1997 by Niels and Nicolai Rømer on a brewery site dating back to 1906. Strong traditional mead is blended with a 7% beer infused with ginger on a bed of Vienna and Munich malted barley. Dark in colour, chewy in body, the sweetness kicks like a stallion in a stall when smoke's in the air, making for a very decent alternative to a dessert wine. Like all the brewery's products, including a 'Blueberry Hill' ale inspired by Fats Domino, a Bock beer, a Weissbier made from 50% spelt, a brown ale and a summer ale made with elderflowers, this is made solely from organic ingredients. Ørbæk also now makes an organic whisky under the name Isle of Fionia.

Refsvindinge
Dansk Skibsøl 2.4%
Nyborg
www.bryggerietrefsvindinge.dk

Revived in 1996 using grain smoked over beechwood, you won't find a more valiantly traditional Danish beer than Skibsøl – literally 'ship's beer'. A bit like a Mild in style, its strength is in its sinewy body of smoke, black treacle and liquorice. It has cultivated cult status among Denmark's craft beer drinking cognoscenti, particularly the older ones not easily impressed with the bluff and bluster of the nation's more esoteric alemakers.

Thisted
Stenøl Beer 7.8%
Thisted
www.thisted-bryghus.dk

A thumping great 'stone' beer from a century-old brewery in North Denmark that uses lava stones heated up to 800 degrees and dipped in the wort four times: originally a method of heating (and sterilising) the wort before the days of coppers heated by a fire underneath. Singed caramel clings to the stones but, after they are placed in the fermenting vessel, loosens its grip in the four-week fermentation. The beer is smooth and rounded, with a palate of Demerara sugar and navy rum and a dry toffee apple finish.

FRANCE

Duyck
Jenlain Ambrée 7.5%
Nord-Pas-de-Calais
www.jenlain.fr

As anyone who has had to endure a French exchange student knows, they are fussy eaters and drinkers. So it is no surprise that in 1978, disillusioned with the homogenous lager on offer locally, hordes of Lille's work-shy tax dodgers began buying lots of lovely Jenlain beer – presumably with a cheque, as étudiants like to do. Were it not for this passionate stand against the bland, the family-owned Duyck brewery's slightly sweet, somewhat spicy bière de garde would have been overrun by lager and Belgian imports. It is now the most renowned and readily available bière de garde in France, caged and corked Champagne-style since the early 1950s. Duyck has smoothed some of its rustic edges but it still remains a very safe bet in supermarches all over l'Hexagon.

Heineken
Pelforth Brune 6.5%
Lille
www.pelforth.fr

There may be those who do not consider this a classic but, originally created in 1935, it is a legendary Lille liquid among French beer drinkers. As a student in France, disillusioned with bland Alsatian lagers, I drank a lot of this deep russet-coloured swirl of autumnal fruit. Its strength gave me both the courage to approach lovely local ladies and, after two or three bottles, several reasons for them to demand my departure. Today it's like that madeleine dipped in tea was for fellow Frenchman Marcel Proust, only tastier.

AUSTRIA

Hofstetten
Granitbock 7.3%
St Martin
www.hofstetten.at

Black Death, the drowning of witches, jousting and fighting with bows and arrows: there's lots of stuff from the Middle Ages that civilisation has, for the most part, deemed unnecessary. Another is Steinbier. The widespread use of metal in brewing today means that very few breweries still throw enormous white-hot stones into their beer. But brewers are a nostalgic, nonsensical bunch and a small brewery in Austria has revived the primitive process. After making the wort for a Bock in a traditional brewkettle, the Hoffstettners cool that wort and pour it into open-air stone troughs, where it awaits the arrival of seriously scorching white-hot granite rocks, heated on open flames. Caramelized sugar from the wort sticks to the granite, aerated yeast is added, a frenzied open-fermentation follows and, once the hullabaloo has calmed down, the beer is taken to cellars, where it chills out for several months. Granitbock is a big beer that gets Medieval on your palate. It is, rather aptly, nutty with a quirky caramelised, campfire character, incorporated with molasses, crème brûlée and Christmas cake.

Stift Engelszell
Gregorius 9.7%
Upper Austria
www.stift-engelszell.at

In May 2012, Engelszell was anointed the eighth brewery of the Trappist Order. With annual output of just over 1,500 barrels, it is by far the smallest, attached to a 13th century monastery tucked away in hills-are-alive Upper Austria. Located more than 500 miles from Belgium, the monks make two beers, both brewed with a drop of local honey and showing early promise. Benno is a hazy golden ale bearing all the fruitiness of a virile Belgian yeast while stewed dark fruits, winter spices and molasses make up its brother, a super-strong brown ale.

NORWAY

Haand
Norwegian Wood 6.5%
Drammen
www.haandbryggeriet.net

A quartet of esoteric ale enthusiasts carve quirky beer styles in a small quasi-amateur brewery situated half an hour south of Oslo. Rustic, neglected Norwegian farmhouse beers are the speciality and this smoky, spicy beer is sensational. An ode to an unindustrialized era when farmers would smoke malt over an open fire, barley from Bamberg brings a sweet leather note that is soothed and seasoned with berries and bittersweet juniper twigs, giving it a delicate pine, slightly menthol finish. One of several awesome, esoteric efforts from Haand.

ESTONIA

A Le Coq
Porter 6.5%
Tartu
www.alecoq.ee

This scorched, oily imperial porter was originally imported from London by Albert Le Coq, a company founded by a Prussian Hugenot. Le Coq bought a brewery in Estonia to brew porter itself, starting in 1913, but wars and revolutions got in the way until 1999, when Le Coq's flagship beer was brought back to life, using German hops and black and chocolate malt coupled with toasted grain. This is an iconic ale, laced with notes of espresso, stewed plums and molasses.

FINLAND

Lammin Sahti
Lammin Sahti 7.7%
Lammi
www.sahti.fi

From Finland's most elderly micro ale-maker, this superb Sahti fired the starting pistol for more micros to follow suit, ensuring that the strange style survives. The brewery, formed in 1985, secured 'protected designation of origin' in 2002 and follows traditional Finnish farmhouse methods. Basic baking yeast ferments wort made from rye, wheat and

barley before being filtered through a bed of juniper twigs and seasoned, along with old hops, with juniper berries. Funky, fiery and very floral, with a dark brown body, it can only be drunk fresh – either from the brewery or a few specialist beer bars in Helsinki.

Sinebrychoff
Porter IV 7.2%
Kerava
www.sinebrychoff.fi

The Sinebrychoff Brewery is a beast of a brewery now, a major northern outpost of the Carlsberg empire. As well as some strong selling lagers, ciders and soft drinks, it is also Finland's biggest bottler of Coca-Cola. But it is another dark liquid for which Syebrychoff is rightly celebrated. The first beer that Russian founder Nikolai Sinebrychoff brewed after opening his Helsinki brewery in 1819, was a powerful porter. But alcoholic production was curtailed in 1919, as Finland freed itself from Russian rule and immediately enacted prohibition for 13 years (exactly the same span of time, strangely, as prohibition lasted in the United States). It was not until after World War II, using yeast pilfered from a bottle-conditioned Guinness, that this Baltic Porter, inspired by the beers London brewers exported east, was brought back, and it is still there after production shifted to the town of Kerava. Its strength shrouded by a soothing, cushion softness, there is dark chocolate compote, mocha and, some may say, a bit of Coca-Cola sweetness.

POLAND

Pinta
A La Grodziskie 2.6%
Wroclaw
www.browarpinta.pl

Undoubtedly one of the front-runners in Europe's most obscure beer-style race, Grodziskie is a smoked wheat beer named after the Western Polish town of Grodzisk, a big 18th-century beer centre which, at its peak, had more than 50 brewers. High in hop, low in strength, A La Grodziskie's grist is made from 100% smoked wheat malt. It is fermented with an ale yeast, then left unfiltered and unpasteurised. With smoked wheat in scarce supply, however, Grodziskie ceased to exist in the mid-1990s and has only recently been revived by the odd homebrewer and Brouwar Pinta, a cuckoo brewer that like to bring back abandoned beer styles. Brewed at Browar Na Jurze in Southern Poland, it is a dry, delicate refresher with a sniff of Gouda and Mezcal smokiness. The beer is fighting a fairly lonesome fight at the moment, but more Grodziskies are sure to follow. Perhaps.

LITHUANIA

Aldonos Udrienes
Jovaru Alus 6%
Jovarai
(no website)

The largest of the Baltic States boasts the best craft scene, yet you will have to venture well beyond Vilnius's brewpubs to discover why. It's in the countryside where they brew kaimiskas alus, meaning 'rustic ales,' in barns, basements and sheds. Kaimiskas is not a style in itself, more an umbrella term for an eclectic array of Saison-style dark and light ales brewed with a big barley backdrop, slightly unhinged yeast strains and local, sometimes wild-growing, hops. Most Kaimiskas are unavailable beyond the back door of the 'breweries' and that is where they taste best, too. An earthy, dark amber cloudy beer starts with straw and citrus, a touch of horse blanket and hay, with a burst of fresh herb on the finish.

KUPIŠKĖNŲ ALUS

Kupiškenu Alus
Magaryciu Alus 5.8%
Kupiškis
(no website)

From the north-eastern town of Kupiškis and one of the more switched-on commercial concerns, comes this hazy rustic country ale, brewed with the early addition of hazelnuts. Nutty of course but natural fermentation gives the beer a fresh and funky farmyard character and a charming shambolic chic.

Ceylon Breweries
Lion Stout 8.8%
Colombo
www.lionbeer.com

Some 66 years after the island now known as Sri Lanka became the British colony of Ceylon in 1815, the explorer Sir Samuel Baker started a brewery high up in the hills in Nuwara Eliya. Its comparatively cool

climate suited both the British and the brewing of beer. But after more than a century of ingredients being hauled up mountain passes, the brewery was phased out a few years ago and brewing now takes place in the capital, Colombo. While Lion Lager is its biggest selling beer, a welcome respite in the heat and the humidity, the landmark Sri Lankan stout is rightly more revered. It conjures up the richness of a Lebanese Chateau Musar, velvety and voluptuous in body with an earthy plummy middle leading to a dry acerbic finish of burnt marshmallow, espresso and spicy red berries.

John Keeling
Fuller's Head Brewer
London

�֍ Brooklyn Lager
This is the lager I give to people who say they hate lager. They then tell me it's not a lager. I say 'read the label.' The lager that said you can experiment even when the rules say you can't . Everybody who tries this understands immediately that just as ales can use American hops then so can lagers too. I find this beer so refreshing that it is my go-to hammock beer on a hot summer's day. Wish we had more days like that in England.

✖ Boddingtons Cask Bitter 1974
In terms of great beers, I think of the times I have drunk them. In 1974 at the start of my brewing career there was no better drinking beer than Boddingtons. Unfortunately this beer was successfully destroyed a number of years later, but for a period was one of the world's greatest beers.

✖ Redemption Trinity
Although it's only 3% this beer drinks with a lot more backbone, with some great orange aromas. I also really love low-gravity beers. This is a signal of the resurgence of craft brewing in the capital, but above all it's a really tasty beer.

✖ Timothy Taylor Landlord
During the 1980s this was the 'beer of the North.' I first started drinking this in Manchester where it was a rarity. This was another marvellous drinking beer designed to be enjoyed in the pub. I guess all my best experiences of drinking have been in the pub with friends and Landlord has contributed to many of those occasions.

✖ Victory Brewing HopDevil
The first American beer I got into, which opened my eyes to American hops. I first got into this beer at the beer and whiskey festival in Sweden where I tried this and several other non British beers. This stood out because as well as having tremendous and powerful hop notes it had a valence to it that gave it great drinkability.

BELGIAN TRAPPIST BEERS

Tights-wearing, gout-riddled, ironic post-modern feminist Henry VIII liked a drink. In fact, he liked a lot of drink, a lot of the time. At Hampton Court Palace, his primary residence, 4.8 million pints of ale and beer were drunk each year.

While Henry loved a drink, unfortunately, he loved the ladies a little bit more, and the ensuing Dissolution of the Monasteries (1536–41) brought the country's monastic brewing to a rather abrupt halt. On reflection, he should have just sent a text: 'It's not you, it's me.'

Much of British brewing had hitherto been undertaken by monks and, indeed, nuns. With no monks around to work magic with their mash-forks, British brewing passed into the secular hands of landowners and farmers, and there it stayed forever. Amen. So there you are – that is why Britain doesn't have a Trappist beer.

But Belgium does. Monks still brew beer in Belgium. They are thought to have started in the 6th century, when beer, safer than water, was sold from abbey inns. Not only was it profitable, it was great PR and helped pimp up the monasteries and fund good causes like the local dolphin orphanage.

After 1783, however, the troubles of the French Revolution spilled over into neighbouring territories, ending the influence of the abbeys and, as a result, monastic brewing stopped.

But, unlike in Britain, it started again when, close to Antwerp, the abbey of Westmalle fired up its kettle in 1836 and began brewing beer exclusively for the monks.

Five more Belgium monasteries followed, and another in the Netherlands, and, in 2012, an Austrian brewery was anointed the eighth brewery of the Trappist order.

WESTMALLE

The largest Trappist brewer in terms of capacity and the most clued-up commercially, Westmalle was founded in 1794 as a religious priory, north-east of Antwerp. Its holy trinity of beers, including a blonde (Extra), a Dubbel and a Tripel, provided the

Above: Orval's iconic chalice.

stylistic template for Belgium brewers of abbey ale, some more authentic than others.

Its famous, phenomenally fruity yeast strain can be found in Westvleteren and Achel beers, while its Tripel, brewed in 1934 and redesigned in 1956, is considered to be the beer that first popularised the style.
www.trappistwestmalle.be

ORVAL

So, here's what happened. At some point in the 11th century, a rather attractive and recently widowed Princess by the name of Mathilda of Tuscany inadvertently dropped her wedding ring into a spring.

She was rather upset about this and, in a desperate attempt to retrieve it, prayed to God, offering him a deal. In exchange for the ring's safe return, she promised to build an abbey on the site of the spring.

Not one to peer at the molars of a gift horse, the Almighty shook on it, metaphorically of course, and within minutes a trout had emerged from the water clutching Mathilda's ring in its mouth. 'This place really is a "val d'or"', she proclaimed to herself, and the trout.

Val d'Or, meaning 'golden valley', was then switched around to give us Orval, the name of Mathilda's new abbey, which Benedictine monks began building in 1070. After being converted to the Cistercian order 62 years later, it endured an array of inconveniences including war, fire, the French Revolution and, from 1887 with little left of the original abbey, half a century in the secular hands of the Harenne family.

Between the World Wars, Orval was rebuilt as an incredible religious centre bringing together Romanesque ruins and Art Deco ambition, designed by architect Henry Vaes who also created the classic Orval beer glass, or 'chalice'.

Orval makes two beers* but only one is readily available to the public. What a beer it is, though. Like a good Bordeaux, it is difficult to discover Orval's genuine greatness until it has been aged for a while. Fresh from the brewery, it is pretty much peerless among pale ales. But leave it alone for a while, the longer the better, and it becomes a uniquely inspirational imbibing experience that goes beyond beer.

*Petit Orval is a less potent Orval made only for the monks.
www.orval.be

Far left: The dark and spicy Westmalle Dubbel.

Left: The Orval Monastery.

Above: Rochefort's ales from the Ardennes.

Below right: Chimay, brewed at the Abbey of Our Lady of Scourmont.

Opposite: Elusive examples of Westvleteren's wares.

ROCHEFORT

The Abbey de Notre-Dame de Saint Remy, near Namur in the Ardennes region of Wallonia, nearly burned down in 2010. A blaze caused by a dodgy power generator ripped through several buildings but, thankfully, the brewhouse was undamaged, and no one died or was injured. The monks did, however, have to flee halfway through their supper.

It was third time 'lucky'. Rochefort has been destroyed twice before; first in 1653 by the troops of Lorraine and then again during the French Revolution. Little surprise that the monks are still slightly suspicious of visitors.

The two dozen or so monks may be shy but Rochefort remains one of Belgium's most attractive ale-making abbeys to visit. Sunk deep in the undulating valleys of the Ardennes, an epicurean utopia, it boasts one of the most handsome copper brewhouses in the world.

It was built in the 1960s, just a decade or so after the abbey began selling its beer in 1952. Before then, the monks had rather selfishly been making it purely for themselves, something they had been doing, disasters notwithstanding, since 1595.

They still don't sell much, but they don't really want to. Rochefort restricts itself from making more than 25,000 hectolitres annually even though the brewery has the ability to brew nearly twice as much.

Lest we forget, monks are not in the habit of making massive money, they're in the habit because they're monks. www.abbaye-rochefort.be

CHIMAY

The abbey of Our Lady of Scourmont was set-up by 17 Cistercian monks from the Westvleteren abbey in 1862. While its discreet neighbours restrict availability to a dedicated few, Chimay has gone the other way.

Not the largest in terms of capacity (Westmalle is bigger), Chimay is considered the most commercially minded of the Trappist breweries, churning out nearly 125,000 hectolitres of beer every year through its secular arm called, rather unoriginally, Bières de Chimay.

Commercial concerns have done little to corrupt the quiet contemplation at the abbey – it remains an extremely peaceful place to visit. But it has encouraged accusations of corner-cutting among aficionados; such as conical fermenters replacing original open ones, making the beer less complex; the use of both malt and hop extract; the addition of wheat starch; and a tangible sweetness that, it is claimed, simply wasn't there 'before'.

These are charges the monks, of course, deny. While fermentation is certainly swifter using tall conicals, the monks maintain it has not diminished the beer's depth of character. As for the accusations of adjuncts, they may well

Trappist Talk

- Trappists are a descendant of the Benedictine Movement founded by St Benedict in the 6th century.

- A derivative of the 'Cistercian Order of the Strict Observance', Trappist monks are renowned for their rigorous religious obedience, a vow of silence and their brewing of beer.

- They are allowed to talk a bit but it can't be the kind of tittle-tattle that less devoted folk indulge in.

- Trappist is not a style of beer. While generally strong and nourishing, the beers cover a range of styles from dark dubbel beers to light tripel ales. Stronger beers tend to be lighter, the dark beers less potent. It is confusing but, remember, God is in charge so don't question it.

- Trappist is a legal designation that was firmed up by the Belgian authorities in 1992. To be deemed an 'Authentic Trappist Product', the beer must adhere to three key rules:

  Monks must make or oversee its production

  It must be made within the confines of the Trappist abbey

  Any profit made must be used for social or charitable work

rue the entirely discretionary decision, in 1990, to list the ingredients on their bottles – a move that has left them exposed to a level of scrutiny that other Trappists brewers do not have to endure.
www.chimay.com

WESTVLETEREN

Since 1839, more than two dozen Cistercians have been brewing their beer at the Saint Sixtus monastery in Flanders, 50 miles from the coast. Small, secretive and silent, the order only makes enough beer to provide sufficient funds for the community.

The monks only brew for around 10 weeks a year and output is a paltry 4,500 to 5,000 hectolitres. They could, of course, brew more beer, sell more beer and make more cash, but they choose not to. They have better things to do, like praying for six hours a day, studying and doing good deeds.

The monks play more than a cameo role in the making of the beer. Within the monastery's high walls, brothers involve themselves in the brewing, man the basic bottling plant and pack the pallets. For all I know, they may be having races in forklifts and playing air guitar to AC/DC atop the coppers, because I have never made it into the monastery and nor has anyone I know. That privilege is restricted to a very fortunate few.

The beers themselves remain the most elusive of all the Trappist ales. Getting hold of the beer is an enormous hassle, as it is only really available from a 'drive-through' shop.

Buying the beer is an absurd undertaking. First you have to call ahead and, if answered, you then give the number plate of your car and an exact date and time. Assuming you are punctual, your number plate is then verified and you can pick up your beer, often restricted to 24 bottles. Phone numbers and number plates are then logged to ensure you do not return within 60 days.

While they say that Westvleteren don't do marketing, practitioners of the dark art must marvel at the air of mystery the monks have created, inadvertently or otherwise.

But they would baulk at the price. Two euros for what many declare to be the best beer in the world is quite ridiculous. If Westvleteren was a wine, it would be sold en primeur to avaricious investors for absurd amounts, cellared and then sold on for huge profit.

Cellaring certainly suits the beers, especially the Westvleteren Abt 12, a voluptuous port-like barley wine that ages with elegance. The dark dubbel, accented with aniseed, also develops and deepens in complexity when left alone for a few years. For immediate appreciation, however, perhaps the profound pale ale is best, a sprightly, floral blonde that belies its strength.

The best beers in the world. Or so they say.
www.sintsixtus.be

KEY BEERS

ACHEL
Achel Blonde 5 5%
Achel Bruin 5 5%
Achel Blond 8 8%
Achel Bruin 8 8%
Achel Extra 9.5%

WESTMALLE
Westmalle Dubbel 7%
Westmalle Extra 4.8%
Westmalle Tripel 9.5 %

ORVAL
Orval 6.2%
Petit Orval 4.5%

ROCHEFORT
Rochefort Trappistes 10 11.3%
Rochefort Trappistes 6 7.5 %
Rochefort Trappistes 8 9.2%

CHIMAY
Chimay Bleue/Grande Réserve 9%
Chimay Rouge/Première 7%
Chimay Triple Cinq Cents 8%
Chimay Dorée Spéciale du Potaupré 4.8 %

WESTVLETEREN
Westvleteren 12 (XII) 10.2%
Westvleteren Blond 5.8%
Westvleteren Extra 8 8%

JACK McAULIFFE

Fritz Maytag, Ken Grossman and Jim Koch are often hailed as the founding fathers of the American Craft Brewing movement. But all will say the real pioneer of modern American craft brewing is a quiet, unassuming man called Jack McAuliffe, founder of New Albion Brewing Company.

Every beer in the craft beer movement in North America, and quite a few in Europe too, is a liquid legacy of his pioneering efforts. Back in 1976, Jack created America's first modern craft brewery in Sonoma, Northern California. Using rudimentary equipment, he welded and hammered New Albion Brewing Company together by hand and, using recipes honed while a home-brewer, he began making bottle-conditioned beers of British character.

At the time, amid unease over the ethics of big business and general disenchantment with corporate America, boutique wineries were cropping up along the Pacific Coast, and in the Napa Valley region where the small town of Sonoma is situated.

But while other breweries were not far behind, following the legalisation of home-brewing in 1978, McAuliffe found himself a little too far ahead of the curve. With no money and no craft brewing cohorts, and surrounded by a sea of light lager, Jack set sail in a one-man sieve. And, after a remarkable six years, the business sank.

Ken Grossman, founder of Sierra Nevada, now one of the biggest craft brewers in the US, which started in 1979, says: 'Jack inspired me to open my first brewery. He didn't last that many years but he was really instrumental in showing that on a fairly small budget, a homebrewer could become a commercial brewer, make good beer and hopefully make a living.'

After New Albion was closed in 1982, McAuliffe stopped brewing and for years remained distant from the thriving American craft beer scene he had helped create. In 2007, at its annual conference, the American Brewers Association recognised his efforts with an award. But, not one for crowds, he refused to attend the conference, sending Don Barkley to accept the award on his behalf. Barkley, currently brewing at the Napa Smith brewery, was McAuliffe's assistant brewer in the late 1970s, who was paid in beer, and went on to brew some great beers at Mendocino Brewing in nearby Ukiah.

In recent years, however, McAuliffe has edged closer to the craft brewing community, thanks in no small way to its leading protagonists. He came back to collaborate with Ken Grossman of Sierra Nevada, making a black barley wine called 'Jack & Ken's Ale' in 2010.

More latterly, McAuliffe resurrected his original New Albion Ale with the help of Boston Beer Company's Jim Koch, who had kept the New Albion Brewing Co trademark alive on McAuliffe's behalf, preventing it from being exploited by others.

From the recipe in McAuliffe's memory, using Cascade hops and the same yeast strain which had been kept, after all these years, at a laboratory at University of California Davis, they brewed the single-hop ale in Cincinnati and released it in both bottle and draught at the beginning of 2013, with all profits going directly to McAuliffe.

Koch said: 'It's because of Jack that so many of us have such enjoyable and comfortable lives. When Jack started brewing, there was no infrastructure and no one to call and ask for advice. Now there are more than 2,000 breweries in America, and each is very thankful.'

Q&A WITH JACK MCAULIFFE

What inspired you to start brewing back in the 1970s?

I was a homebrewer and people liked my homebrews so I thought I should start a brewery and start selling it. I was inspired to brew English style beers after reading a number of books about British brewing and after being stationed in Scotland in the 1960s and trying great brews.

I was in the Navy from 1964 to 1968 and we'd get our first liberty and we'd go to the pub and a have a pint of heavy. It was a really different beer and I realised that when I got back from the States I would not be given that choice – so the only option was to learn to make it myself. Of course I could start a brewery, the thought that it wouldn't work never entered my mind.

Back then, there were no off-the-shelf brewing kits so what did you make the brewery from?

I bought 55-gallon stainless steel tuns that were originally used to ship Pepsi-Cola syrups. When Pepsi-Cola decided to go into bulk shipping, they put them on the market and I bought 15 of them from Wine & The People in Berkeley, California. From these tuns, I made our brewing vessels.

What did the brewery look like? Did you make it yourself?

I built it myself and it was a proper tower brewery. We had no pumps and used gravity to feed the brewing stream to the brew kettle and then to the fermenting cellar. Nothing was automated. It was all manual, unlike many breweries today.

Can you describe the beers you brewed?

I brewed a classic English-style stout, porter and pale ale. I wanted to start with the basics. The pale ale is the same recipe that we brewed this year.

What would you have done differently?

I did everything I possibly could and would not do anything differently. I didn't have an option to do anything differently – I would have needed enormous sums of money. I did what I could with what I had.

What do you think about the American craft brewing scene that you started?

It's totally amazing. I never imagined anything like this. Craft beer didn't exist when I first started out, so my ale was the hoppiest, most full-flavoured beverage that anyone at that time had ever experienced. Drinkers would not have been prepared for the big beers like IPAs that brewers are making now.

Do you still (home) brew today?

No, but I offer brewing advice to anyone who needs it.

And what advice would that be? What do you need to start a brewery today?

You need a lot of money to start a brewery today. The brewery, equipment, ingredients … it all adds up.

What are the skills you need to start a brewery?

You need the scientific knowledge behind brewing and the manual or trade skills to maintain it.

Above: Jack McAuliffe and a bottle of New Albion ale.

Opposite: New Albion ale.

Below: Jack with Jim Koch of the Boston Beer Company.

*CURIOSITIES

---

* experimental

* alternative

* leftfield

* innovative

* off-centre

Roll up, roll up, for the carnival of curiosities. Pay homage to the peculiar at this quirky curation of craft beer's oddities; an unabashed endorsement of the eccentricity, the individuality and the sheer madcap derring-do currently shaping beer at its most unusual and extreme.

You would be forgiven for thinking that the white coats worn by the brewers of these beers have those arms that tie up at the back. An unconventional bunch at their most strait-laced, here they push more envelopes than a drug-fuelled Lance Armstrong locked in a mailroom, paying back the multi-million dollar sponsorship owed to the US Postal Service.

These guys twist and bend beer like a circus strongman with an iron bar; they cheekily pull down the pants of the Reinheitsgebot purity law before walking it through the centre of town; they undermine and unsettle the common perception of what beer is supposed to be, leaving it sitting on the edge of a chair, blankets wrapped around its shoulders, sipping herbal tea from a cup that it can't stop rattling against the saucer.

In the beer world, this is the mysterious state run by a potty dictator wearing a hardly thought-out hat. These are the beers that David Lynch would drink. These beers baffle like a French teacher asking you to conjugate the verb 'aller' into all the compound tenses; this is brewing outside the box where unusual, esoteric ingredients are embraced with wild-eyed gusto.

Here beers are brewed with bacon and beetroot; Egyptian bread and Turkish figs; South American leaves laced with caffeine and sea buckthorn; wormwood; asparagus; chilli and bog myrtle. There are banana beers brewed in an old shoe factory; a cherry porter made on a former boot camp; and ales filtered through a tree trunk.

Take leave of your senses and step inside the chapter of curiosities.

LAUGHING IN THE FACE OF BREWING CONVENTION, THESE BEERS EPITOMISE THE ECCENTRICITY, THE INDIVIDUALITY AND THE SHEER MADCAP DERRING-DO CURRENTLY SHAPING BREWING AT ITS MOST UNUSUAL, ITS MOST IRREVERANT AND, SOMETIMES, ITS MOST EXCITING.

UK

Red Willow
Smokeless 5.7%
Cheshire, England
www.redwillowbrewery.com

Unlike Plaxico Burress, the American Football star who accidentally shot himself in the leg with a gun that he had stuck down his pants, Smokeless packs heat in a far more sensible manner. Spice and smoke comes courtesy of chipotle, a smoked jalapeño that this creative Macclesfield-based micro chose instead of smoked malt. Silky and softly spiced with a haze of smoke over the palate.

Saltaire
Hazelnut Coffee Porter 4.6%
Yorkshire, England
saltairebrewery.co.uk

From an impressive stone hall that formerly provided power for the trams of Bradford, Saltaire regularly ventures off-rail to great effect, especially with darker beers. This is a deep maroon porter pert with fresh coffee and hazelnut syrup. Note that I have fought the urge to write 'Nutella on toast'. Eh? Oh.

Waen
Blackberry Stout 3.8%
Powys, Wales
www.thewaenbrewery.co.uk

There are lots of British brewers who fling fruit into their beers but few achieve the subtlety and balance of this gorgeous blackberry stout, which punches well above its modest ABV. A quality calling card from one of Wales's many excellent micros.

Butternuts
Porkslap Pale Ale 4.2%
New York
www.butternutsbeerandale.com

A cult canned beer brewed in a barn on the outskirts of Cooperstown, this ginger-infused pale ale hangs out in New York's hipster haunts. Chucking the palate a curveball with the addition of spice, it's a little reminiscent of root beer and, a little like its website, a bit strange.

Craftsman Brewing
Triple White Sage Ale 9%
Los Angeles
www.craftsmanbrewing.com

From an industrial unit in Pasadena, Mark Jilg has been quietly fighting the good fight since 1995, delivering his softly-spoken idiosyncratic creations to local bars in a retro-1940s Studebaker truck. Other Craftsman ales have been accented with whole grapefruit and grapes, fresh lemons and lavender. This seasonal summer beer is a sinewy Belgian Tripel perked up with hand-picked white sage; the result is clean and perfumed, with hints of pine and grass.

Dogfish Head
Chateau Jiahu 9%
Delaware
www.dogfish.com

In 2006, as part of its Ancient Ales series and in cahoots with a molecular archaeologist, Dogfish sparked a 9,000 year-old Chinese recipe back to life. Like the original, the sugars come from mixed sources: rice, grapes and hawthorn berries, as well as malt, fermented with sake yeast, giving a dry tartness similar to a farmhouse cider and the tongue-tingling potency of sake.

Elysian Brewing
Avatar Jasmine IPA 6.3%
Seattle
www.elysianbrewing.com

It has been more than 15 years since Dick Cantwell, a huge figure in American craft brewing, opened a 20-barrel brewpub in Seattle's Capitol Hill neighbourhood. Further brewpubs followed and in 2011, a standalone brewery was unveiled in the city's Georgetown district. Despite its growth, Elysian still fields an acutely experimental, innovative and expansive team of great beers. This one is a fantastically fragrant and floral IPA dry 'hopped' with jasmine, which lifts the hop bitterness off the palate.

Left Hand
Good JuJu 4.5%
Colorado
www.lefthandbrewing.com

Known for its nitro milk stout, the first American nitro craft beer in a bottle, Left Hand Brewing has, for the past 20 years, been gradually growing into one of Colorado's more macro micros. While the stout is a landmark brew, an equally impressive achievement is brewing a balanced ginger beer. Here the ginger is gentle, with a lovely low heat to supplement the citrus notes of the hops – Centennial, US Golding and Sterling.

MateVeza
Morpho 6.5%
California
www.mateveza.com

Yerba mate, a highly caffeinated tea, is ubiquitous in Argentina but rare among beers. So bitter are its green leaves that Jim Woods, founder of MateVeza in 2007, adds them to the grain bill, since 'hopping' with yerba mate in the copper would make this organic hopless ale undrinkable for all but the most extremophile IBU-loving Imperial IPA drinker. The addition of hibiscus flowers and bay leaves evens out the astringency.

Maui Brewing Company
CoCoNut Porter 6%
Hawaii
www.mauibrewingco.com

If you've been looking for a rich, roasty and refreshing porter brewed in Hawaii using hand-toasted coconut and half-a-dozen varieties of roasted barley, and if you want all that delivered in a fine-looking funky can then this, my dear book-reading beer drinker, is what you've been waiting for. Supple and not overly sweet, it's a bit like an alcoholic Bounty bar in a tin.

Saint Somewhere
Saison Athene 7.5%
Florida
www.saintsomewherebrewing.com

Saint Somewhere's Belgian beers are more Belgian than the Belgians. Belgian malt is flown into Florida, where they create their own dark candy sugar and ferment their bottle-conditioned beers with a bespoke house yeast and, just before bottling, a burst of Brettanomyces. Whole leaf hops are joined by black pepper, rosemary and chamomile to leave a cider-like sourness, a peppery prickle on the palate and a dry, concise finish.

BEER VENUE
White Labs Tasting Rooms

Welcome to the White Labs tasting room; the ultimate chic beer geek experience.

An annex to one of the largest suppliers of brewing yeast in the United States, this not like any other bar or tasting room in the world and neither are the beers that it serves.

The tap handles are test tubes, chandeliers are fashioned from conical flasks and the walls are illustrated with the DNA of various yeast strains. On a 20-gallon brew system, small batches of beers are brewed and then divided into a number of individual demijohns and inoculated with separate yeast strains taken from White Lab's abundant bank.

After fermentation, each is connected to one of 32 taps and three handpumps so that drinkers can appreciate yeast's undeniable and individual influence on beer's flavour. Tasting the same beer fermented with half-a-dozen different strains is a unique beer-drinking experience and liquid proof that the magical micro-organisms can account for around 70% of beer's character.

As well as house beers and generic styles, White Labs also works with local Southern Californian brewers such as Alesmith and Ballast Point, taking their recognised beers, separating them into small batches before fermenting them with different yeast strains.

White Labs Tasting Room
9495 Candida Street
San Diego, CA 92126 USA
Tel: (858) 693-3441
www.whitelabs.com
Hours: Monday-Saturday: noon to 8 p.m.

Salmon Trout Fillet in Raspberry Beer

'A professional kitchen is a small world and every good chef has a mind of his own. Every once in a while this leads to interesting situations, when egos battle for preference. This recipe is the result of a bet that the combination of ingredients listed below would be a good one. Professional pride dictated that it be put on the menu and not be tried out beforehand. I won the bet.'

Peter Paul Stil of Eet & Bierlokaal de Molen.

Ingredients
• 1 salmon trout fillet with skin per person
• 1 tablespoon of raspberry vinegar
• 1 bottle of Framboise
• 1 sprig of fresh thyme
• Salt and pepper

Method
Rub the fillets with salt and pepper, put in a bowl. Add vinegar, beer and thyme until the fish is covered and keep cool for 24 hours.

Carefully pull off the skin. Serve at room temperature with a salad. Toss the salad with fresh herbs and good olive oil: don't add vinegar to the salad, the fish is good for that.

Uncommon Brewers
Bacon Brown Ale 6.8%
California
www.uncommonbrewers.com

Correct. A beer brewed with pork, no less. While others create a cured meat effect with smoked malt, Uncommon brewmaster Alec Stefansky goes the whole hog and drops actual pieces of applewood-cured bacon into the boil of a nut-brown ale at his Santa Cruz brewery, bolstering it with buckwheat. The swine presence is subtle, savoury with a smooth smokiness that shifts to the back on the finish. Light leather with a nutty undercurrent.

Westbrook
Vanilla Tree 7.5%
South Carolina
www.westbrookbrewing.com

A sexy-looking and sizeable stainless steel micro in Mount Pleasant, South Carolina, Westbrook is young but belies its age in the shape of some wonderful beers that emulate old-world European beer styles with an energetic, unabashed American accent. This one is a seamless, silken and very soft Belgian dubbel laid down on a bed of vanilla beans and toasted oak chips.

Short's Brewing
Cornholio 7%
Michigan
www.shortsbrewing.com

Like the three wise men but with smaller beards and less adventurous millinery, a triumvirate of craft brewers converged on Michigan bearing gifts from each of their home states. Dogfish Head brought beach plums from the sand dunes of Delaware, Three Floyds bequeathed roasted red popcorn, while horehound, a menthol-like herb that sounds like a brothel-creeping ne'er-do-well, was the gift from Short's. All three indigenous ingredients were added to the boil of this beefy Baltic-style porter (though it calls itself a dark lager) rich in ripe fruit, mint chocolate and a dusty, dry cocoa finish.

Stone Brewing/Dogfish Head/ Victory
Saison du BUFF 7.7%
San Diego
www.stonebrew.com

Fresh, funky and gorgeously grassy, Saison du BUFF was born in 2010 of three fathers; Greg Koch of Stone Brewing in California, Sam Calagione of Dogfish Head in Delaware and Bill Covaleski of Victory Brewing in Pennsylvania, who came together as Brewers United for Freedom of Flavor. Brewed three times, by each brewery, to the same recipe, this is a Belgian-style Saison seasoned with parsley, sage, rosemary and thyme (say — wasn't there a song about that?). The result is a beer that is herbal, a little bit menthol, with a gentle grainy dry wood finish.

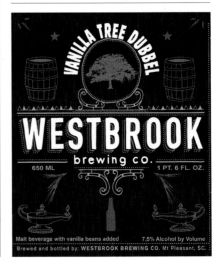

CANADA

Amsterdam Brewing Company
Framboise 6.5%
Toronto
www.amsterdambeer.com

Born as Toronto's first brewpub back in 1985, Amsterdam Brewing has blossomed into something bigger, and hits the right notes with this Belgian-inspired fruity flute-filler, which is fermented twice and brewed with six pounds of Canadian raspberries. Strikes a sublime balance between sweet and sour.

Garrison Brewing Company
Spruce Beer 7.5%
Nova Scotia
www.garrisonbrewing.com

Unwilling or unable to source imported European ingredients, colonial American brewers regularly went native and used fir, pine and spruce tips in lieu of hops, while fuelling fermentation with molasses instead of malt. This rich, honeyed treacle-like beer is a loyal resuscitation of a common colonial beer style: a palate of baked toffee apple, black pepper and stewed dried fruits. It's a little weird, but in a good way.

Muskoka
Winter Beard Double Chocolate Cranberry Stout 8%
Ontario
www.muskokabrewery.com

When winters in Ontario get whisker-whitening cold, this cracking cockle-warming cranberry stout is what's called for. A chewy, chocolate seasonal from the town of Bracebridge by a brewery whose ales are all unpasteurised, it brings together real cocoa, slightly bitter dark chocolate and local cranberries. Oily, elegant and erudite.

Spiritual Enlightenment

Monogamy tends to be the best policy with regards to one's love life, and it is certainly a must in the use of type fonts, but sticking just to the one simply does not make sense when it comes to discerning drinking. A growing number of brewers, increasingly unable to resist the Rubensesque allure of the alembic still, are playing the field with other fermentable forms and using beers as an inspiration for their spirits.

SPIRITS INSPIRED BY BEER

Adnams Brewery, Suffolk, England
Spirit of Broadside, 43% ABV
Adnams has created an eclectic selection of artisan spirits from its small seaside stills, situated opposite the brewery. As well as an absinthe, a limoncello, an oak-aged vodka and a gin, beer lovers should seek out 'Spirit of Broadside', a so-called bière-de-vie that uses the brewery's rich, red Broadside beer as a base.

Anchor Distilling, California, United States
Hophead Vodka, 45% ABV
Fritz Maytag was ahead of the rest when he set up a micro-distillery beneath the brewery back in 1993. Maintaining the small-batch philosophy that served Steam Beer so well, Anchor's Junipero gin and Old Potrero rye whiskeys have won myriad medals at spirits competitions. 2012 saw the launch of Hophead, a vodka infused with hops from Washington State.

New Holland Brewing, Michigan, United States.
Hatter Royale, 80% Proof
Centennial hops are steeped in a double-distilled spirit, made with a 100% barley wash, to create this herbal, aromatic white whiskey. It is one of several spirits made by New Holland, including a rum, gins and a bourbon matured in barrels that its beers previously called home.

Corsair Artisan Distillery, Nashville, Tennessee, United States
Rasputin hopped whiskey, 46% ABV
Down in Nashville, Tennessee, this hedonistic beer-spirit hybrid begins life as an Imperial Stout before being run through a column still stuffed with aromatic hops. It is then aged in charred oak barrels to create a very rare, rich, slightly hoppy and spicy whiskey.

G. Schneider & Son, Bavaria, Germany
Edelster Aventinus, 40% ABV
The legendary Bavarian weissbier brewer teamed up with the Schrami distillery nearby to turn its banoffee-pie–tasting Aventinus Weizenbock into a 'beer brandy'.

Kiuchi Brewery, Naka, Japan
Kiuchi No Shizuku, 43% ABV
Loosely translated as the 'initial drop from the still', this oak-aged woody distillate is created from Kiuchi's Hitachino Nest White Ale, a Belgian-style witbier brewed with nutmeg, orange peel, coriander and orange juice.

Wild Rose Brewery
Cherry Porter 6.6%
Alberta
www.wildrosebrewery.com

A boundary-bending brewery based on a former Canadian army boot camp in Calgary where Jackie Chan once filmed a movie, Wild Rose, founded in 1996, is self-described as the wildest ale-maker in Alberta. Yet this perfectly weighted porter, enriched with ripe and fleshy British Columbia cherries, and hinting at chocolate and plums, is a highly cultured, refined affair. It's Black Forest gateau in a blender: try it with ice-cream. Or even Black Forest gateau.

NETHERLANDS

De 3 Horne
Bananatana 7%
North Brabant
www.de3horne.nl

Bananas. A very funny-looking fruit. But brewers tend to lose their sense of humour when attempting to make beer with them, confusing fermentation and bringing wild yeast to the brewhouse. At his home in an old shoe factory in Kaatsheuvel, Sjef Groothuis is fearless when it comes to fruit beer, and he flings whole bananas and golden sultanas into the fermentation tanks to create this hazy, dark yellow beer with a name that sounds a bit like an all-girl pop group. There is big banana here, yet it's not too sickly, with more balance than one would expect. Best drunk while swinging in a tyre, blowing raspberries and doing a double armpit scratch.

GERMANY

Broumov Olivetin
Kvasnicák Coriander 5%
Eastern Bohemia
www.pivovarbroumov.cz

Originally a 14th-century monastic brewery, the beautiful brick Broumov brewery, set in bucolic countryside near the Polish border, has recently been passed round different hands like a hot car radio in a backstreet boozer. But in 2006, Opat (Abbot) was taken on by Jaroslav Nosek, who malts his own barley and brews several unfiltered lagers using esoteric ingredients such as black pepper, raspberry, laurel and honey. This great, grassy-kneed golden soft beer calls on coriander oils, which add spicy notes to a light cookie-dough base.

Freigeist Bierkultur
Deutscher Porter 8%
Cologne
www.braustelle.com

Freigeist means 'Free Spirit' and founders Sebastian Sauer and Peter Essel, inspired by Belgium and the United States, have placed a grenade down the lederhosen of conventional German brewing. Using the kit belonging to the Gasthaus-Brauerei Braustelle, a corner brewpub in Cologne, a city synonymous with clean and crisp Kölsch, Friegeist brews a wide gamut of German styles and resurrects historical native beers that have long vanished. As well as an unfiltered Kölsch (meaning it can't be called a Kölsch by law), a smoked Berliner Weiss and an awesome Alt, Sauer and Essel make this modern interpretation of a beer once brewed by the Dressler Brewery in Bremen and inspired by oak-aged 19th-century English porters, with a strong wood-dwelling Brett character. Both Brett and salt are used to funk up this tart, highly individual black porter.

Störtebeker
Glühbier 5%
Mecklenburg
www.stoertebeker.com

The brewery, in Stralsund on the German Baltic Coast, is named after a pirate in the Middle Ages who was like a seafaring, boozing Robin Hood – Störtebeker meant 'empty the mug with one gulp' in Low Saxon. From a solid stable of seven Störtebeker brews , the Schwarzbier is a stand-out, while this 'mulled' beer, served warm, works wonderfully as a spicy winter warmer, with flavours of cinnamon, cloves, honey and gingerbread. It MUST be heated up: it's not designed to be drunk cold.

CZECH REPUBLIC

Chodovar
Prezident Premium 5%
Chodová Planá
www.chodovar.cz

Drinking large quantities of beer can be bad for you. And can make you do and say silly things that you will often forget. But at Chodovar, a brewery dating back to 1473 and located in a region renowned for its hot springs, it is beer's health-giving properties that are championed in a soporific beer spa, where one's mind, body and soul are pampered with malted barley, hops, yeast and herbs. When not grinding grain into butt-cheeks, Chodovar brews this pleasantly creamy, citrus-kissed Pilsner made with malt from its own maltings. You have to find your own company to share a beer bath with, though.

DENMARK

Fanø
Coffee Grinder 11%
Nordby
www.fanoebryghus.dk

Much like the eponymous island on which it is situated, a mile west of the Danish mainland, Fanø brewery is a little out there. Set up in a former power station in 2006, it hit hard times and hibernated for six months in 2008 before getting a new lease of life a year later. Now firmly established, the brewery regularly collaborates with Copenhagen's famed flock of cuckoo brewers, and the occasional adventurous American, such as Hoppin' Frog of Ohio and Grassroots of Vermont. This is the Barry White of the imperial stout world; dark, deep in tone, enormous in every way, smooth, great with chocolate cake and sure to get you laid on a first date.

Herslev
Aspargesøl, 6.5%
Roskilde
www.herslevbryghus.dk

Asparagus is a very versatile vegetable. Not content with adorning one's bodily fluids with a distinct bouquet and actively encouraging their exchange in its role as an aphrodisiac, asparagus is also very good for you. Usually, in beer, however, asparagus aroma suggests a drop of diacetyl may be present. Here it is entirely intentional. A twist on Herslev's mellow Bavarian-style wheat beer, crisp spring asparagus is added during fermentation to give the beer a flavour akin to … er … asparagus. I'll level with you: you really do need to like eating asparagus to enjoy drinking this one.

Nørrebro
Little Korkny Ale 12.25%
Copenhagen
www.norrebrobryghus.dk

Nørrebro is a cracking brewpub and brewery founded in 2003 by Anders Kissmeyer, formerly of Carlsberg. Inspired by the American microbrewery explosion, Kissmeyer combines Carlsberg's scientific scruples with the rule-book ripping of a small brewer. Here in this Beer World Cup winner, Kissmeyer creates a voluptuous vintage ale, glowing dark gold and grainy, proudly parading port, molasses, fruitcake and crème caramel on the palate. Lay it down and wake it up when something special happens.

Skagen
Porse Øl 5.5%
North Jutland

www.skagenbryghus.dk

The Skagen brewpub, built into an old power station at Denmark's northern tip and hewn like a ship's hull, does not normally veer too far from standard styles, but pushes the boat out when it comes to its seasonals. This soft-bodied retro-revival of a traditional bog myrtle-flavoured ale has a pine-like perfume and a dry finish.

To Øl
Moccachino Messiah 7%
Copenhagen
www.to-ol.dk

To Øl, founded by Tobias Emil Jensen and Tore Gynther, two former school pupils of Mikkeler's Mikkel Borg Bjergso, are another 'cuckoo' or 'gypsy' brewer from Copenhagen. Their efforts range from accessible to extreme and many of their beers are, wisely, produced at the prolific De Proef Brewery in Flanders, Belgium. Coffee percolates through this buzzy brown breakfast ale, fleshed out with flaked oats, spiced with four aromatic New World hops and given creaminess with a generous splash of lactose.

ITALY

Birrificio Barley
BB10 10%
Sardinia
www.barley.it

Every year, immediately after the Sardinian vineyards are harvested, Birrificio Barley's brewmaster, Nicola Perra, takes Cannonau grapes (aka Grenache) and boils them at his brewery near Cagliari, for 16 hours, after which the sapa (a wine-like wort) is blended with 6 types of British barley before undergoing late-hopping with Cascade. This is a well-rounded, rumbustious dark maroon full-bodied sipper wonderful with roast lamb.

Del Ducato
New Morning 5.8%
Parma
www.birrificiodelducato.net

Brewer Giovanni Campari lives up to his surname with some unabashed bitter beers, including the blistering Machete IPA. But in New Morning, a Bob Dylan-inspired celebration of spring, Campari conjures up a field full of flowers using chamomile, ginger, green pepper and coriander. Layered on a bed of barley, flaked wheat and flaked rye, it is bracing, fabulously fresh, with a late flowering of Lambic-like funk.

Piccolo
Chiostro 5%
Liguria
www.piccolobirrificio.com

The tiny picturesque Alpine town of Apricale, not far from the French border, harbours a picturesque tiny brewery that is home to some handsome looking bottle-conditioned beers infused with herbs, fruits and spices. *Artemisia absinthium*, otherwise known as wormwood and infamous for making a mess of Fin de Siècle Paris, adds a bracing bitterness to the soft, mineral blonde ale.

FRANCE

Pietra
Colomba 5%
Corsica
www.brasseriepietra.com

Brasserie Pietra from the feisty island of Corsica is usually credited for inventing chestnut beer back in the 1990s, with the not very chestnutty Pietra amber lager. Colomba is possibly a more interesting beast: a blanche spiced with 'maquis' herbs that add an intriguing fresh thyme and rosemary edge to the dry fruity-citrusy wheat beer base.

Puisaye
La Grenouillette Cassis 5%
Burgundy

Such is the expectation in France that a fruit beer must be sweet, brewster Kate Hallett, who was a home-brewer for 10 years before going professional in 2007, likes to warn prospective drinkers that this balanced maroon mouthful from a farmhouse brewery in Yonne is dry and tart. It drinks remarkably easily though, the blackberries giving it a crisp, quenching character.

FAROE ISLANDS

Okkara
Rinkusteinur 5.8%
Velbastaður
www.okkara.fo

An ancient and acutely dangerous brewing technique is used to make this lush, smoky lager. An enormous lump of lava is heated in a ceramic oven up to a temperature of 800°C/1472°F before being dramatically dropped into the boil to heat up the wort. Once coated in rich, sticky caramelised malt sugars, the stone is taken out of the kettle, cooled down and reintroduced to the lagering tank, where it gets to reacquaint itself with the beer for six weeks. Hopped with Columbus and Nelson Sauvin, the beer is fragrant and phenolic.

LITHUANIA

Su Puta
Paliuniškio medutis 5.5%
Panevežys

Bubbling under the surface, barely acknowledged by the beer boffinsphere, lies the unlikely and relatively undiscovered Lithuanian craft brewing scene. The beers on the lips of locals range from dark lager and wheat beers to old-fashioned, rustic farmhouse ales, incorporating ingredients that surround the brewhouse. This copper-hued honey ale, herbal with a pinch of pecan nut, is one of myriad lesser-known Lithuanian gems.

AUSTRALIA

Red Duck Brewing
Queen Bee 6.6%
Victoria
www.redduckbeer.com.au

If you were to swing a cat in Red Duck's small brew house, you'd knock it out cold within a few seconds. So don't do that. Instead, marvel at a brewery that while diminutive in output, is big in brewing ideas. Rhubarb jam, Egyptian bread and gruit star in Red Duck's limited-release resuscitations of ancient recipes but this unfiltered, bottle-conditioned porter, infused with bush honey, is especially sought after. Nutty, jammy plum notes with a figgy finish.

Redoak Boutique Brewery
Framboise Ferment 5.2%
Sidney
www.redoak.com.au

Redoak has been flying the flag of flavoursome beers since 2005. Founder David Hollyoak began homebrewing long before it was legal to do so and his first beer was this one – a dry, tart and lovely layered raspberry beer now brewed with hand-picked fruit from the Yarra Valley in Victoria. It has an initial big, sweet raspberry character, followed by a long, satisfying, sour send-off. Serve in a Champagne flute with chunks of dark chocolate.

NEW ZEALAND

Epic Brewing
Epicurean Coffee & Fig Imperial Oatmeal Stout 8%
Auckland
www.epicbeer.com

Kelly Ryan, formerly of the UK's excellent Thornbridge Brewing and now late of Epic, was the brewing brains behind this exotic imperial stout. He mixed caramelised Turkish figs into the boil alongside a healthy crop of Cascade, then added Ethiopian coffee to the wort before sprinkling toasted fresh coconut, prior to lengthy cold-conditioning. Its legs strengthened by eight different malts, including CaraAmber and CaraAroma , this is a broad-set, brooding black stout with Camp coffee and chicory on the nose, and a touch of aniseed and liquorice too. On the palate, stewed dark fruit stir in the background while espresso gives you the eyeballs up front. A sublime shapeshifting stout.

Garage Project
Venusian Pale Ale 7.3%
Wellington
www.garageproject.co.nz

Founded in 2011, Garage Project is a young whippersnapper on Wellington's rich craft beer scene whose output is prolific, precocious and pushes the perceptions of what beer can be. After a full-on local forage, brothers Pete and Ian Gillespie and Jos Ruffel created a fragrant, zesty Saison-style summer beer seasoned with kaffir lime, lemongrass and grapefruit peel.

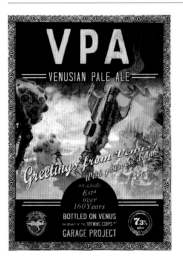

Moa Brewing
Breakfast 5.5%
Blenheim
www.moabeer.com

Using only locally grown New Zealand hops, Moa treats its beer to barrel-ageing and Methode Champenoise refermentation in the bottle, but please don't tell the French as they get a bit moody about things like that. While Moa Pinot and Moa Blanc are wonderful beers, this is the most different – a crisp, clear lager brewed with wheat and bursting with cherry freshness. Almond and vanilla do a Hakka on the hooter with some strong, juicy cherry notes on the palate, as sweet and sour swing each other round. Unique and lovely.

JAPAN

Coedo
Beniaka 7%
Saitama
www.coedobrewery.com

Coedo's home city of Kawagoe, about 30km outside Tokyo, is mainly famous for one thing: purple-skinned sweet potatoes known as Kintoki. On Kawagoe's main drag, street vendors sell sweet potato ice cream, sweet potato coffee and sweet potato crisps. So it was no surprise when Coedo used sweet potatoes in its first beer back in 1996. Beniaka is a crisp, crimson and surprisingly full-bodied nutty lager.

Sekinoichi
Iwate Kura Oyster Stout 7%
Ichinoseki
www.sekinoichi.co.jp

Sekinoichi, a sake and beer brewer in the northern prefecture of Ichinoseki, sources oysters from Hirota Bay, a region renowned for Japan's most beautiful bivalve molluscs. A quartet of malts, some roasted, gifts this stout its deep dark brown hue, but it is the addition of oysters and a striking alcohol content that give the beer its robust body and mouth-filling rich flavour.

BRAZIL

Bodebrown
Perigrosa Imperial Milk Stout 21%
Paraná
www.bodebrown.com.br

Both a brewery and a brewing school, Bodebrown, based in the southern Brazilian city of Curitiba, provides instruction and inspiration to Brazil's embryonic small beer scene. While adhering to the Reinheitsgebot, Bodebrown's beers aren't slaves to style, nor do they play it safe. This is Bodebrown's biggest beer, an imperious ink-black lactose-laced milk stout that also comes in a more potent, viscous and velvety bourbon barrel-aged version.

MEXICO

Cucapá
Tequila Barrel-Aged Ale 10%
Mexicali
www.cucapa.com

Not far from the Californian border, in the town of Mexicali, the Cucapá brewery has created what it claims to be the world's first and only beer aged in tequila barrels. 'Green Card', Cucapá's flagship no-nonsense West Coast barley wine, is put in wood for 6 months to produce a beer with tight tannins, Mezcal-like dusty notes, a touch of smoke and lots of wood.

La Chingonería
Házmela Rusa 7%
Mexico City
www.lachingoneria.com.mx

In 2012, this chipotle-noted imperial stout crossed the border, scooped a gold medal for the chocolate beer category at the World Beer Cup in San Diego, then came back again.

MY TOP 5 CRAFT BEERS

Bryan Baird
Baird Brewing
Nomazu, Japan

✳ **Anchor Liberty Ale**
Really the first true American west coast style hoppy ale. Every beer that Fritz Maytag put out at Anchor was notable and each served as inspiration for the next generation of craft brewers.

✳ **Sierra Nevada Pale Ale**
This wonderful ale, more than any other, has paved the way for the world craft beer renaissance. It is so flavourful in such as clean, balanced and nuanced way. I could drink several every day for the rest of my life.

✳ **Orval**
The most idiosyncratically complex, fascinating beer I have ever imbibed. This beer woke me up to the glories of Belgian beer culture.

✳ **Victory Prima Pils**
A perfectly balanced, refreshing Pilsner lager with loads of flavour and character. This is what a Pilsner should be.

✳ **Russian River Pliny the Elder**
Vinnie Cilurzo is the master of hop-forward beers. They burst with hop character without ever losing balance. This beer inspired our own Suruga Bay Imperial IPA.

BEER COCKTAILS

There are those who refuse to give beer cocktails their blessing, believing them to be an unnecessary and unnatural union.

And given the acutely average offspring produced in the past, such caution is understandable.

But, as history shows, the coming together of beer and other ingredients in the form of a cocktail can be a harmonious one. As far back as the 1400s, people were drinking possets, (a mix of beer, milk and spices), while the traditional wassail bowl was a mix of ale, sweet wine (or sherry), ginger and sugar, and the 'lambswool wassail', which featured in Robert Herrick's 1640s poem 'Twelfe-Night', added grated baked apples and nutmeg to the mix.

In *How to Mix Drinks*, the first ever true cocktail tome, written by the legendary Jerry Thomas in 1862, beer-based beverages abound.

The book features the ale flip, hailed as a 'finely frothed' cure for a cold, which was served hot by thrusting a glowing poker into a concoction made of beer, eggs and sugar fortified by sherry, rum or Madeira.

The potent porter cup saw a bottle of porter mixed with a bottle of ale, a glass of brandy, some nutmeg, sugar, cucumber, bicarbonate of soda and ginger syrup. Once covered up, Jerry wrote, 'expose it to the cold for half an hour'.

Today there are several classic beer cocktails: the Black Velvet, a simple yet sublime embrace of strong stout with Champagne; the Mexican Michelada, light lager served in a salt-rimmed highball and seasoned with Tabasco sauce, salt and pepper and Worcestershire sauce; and the Boilermaker, a shot of whisk(e)y plunged into a glass of Pilsner or alternatively, drunk alongside each other.

But in these times of increasingly daring drinking derring-do, bartenders and mixologists are finding inspiration in their fridges, pushing the boundaries of creativity and increasingly bringing beer into the mix.

Above left: Shaky Pete's Ginger Brew.

Above right: Lagerita.

Right: Lambswool.

Oskar Kinberg, Dabbous Bar

Oskar Kinberg, bartender and director of Dabbous Bar & Restaurant in Fitzrovia, London: 'Beer boasts a broad spectrum of flavours and styles, so why shouldn't it be considered an integral ingredient in cocktails? It can be used simply as a lengthener or a sweetener; it can smooth out hard edges of spirits. The thing to avoid is over-complication. Keep it simple and let the beer and spirit combine rather than clash. If you're thinking of mixing a delicate elderflower liqueur with an imperial stout, then may I suggest, you have a rethink.'

BEER GRYLLS

- Shake 20ml Diplomatico Blanco, 20ml crème de banana, 15ml Domain de Canton liqueur, 5ml manuka honey 15ml lime juice
- Strain into a wine glass and top up with Einstok white ale

BLUE MOON LAGOON

- Shake 35ml Mezcal, 25ml Golden Falernum, 10ml lime juice, 10ml agave and 25ml orange juice
- Strain into a tankard and add 330ml of Blue Moon wheat beer

GIDDY UP

- Shake 25ml Tapatio Blanco; 10ml elderflower cordial, 25ml Bramley and Gage Slider, 10ml lemon juice; 20ml chamomile-infused acacia honey
- Strain into a tankard and top up with 330ml Sierra Nevada Pale Ale

MUMMA

A twist on a Swedish Christmas drink

- Mix together 330ml light lager, 330ml porter, 200ml ginger ale, 50ml gin infused with cardamom, 25ml Akvavit, 50ml port
- Make sure it's all cold and serve

DEAD COBBLER

Designed by Ryan Chetiyawardana, an award-winning barman and world-class bartender from Edinburgh

- Muddle 2 slices orange and one slice grapefruit.
- Add 15ml redcurrant syrup and 30ml gin.
- Short shake, dump all into a Singapore sling and top with Brewdog's Dead Pony.
- Garnish with a skewered slice of pink grapefruit.

BOIL YOUR MAKER

- Stir two parts whisk(e)y with one part beer vermouth* over cubed ice.
- Strain into a chilled coup and garnish with a cherry.
- Strain and chill.

* Beer vermouth is made by vac-packing beer with sugar, botanicals and spirit and then blasting in the microwave.

LAMBSWOOL

A centuries-old concoction taken from Robert Herrick's 1640s poem, 'Twelfe-Night'.

- Core 6 apples and bake at 100°C/212°F for an hour.
- Dissolve 150g/5oz brown sugar with two litres of stout or porter in a pan and add 1 tablespoon of pureed ginger and one freshly grated nutmeg.
- Stir and simmer (do not let the beer boil: it makes the bitterness too harsh).
- Remove the flesh from the apple, blend, and stir into the ale.
- Pour the mixture between two pans to get a bit of froth going and serve in a heated tankard.

SHAKY PETE'S GINGER BREW

Created by Pete Jeary, the head drinks honcho at the legendary Hawksmoor Restaurants in London.

- Shake 50ml lemon juice, 50ml ginger syrup and 35ml Beefeater gin with 4 or 5 ice cubes.
- Strain into a tankard.
- Top up with 100ml London Pride and stir twice.

MEAT LIQUOR LAGERITA

Invented by Soul Shakers, UK-based designers of devilishly dapper drinks, this twist on a Margarita is a favourite at Meat Liquor, the finest burger joint in all of London town.

Glass: highball or tankard

- Blend 35ml Blanco Tequila with 15ml Cointreau and 10ml simple syrup in a cup of crushed ice.
- Pour into a chilled highball or tankard and top with 50ml Hobo Craft Czech Lager

RUM FLIP

A creation from New England dating back to 1690.

- Mix 140cl beer with 24cl aged rum in a 2-litre pitcher.
- Sweeten with molasses or dried pumpkin.
- Stir with a red-hot poker.

Serve after cancelling all next-day appointments.

DEL DUCATO

Parma, Italy www.birrificiodelducato.net

Not content with their hi-falutin' ham and wheels of elegant cheese, their tasty tortellini and wonderful wines, Parma's swinging basket of gastronomic goodness now includes some rather decadent beer too.

Birrifico De Ducato, perched on Italy's upper thigh, in the small town of Le Roncole, is one of the country's classiest, most creative craft breweries. Brewmaster Giovanni Campari, handsome and hirsute, with a build that belies the epicurean enticements around him, exemplifies all that is enchanting and unique about Italian beer culture.

Campari is a former food scientist whose fondness for fermentation took him from the kitchen to the brew kettle, and his beers, like many others that have been instrumental in the Italian craft beer renaissance, sit hand in glove with the nation's 'slow food' movement.

Like many of his craft brewing countrymen, Campari uses an array of indigenous and inventive ingredients including chilli, chamomile, green pepper and liquorice. But it is not just in the pantry where he reaches for his inspiration.

Fittingly for a brewery based in the birthplace of Giuseppe Verdi, Campari calls on music as his main muse. 'Music evokes feelings and ideas that materials find difficult,' he says. 'I always draw comparisons with music when I talk to people about my beer. Everyone has their own sense of harmony within them. Someone who is educated in music will discover the nuances of a symphony by Mozart or Beethoven at a deep level but, equally, the "man of the street" will be touched by the warm beauty and harmony of the music.'

His father was a professor of cinema and his mother a teacher of Italian literature, and Campari studied classics at high school. But he was seduced by science, and began homebrewing at University.

Campari was then taken under the wing of Agostino Arioli at Birrificio Italiano, one of the key characters in Italy's genteel brewing revolution, and the creator of the legendary Tipopils.

'Agostino inspired me a lot,' Campari says. 'He taught me how to manage fermentation. But above all I was fascinated more by the man than the brewer. He has an admirable philosophical approach that is reflected in his beers.'

The DNA of many of Campari's beers date back to in-depth discussions with Agostino, whose Germanic leanings can be traced in Ducato's Via Emilia, an award-winning kellerbier named after the ancient Roman road that ran north from the Adriatic coast to the River Po.

This award-winning best-seller is dry-hopped with Tettnang hop that Campari hand-picks just before the harvest. Lagered for three weeks, it is floral and faintly fruity with just enough bitterness to challenge the local cheese and charcuterie.

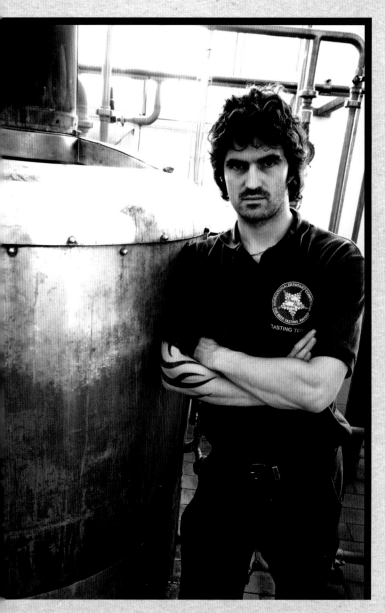

As his surname would suggest, Campari likes a bit of bitterness in there, too. Machete Double IPA is an aggressive ode to America while Bitter Ale is a more discreet doff of the bowler hat towards England's session style.

after its disaster in 2009 (see pages 196–97), he drove to Belgium, siphoned three barrels of 18-month-old Lambic into his tanker, and drove it back again.

It now forms the base beer of Beersel Morning, a subtly sour Saison made up of a blend of Lambic and New Morning. La Luna Rossa, meanwhile, is a Flemish Red-cum-kriek made from a blend of different aged barrels, some of which have held local, sour Morello cherries for a minimum of 6 months.

'It's the most difficult beer I brew,' Campari admits. 'The process is closer to wine than beer. When it's time for blending I turn myself into an oenologist, I try to keep my style every year but every cuvee is quite different from the others.

'The most difficult part of the job is trying to predict how the blend will develop in the years to come. But, to be honest, that's the bit I love most about my job!'

Unlike some other Italian brewers, Campari's stylistic embellishments are neither gimmicky nor gratuitous. 'Sometimes I want to be loyal to traditional beer styles and sometimes I want to push the boundaries and explore new frontiers,' Campari says. 'But what else is tradition if not a successful innovation?'

Grounded in Campari's scientific schooling, each unusual ingredient comes wrapped in reason: oats for a smoother mouthfeel; peppercorns for freshness; and hot pepper in the Verdi Imperial Stout because, he says, chocolate and chilli is a classic match: 'The heat of the chilli deconstructs the fullness of the beer, giving a better finish and leaving the throat ready for another sip.'

Beer, Campari insists, is an articulation of the individual. Wine is a mere idiom of its ingredients. 'Wine is first of all an expression of the terroir, while beer is more an expression of the brewmaster,' he says. 'In the brewing process there are many variables that we can adjust to obtain an infinite range of results. Making beer is a way to express myself, like a novel is for a writer.

'My intention is to create a beer that delivers insights,' Campari says. 'I am truly fulfilled when, after a long research, I can finally "taste" those same emotions in my glass of beer – and it is even more gratifying when others are able to describe, in their own words, what I wanted to express. It makes me feel I was able to communicate something meaningful.'

While European influences abound in his beers, Campari, like Italy itself, has developed a style distinctive in its diversity. 'I have no brewing style, like I don't have a favourite meal,' he says. 'Our beers are very balanced and fine. They are not ordinary, they have culture, style and a special touch that make them different. Our brewing philosophy is to brew beers that, no matter how complex they can be, are always balanced and easy to drink.' As his surname would suggest, Campari likes a bit of bitterness in there, too. Machete Double IPA is an aggressive ode to America, while Bitter Ale is a more discreet doff of the bowler hat towards England's session style.

But of the European brewing nations, it is Belgium that energises Campari the most. Keen to help out Drie Fonteinen

Left: The brewery and beer bottles at Le Roncole.

Above: Del Ducato's Giovanni Campari.

KEY BEERS
Verdi Imperial Stout 8.2%
Nuova Mattina 5.8%
VIÆMILIA (Via Emilia) 5%
Winterlude Tripel 8%
Chimera 8%
L'Ultima Luna 13%

Above: The brewery in Amsterdam's red light district.

Above left: Fer Kok (left) and Arno Kooy.

Left: Johnny is an easy-sipping salute to Johnny Jordaan, a Dutch soprano who specialised in tearjerkers. He was known as 'The Pearl', or De Parel in Dutch, and his nickname was the name initially adopted by the brewery, 'We thought it worked well, as those with mental issues have a hard life but there's the odd laugh along the way - and you shed a tear when you laugh and cry,' Fer said. Bottles were made, labels were printed and beer mats were ordered. And then came a letter from lawyers at another Dutch brewing concern, Budels Brewery, insisting that, as Budels had a Parel beer, Fer and Arno would have to rename their operation. So they shuffled the letters around. The choice was either De Prael (an old-fashioned word meaning 'extravagant') or De Lepar. They opted, rather wisely, for the former.

DE PRAEL

De Wallen, Amsterdam, The Netherlands deprael.nl

Fer Kok is sat opposite in the bar of the De Prael Brewery. He's a tall man. He's proudly plonked his Willy on the table and there is an unopened Johnny sat next to it. It's 10am in Amsterdam's red light district and we have only just met.

Even for Europe's most notorious neighbourhood, this seems a surreal scenario. Then again, De Prael is not a normal brewery. Surrounded by peddlers of pleasure and coffee shops hawking herbal highs, De Prael offers people a different kind of escape.

While Willy (a dark Dubbel) and Johnny (a crisp, unfiltered Kölsch-style beer) do a fine line in lightening life's load a little, De Prael's ale-making altruism extends well beyond the beer.

Those that work here, from brewing and bottling the beer to cleaning the canteen and delivering kegs to bars, suffer from varying degrees of mental illness and have all experienced psychological problems of some kind. For them, the brewhouse serves as a safe place, a source of solace for those who find life rather frightening. 'People feel that the world is a nasty place and they want to feel safe,' said Fer, the brewery's co-founder. 'Not feeling safe is a problem for a lot of people. I like to think people feel this is a safe place to be.'

De Prael was started in 2002 by Fer and Arno Kooy, two psychiatric nurses working in an Amsterdam hospital, helping patients back on their feet and finding them voluntary work. 'Back then, we needed money,' Fer said, 'and we liked hanging out with strange people.'

Fer and Arno also liked making unusual ales. Disillusioned by taste-a-like Pilsner beers, the duo brewed in pots and pans for people's birthdays and weddings. Before long, they dovetailed their hobby with the work at the hospital, and De Prael was born. 'The jobs we'd been sending patients to do kept people occupied, but they kept coming back to the hospital,' Fer said. 'There was very little pride in what they were doing. We wanted to create a business that people could genuinely be proud of.'

Using second-hand dairy equipment, they built a basic brewhouse in west Amsterdam. The makeshift micro provided a haven for more than 50 people, some suffering from schizophrenia, others manic depressives or with personality disorders. But while the priority remained the people, the beers were selling extremely well.

'The beers were merely a by-product of the business,' Arno said. 'But more people wanted to drink them and, crucially, more people wanted to work with us.' The pair, no longer able to survive solely on social funding, realised the beers needed to make money, and a bigger brewery was required.

In 2008, De Prael relocated to De Wallen, Amsterdam's red light district, moving into a former paper mill and auction room that, more recently, had been the Last Watering Hole, a gritty good times bar notorious for being a little bit naughty.

Now it houses a brewery, a pub, a tasting room and a shop, as well as a hop garden, where employees grow Tettnang, Saaz, Magnum and Challenger. It is, however, a crazy place to build a brewery – cramped, small, with little or no access. All the ingredients arrive by a canal boat which then takes the beer away. An out-of-town industrial estate, however, wasn't an option. 'We needed to be in an area where the issues surround us and we fitted in. Historically, this area has been very bad – lots of hookers and junkies struggling to get it together,' Fer said. 'We bring structure and a culture here. It's been a bad neighbourhood but efforts are being made to clean it up.'

A brewery run by mental patients in the red light district surrounded by drugs and debauchery? 'A lot of people think it's a crazy idea,' grinned Fer, gesturing out of his window at the working women in their windows. 'But somehow it works.' Is working with alcohol, a well-known depressant, appropriate employment for the mentally ill? 'We are strict from day one. If you drink on the job, you lose the job,' Fer said. 'This is a professional business,' Arno added, 'not a party or a prison.'

Of the hundreds of people De Prael has employed, five have an alcohol dependency. 'The difference from any other business in the world, is that we know exactly who they are – it's in their files,' Fer said. 'Walk into any other business on the planet and there'll be those with drinking problems, but they'll be anonymous.' Only four employees have been dismissed. 'Two were drinking, one was discovered smoking a joint outside the brewery,' Arno said, 'and then there was another guy who, for some reason, liked standing in water and playing with the electricity. So he had to go too.'

Training workers is difficult, as concentration levels tend to be low. Focusing is a challenge for some, and people forget things. 'The strength of the brewery is being a warm, welcoming place,' Arno added. 'That has to be the main focus: to create a safe place where people are proud of their beer.'

There is plenty to be proud about. De Prael is inspired mainly by Belgian brewing traditions, with the odd American or German influence. All the beers are unfiltered, and each is named after a famous Dutch crooner.

'Our beers are romantic, they're little dreams in a glass,' Fer said. 'Brewing is more than a profession, it should be fun. The philosophy with the beers is that people must enjoy them. Life's hard, but drinking a beer shouldn't be.'

KEY BEERS

Mary 9.6%
Johnny 5.7%
Willeke 7.5%
Heintje 5.4%
Nelis 7.7%

* SIPPER

---

* baltic

* tripel

* barley wine

* imperial

* coffee beer

Given that the beers found within the following pages range from 7% to 12% ABV, it would be irresponsible to not alert you to the dangers of alcohol when imbibed in excess.

Alcohol, as we all know, is a fickle friend who can fast become a foe. Like a dwarf who flunked out of college, it is neither big nor clever to drink too much.

Alcohol impedes the function of the central nervous system. In lesser quantities, it can induce a sense of euphoria and diminish inhibitions, while in larger doses, it will generate sluggish brain activity, decreased motor function, slurred speech, lethargy and memory loss. It can also generate memory loss.

But it would be an error to assume that alcohol's only role in brewing is as a mere problem-solver. As well as being an affability accelerator, a highly effective ennui eraser, beer of higher strength is beloved by brewers for its ability to carry more character.

As anyone who has drunk non-alcoholic beers can vouch, it is almost impossible to coax the best out of barley, yeast and hops without alcohol on the scene. Brewing beer with no alcohol is like taking Picasso's canvas away and asking him to paint a masterpiece on cellophane, or requesting the Philharmonic Orchestra to create a concerto using just a kazoo and a kettle drum.

Not only is alcohol the vehicle on which other ingredients deliver depth and bring breadth, it is also an important flavour contributor without which beer would be bereft of fruity esters and that wonderful warming sensation which makes everything seem a lot better.

'Sipper' spans a gamut of styles ranging from smoked beers to Tripels, robust rye ales and Baltic stouts to imperial porters and big Belgian darks. These may be big beers but they all have a deftness of touch and a complexity deserving of quiet and considered contemplation.

Oh, and if you're reading this while operating heavy machinery then please, for everyone's sake, stop.

POTENT, PROFOUND AND IN NO WAY INTENDED FOR OPERATORS OF HEAVY MACHINERY, THESE BEERS ARE ALL IMMENSE, INTENSE AFFAIRS WITH CONSIDERABLE STRENGTH AND DEPTH, DESERVING OF MATURE AND MEASURED CONTEMPLATION.

UK

Green Jack
Baltic Trader 10.5%
Suffolk, England
www.green-jack.co.uk

While this sizeable Suffolk brewer is home to several hop-heavy brews, using both old world and new world varieties, it is not averse to knocking one off the grist now and again. Served from a 70cl swing-top with a ship on the label, this is a classic Baltic porter from the crown of its big mink hat to the toes of its leather slip-ons. Bigger than a dancing bear and just as sweet, there is a smouldering smokiness with a grainy undercurrent.

Marble
Chocolate 5.5%
Manchester, England
www.marblebeers.co.uk

Marble is a Mancunian brewer that goes about its business with a quiet, and entirely justified, confidence. Even down in that London town I've never met a 'meh' Marble pint, and its excellent Earl Grey IPA, a collaboration with Emelisse from the Netherlands, is a great beer. Of Marble's core craft beers, though, this beautifully balanced porter-mild, all mocha and liquorice, attains all its chocolate notes solely from heavily kilned malts. A fantastic dark beer.

Sharps
Honey Spice Tripel 10%
Cornwall, England
www.sharpsbrewery.co.uk

When the massive multinational Molson Coors bought Sharp's Brewery back in 2011 for a whopping £20m, many wondered whether its head brewer, Stuart Howe, would be allowed the freedom to flex his creative muscles. Making beers for the 'Connoisseurs Choice' line is where Stuart can go a little maverick with the mash fork. The honey here is subtle and soothing, enlivened by an untethered Trappist yeast, coriander and citrus peel. Dry and drinkable for a beer of such strength, it is warming with notes of bubble gum and a waxy, resinous finish.

IRELAND

Franciscan Well Brewing
Shandon Export Stout 7.5%
Cork
www.franciscanwellbrewery.com

The story goes that this brewery and brewpub is built on the site of a Franciscan monastery whose well water was supposed to cure everything from gout and tuberculosis to smallpox and itchy balls. This dark and deep

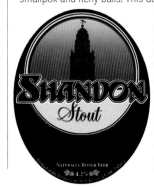

Irish export stout certainly makes you feel better, with its briny palate, chocolate compôte-like texture and treacly finish of Demerara rum.

US

Dark Horse
Reserve Special Black Ale 7.5%
Michigan
www.darkhorsebrewery.com

As with all dark horses, one to watch. Started as a small brewing stable by Aaron Morse back in 1997, this micro and taproom in Marshall, Lower Michigan has made its name with bold, balls-to-the-wall beer that is big on balance, too. Somewhere between an imperial porter and a strapping stout, this ink-black bruiser tumbles thickly over the tongue, with rich roasty notes, coffee cream and vanilla and a late lacing of liquorice.

Flying Dog
Gonzo Imperial Porter 9.2%
Denver
www.flyingdogales.com

Flying Dog has howled in the face of conventional brewing wherever it goes. Its beer filled the fridge of the late, great Gonzo journalist Hunter S Thompson and in 2005, after Thompson took his own life and his ashes were fired out of a cannon, Flying Dog released this special beer in his honour. A black oil slick of chocolate, chicory and heavily roasted coffee with a coarse smoky farewell, it makes a rambunctious boilermaker with a shot of Stranahan's Colorado Whiskey dropped down into the dark abyss. Now a year-rounder, its bottles are, like all the beers in Flying Dog's kennel, adorned with the anarchic art of Hunter's English illustrator, Ralph Steadman.

Durden Park Beer Circle

It was easy to be a disillusioned British beer drinker in 1971. Cask ale sales were shrinking like a crisp packet in a fire, gormless British brewers were cosying up to keg beer and faceless yellow fizz was gaining a foothold.

With conformity replacing charisma and character, miffed groups of men began to sow the seeds of mutiny. The most famous uprising occurred in a pub on the most westernmost point of Ireland where four men formed CAMRA (then standing for Campaign for the Revitalisation of Ale), whose fame at the forefront of the fight against bland beer is well-known.

But in West London, meanwhile, a more refined revolt was occurring. A group of homebrewers had begun to regularly gather in a tin shed perched on the edge of Durden Cricket Club in Southall, a suburb known more for its Asian community than its ale.

While they shared CAMRA's contempt for characterless beer, the mission of these men was less frontline fighting and more one of retro reconnaissance. With the late Dr John Harrison at its helm, the Durden Park Beer Circle blew the dust from old brewing tomes and began faithfully recreating beers from the 18th and 19th centuries.

Like the Bletchley Park of beer, the circle's members meticulously unravelled complicated codes, these ones composed centuries earlier by brewers worried that their recipes would be stolen by rivals. Some even breathed life back into types of barley malt that were, by then, no longer being commercially made.

The Durden Park Beer Circle is still spoken of by homebrewers in hallowed terms and its book *Old British Beer and How To Make Them*, refreshingly straightforward in its title, remains the last word on little-known, long-forgotten British beer styles.

Demystifying the brewing techniques of yesteryear, it includes more than 120 recipes ranging from Imperial Double Stouts and Mild to Irish Porters, London Porters, Scotch ales and even the lesser-spotted March and October ales.

The Durden Park Beer Circle, still a rich source of historical and brewing endeavour, continues to accurately recreate old ales and inspire a new breed of brewers increasingly looking to the past for inspiration.

Midnight Sun
Panty Peeler 8.5%
Alaska
www.midnightsunbrewing.com

Midnight Sun is an incredibly accomplished and ambitious South Anchorage brewer with an extremely loyal local cult following. One of many bottle-conditioned beers brewed with a distinctly Belgian burr, this Tripel is fuelled by a funky, fruity Belgian yeast and emphatically seasoned with orange peel and coriander: a gorgeous blonde that goes down very easily. Stop sniggering at the back.

Oskar Blues
Ten Fidy Imperial Stout 10.5%
Colorado
www.oskarblues.com

Founded in 1997 as a brewpub in Colorado, and considered the creator of canned craft beer, Oskar Blues has extended its reach beyond the Rockies and in 2012 broke the 100,000 barrels barrier to become one of America's top 50 biggest craft breweries. While Dale's Pale Ale may be the commercial powerhouse, malt advocates migrate towards this viscid, nutty vortex of flaked oats and chocolate malt. There is hop here too though, with nearly 100 IBUs adding chilli to the chocolate character.

Pretty Things
Jack D'Or 6.5%
Massachussetts
www.prettythingsbeertoday.com

A misty, slightly sour and smoky Saison-style sip from Dann and Martha Paquette, a couple of cuckoo brewers who create some truly magnificent beers in Massachusetts. Grainy with green apple and Belgian funk lifted on a tide of tight carbonation. Watch out for the Once Upon A Time Series, too, a growing range of historical retro-recreations that have been brewed in association with beer historians such as Ron Pattinson.

Southern Tier Brewing
Mokah 11.2%
New York
www.stbcbeer.com

The barista and the brewer come together in this lovechild born of two of Southern Tier's enormous imperial stouts, Choklat and Jahva. Dark chocolate from Belgium and roasted coffee from New York percolate through this decadent perk-me-up best drunk once pretty, fragrant womenfolk have withdrawn to do the dishes and the discussion turns to the gold standard and other such masculine affairs.

Victory
Storm King Stout, 9.1%
Pennsylvania
www.victorybeer.com

It calls itself a stout but dances dangerously close to an astringent dark IPA courtesy of copious Pacific Northwest hops. Sweet and spicy, it's a turbulent swirl of cigar box wood, molasses and a port-like finish.

CANADA

Charlevoix
Dominus Vobiscum Double 8%
Quebec
www.microbrasserie.com

From the copper-clad brewhouse in Baie-Saint-Paul that sprang out of the town's Le Saint-pub, founded in 1998 and shifted to larger premises in 2009, Charlevoix brews with a broadly Belgian bent, and this dark brown Dubbel with a name that means 'the Lord be with you' in Latin draws from the fine monastic brewing traditions of the Lowlands. Spice, sweetness and hop bitterness all work in tandem; it's a deep swirl of star anise and liquorice, Madeira and cinnamon, with a soft cedarwood finale. Bottle-conditioned, it will evolve happily over three years. Try the brewery's Tripel, at 9% alcohol a fruity, peppery, warming snorter.

Dieu du Ciel
Péché Mortel 9.5%
Montreal
www.dieuduciel.com

First brewed in Montreal back in 2001, and with a name meaning 'Mortal Sin', this cult coffee stout from Quebec comes courtesy of head brewer and co-founder Jean-François Gravel, a highly imaginative Canadian brewer unafraid to experiment with intriguing ingredients. Fair Trade coffee adorns this jet black beer with an acutely intense freshly ground espresso aroma, while melodious malts and a strong hop presence lend it labyrinthine layers of mocha, chocolate, cherry, cocoa and chicory before a sultry smoky stretched out send-off.

RJ
Snoreau 7%
Montreal
www.brasseursrj.com

A Quebecois Christmas beer brewed with cranberries from a big Montreal brewer that was formed when three micros merged in 1998, naming the new concern after the bossman, Roger Jaar. Somewhat sour with a rich cranberry backdrop and a scent of cinnamon and clove, this bottle-conditioned beer's tartness ties in perfectly with cold turkey sandwiches.

BELGIUM

Abbaye du Val Dieu
Triple 9%
Liège
www.val-dieu.com

Unique among abbey brewers who brew elsewhere, Val Dieu's brewhouse can, since 1996, be found within the walls of a Cistercian Abbey that dates back to the 13th century. The only reason it cannot title itself as Trappist is that laymen rather than monks brew the traditional trio of beers: a Blonde; a Brune and a tight and tidy Triple. Warming, banana and apricot, custard cream and honey.

Affligem
Tripel 9.5%
Brabant
www.affligem.biz

Affiliated to an eponymous monastery formed back in 1074 and with a strong history in both the Belgian and British hop trade (it owned hop gardens in Kent), Affligem is an impressive abbey brewery now situated in nearby Opwijk. It is currently owned by Heineken but, if anything, consistency and quality has improved considerably, with the Tripel an especially alluring affair. Huge herbal hop character; a golden rum-like finish with peach and pepper on the palate.

Beer Chocolates

'Good brewers make good barley wines, strong and sweet, with the fruit and the bitter flavours of the hops. This recipe originated after a discussion about the Bommen & Granaten. Menno [Olivier] declared the beer was so sweet you could pair it with chocolate. I had an enthusiastic apprentice in the kitchen I had to keep busy.In an inspired moment I dictated this recipe. It has been one of our most closely guarded secrets but so what.'

Peter Paul Stil of Eet & Bierlokaal de Molen

Ingredients
• 75g/3oz butter
• 150g/6oz milk chocolate
• 100ml/4 fl oz cream
• 2 tablespoons Golden Syrup
• 1 teaspoon vanilla essence
• 200ml/7 fl oz Bommen & Granaten
• Empty dark chocolate cups
• Dark chocolate to top off

Method
Melt the butter, milk chocolate, cream, syrup and vanilla essence in a bain marie or in a glass bowl placed over a saucepan of just-simmering water.

Remove from heat and add the beer. Let cool down and fill the cups just below the top. Freeze to solidify.

Melt the dark chocolate and spread over the top. The first time your kitchen will be covered in chocolate as well but the result is worth it.

St Bernardus
St Bernardus Abt 12 10.5%
West Flanders
www.sintbernardus.be

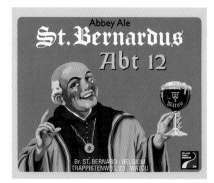

Like restaurants that show photos of their meals on the menu, I'm always a little suspicious of brewers who put pictures of smiling monks on their bottle labels: I can't help think that there must be some hoodwinking happening beneath the habit. But that is not the case with St Bernardus, an honest, hard-working and handsome-looking brewery founded in Watou, in 1946. For years it was known as St Sixtus, when it was licensed to brew a trio of well-made Westvleteren clones, but when the licence was revoked in 1992, it brewed its own brand of beers. While strikingly similar to the St Sixtus range, they have grown in stature over the years, and this brownish-bronze barley wine broadens out when left to its own devices. Not shy in its candi sugar content, it revels in long periods of fermentation and maturation where the bitterness and dark fruit conjoin to create several strata of sweetness; ripe plums, pistachio, dried figs, raisin and a leathery, liquorice finish.

Silly
Scotch Silly 7.5%
Hainault
www.silly-beer.com

Only just beating Dave for the title of Belgium's daftest town name, Silly is home to an excellent eponymous brewery. The presence in Silly of a Scottish regiment after World War I inspired this Walloon Wee Heavy, brewed with Kentish and Hallertau hops and a trio of malts. Rich and robust with an earthy, nutty aroma, its malt-driven mahogany-coloured body flexes full-on fruit flavours – plums, cherries, prunes and a touch of toffee apple.

Verhaeghe
Duchesse de Bourgogne 6.2%
West Flanders
www.brouwerijverhaeghe.be

The Verhaege family, a key Flanders brewing clan since the 16th century, has a rightly renowned reputation for its exceptional oak-aged brown ales and is a grand master in the Flemish art of beer blending. Echt Kriekenbier, matured on a bed of whole cherries, is a classic tart kriek while Vichtenaar is a terrific toe-in-the-door introduction to the style. The Duchesse, meanwhile, is rich, gently sour and velvet smooth with a sweetness that seems to have been tempered in recent times.

NETHERLANDS

't Ij
Struis 9%
Amsterdam
www.brouwerijhetij.nl

An organic, unfiltered, dry, heavily toasted dark beer that swings stylistically between stout and a barley wine. The strongest (in both senses of the word) served up at this great little brewpub in east Amsterdam, located beneath a windmill. Ij sounds a bit like the Dutch word for ostrich – hence the presence of the long-legged, large egg-laying bird which, like Dutch football legend Dennis Bergkamp, doesn't fly.

Klein Duimpje
Erik de Noorman 9.5%
South Holland
www.kleinduimpje.nl

As a rule of (small) thumb, this miniature micro situated just south of Haarlem tends to perform well despite a quite prolific output of different styles. Blue Tram Tripel is an appealing abbey beer, but brewmaster Erik Bouman cranks up the complexity here: herbal notes, stewed apples, golden syrup and, somehow, soy sauce. Leaner in body and booze than most barley wines.

Mommeriete
Special Rookbock 7%
Overijssel
www.mommeriete.nl

Started in 2004 by Gert and Karina Kelder and situated on the River Vechte, near the German border, this most diminutive of Dutch brewers has earned plaudits for both its Belgian beers. But its Bocks, brewed on its German-built Kaspar Schulz brewhouse, are worth seeking out at Dutch beer festivals too, especially this hybrid hazelnut-hued smoked beer brewed with Bamberg malt. A sweet Rauchbier with soft smoke, molasses, dried fruit and a clipped bitter finish.

De Pelgrim
Mayflower Tripel 7.3%
Rotterdam
www.pelgrimbier.nl

Rotterdam is not the most picturesque of places. But ale lovers should head to Delfshaven, where the Pilgrims moored before setting sail for America in 1620 on the Mayflower. They have inspired the name of a cosy, wooden-beamed brewpub steered by a former Heineken brewer. It crafts an array of robust ales, including a superb heavy stout, and VSOP, a broad-shouldered barley wine. But this blonde Belgian beer, exhilarated with coriander and orange peel, is a distinctively fruity and floral Tripel. Superb with De Pelgrim's own bread and cheese.

De Prael
Willy 7.5%
Ansterdam
www.deprael.nl

The original De Prael ale, a strong yet subtle winter warmer, ideal after a long day window shopping in Amsterdam's red light district. Rich, spicy and warm with a dark fruit finale – get your gums round those plums.

Texels
Bockbier 7%
Oudeschild
www.speciaalbier.com

The peaceful and picturesque island of Texel is the largest and most western of the Friesian islands, an archipelago that dots itself from the Netherland towards Denmark. People go there to get away from it all, gawp at birds through binoculars, cycle about,

saunter in sand dunes and kick back with a beer. Its eponymous microbrewery, pronounced Tessel, is based in the fishing village of Oudeschild and brews on a copper brewhouse using barley grown on the island and dune-filtered water. This bock is top beer in a terrific trio of top-fermented beers that go with the grain rather than the hop. Long lagering and a rich mix of roasted malt deliver depth that develops in the bottle. Fresh supplies are released every autumn.

ITALY

Amarcord
Riserva Speciale 9%
Rimini
www.birraamarcord.it

Like Tony Soprano, Jake La Motta and Yogi Berra, this is a complex, potentially dangerous Italian-American with lots of character. A well-built, wistful wheat ale flavoured with local fruits and honey, it was created by Garrett Oliver of Brooklyn Brewery, one of America's most inventive ale-makers, and inspired by Tonino Guerra, Federico Fellini's screenwriter on the film after which the brewery is named. Tonino designed the labels and lived locally until his death in 2012. Summer fruits and a fine 'Champagne' fizz, with hints of almond, apricot and aniseed.

Bi-Du
Artigian Ale 6.2%
Como
lebirredelbidu.altervista.org

Begun as a brewpub by the illustrious Beppe Vento, and now a stand-alone micro near the Swiss border, Bi-Du elicits admiration for its archetypal Italian out-there ales. A very well-balanced ruby-bronze Extra Special Bitter bedecked in dry fruit and a whole load of hop fragrance.

Karma
Cubulteria 6.8%
Campania
www.birrakarma.com

Many of Italy's most impressive breweries hail from the north, but there is some super stuff being brewed down south too.

Unpasteurised, unfiltered and conditioned in some sexy-looking 33cl bottles, Karma's beers embrace esoteric, indigenous ingredients where they deem it right to do so. Orange peel and coriander are what give this assertive hazy golden Tripel, brewed with a little bit of wheat, its spicy citric swagger, before ending dry and assertive.

DENMARK

Hornbeer
The Fundamental Blackhorn 11%
North Zealand
www.hornbeer.dk

Jurgen Fogh Rasmussen is a former homebrewer with a hugely fertile brewing imagination and, since turning professional in 2008, his crop of craft beer is as vast as it is varied. Displaying typical Danish chutzpah, this smooth Sasquatch of an imperial stout hits you hard with wholesome hop and then dabs your bewildered taste buds with real honey and gentle pecks of soothing chocolate. Maturation over oak and walnut acts as ballast to the bitterness, bringing in tobacco, liquorice, fig, caramel and vanilla.

Ugly Duck
Imperial Vanilla Coffee Porter 10%
Funen
www.uglyduckbrewing.dk

Ugly Duck is the 'cool' arm of the Indslev Bryggeri, a daring Danish brewery that replaces barley in a lot of its beers. It makes quite the impression here, however, coming together with copious amounts of coffee and a decent dash of vanilla. A bit shouty at first, it simmers down and settles with a bit of warmth to make a smoky, post-prandial porter, perfect with a shot of rum and a chunk of dark chocolate.

NORWAY

Nøgne Ø
Dark Horizon 18%
Grimstad
www.nogne-o.com

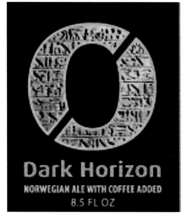

Kjetil Jikiun and Tor Jessen never brew this satin-cloaked sledgehammer of a stout the same way twice. All you know is that it's going to be intense, immense and both imperial and international in its ingredients. Powered by an enormous English malt cake and dollops of dark molasses devoured by wine yeast from Canada, the original Dark Horizon was perked up with Columbian coffee before being hopped long and hard. Designed for those days when the weather gets a little grim in Grimstad, which it does up there in the northern nosebleed that is Norway.

SWEDEN

Slottskällans
Slottskällans Imperial Stout 9%
Uppsala
www.slottskallan.se

Slottskällens, a seriously solid brewery, was started in 1997 after duty-free salesman Hans Finell experienced a beer-drinking 'awakening' on the west coast of America. This burly, black beauty of a porter belongs to the Baltic and is brewed in Uppsala, 45 miles north of Stockholm, home to thousands of students.

FRANCE

L'Agrivoise
Sans Dessus Dessous 7.5%
Ardèche
www.lagrivoise.fr

The Ardèche is France's version of the G-spot. People tell you how wonderful it is but not many really know where it is and, let's be honest, even fewer have ever been there. But deep in the north of the region, in Saint Agrève, Xavier Clerget brews this innuendo-laden dark ale meaning 'topsy-turvy' and, in more common parlance, head-to-toe hanky panky. It is brewed at an original gravity of 1069, mashed at 69°C and hopped at 69 IBU – do you see what the cheeky chap has done there? It is, unsurprisingly, exceptionally fruity, and finishes with a bitter taste in the mouth.

SWITZERLAND

Ticinese
Two Penny 8.15%
Ticino
www.badattitude.ch

Based literally yards away from the Italian border, in Stabio, at the southernmost tip of Switzerland, the Birrificio Ticinese radically overhauled its beer range in 2010, introducing the Bad Attitude range, fronted by Two Penny, a very rounded, slightly heretic porter with a rich roasty profile.

AUSTRIA

Schloss Eggenberg
Urbock 23° 9.6%
Gmunden
www.schloss-eggenberg.at

Aged for nine months, this Doppelbock deviously emanates an amber innocence which disguises an intense array of flavours and rich fruity esters: cooked pear and stewed apple with a middle of mulled cider and cloves. Check it with a good mature cheese.

Beer and Snails

Squirrels that sink their nuts into the soil; weeds; insouciant urban foxes; the next door neighbours' uninvited ivy; and slugs and snails. Of all these infamous garden vandals, only the last one can be banished with beer.

Snails love a saucer of ale, but as hopeless swimmers (it can't be easy doing breaststroke with your house on your back), drinking inevitably turns into drowning, and their affection for ale ends up being a fatal one.

What green-fingered grim reapers may like to know, however, is which beers are snails particularly susceptible to? Findings from an experiment in 2012 (unprecedented in its scientific rigour) offered searing insight into their drinking habits.

Lacklustre lagers simply will not do (they're snails, not morons), and while golden ales and hoppy pale ales caught the odd antenna, the beers they liked most were those that really go with the grain, malty mouthfuls full of fruity esters with a decent slug of alcohol in them. Several made speedy glistening tracks to Marston's Pedigree (a soft spot for the Burton Snatch perhaps?), while Theakston's Old Peculier and Robinson's Old Tom proved similarly popular.

Think Extra Special Bitters, Bocks, strong stouts and maybe, at a push, a Vienna lager. But remember, they're drinking in the last chance saloon, so give them something decent, give them a beer to die for.

SLOVAKIA

KALTENECKER
Pivovar BIER Rožňava

Kaltenecker
Archa 9%
Košice
kaltenecker.sk

Founded in 1997, this small micro in Slovakia's mining region leaves its enormously impressive imperial stout to mature for 11 months. English Challenger and Northdown hops hand this huge heavyweight Baltic-style stout an earthy citrus spice that livens up a backdrop of roasted barley and smoked malt. Ash-like bitterness on the finish.

ICELAND

Ölvisholt
Lava 9.4%
Suðurland
www.brugghus.is

This farmhouse brewery-cum-dairy in an isolated idyll in southern Iceland endured an enormous earthquake when it opened in 2008. From the brewery's front door, the oft-erupting Hekla volcano can be seen in the distance, and, inspired by Hekla's viscid flow, brewer and proprietor Jón Gunnlaugsson created this smoky imperial stout, fuelled by half-a-dozen varieties of barley malt and two English hops, the modern First Gold and the older, earthy Fuggles. Tightly packed fruit cake flavours, dry bitter espresso notes, rum-soaked cherries, black leather and a soothing smoky finish.

AUSTRALIA

Holgate
Beelzebub's Jewels 12%
Victoria
www.holgatebrewhouse.com

In the Macedon Ranges, 40 miles from Melbourne, Paul and Natasha Colgate create classy, classic ales inspired by their travels in America and Australia in a brewery inside a restored 19th century hotel. A brooding Belgian quadrupel, created in honour of Holgate's sales manager, 'Jules' Nelson, unleashed once every year and aged in Pinot Noir barrels (the 2011 release was aged in French oak barrels from the award-winning local winery Curly Flat) this beer reveals red berries beneath its deep cloudy, rusty reddish hue, along with toffee, caramel, raisins, vanilla and dried fruit, and a warming, tart tannin to finish. Beelzebub means 'Lord of the flies' – but you'll find no flies on this beer.

NEW ZEALAND

8 Wired
iStout 10%
Marlborough
www.8wired.co.nz

Kiwis use No 8 wire to pretty much fix anything, it's like Down Under's version of duct tape, and also the name given to a practical Kiwi chap who, with the most basic of tools, can turn his hand to anything. Søren Eriksen, a Dane brimming with creative derring-do, does the bulk of 8 Wired's work at Renaissance Brewing in Marlborough on the South Island. Even Eriksen's most idiosyncratic interpretations of classic styles, such as the acutely acerbic Super Conductor Double IPA, bear plenty of balance. But it is on the darker side of the beer world where the Dane particularly excels, such as with this mammoth, tumbling All Black beer, a seven-strong mix of pale and dark malts that pours a thick, viscous dark brown. With roaring, roasty, toasty aroma and resinous molasses on the finish, it still manages to drink a lot easier than its double-digit ABV might suggest.

Yeastie Boys
Rex Attitude 7%
Wellington
www.yeastieboys.co.nz

Sam Possenniskie and Stu McKinlay are a couple of Kiwi cuckoo brewers creating craft beers unprecedented in their cunning. The Invercargill Brewery, on the southernmost tip of New Zealand, is where the duo bring their unique beers to life including an IPA brewed with Earl Grey Blue Flower Tea; and this, proclaimed to be the first beer brewed using entirely peat-smoked malt. One for the Islay whisky lovers, this phenolic phenomenon evokes images of a Lapsang Souchong-sipping, iodine-soaked smoked kipper doing laps in a loch of Laphroaig. Think the elbow-patches on a geography teacher's jacket, the hot knees of campfire trousers, and the whiff of Winston Churchill's leather-topped desk after a long night drinking drams and chomping on cigars. Smoky doesn't even comes close.

BRAZIL

Anner
Maria Degolada 10.5%
Porto Alegre
www.cervejaanner.com

A wonderfully well-appointed Triple first brewed to honour the Bierkeller in Porto Alegre (considered by many to be the best beer bar in Brazil), which is pretty much the only place you can buy it. Grainy and golden with a rounded earthy edge, it is tricky to tell whether the beer gets its peppery tang nose from the gruit or the bittering hops. An irritatingly rare beer but very well spoken of by those who have found it.

Baden Baden
Double Red Ale 9.2%
São Paulo
www.badenbaden.com.br

So good they named the brewery twice, Baden Baden is situated in the Swiss-themed chocolate-box town of Campos do Jordão, the highest city in Brazil, at more than 5,000 feet above sea-level. Opened in 1999, it blazed a stylistic style with this ballsy barley wine, the maroon hue of a sun-kissed fairground worker. Full-bodied, and filled with fruitcake and Amontillado sherry.

ARGENTINA

Antares
Stout Imperial 8.5%
Buenos Aires
www.cervezaantares.com

Brewpub operators do not always deliver quality craft beer but Antares, dotted all over Buenos Aires, is more than just a cookie-cutter chain churning out unambitious ales. The most impressive all-year effort is this rich and mellow muscular roast malt-driven stout, which works wonders with succulent steaks and cold meats.

Beagle
Beagle Negra 7.8%
Tierra del Fuego
www.cervezabeagle.com.ar

Located in Ushuaia, Tierra del Fuego, the southernmost city in the world, and named after the ship that brought Charles Darwin to Argentina in the early 19th century,

the Beagle brewery is home to three classically-trained ales. After five days hiking in the Martial Mountains and clambering over glaciers and watching penguins muck about, I drank this soporific, silky tawny porter with my feet in a bowl of hot water while watching the sun drift down below the Beagle Channel. The bowl of hot water is by no means essential to appreciate its charms. Nor, for that matter, the charms of any of the brewery's other beers, which include an IPA and a golden ale.

Jerome
Diablo 7.5%
Mendoza,
www.cervezajerome.com

Deep in Argentina's Malbec country and very much part of the local epicurean slow food movement, Jerome was begun by the late Eduardo Maccari in 1983. Having helped rescue a Czech man who had got into trouble in the Andes, Maccari visited Pilsen where, drinking Pilsner Urquell, he experienced an alcoholic epiphany. Now in the hands of Eduardo's son, the small five-barrel plant deftly apes European beers and works wonders with wine-soaked wood sourced from local Malbec wineries. While many of the best beers can be found at the brewery tap, this perky, balanced Belgian pale ale with the devilish name performs perfectly well in bottle.

JAPAN

Minoh Beer
Imperial Stout 8.5%
Osaka
www.minoh-beer.jp

Half an hour outside Osaka, the epicurean epicentre of Japan, Minoh is one of the more maverick micros in Japan. It is run by two sisters, Mayuko and Kaori Ohshita, and they craft some excellent eye-catching

beers, including a wonderful weizen and a heady, hoppy IPA, all with great-looking labels. This orbicular Imperial stout is a maelstrom of rich chocolate malt, cocoa powder and dark cherry which won three top prizes at the World Beer Awards in 2010, including World's Best Stout & Porter.

EXTREME BEERS

Considered by some as courageous, cutting-edge creativity, yet wearily dismissed by others as an indulgent, attention-seeking affectation, extreme beer tends to excite and exasperate in equal measure.

But every art form needs its iconoclasts and brewing is no different. Just like fine art, cinema and theatre, beer has its very own versions of Jackson Pollock, Lars von Trier and Samuel Beckett. An impish, unruly element, they rattle craft beer's cage, explore new genres, loosen the screws of stylistic convention and peer at beer through an alternative prism, taking it to places where it's never been before – or ever really dreamt of going.

They are the envelope-pushing practitioners of 'extreme beer', employing unorthodox ingredients, twisting on traditional brewing techniques and cajoling yeast and hops to achieve unprecedented levels of alcohol and IBUs.

While firmly entrenched in the modern craft brewing lexicon, extreme beer is by no means a new phenomenon. Brewing with heather, white hot stones and juniper twigs may appear acutely idiosyncratic now but, rewind a few, and it was considered craft brewing at its most conventional.

Back in 2001, archaeological boffins on the Scottish island of Orkney excavated a 5,000 year-old pub and brewery whose beer was brewed using hemlock, nightshade and baked cow dung. At the time of writing, no 21st-century brewery has yet unleashed an extreme beer made from poison and excrement, even though some may taste as if they have.

Scottish tribes aside, the birthplace of extreme beer was most definitely Belgium. Unlike their neighbours in Germany, Belgium refused to be strait-jacketed by purity laws. They may not be the craziest craft brewers now, but the Belgians are the original punks of brewing, anarchic creators of esoteric ales whose brewing traditions embraced the unusual in both ingredients and approach.

Yet, today, it's the Americans where 'extreme beer' is extolled with the most enthusiasm and, it is claimed, where the term was first coined when, in 1994, Jim Koch of the Boston Beer Company released 'Triple Bock'. It was a beer Jim – but not as we know it. Packaged in a 250ml cobalt blue bottle, aged for several months in whiskey barrels and weighing in at 17.5% ABV, it was dark purple, flat and served like a spirit in small measures from crystal glasses. It wasn't just the strongest beer in history at the time, it was arguably the most unusual.

Five years later, Samuel Adams pushed its yeast further with the rare Millennium (20% ABV) before unleashing Utopias, a beer brewed at high gravity and kept in a combination of casks that have previously contained port, whiskey, cognac or Scotch. Blended and released every year in a copper-shaped, decanter-style bottle – and sipped from a special snifter glass – its peers are not beers but top-shelf spirits.

Mikkeller Craft Beer Bar

It is very difficult to dislike the cut of Copenhagen's jib.

From the furniture to the fashion, and even the food, everything looks incredibly at ease with itself. Gorgeous blondes float by on bikes, there are cobbled streets, impressive architecture, artisan shops run by handsome hunks called Hans and, of course, some rather remarkable beer venues.

Mikkel Borg Bjergsø is the main man of Copenhagen's craft beer scene. Not content with being the world's most renowned gypsy brewer and the brains behind some of the most innovative collaborative beers, the man known as Mikkeller has created the Copenhagen Beer Celebration, a two-day craft beer ballyhoo featuring Bjergsø's artisan associates and like-minded craft brewers.

Unsurprisingly, he has also opened a splendid craft beer bar in Copenhagen's Vesterbro district. Disillusioned with boorish beer venues, he teamed up with the Danish design bureau Femmes Regionales to create a craft beer venue where the uncompromising approach to the drink is paralleled by the design.

Sunk down below street level, it walks the right line between cool and cosy, with bare tungsten bulbs, vases filled with flowers, low lighting and wooden tables and benches set against white-washed walls. Shiny black tiles mark out the bar, where a forest of taps dispenses a regularly rotating range of beers running the full gamut of styles.

Beers classic and contemporary are chalked up on the blackboard above the bar. As well as Mikkeller's own beers and one-off exclusives, the likes of Rodenbach and Cantillon rub shoulders with global Mikkeller collaborators such as Stillwater, Kernel, Fanø, De Molen and Nøgne Ø.

The bar, regularly awash with impressive facial hair, tattoos, skinny jeans and ambitious millinery, really comes to life during May, when the Copenhagen Beer Celebration and the separate Copenhagen Beer Festival draw craft beer cognoscenti from all around the world.

Mikkeller
Viktoriagade 8
1620 Copenhagen
Denmark
mikkeller.dk/the-bar

Alcoholic Arms Race

Utopias has long been usurped in strength by Brewdog in Scotland and the German brewer Schorschbrau. Their pursuit of even greater ABV escalated into an attention-grabbing, and some would say unseemly, game of alcoholic one-upmanship fuelled by freeze distillation (a process originally used for Eisbock, whereby water is frozen and removed from the beer to make it stronger).

The first potent punch was thrown in 2008 when Schorschbrau unveiled an Eisbock-style effort (31% ABV) lagered for six months at very low temperatures. Within a year, Brewdog raised the bar by 1% with Tactical Nuclear Penguin, an imperial stout stored in an ice cream factory at -20°C/-4°F.

The German retort, an even bigger bock beer at 40%, was almost instantly excelled by an antagonistic 41% IPA called Sink The Bismarck, which, in turn, was outdone by Schorsbrau's 43% Schorschbock.

Brewdog then blew the doors off with The End of History, a 55% elixir packaged in various forms of taxidermied weasels, squirrels and rodents. Many expected, and hoped, that would be it. But the stubborn Schorsbrau came off the ropes to release Finis Coronat Opus, a 57% final word on the matter… for now.

Predictably, righteous indignation and faux media outrage followed each and every release while many doubted whether new-fangled fermentations of this strength can be considered 'beer'.

Arguably the most infamous advocate of the extreme is Dogfish Head's brewer Sam Calagione. Wackiness can be irritating in the hands of some, but Sam's unconventional approach, more wily and worldly than most, is rooted in reason and research.

Starting in the mid-1990s with a stout steeped with St John's Wort and organic Mexican coffee, his 'out-there' ales are brewed with justified chutzpah and a fearless quest to create new flavours. Gregarious and genuinely gonzo, he famously partnered with a molecular archaeologist to unearth several ancient ale recipes featuring chrysanthenum flowers, Aztec cocoa powder, Arabic herbs and loaves of baked bread.

Other ingredients have included arctic cloudberry, algae, agave nectar and Viognier grapes, while one beer, a brew inspired by Peru called Chicha, was created using masticated maize that is chewed into small caked mouthfuls, spat out, dried and thrown into the sterile mash.

'The Reheinstgebot is nothing more than a relatively modern form of art censorship,' said Sam Calagione. 'Long before the Bavarians told us what we should all be drinking, every culture was making beautiful, exotic beers made with indigenous ingredients.'

Yet, amid the esoteric efforts, traditional hops are at the heart of Sam's headline beers. Inspired by a TV chef who found fuller flavours from seasoning his soups at various stages, rather than at the beginning and the end, Sam created 'Sir-Hops-A-Lot', a custom-built juddering gadget made from an old gridiron game that continuously hopped his beers for the duration of the boil.

Not content with his 90 minute, 60 minute and 120 minute (18% ABV) IPAs, Sam heralded his hoppy hedonism with the creation of Randal The Enamel Animal, a kind of fresh leaf hop bong that is filled with beer in the bar, infusing it with extra hoppiness and aroma.

Even though the human palate struggles to distinguish hop bitterness beyond a certain IBU (thought to be around 70), that hasn't stopped brewers, mostly of American origin, engaging in a chest-beating IBU arms race culminating in Alpha Fornication, an imperial IPA with 2400 IBUs and brewed by the Flying Monkeys Brewery in Canada.

Elsewhere, Ithaca Brewing scorched the Scorville scale with a beer aged in Tabasco barrels; Mikkeller blended Beer Geek Brunch using coffee made with beans that have been passed through a weasel; while the Uncommon Brewery even brews beer with bacon.

While a little daft and not always designed to be drunk, extreme beer does add drama and dynamism to one of the oldest drinks in the world. Those that seek to diminish such daring derring-do would do well to remember that some of the best ideas are borne out of a carefree creative climate.

And lest we forget, the likes of Josef Groll, Gabriel Sedlmayr and Ken Grossman were all considered 'extreme brewers' once.

Above: The weekly 'Agoraphobics Anonymous' meeting at Mikkeller's in Copenhagen.

Above: Just some of Nøgne Ø's eclectic range.

Below: Nøgne Ø's brewhouse in Grimstad, at night.

Below right: Where Kjetil Jikiun ages his beers.

NØGNE Ø

Grimstad, Norway www.nogne-o.com

Nurg Nay Eurrr: An early morning mumble into a pillow; the groan exhaled on being winded; or an incoherent, awkward introduction of Nigel to Naomi – unsure of who's who.

This is how you say it: Nøgne Ø, meaning 'Naked Isle'. Try not to imagine chubby Swedish chaps playing badminton in their birthday suits but rather romantic barren outcrops off Norway's southern coast that nose their way out of the stormy North Sea.

The name is taken from 'Terje Vigen', a poem by the 19th-century Norwegian playwright Henrik Ibsen, who lived in Grimstad, home of Nøgne Ø, and who, if you take a peek at some old pictures, bears a canny resemblance to its brewmaster, Kjetil Jikiun.

Not just the burly build and shock of rowdy coarse hair but the remarkable booming beard too, their wild whiskers tied into two neat pigtails. But it's there that the resemblance runs aground. If accounts of Ibsen are to be believed, Jikiun is of a far more upbeat disposition; charming and chucklesome, the kind of chap you would like to go for a beer and a chat with.

Before he was a brewer, Jikiun flew planes, and still does. First a flight instructor and then working long-haul with Scandinavian Airlines, he was stationed in Malaysia for two years and also spent six months living in Pakistan, flying for the Red Cross to Afghanistan.

Twenty years of travelling opened his eyes to better beer. It was the flights to the United States, he says, that were most crucial. 'At that time, in the late 1990s, America was the only place in the world where you could walk into a bar and find beers from Britain, Germany and Belgium, all under one roof.'

With nothing like that in Norway, Jikiun started homebrewing in 1996. Norway had no homebrew shops, so Jikiun had to make do with malt extracts and any grains, hops and yeast he could source overseas. He would brew different styles, picking one, 'brewing it until I thought I'd perfected it,' and then moving on. The epiphany was my first successfully homebrewed IPA,' he says. 'It made me so happy, joyful and proud. I thought, "If I can make this, then I can make other people happy." I can make them feel good – and I am not talking about alcohol here,' he says. 'I'm talking about flavour.'

At a Norwegian homebrewing competition in 2000, however, the beer bombed. His American IPA, of which he was so very proud, limped home in second to last place in the 'light coloured ales' category. The judges, recalls Jikiun, declared it too hoppy and not in style. 'They simply were not exposed to the American interpretation of the style,' he says. 'It made me realise the distance between my perception of good beer and that of the Norwegian beer drinking public. I absolutely hated it and realised that I had to go professional,' Jikiun says. 'Someone had to take the responsibility of exposing these ignorant people to new beer experiences.'

In 2002, the year Nøgne Ø was launched, Norway's brewing landscape was dominated by light lagers, with little else other than the odd ersatz Irish stout and a seldom-spotted German Weissbier. 'This is the other reason we called it Naked Isle,' Jikiun says. 'It was a barren, bare beer scene and we were ignorant amateurs with homebrewing equipment who didn't know how to run a company.'

Everything about Norway said 'No'. Jikiun and co-founder Tor Jessen faced the highest alcohol taxes in the world; some of Europe's most expensive labour costs; a ban on alcohol advertising; and a law that bans the sale of strong beers in grocery stores, regardless of how flavoursome they are.

Norwegians weaned on tasteless lager, did not understand Nøgne Ø's ales. 'People said our products were not beer, but some weird foul-tasting stuff we had invented,' Jikiun says. 'But we kept our faith in flavour, and 7,000 hectolitres of our beer were consumed in Norway last year.

'I am very proud that we have changed the Norwegian beer culture,' he says. 'We have had an impact on a whole nation's relationship with beer.'

From its base in an old hydroelectric power plant built in 1914, perched on a river and surrounded by farmland and forest, the 'Uncompromising Brewery' exports a lot of its beers too, and Jikiun has collaborated with a veritable who's who of craft brewers: Jolly Pumpkin, Stone, Brewdog, Renaissance and 8 Wired.

Assertive yet balanced, Nøgne Ø's style is stationed somewhere in the middle of the Atlantic, yet it casts its stylistic net far and wide; from a light session British bitter to a smoking Bamburg Rauchbier via imperial stout, Belgian wits, an unfiltered Czech Pilsner primed with a liberal smattering of Saaz and, its best seller, a classic American IPA brewed with Maris Otter barley and American Cascade hops.

The beer, Jikiun says, should have integrity and drinkability: 'You should always be clear what beer style you are drinking and the beer should taste well all the way to the end.

'When you are finished, then you should feel like having another. But most of all I want people to have that same magical feeling I had when I tasted my first successful IPA.'

Assertive yet balanced, Nøgne Ø's style is stationed somewhere in the middle of the Atlantic, yet it casts its stylistic net far and wide; from a light session British bitter to a smoking Bamburg Rauchbier via imperial stout, Belgian wits, an unfiltered Czech Pilsner primed with a liberal smattering of Saaz and, its best seller, a classic American IPA brewed with Maris Otter barley and American Cascade hops.

SAKE

Nøgne Ø is Europe's first sake brewery. After several years of talking and working with sake producers all over Japan, Jikiun began brewing acutely traditional, old-style sake using the Yamahai method.

'It's the hardest fermented drink to make in the world,' he says. 'Yamahai sake has very low acidity and ferments with naturally occurring lactic bacteria.'

Jikiun brews half-a-dozen sakes which, like his beers, are bold and equally uncompromising. 'When we took it to Japanese restaurants, we got the same reaction that we did all those years ago when we took our Norwegian IPA to bars,' he says. 'Production is very small but I've fallen in love with sake and I want others to discover it too.'

… if only for old time's sake.

Left: Some of Nøgne Ø's beers are best served on the rocks.

KEY BEERS

Imperial Stout 9%
Dark Horizon 16%
IPA 7.5%
Saison 6.5%
Two Captains Double IPA 8.5%
God Jul 8.5%

MINOH

Osaka, Japan www.minoh-beer.jp

Some teenagers dream of fanciful careers, only to be frustrated by their parents, who tell them to find proper jobs. But for Kaori Ohshita, who was set on a sensible 9–to–5 earner, the roles were reversed, when her father announced he had other plans for her.

'I'd always wanted to be a school teacher,' she says. 'But one night, when I was still a high school student, my parents, me and my two younger sisters were out for dinner, and on the way home, my dad pointed to this empty place and declared: "Tomorrow, you'll start brewing beer there."'

'We all thought it was a joke.' She laughs abruptly, then stops. 'It wasn't.'

'My dad was …' begins Ohshita, Minoh Brewery's glamorous but matter-of-fact head brewer, before pausing and grinning at a private recollection. 'You could say he was a dangerous person. Impulsive. He'd make these spur-of-the-moment decisions. He said we'd run a brewery, and we did.'

It was 1994, and Japan had just relaxed strict tax laws to allow small-scale commercial brewing for the first time. Masaji Ohshita had run a successful liquor store in Osaka for 30 years. But he was restless. Now was the time to expand his family business, to take on a challenge.

It sounds like the stuff of every beer boffin's wildest dream, but the brewmistress, Kaori, is quick to disabuse envious parties of the idea everything's been handed to her on a platter. At the outset, she knew precisely nothing about brewing and had to teach herself 'more or less the whole lot', first at a plant in Kobe, not far from Osaka, and then on

a tiny system run by the National Tax Agency (of all things) in Hiroshima. The most useful training came through hard graft and countless mistakes on the brewery system her father imported from New Zealand and installed at the plant, housed in a nondescript warehouse in the Minoh district, a quiet neighbourhood on Osaka's northern fringe.

By the time the brewery was producing beer for sale, in 1997, Japan's initial microbeer boom was already stalling, mired in the dregs of so many insipid throw-downs from misguided micro ventures. 'There was a backlash, because people saw craft beer as overpriced and inconsistent in quality. Mostly it was a novelty to be bought from gift stores,' Ohshita says. 'So for us it was a struggle to be taken seriously through those years.'

It was a lonely time to be starting out: 'I didn't have anyone to guide me, so I had to teach myself how to make new styles through trial and error. I was working around the clock back then. It was so hard.'

It still is. After spending the morning bottling, kegging and overseeing a new brew, Ohshita is taking a quick break in the miniature bar and bottleshop attached to the brewery before racing off to a meeting of female brewers from the region. In recent years, she has become a pin-up girl among the growing ranks of Japanese beer otaku (obsessives), but she doesn't feel comfortable with this, or with her role as a pioneer for female brewers in a country that still embraces old-fashioned ideas about gender roles. 'I want people to like Minoh for the beer, not because it's run by women,' she says.

Below far left: Minoh HQ in Osaka.

Below left: Kaori Ohshita checks her brews.

Below: Minoh's award-winning beers.

Below right: The Minoh team celebrate the release of their new 'helium' beer.

Minoh's Imperial Stout, a pitch-black 8.5% beast, is a perfectly balanced rich concoction that blends notes of roasted coffee and hazelnut with strains of beef jerky and Worcestershire sauce.

Later she plans to stop by one of the family company's three Beer Belly pubs in central Osaka to talk to a business partner about the tap line-up, devoted mostly to Minoh's extensive range.

For the first five years, Ohshita and her two younger sisters, Mayuko and Nozomi, only made Pilsners, dark lagers and light stouts, always using extract. The early efforts, she readily admits, were a very distant relation to the big, bold numbers for which Minoh has become the most awarded craft brewery in the Kansai region of western Japan, and, alongside Baird Brewery, the most celebrated small-scale operation in the country.

Minoh's Imperial Stout, a pitch-black, 8.5% beast, is a perfectly balanced, rich concoction that blends notes of roasted coffee and hazelnut with the faintest strains of beef jerky and Worcestershire sauce. The brewery's equally beloved W-IPA (in Japan, 'W' is pronounced 'dabaru' and used as an ideogram to mean 'double') is a 9% belter with a delicate nose of white peach and bubblegum and a dense body of sticky toffee malts and earthy hops. It was one of the first double IPAs in Japan, but, despite the appellation, it lies somewhere between the oily, semi-sweet double IPAs of US east coast brewers, and the punchiest American strong ale. Regardless, it is a treat.

Some of Minoh's more adventurous brews, including the Cabernet Ale, a fruit beer made with cabernet grapes, and the award-winning Yuzu White Ale, a witbier infused with Japanese citrus fruit, take their cues from the relentlessly experimental approach of brewers in the US. Ohshita admits she particularly respects Greg Koch at Stone in San Diego. But whereas many American breweries aim for towering ABVs and brutal flavours, Minoh prioritises balance.

'In Japan we have a word – shokuchushu – which means alcohol that is designed to be drunk with food,' she says. 'This is what I'm mindful of when I create recipes for beers: I want to make them to complement food and not overpower it, no matter how high the alcohol content. Even the W-IPA shouldn't be too bitter, because then you can't taste anything else. At Minoh, balance is the guiding principle.'

KEY BEERS

Minoh W-IPA 9%
Minoh Stout 5.5%
Minoh Imperial Stout 8.5%
Minoh Pale Ale 5.5%
Minoh Cabernet Ale 7%
Minoh Weizen 5.5%

* WILD & WOOD

---

* barrel-aged

* lambic

* sour

* brettanomyces

* spiritual

Welcome to the bit of the book that rejoices in the beguiling blend of boisterous bacteria and the wonders of wood over time.

This chapter is where the wild yeasts roam, where the most maverick and mysterious of microorganisms such as Brettanomyces, Lactobacillus and Pediococcus work their magic and where Lambics, sours and Gueuze reside.

For more than a century, wild yeast has been considered an irksome contaminant by conventional brewers but, in their tenacious pursuit for new flavour experiences, an increasing number of craft brewing cognoscenti are welcoming wild yeast into their breweries with open arms . . . and an increasingly open mind.

Of course, letting wild yeast loose on one's liquids is by no means a new phenomenon: the Lambic brewers and blenders of Belgium have been doing it for years. With all the resignation of a cat herder, they have long given up trying to tame the capricious little fellows and accepted that all the brewer can do is keep them as content as possible.

Placing beer in wooden casks is not a new trend either. Prior to the advent of metal, coopered vessels made from staves of oak were the common containers for not just beer, but pretty much any libation. Yet, back then, little attention was given to the array of influences and flavours from the wood that might be shaping the liquid inside.

But just as they have with spontaneous fermentation and naturally occurring yeast, modern craft brewers are taking barrel-ageing to an entirely different level. Dovetailing tradition with all the latest scientific techniques, they are playing homage to the past, yet have no intention of getting stuck there.

Inspired by both winemakers and distillers, brewers are eagerly exploring the effect of wood on the flavour and aroma of their beer by using casks previously filled with anything from port and pinot noir to whisky, sherry and even tequila.

THE BARREL-AGED, BACTERIA-LADEN BIT OF THE BOOK THAT UNVEILS THE MAGIC OF MICRO-FLORA AND MATURATION, REVELS IN THE WONDROUS EFFECT OF WILD YEAST AND WOOD AND CELEBRATES BEER'S SPIRITUAL SIDE. THERE'S SOMETHING IN THE AIR, AND IT'S FLAVOURING YOUR BEER.

UK

Hardknott
Aether Blaec 2011
Epsilon 8.5%
Cumbria, England
www.hardknott.com

This mould-breaking craft brewery began life in the Woolpack Pub at the foot of the Hardknott Pass, in the Lake District. In 2010, founders Dave Bailey and Ann Wedgwood moved to the nearby small town of Millom. Aether Blaec is a series of whisky cask-aged imperial stouts, released annually in small batches. After six months in barrels that have housed Aultmore whisky for 28 years, the 2011 Epsilon attains a dusty, oak-edged, toasty, charred character, with vanillin and a tarry whisper on the finish.

Hawkshead
Brodie's Prime Reserve 8.5%
Cumbria, England
www.hawksheadbrewery.co.uk

After years as a BBC foreign news correspondent, Alex Brodie really needed a beer. So, in 2002, he swapped his microphone for a mash-fork and, in an old dairy on the Cumbrian fells, created his own craft brewery. Within four years, the dairy was deemed too small and Hawkshead was relocated to the other side of Lake Windermere. Here, head brewer Matt Clarke pimps up his 'Prime' porter by laying it down for six months in Bladnoch Lowland whisky barrels. The result is rich and seamless, with touches of treacle and tobacco, while the oak plays only a background role.

Lovibonds
Sour Grapes 4.6%
Oxfordshire, England
www.lovibonds.com

The haughty but nice town of Henley-on-Thames once boasted Brakspear's brewery before it was, sadly and scandalously, closed down in 2002. Within three years, Wisconsin native Jeff Rosenmeier had filled the void with a very different offering, on keg rather than cask. From the bucolic heart of Oxfordshire comes this sensational Brettanomyces-brushed Berliner Weiss aged in Pinot Noir wine barrels. Born as a batch of Henley Gold wheat beer that accidently went wild, it recently won gold in the 2012 World Beer Cup 'Wood Aged Sour Beer' category. Extremely impressive.

Magic Rock
Bourbon Barrel-Aged Bearded Lady
10.5%
Yorkshire, England
www.magicrockbrewing.com

All hail this hirsute Huddersfield-hewn barrel-aged version of an imperial brown ale, which will happily put hairs on your chest, legs, face and, if you drink enough of it, palms and eyelids too. Immense and intense, it emerges from six months in bourbon-soaked American oak tasting significantly more suave and seductive than when it went in there. Hang it under your hooter and it will send informative stuff like 'rich black chocolate', 'vanilla and oak', 'chipotle' and 'black cherry' to your brain box. From one of the most inspiring British micros to emerge in the past couple of years – and there have been a few.

Wild Beer Company
Bliss 6%
Somerset, England
www.wildbeerco.com

Californian Brett Ellis and Englishman Andrew Cooper, both formerly of the Bristol Beer Company, are bringing wild yeast and wood to the West Country beer scene. Big on barrel-ageing and blending with a soft spot for sour flavours, some of their early efforts were a little too wild, but the tartness has been tamed here. It's a smooth, softly sour Belgian Saison with a gentle funk which will find favour with cider drinkers.

Harviestoun
Ola Dubh 16-year-old 8%
Clackmannanshire, Scotland
www.harviestoun-brewery.co.uk

This is the beer I crack open at Christmas wondering why Santa has, yet again, insisted on stuffing my stocking with satsumas and not, as I specifically asked, toys. Viscous and velvety, 'Black Oil' is a whisky-finished collaboration between Harviestoun and Highland Park single malt whisky. A sensational swirl of chocolate, espresso and cardamom, it glides through Gentleman's Relish and is sublime with stilton and oatcakes.

Orkney
Dark Island Reserve 10%
Orkney Islands, Scotland
www.orkneybrewery.co.uk

With the Ring of Brodgar on its label and housed in a former schoolhouse in Quoyloo, just a mile from Skara Brae, in the heart of the eponymous archipelago, the Orkney Brewery sounds like something from a JRR Tolkien novel, with a history that is just as convoluted. Set up by former publican Roger White in 1988, on merging with the Atlas

Brewery in 2004 it became the Highlands & Islands Brewery and, two years later, it was taken over by Sinclair Breweries. Its flagship beer is Dark Island, darker than Middle Earth and scooper of several awards, a not-so-wee Heavy chunked up with chocolate malt. Head brewer Andrew Fulton makes it even more fantastical by finishing it in old Orkney single malt whisky casks for three months, with each small batch filling just over 3,500 75cl swing-top bottles. Each lovely-looking bottle is signed by the brewer alongside an individual gyle number and the date of bottling – 3rd April 2012 in this case. After just a year in the bottle, there is genuine depth to this massive mouthful, which pours deep black with a dark plum tint. Chocolate compôte, molasses, distinct dry-roast coffee notes, mocha and vanilla combine with a tobacco note on the finish.

Ale Apothecary
Sahalie 9.3%
Oregon
www.thealeapothecary.com

After years of designing some of Deschutes Brewing's most distinctive beers, Paul Arney withdrew to the wilderness and the woods of Oregon in 2012 where, on a primitive brewhouse, using brewkit hewn from wood, he creates some sensational, small-batch old style ales and spontaneously fermented sours. Found somewhere between the farmhouse and the funk, there's a refinement to this raw and rustic wild ale that can be likened to Lambic in its aroma yet drinks closer to a slightly unhinged Orval.

Alesmith
Speedway Stout Barrel-Aged 12%
San Diego
www.alesmith.com

Back in 1995, Alesmith was instrumental in sowing the seeds of San Diego's blossoming beer scene. Current brewmaster Peter Zein, having formerly volunteered at the brewery, took it over in 2002 and swapped a career in law for a cobbled-together out-of-town brewhouse made up of old dairy equipment. Inspired by the beers of Britain and Belgium, he was soon bringing home the bling from prestigious beer competitions. Alesmith keeps things extremely classic and seldom

releases more than one new beer every year. The 'standard' Speedway Stout, smoother than a cashmere codpiece, is given plenty of Brazilian coffee percolating through its veins, and then develops a new dimension when it beds down in Heaven Hill bourbon barrels. The barrel-aged version is released each year in very limited quantities, the Kentucky cask adding vanillin, tobacco and a distinctive dryness to a stunningly smooth oak-aged imperial stout.

Allagash
Coolship Resurgam 6%
Maine
www.allagash.com

Allagash pride themselves on their brilliant Belgian-style beers. But in 2008, they became even more Belgian by creating a coolship, a shallow copper bath that cools the wort and invites wild yeast to come down and have a special cuddle. There are now four very limited-edition 'coolship' Lambic-style beers: some are fruited, but this one is blended like a Gueuze. Stateside stabs at Gueuze can go a little wrong but Resurgam feels and tastes just right: wild and a little weird, funky fruit-bowl flavours and a shiver-inducing sourness. Very clever.

Boulevard
Rye-on-Rye 12%
Missouri
www.boulevard.com

Keeping it real in Kansas City since 1989, Boulevard is now Missouri's biggest independent brewer and the 10th largest in the US. While its success is built on the pull of its Pale Ale and Unfiltered Wheat Beer, purists salivate about its exploratory Smokestack series. Conditioned in 75cl bottles, several are rested on different wood including this ochre-hued, spicy, tangy sipper built on two types of malted rye and laid to rest in rye whiskey barrels sourced from a distillery in Indiana. Soft honey up front, dusty, with touches of spruce, fennel and tobacco.

Beard Beer

From serving its hazelnut beer with a condom encased in a nut to owning its own beehives in order to provide honey for its ales, Rogue has always lived up to its name and been a bit different.

But in the summer of 2012, the Oregonian brewery took its cheeky chutzpah to the next level when it brewed a beer cultivated from wild yeast taken from the whiskers of its famous brewmaster, John Maier.

The idea was initially born out of disappointment. A joint project with White Labs, the go-to guys for all brewing yeast, to create a beer with real terroir, including local yeast, had shuddered to a halt after strains collected from Rogue's hopyard were declared unsuitable for brewing beer.

Undeterred, their eyes fixed on the hirsute face of Maier, Rogue's head brewer since 1988. Nine hairs were plucked from his chin and carefully placed in a petri dish. A Q-tip swab was then sunk into its furry depths and both were then sent off for testing.

And then they waited, more in hope than expectation. But to the surprise of White Labs, Maier's beard samples proved positive: the hairs contained yeast that was suitable for brewing beer. And it wasn't Rogue's house yeast either.

After Rogue cultivated the yeast with White Labs and experimented with different styles, the beard beer – New Crustacean, a 10.8% alcohol, fruity, honeyed golden barley wine – was released in early 2013.

John, who had been growing his beard since 1978, said: 'I can't believe it was in front of me the whole time. Yeast is everywhere and so it kind of makes sense.'

The Bruery
Oude Tart 7.5%
California
www.thebruery.com

This phenomenal Flemish Red from Orange County's little bit of Belgium brings dark cherry, worn leather, tannin and tartness to your tongue. A consecutive gold medal winner at the biennial World Beer Cup in 2010 and 2012, it's a tongue-tightening sour, dark brown blend which meditates in oak for up to 18 months.

Cambridge
Cerise Cassée 9%
Massachusetts
www.cambrew.com

The only bad thing to say about this brilliant brewpub is that you have to go to Massachusetts to drink its beer. Selfish so-and-so's. Cambridge Brewing is most definitely worth the trip though. It's a gastronomic guardian of all that is good and local, the food is phenomenal while its taps are upstanding pillars of diverse, discerning beer.

An unfettered epicurean iconoclasm drives much of what it does, no more so than this aggressively acidic kriek brewed using America's first solera system, a complex mesmerising maturation technique more readily associated with sherry.

It all starts with a three-day anaerobic sour mash. Stirring in raw malt, beset with natural microflora, inoculates the mash and, in conditions perfect for lactobacillus to thrive, creates a very clean, concise acidity. The raw beer is then inducted into a 'endless' solera system consisting of French oak wine barrels stacked on top of each other. The youngest 'cradle' cask sit at the top and the oldest at the bottom. Each year, 25–75% is taken from each 220-litre barrel to create a blend made up of cherry beer aged between one and eight years old. As beer is drawn, each barrel is filled up with beer from the younger barrels above – all part of an oak-ageing process that never ends.

Within the solera system, ambient yeast strains such as Brettanomyces, Lactobacillus, and Pediococcus work in tandem, politely taking turns to create alcohol and a soft and silky acidity, cleaning up after the other, as part of a magical, mysterious symbiotic relationship.

The tongue-twisting tartness and acidity comes from a combination of the sour mash and the solera system, while the fruity finesse comes from the 300 pounds of sour cherries in each brew. Maroon, with a magnificent mousse head, it is fruity, gently funky and seriously sour, adorned with aniseed and a dry oak tannin on the finish: an incredible aperitif best drunk from a Champagne flute.

Cigar City
Humidor India Pale Ale 7.5%
Florida
www.cigarcitybrewing.com

Wayne Wambles, the wonderfully named head brewer, makes a mockery of Tampa's high-riding mercury by manufacturing a medley of great brews in a region not renowned for quality craft beer. Tampa is synonymous with cigars and homage is paid to its past with the Humidor series, a range of beers fermented for a second time with Spanish cedar, the wood used to make cigar boxes. Here Jai Alai, a fabulously floral IPA, is made further fragrant with notes of jasmine, sage and the woody fustiness of a gentleman's barber's.

Clown Shoes
Tramp Stamp 7%
Massachusetts
www.clownshoesbeer.com

Inspired by the craft beers shuffling onto the shelves of his liquor store, Gregg Berman , linking up with manager Jesse Dooley, decided to begin brewing. Without a brewhouse of their own, they teamed up with the Mercury Brewing Company in Ipswich and started Clown Shoes. The brewery name is simply brilliant, and so are a lot of the beers. This bare-cheek Belgian IPA, like the lower back tattoo after which it is named, doesn't do subtlety. An in-yer-face amber, highly hopped with Centennial, Amarillo and Columbus, sweetened using orange peel with further fruit furnished from the rapacious Belgian yeast, it has the texture of a Tripel with the nose of an American IPA.

Crooked Stave
Wild Wild Brett Rouge 5.2%
Colorad,
www.crookedstave.com

At the time of writing, the chaps at Crooked Stave were building a new brewery in Denver having brewed their embryonic beers elsewhere. They had also just won an award at the 2012 World Beer Cup for this acidic elixir, brewed using 100% Brettanomyces. Part of a series of beers bigging up Brett, it includes hibiscus, rosehips and hawthorn berries to produce a delicate, complex drop.

Dogfish Head
Palo Santo Marron 12%
Delaware
www.dogfish.com

Dogfish Head needs little introduction to in-the-know craft beer connoisseurs. Founded in 1995 by Sam Caglione, a former underpants model described as the Johnny Knoxville of American brewing by some, Dogfish does things very differently, even by American craft beer standards.

The 'off-centred ales for off-centred people' tagline that adorns its bottles is an acute understatement and, despite impressive expansion in recent years, Dogfish Head has not lost its edge. Sam's are unashamedly unusual ales, especially the ancient ones. The core Dogfish Head range, spearheaded by two amazing examples of American IPAs, is equally as enthralling, and featured in the Hop chapter.

Even by Dogfish Head's extraordinarily high standards, though, this after-dinner ale really is something rather special. After brewing a bold, malt-driven brown ale, Dogfish ages it on Paraguayan Palo Santo wood. More readily associated with wine-making, the wood imparts notes of vanilla, figs and dark fruit and softens the malt flavours to produce an immensely complex oak-aged ale, smoky and oaky with some cherry and cinnamon too.

Evil Twin
Femme Fatale Brett 6%
New York
www.eviltwin.dk

Now headquartered in Brooklyn, though brewing all over the world, Evil Twin is Jeppe Jarnit-Bjergsø, the Danish gypsy-brewing twin brother of Mikkeller's Mikkel. Initially an adventurous homebrewer, Jeppe began collaborating with craft brewers while working at Ølbutikken, Copenhagen's cult bottled beer shop. Brewed with Amager, Fanø, De Molen and Westbrook among others, Jeppe's beers are a broad, iconoclastic church spoken of in hallowed terms by the hipster craft beer crowd, especially Blåbær, his lush bilberry Lambic collaboration at Cantillon. Back in Denmark's Fanø brewery, using 100% Brettanomyces, Jeppe conjures up aromas of countryside in this amber-coloured IPA. Excellent attenuation and similar to a citric Saison, it's musty, a tiny bit tart with a medicine cabinet finish.

Founders
Kentucky Bourbon Stout 11.2%
Michigan
www.foundersbrewing.com

After several expansions in recent years, Founders broke into the top 50 craft breweries in the United States in 2011 and, as any beer-related venture onto the information super highway will reveal, it commands a cult following among advocates of the esoteric and the extreme. Founders (pun very much intended) Mike Stevens and Dave Engbers have been instrumental in making Michigan the supreme state for barrel-aged stouts thanks to both CBS (Canadian Breakfast Stout), brewed with maple syrup, and KBS, an epic imperial stout brewed with real coffee and posh chocolates before being laid down for 12 months in bourbon barrels and released at the beginning of spring.

Goose Island
Bourbon County Stout 15%
Chicago
www.gooseisland.com

When, in 2011, the enormous brewing behemoth AB-InBev stumped up $38.8m to buy Goose Island Brewing, the craft brewing community widely condemned the move. John Hall, who founded the oldest brewery in Chicago as a brewpub in 1988, and is no longer involved, was accused of selling out to global brewing's version of Beelzebub, and alarm bells chimed when the brewing of 312 and other year-round beers moved to bigger AB-InBev breweries on the East Coast.

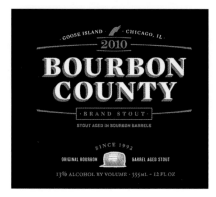

What critics could consider is that capacity has been freed up at Goose Island's Fulton Street Brewery in Chicago, which remains a Midwestern mothership of more innovative, ambitious small-batch brewing. Home to a state-of-the-art laboratory which works wonders with wild yeast, it has spawned several impressive Belgian-style, Brett-laced sour beers such as Lolita, Matilda, Madame Rose, Juliet and Sofie.

Opposite the brewery sits America's biggest barrel-ageing programme: three warehouses holding more than 150,000 barrels sourced from distilleries and winemakers. One entire warehouse is dedicated to Bourbon County Stout, regarded by many as the beer that pioneered barrel-ageing in America and still, nearly 20 years after its release in 1995, a very special strong stout. It's a mellifluous mash made up of roasted barley, Munich, chocolate and caramel malts, embroidered with deep fruity Willamette hops, fermented out for a fortnight before spending nine months hibernating in a variety of wood sourced from different American whiskey distilleries.

Surely not even the Darth Vader of global brewing would dare dilute this velvety vortex of vanillin, dark chocolate-orange and charred, smoky campfire coffee? After five years filling out in the bottle, you will find it even more phenomenal. When it's let out on rare release, get hold of it and pray the boys from Brazil don't start meddling with it.

Great Divide
Oak Aged Yeti Imperial Stout 9.5%
Colorado
www.greatdivide.com

A well-thumbed thesaurus offered no better adjective to describe Great Divide's beers than big. Exalted in both attitude and altitude, it creates colossal Coloradoan quaff on the edge of downtown Denver, having being founded by Brian Dunn in an old dairy (what is it with these old dairies?) back in 1994. Its locker of large liquids boasts enormous IPAs (Titan and Hercules), behemoth Barley Wines (Old Ruffian) and full-on fruit beers (Wild Raspberry Ale) but this Baltic, balletic Imperial stout, aged on oak and released each year as the evenings draw in, is correctly considered the classiest. Intense in alcohol yet not without nuance, it's a mesmeric mix of chocolate, roasted coffee, liquorice, vanilla and chipotle, with a massive 75 IBUs for those who like their stouts a bit bitter.

Heavy Seas
Plank II 8.5%
Baltimore
www.hsbeer.com

A conglomeration of three Maryland micros, Heavy Seas has formed a guerrilla splinter group in the world of wood experimentation. Working with a local wood expert, the brewery eschewed oak barrels in favour of six foot staves of yellow poplar and eucalyptus that have been heated and fortified to coax out extra flavour. Steeped in a toffee-tinged Doppelbock for six months, the eucalyptus staves exude spicy chocolate notes while poplar adorns it with a smoky, dry finish. A captivating coming together of craft brewing and, er … carpentry.

Hill Farmstead
Fear & Trembling 9.3%
Vermont
www.hillfarmstead.com

In 2010, after two years brewing in Denmark, brewmaster Shaun Hill returned home to his family farmstead in a remote hamlet in Vermont. Using his own well water and house yeast, he brews soft, elegant and succinct ales (more than 200 casks). Shaun showcases his creativity using whiskey, port, wine and sherry barrels. In this collaborative creation, Shaun's rich and rounded Baltic porter, perked up with malt hand-smoked over maple wood, is sent to sleep in both cabernet barrels and bourbon casks before being blended. A forceful up-front fireside fragrance subsides to reveal bourbon, bacon, black cherry and Nutella (other chocolate-based breakfast spreads are available).

Jolly Pumpkin
Oro de Calabaza 8%
Michigan
www.jollypumpkin.com

Yeast simply won't find a warmer American welcome than at Jolly Pumpkin. Founder Ron Jeffries allows a variety of Belgian and French Saccharomyces to frolic in his open fermentation vessels while, over a period of months and years, wilder strains creates complexity from deep within the crevices of hundreds of wine and spirit barrels before further fermentation occurs in the bottle. Oro de Calabaza is a gorgeous, graceful Belgian Golden ale with a whole load of funk in its treasure trunk. Grape skin on the nose, tart tropical fruit, a bit of banana and sparkling sourness: incredible stuff.

Logsdon Farmhouse Ales
Seizoen Bretta 8%
Oregon
www.farmhousebeer.com

In 2011, deep in the Oregonian outback, Full Sail founder David Logsdon set up a farmhouse brewery in a red barn. His

bucolic vision? To brew organic beers using the ingredients that surrounded him, including hops, pears and cherries grown on trees specially imported from Flanders. Brettanomyces brings the dryness, pear juice brings natural carbonation in the bottle and whole locally sourced hops bring the delicate aromatics. The result is a fabulous bottle-conditioned farmhouse ale.

Lost Abbey (Port Brewing)
Cuvee de Tomme 11%
California
www.lostabbey.com

Barrel-ageing, blending and working wonders with wild yeast and wood is what native San Diegan Tomme Arthur likes

doing best. Inspired by the Belgians, Port Brewing began in 2006 when it took over the brewery in San Marcos previously inhabited by Stone Brewing, and soon became famous for the Lost Abbey line of Belgian-style brews.

Lost Abbey's lair of oak barrels is a magnificent, musty place of worship, its entrance adorned with an enormous eight foot Latin sign declaring: 'In Illa Brettanomyces, Nos Fides' – 'In Wild Yeast We Trust.' Brett runs the show here, its funky fingers gently feeling their way into Lost Abbey's

forest of oak barrels, collaborating with other feral fungi and microcritters cohabiting within the wood's crevices.

Lost Abbey's barrel room has borne numerous one-off releases such as the über-exclusive Veritas range, where grain met the grape in oak wine barrels, and rare blends such as Phunky Duck, En Garde and the peachy sour ale Yellow Bus.

While these may remain out of reach, do yourself a favour and jot down Tomme's regular releases in your drinking diary. From January to October, bespoke blended barrel-aged beers are unleashed, highlights being the bourbon-blessed barley wine Angel's Share in January and the funky Flemish Red Poppy blend, released in February.

Each May, however, the quirky sour kriek Cuvee du Tomme comes out to play. Using Judgment Day as its genesis, the beer is tucked up nice and tight in American bourbon barrels. Raisins and a dose of dextrose seed a stewed sweetness up front. But its unique appeal is its tight tingle of tartness, courtesy of sour cherries and unshackled secondary fermentation. Any sharpness is smoothed by the oak, adding a veneer of vanilla and tannin. A remarkable digestif and dessert beer.

Lost Abbey's Box Set Beers

Each month throughout 2012, Lost Abbey unveiled a new beer inspired by classic rock anthems that referenced either Heaven or Hell. Representing Lost Abbey's full repertoire of wood-aged beers, wild beers, sour ales and spontaneous fermentations, each 'track' was limited to a total of 450 375ml bottles and, to avoid black market profiteering, bottles were only available in the brewery's tasting room.

Fresh Tracks: completely new beers designed specifically for the Box Set

Van Halen 'Runnin' With The Devil', 7.66%
A brown beer spiked with 30 pounds of Cabernet Sauvignon grapes and house-raised Brettanomyces cultures, then aged in three red wine barrels.

AC/DC 'Highway to Hell', 14.3%
A brooding dark beer blending brandy barrel-aged Serpent's Stout and bourbon barrel-aged Angel's Share.

Iron Maiden 'Number of the Beast', 13.7%,
Empty bourbon barrels are filled with Judgement Day and infused with cinnamon stick and dried chilli pepper.

Meatloaf 'Bat Out of Hell', 13.5%,
Bourbon barrel-aged Serpent's Stout mellowed with coffee and cacao nibs.

Re-mixes, bespoke blends created from The Lost Abbey cellars.

Led Zeppelin 'Stairway to Heaven', 12.5%
One part Cuvee Tomme from bourbon barrels; three parts The Angel's Share (bourbon) with peaches; and one part Project X, a wild fermentation project which spikes the sweetness with acid.

AC/DC 'Hell's Bells', 7.55%
Phunky Duck, the base beer in 'Duck Duck Gooze', is dovetailed with two barrels of the lactic-laced Mellow Yellow to make a pale sour beer.

Rolling Stones 'Sympathy for the Devil', 11.33%
Tomme has taken two barrels of Hot Rocks lager aged in French oak red wine barrels, which developed a Brettanomyces note, and some barrel-aged black beer that was to have been part of 2011's Veritas 009. The result? A dark vinous blend of tobacco, leather and ripe fruit.

Motley Crüe 'Shout at the Devil', 7.7%
Framboise de Amorosa is infused with more fruit, then laid down in French oak with the cherry-laden Red Poppy, to create a sensational sour duet.

INXS 'The Devil Inside', 8.12%
A tannin-tastic twist on Veritas's legendary 006, a base sour beer layered with orange peel, mandarin and orange zest, raspberry and cherry.

Guns 'n' Roses 'Knockin' on Heaven's Door', 9.7%
Barrels of Cuvee de Tomme were laced with more Brettanomyces and bulked with currants: like a punked-up port.

Charlie Daniels 'The Devil Went Down to Georgia', 12%
Inspired by Hell yet aged in Heaven Hill whiskey barrels for nine months, this is Angel's Share joined by fresh peaches and a touch of Brettanomyces.

Black Sabbath 'Heaven & Hell', 8.69%
A gently funky blend of Lost Abbey's Gift of the Magi golden ale, Avant Garde and an anonymous sour base beer, all aged in oak barrels.

Nebraska
Melange a Trois 10%
Nebraska
www.nebraskabrewingco.com

This expressive brewpub from Papillion, a suburb of Omaha, is no corporate cookie-cutter set-up, and makes some award-winning oak-aged efforts. During six months sitting in French oak Chardonnay barrels, this fruity blonde Belgian acquires crisp apple notes, a peachy depth and a whole load of drying tannin touches on the finish.

New Belgium
La Folie 6%
Colorado
www.newbelgium.com

It is no surprise that brewmaster, Peter Brouckaert, having made the move from Rodenbach to the Rockies, is eager to experiment with oak. This was his first Colorado-based creation, a robust brown ale laid down in French wine barrels for between one and three years. La Folie puckers and pouts your laughing gear with ripe plums, sour cherries and pear drops.

New Glarus
Serendipity 4%
Wisconsin
www.newglarusbrewing.com

Seldom seen beyond Wisconsin's borders, there is certainly nothing parochial or neutral about its beer. Few other microbreweries have a cloudy, corn-tinged farmhouse ale as their flagship beer and even fewer manager to create such near-flawless fruit beers as Raspberry Tart and Wisconsin Belgian Red. Serendipity, released in 2012, is a phenomenal fruit beer borne out of a catastrophe. Faced with a famine of local cherries, brewmaster and co-founder Dan Carey was forced to replace the recipe for Belgian Red with a bumper crop of cranberries and apples. Fermented with unruly Belgian yeast and lagered in oak for a year, the 'happy accident' is tart and vinous, an ideal aperitif which switches between sweet and lip-smacking sour with every sip, culminating in a sharp, bitter, berry finish.

New Holland
Dragon's Milk 10%
Michigan
www.newhollandbrew.com

Tulips, Calvinist churches, wax-covered cheese, windmills, a very relaxed attitude to prostitution and shops hawking A-grade marijuana. All these things, apart of course from the last two, can be discovered in this prim and proper Dutch enclave on the Michigan coast. A staunchly conservative town with more than 170 places of worship and a Sunday ban on beer sales may not appear the most logical location to start a brewery but that is what Jason Spaulding and Brett VanderKamp did in 1996. And, by golly, it has worked out rather well. New Holland was one of the first Michigan micros to get behind barrel-ageing, and it is with the experimental oak-aged offerings where New Holland excels. Hop-heads hanker after the excellent India Pale Ales slumbered in Kentucky bourbon casks, while those into a taste for the tart are steered towards the fruity, sour Cellar series. But the brewery's best known 'art in fermented form' is this imperious, ink-black stout, aged for three months in bourbon barrels. Flexing flavours from both the whiskey and the wood, it is an intoxicating eddy of espresso, praline, vanilla-coated raisins and bitter dark chocolate with a nutty background, rich and wonderfully rounded.

Rivertown
Lambic 6.3%
Ohio
www.rivertownbrewery.com

I have no idea whether the yeast circling Cincinnati is similar to that floating around in Flanders, and purists may question whether it can be called Lambic, but this is a super-duper spontaneously fermented sour beer. Aged in port oak barrels for a year and only released once a year, in May, it is hard to get hold of yet easy to like.

Russian River
Supplication 7%
California
www.russianriverbrewing.com

At both his brewpub and brewery, Vinnie Cilurzo is a renowned guru at grafting the grape with the grain. For this beer, Vinnie packs Pinot Noir barrels, sourced from Sonoma County wineries, with 25lbs of fresh sour cherries, a trio of wild yeast strains (Brettanomyces, Pediococcus and Lactobacillus) and, lest we forget, a Belgian-style brown ale. He then lets all these ingredients introduce themselves to each other over 12 months. The beer is subsequently decanted into a corked and caged bottle, where it re-ferments to create something that is funky, fruity, tart and teeming with tannins. Incredible.

Shorts
Bourbon Barrel Sustenance 6.5%
Michigan
www.shortsbrewing.com

In 2004, Joe Short opened a brewpub in an old hardware store in the small town of Bellaire. A new brewhouse brewed its first beer in 2010, just across the river in Elk Rapids. Short's fertile imagination and fleetness of foot has led to some lush leftfield liquids, including the brisk, herbal India Spruce Pilsner. This, a rare example of a barrel-aged bottom-fermented beer, is a stupidly sippable Schwarzbier held captive for 11 months in oak casks previously filled with American whiskey. It is reminiscent of old-fashioned root beer, dry and firm, with a touch of light smoke there too: different yet very drinkable.

Stillwater Artisanal Ales
De Bauched 6.7%
Baltimore
www.stillwaterales.com

As a leading techno DJ and producer, Brian Strumke would spin vinyl and make music in studios all over the world. He now does the same as one of the most creative gipsy brewers around. Inspired by a Belgian brewpub in his native Baltimore, Strumke began homebrewing in 2005 and, having traded in his Technics, he brewed his first

professional batch in 2008. Within the first two years, he brewed 36 different beers in four different countries, and developed a core range of six beers at the Dog Brewery in Maryland, including Debutante, a slaking Saison-esque spring beer brewed using rye and spelt and 'hopped' with honeysuckle, hissop and heather.

More recently, his travels have spawned elaborate and increasingly inventive collaborations. He breathed life into one of his most rambunctious yet remarkable recipes at the Fanø bryghaus in Denmark. Made in association with ex-pat American brewmaster Ryan Witter-Merithew, it is a Brett-kissed 'Viking Saison' made of spelt, Pilsner and smoked malt, hopped with Pacific Gem and East Kent Golding and seasoned with juniper bushes. It shouldn't work but, somehow, it does.

Telegraph
Gypsy Ale 8%
California
www.telegraphbrewing.com

A riot of flavours inspired by the Romany community and brewed with unmalted wheat, Californian plums and rye. The yeast works its magic – so the Santa Barbara-based brewery claims – to the tune of gipsy folk songs blaring out in the brewery. An untamed imbibing experience that takes you here, over there, there and back here again.

21st Amendment
Monk's Blood 8.3%
California
www.21st-amendment.com

A stalwart of San Francisco's beer scene and a pioneering proponent of canned craft beer, 21st Amendment is a legendary brewpub situated just a wayward pitch from the Giants' baseball stadium. Its Watermelon Wheat is wonderful during the summer but when Frisco's fog comes in, it's this marvellous bit of monky business that locals reach for. Dark ruby, decadent and rich, Monk's Blood is spiced with cinnamon, dried figs, vanilla bean and candi sugar before being aged on oak. The kind of beer that Belgian monks would shout about … if they were allowed.

Weyerbacher
Insanity 11%
Pennsylvania
www.weyerbacher.com

Easton, a small town situated between Philadelphia and New York, has borne two things with an insatiable appetite for the considerable. The first is art-house actress Lisa Ann, while the second is Weyerbacher, a modest-sized micro that has been making massive beers since 1995. Founders Dan and Sue Weirback don't do things by halves, taking a firm grasp on the slack leash of any given beer style and giving it an almighty yank. Here, the scandalously bitter Blithering Idiot IPA is further amplified by a spell in bourbon barrels, where it undergoes mellow metamorphosis into a big, big barley wine: Christmas cake, rich rummy malt and a spicy, sharp citric bitterness.

Central City
Bourbon Barrel-Aged Thor's Hammer 11.5%
British Columbia
www.centralcitybrewing.com

Central City was named Canada's 2010 Brewery of the Year, though its big breakthrough came two years earlier when it pulled off a marketing masterstroke of unprecedented guile: putting a picture of a scantily-clad, well-endowed pretty lady on its Red Racer range of cans. Everyone likes nice cans and pretty much everyone liked the liquids inside, especially the flagship Red Racer IPA. Carving a cult and thriving commercial niche, and buoyed by his national gong in 2010, the much-admired brewmaster Gary Lohin expanded from a brewpub to a 35,000 hectolitre brewhouse in 2012, complete with capacity for a barrel-ageing programme. This bomb of a barley wine, made with eight different malts, is matured for 11 months, including a period within American bourbon-soaked oak, to give a slightly sour beer with rum and raisin, walnuts, and, again, a colossal Christmas cake core.

Hopfenstark
Saison Station 10 5%
Quebec
www.hopfenstark.com

Quebec may have arrived late to the Canadian craft beer party but the French-speaking province quickly started playing cool tunes from its iPod and challing to all the sexy ladies/lads. One of the most impressive players is Hopfenstark, a brewpub overseen by Fred Cormier, who has seized upon Saison as the beer style to reflect much of his creativity. The numbered Station series includes a herby, citrus Saison (Station 7), one with rye in the grist (Station 16), and a heavily bittered version (Station 55). Station 10 is a sour Saison gently tapped with the wand of Brettanomyces: hazy and tart with a touch of barnyard, grain and grapefruit.

Storm
Imperial Flanders Red Ale 11%
Vancouver
www.stormbrewing.org

There is a charismatic anarchic element to Storm Brewing, a quirky mash-up of metal cobbled together in 1995 by James Walton. In the first couple of years, stabs at spontaneous fermentation were successful, yet his first foray into sour Flemish Reds was not until 2010. All manner of microflora living in oak Lambic casks chow down on sugars from a maverick mash of dark malt, peated malt and candi sugar. The result is funky and pungent, with a finish of goat's milk.

Le Trou de Diable
La Buteuse – Brassin Spéciale 10%
Quebec
www.troududiable.com

A classy, hugely creative Quebecois craft brewery created in 2005, 'Devil's Hole' is synonymous with some sexy-looking bottled beers, and dabbles deftly in the art of oak ageing. While some of its stable-mates are rested in barrels sourced from American winemakers, the 'Striker' is set down in American oak formerly filled with Michel Jodoin Canadian cider brandy. It is fragrant yet a little funky, with sizeable cinnamon and spice in the centre and brandy-soaked peach and pear on the nose: mellow and musky.

BELGIUM

Alvinne
Mano Negra Oak Aged Bladnoch Barrel 10%
West Flanders
www.alvinne.be

In its home in Moen, Alvinne is one of a handful of new Belgian breweries whose vision is unhampered by blinkers or a rear-view mirror. Petit and pioneering, it embraces hops from England and the Czech Republic, adds New World nous to native beer styles and, for such a small set-up, boasts an impressive barrel-ageing programme. Its array of oak-aged beers, laid down in, variously, Pomerol casks, Bordeaux casks, French Monbazillac wine casks and Scotch whisky casks from Scotland, deserve extensive exploration, no more so than this classy imperial stout imbued with the elegant Lowland influence of Bladnoch single malt whisky. Other iterations include the same beer aged in casks once containing Glenrothes whisky, and bourbon casks.

La Botteresse de Sur-Les-Bois
La Botteresse Ambrée 8.5%
Liège
www.labotteresse.be

Cousins Willy and José Poncin, a former chemist turned brewer, create their wonderful wares with typical Walloon whimsy. Renowned for a richness of flavour and whole-hearted spicing, they debuted with this deliciously dry and cloudy amber ale back in 1998. While less elaborate than other liquids in the brewery's locker, the frank exchange of views between sweet and sour is rather special.

Drie Fonteinen
Oude Geuze Golden Blend 6%
Beersel
www.3fonteinen.be

If you don't 'see' the Lambic light after gracing your lips with this golden Gueuze then, well, your soul is beyond redemption's reach. One quarter of Armand Debelder's blend consists of a four-year-old Lambic, with a secret combination of one, two and three-year-old vintages making up the rest. Aged for four years in oak, entirely natural and unique every year, the 2012 release had everything; dryness, a soft citric sourness, a brush of Brettanomyces and a sharp, acidic send-off.

Cantillon
Kriek Lambic 5%
Brussels
www.cantillon.be

On my first visit to Cantillon, there was a small boy, sat astride an enormous oak barrel, stuffing copious amounts of Schaerbeek cherries into a frothing bung hole with his small hands. It looked suspiciously like child labour but, quite frankly, who cares when the beer tastes this remarkable. Head brewer/blender Jean Pierre Van Roy, a legend among Lambic lovers, works wonders with wild yeast and wood. Cantillon is a terrific, tumbledown time-warp, more musty museum than modern micro.

BEER VENUE Brussels

Whatever you do, don't trust the Belgians. They are a crafty bunch. For years they have been peddling the myth that Brussels is deadly dull. Don't believe the hype, or the lack thereof. It isn't.

The whole 'Brussels is boring' thing is nothing but a conspiracy born of a disorderly past. Belgium has been invaded so often that its people may have deliberately tried to make their country seem as unexciting as possible to any would-be conquerors.

How else to explain the 1960s experiment known as Brusselsisation, during which the city, anticipating its future status as the capital of Europe, demolished lots of lovely old buildings and replaced them with far less attractive modern ones? The ornate and the art deco now awkwardly rub shoulders with sorry-looking modernist structures. It is as if the Belgians purposely made Brussels look plain.

So bountiful are its beery delights, however, the rest of Brussels could be razed to rubble and discerning drinkers would still be content. From classic beer cafes soaked in sepia-tinted tradition to contemporary craft beer venues, here are some Lambic-loving venues to seek out.

A la Mort Subite 7 Rue Montagne Aux Herbes Potagères; + 32 (0)2 513 1318. The family-owned Sudden Death is a beer-drinking institution named after a bankers' dice game. An ornate, fin-de-siècle affair, where Gueuze flows on tap, it's well-touted in tourist guides but a must if you haven't been.

Le Bier Circus 57 Rue de l'Enseignement; +32 (0)2 218 0034. This brilliant beer bar and bistro off the tourist treadmill specialises in Lambics, and many dishes feature beer, from fish and Lambic waterzooi (stew) to chocolate mousse à la Chimay Bleu.

Au Bon Vieux Temps 4 Impasse St Nicolas; +32 (0)2 217 2626. The Good Old Times is an old-school alehouse tucked down the end of an alley in the city centre. Decked out in dark wood and stained glass, it is quiet, classy and quintessentially Brussels.

Delirium 4a Impasse de la Fidélité; +32 (0)2 514 4434. This basement beer cafe stocks a staggering 2,000 beers from around the world. Definitely an unmissable one for beer buffs.

Moeder Lambic 8–10 Place Fontainas; +32 (0)2 503 6068. Modern, minimalist and rated by many as the best beer bar in Brussels, Moeder only serves beers from independent artisan breweries and has 46 draught beers, 200 bottled beers, food, live music and DJs. It also serves a small bowl of malted barley with each beer – a quirky, healthy alternative to more traditional bar snacks and crucially, given all that meat and cheese, one that keeps you regular.

Restobieres 32 Rue des Renards; +32 (0)2 511 5583. Wash down rabbit with a Lambic at this cracking beer restaurant in the middle of the fashionable Marolles

Spinnekopke 1 Place du Jardin aux Fleurs; +32 (0)2 511 8695. Here since 1762, the 'Little Spider's Head' is a tiny restaurant famed for its classic beer list and simple yet hearty Belgian food, often cooked in beer.

De Cam
Oude Gueuze 6.5%
Brabant
www.oudecam.com

You go to the Belgian village of Gooik for two things: folk music and beer. Known as the 'Pearl of Pajottenland', Gooik is 'Graceland' for folk-loving folk: there is an annual folk festival, a folk instrument museum and there is even a diploma in folk music. Yet Brettanomyces-driven funk is what you get in the Lambic and Gueuze created by De Cam, one of Belgium's newest natural beer producers. Blender Karel Goddeau, who took over from founder Willem Van Herreweghen in 2000, serenades his Lambics with an accordion while the Brett throws sexy shapes in old Pilsner Urquell oak casks. A gushing, lively Gueuze that hits notes of lemon tart, with leather and a long finish.

De Dochter van de Korenaar
Embrasse Peated Oak Aged (Whiskey Cask) 9%
Brabant
www.dedochtervandekorenaar.be

Since 2007, Dutch brewer Ronald Mengerink has been transcending traditional beer styles at his characterful brewery situated in the little exclave of Baarle Hertog, a small slice of Belgium completely surrounded by Netherlands territory, where the border is so complicated it sometimes cuts houses in half. The brewery is named after an old Flemish term for beer, 'daughter of the corn ear'. The original Embrasse bears a resemblance to a robust, hoppy Rochefort 10, yet touches of peat, tanned leather and rich fudge emerge after a dozen weeks laid down in Connemara casks from Ireland's Cooley distillery.

De Dolle Brouwers
Oerbier Reserva, 9%
West Flanders
www.oerbier.be

In 1980, a trio of brothers bought a ramshackle brewery and began making mischief with their mashforks. The 'Mad Brewers' moniker is not misleading: their ales are eccentric and unusual, deftly weaving the wonders of wood with wild yeast and old-school equipment, including a traditional koelschip, where the hopped wort cools. The 'original beer', an oud bruin, is brewed with six different malts, three varieties of Belgian hop from Poperinge and, until 2005, inoculated with Rodenbach yeast. The brothers now propagate their own and age Oerbier in a variety of oak barrels that previously housed Cognac, Calvados and wine. Brettanomyces and Lactobacillus star in a sharp, smoky, slightly spicy and sherry-esque sip.

Girardin
Girardin Gueuze Black Label 1882 5%
Brabant
www.specialtybeer.com

While others wavered, Girardin maintained the faith and held the lantern for Gueuze and Lambic until the storm subsided. They are good guys making great Gueuze and this, a gorgeous grapefruit-gilded blend of small-batch one and two-year-old Lambics, is traditional oude Gueuze at its most enticing.

Gulden Spoor
Kalle 8%
West Flanders
www.guldenspoor.be

Kim Olievier and Björn Desmadryl no longer just brew for 't Rusteel restaurant next door to their tiny brewhouse in Gullegem, formerly known as Brouwerij 't Brouwkot. The sprightly, shrewd duo design erudite, concise beers that elude stylistic pigeon-holing. Laced with liquorice and a touch of coriander, this brisk and fresh golden ale tingles with white pepper, sweet honey, soft peach and a dry straw finish.

Hof Ten Dormaal
Blond 8%
Brabant
www.hoftendormaal.com

This small farmhouse brewery in Tildonk makes being green look extremely simple. It grows its own grain and hops, and fuels its basic brewery using rapeseed oil produced on the farm. Honeysuckle, clove, peach and white pepper are coaxed from just one hop, one grain and fruity house yeast. Less a Blond and more a smooth, strong Saison.

Lindemans
Kriek Cuvée Réne 6%
Brabant
www.lindemans.be

Seven generations of Lindemans have been brewing Lambic here since 1809, while Réne, the man after whom the beer is named, has held the reins since 1963. In the 1970s and 1980s, the firm enjoyed export success with sweet Lambics made with apple, blackcurrant and peach juice. In 2007, Réne got back to the tart, and traditional with this cracking, sour, silky Kriek: notes of aniseed and a funky barnyard finish.

De Proef
Flemish Primitive 'Surly Bird' 9%
East Flanders
www.proefbrouwerij.com

De Proef's Dirk Naudts (otherwise known as 'The Prof') is, quite literally, a world leader in his field. In a meadow not far from Ghent, Dirk breathes life into highly original brewing recipes on an impossibly hi-tech boutique brewhouse often borrowed by other brewers. Each of the Flemish Primitive beers owes its edge to a selection of different Brettanomyces yeasts and each is spruced with a different individual hop. Surly Bird is wild yet well-mannered, with signature Flemish funk. It is distinctly dry, yet can be sunk like a Saison.

Sint Canarus
Potteloereke 8%
East Flanders
www.sintcanarus.be

Among the numerous small farmhouse breweries found all over Flanders, this retro-rustic ale-making enterprise in the tiny village of Gottem stands out for being that little bit quirkier and more creative than others. On unconventional equipment, brewmaster Piet Meirhaeghe creates some superb stuff, including this robust, big-bodied deep brown ale resplendent in dark rich fruit, sugared coffee and hazelnut. Comes in a cracking-looking ceramic mug, too.

Strubbe
Ichtegem's Grand Cru 6.5%
West Flanders
www.brouwerij-strubbe.be

Since 1830, seven generations of the Strubbe family have brewed beer in Ichtegem, a small town near Bruges. Grand Cru is an oak-aged, tart and tannin-tastic Flanders sour with the hue of Hugh Heffner's purple dressing gown, a head as fluffy as the tails of his bunny-clad bimbos and more wood, one imagines, than the ageing erotica peddler can manage on his own these days. Think plums, cherries and other innuendo-laden fruit.

Beersel

In 2002, they shut the doors of Oude Beersel, a brewery and Lambic blending business just outside Brussels. Three generations of the Vandervelden family had been making Lambic here since 1882 but the fourth generation wasn't interested.

A year later, word of Oude Beersel's demise reached Gert Christianes and his pal Roland de Bus. 'We always ordered Oude Beersel Gueuze, it was what we liked drinking,' Christianes says. 'As the barman brought them over, he told us they were the last Beersel beers available.'

They liked the beers so much, they bought the business. With no brewing experience whatsoever, they enrolled on a commercial brewing course in Ghent and approached the bank for a loan. 'I made the mistake of telling them that it takes three years for Lambic and Gueuze to make any money,' says Christianes, who was then working as an IT manager. 'They weren't interested.'

In 2005, to conjure up some cash flow, they contract-brewed a Tripel at the nearby Huyghe brewery, calling it Bersalis after the Latin name for Beersel. 'It was crucial to keep the brand alive and the tripel is a good way to get people to move onto Lambic and Gueuze,' Christianes says. 'We needed to brew a beer but we couldn't brew it here – the wild yeast wouldn't allow it.

'The brewery we inherited was too old and dilapidated. We had to choose between buying more wooden barrels or buying a brewery and bottling line. We chose to focus on the traditional part of the process: fermentation, wooden tuns and blending.'

Christianes outsources all the minutiae so he can concentrate on the artisan elements. Boon, half an hour's drive away, tops and tails the process by both brewing wort to the old recipe and bottling the finished blends.

In 2007, after buying out de Bus's share in the business, Christianes unveiled his first batch of Oude Beersel Gueuze and kriek. A year later, the Gueuze scooped silver at the World Beer Cup, and production since has far outstripped what previous owners achieved.

Matured for a maximum of three years, Beersel Lambics are milder than most; delicate, dusty and dry, they do not contort the cheeks with sourness. The Gueuze is soft, with a clean citrus character while the kriek, fermented with Polish cherries, is sharp, effervescent and fabulously fruity.

While Beersel remains faithful to traditional techniques, Christianes craves consistency and quality. 'It's striking a balance between consistency and maintaining the magic. You mix the young with the old,' he says. 'You have to use technology but only to frame the picture.'

'People told me Lambic was for old people, a generation that will soon disappear but, look around you, 25-year-olds are drinking Lambic and Gueuze,' Christianes says. 'That's a new thing. In mature beer drinking countries, traditional styles are coming back. When things are tough, people look behind them.'

De Struise
Struiselensis Wild Ale 6%
West Flanders
struise.noordhoek.com

It is not always a good idea to introduce one yeast strain to another. John Keeling, head brewer at Fuller Smith and Turner by the Thames in West London, equates it to introducing one's wife to one's mistress – a very risky business with potentially disastrous consequences. But De Struise are nothing if not open-minded and are unworried if things turn a little sour, as in this burnished blonde beer, made as a tribute to the brewers of Lembeek, fermented for 14 months using Brettanomyces bruxellensis and Pediococcus cerevisiae sourced from Wyeast Laboratories in Oregon in the United States.

Weird and wonderful, and probably not a beer to offer to someone who has just told you they normally drink sweet white wines: the hint of barnyard aromas, the tartness, the cloudiness is likely to send them screaming from the room.

Gueuzerie Tilquin
Oude Gueuze Tilquin a l'Ancienne 6.4%
Brabant
www.gueuzerietilquin.be

Pierre Tilquin learned about Lambics under two of the masters of the arts and mysteries of wild fermentation, Armand Debelder (Drie Fonteinen) and Jean Pierre Van Roy (Cantillon). In 2009, the grasshopper left the temple and set up what proudly proclaims itself to be the only 'Gueuzerie' in Wallonia. In the small village of Bierghes, in the Senne valley, more than two hundred wooden tuns, brought in from Bordeaux and Burgundy, reside. Once they were filled with wine: today they hold wort sourced from four top suppliers, Boon, Lindemans, Girardin and Cantillon. Early editions of the refined and rounded Oude/l'Ancienne contained one and two-year-old Lambics: now they can be up to three years old before being blended, bottled and refermented for 6 months. It's fresh, funky and a little bit farmyard.

NETHERLANDS

Emelisse
Imperial Russian Stout (Laphroaig BA) 11%
Zeeland
www.emelisse.nl

Not content with boasting arguably the world's best brewer name, Kees Bubberman, a former home-brewer, brews bold and brave at his brewhouse in Kamperland on the western tip of the Netherlands. Very creative and forever welcoming overseas collaborators, Bubberman has a healthy appetite for hops. His dry-hopped Triple IPA,

heaving with Chinook, Simcoe, Cascade and Amarillo, throws herbal haymakers more readily associated with the coffee shops of Amsterdam, while his Dutch boks are big in every way. Equally intense is this bulbous, Baltic-style beer laid down in barrels soaked in Laphroaig, the most medicinal of Islay malts. This is a beer adorned with iodine, dry peat and seaweed, plus a snippet of vanilla.

DENMARK

Amager
Wrath 6.5%
Copenhagen
www.amagerbryghus.dk

Hunkered down in an old air raid bunker, Amager is an acutely on-the-ball brewer for whom pasteurisation, filtration and the use of naughty adjuncts is deemed the devil's work. The funkiest of its Sinner series is a full-on farmyard Saison primed in Pinot Noir wine barrels. Expect toffee apple, pepper, cinnamon and a sherry finish.

SWEDEN

Närke
Konjaks! Stormaktsporter (2008)
9.6%
Örebro
www.kulturbryggeri.se

A trio of honest, principled homebrewers started this small-batch set-up in south central Sweden in 2004 yet sprung to prominence when, in 2011, its Stormaktsporter was voted the number one beer by the hordes of beer buffs who prowl Ratebeer.com.

The Konjaks! version is an opulent, enormously exalted imperial stout aged in cognac-sodden oak casks and unleashed in rationed annual batches, the last being 2009. Rich praline emanates from its tawny top, while an unctuous, elegant dark cherry body sheds tears down the side of the snifter. Log fire smoke, brandy snaps, charred chestnuts, pistachio and an overwhelming desire to drink more of it. Elusive, expensive, yet earns its online admiration.

LoverBeer
D'UvaBeer 8%
Piedmont
www.loverbeer.com

A delightful dark pink sour tailored near Turin by an Italian microbrewer named Valter Loverier (hence the name of the brewery – geddit?) very much in tune with his epicurean surroundings. A number of his ales embrace indigenous ingredients including this funky fruity fellow fermented with Freisa grape must from the Piedmont region. Tart cranberry notes, citric astringency and a flint dry fruit finish.

Maltus Faber
Extra Brune Barricata
10%
Genoa
www.maltusfaber.com

Along with Milan and Turin, Genoa is the third point of Northern Italy's craft brewing triangle and Maltus Faber has been crucial in the cultivation of local craft beer. In a brewhouse jettisoned by Heineken, it crowbars a bespoke, coffee-noted, muscular, malty brown ale into Brunello di Montalcino wine barrels made from Croatian oak. The result is like a Port Sour cocktail blended with a robust porter, satin smooth with a mousse-like mouthfeel and notes of coffee, chocolate and a deep Chateau Musar.

Revelation Cat
Woodwork Series (Acacia) 11%
Rome
tiny.cc/revelationcat

Another 'gypsy brewer' with no brewery of its own uses new casks for its Woodwork series. The beer, an intensely aromatic IPA, seasoned with Nelson Sauvin, is made by the Proefbrouwerij in Belgium, then matured in acacia, which imparts a floral vibrancy and notes of lemon, lime and lychee along a spicy spine with an undertow of tannin.

Toccalmato
Russian Imperial Stout Wild Brett 12%
Parma
www.birratoccalmatto.it

Enthused by the American beer scene, especially the widespread hailing of the hop, gastronome Bruno Carillo began producing craft beer in Parma, the 'larder of Italy', back in 2008. By filling out classic flavours wherever he is able, and shaped with no shortage of chutzpah, his beers have found a following outside of Italy, especially in the UK and the US. A velvety, vinous barrel-aged Baltic beer aged in Sagrantino di Montefalco red wine barrels and hopped with earthy English hops, beneath the black inky, opaque hue of this imperial stout lies a little bit of lactic funk, a rich coffee roast character and a tart chocolate-coated dark fruit finish.

Torrechiara
Panil Bariqueè Sour 8%
Parma
www.panilbeer.com

Brewed next door to the winery by the son of a winemaker, there is a thinly veiled vinous edge to Torrechiara's ales, produced in the Provincia di Parma since 2000. A big fan of Belgian brewing techniques, Renzo Losi rears his creations in an array of oak barrels, works closely with wine yeast and, in Divina, has a Lambic shaped by ambient yeast. This spicy sour is fermented thrice: first in stainless steel, then for three months in Bordeaux barrels bathed in cognac and, finally, in the bottle. With musty mahogany notes, dark cherry and a dry, warm finish, on form, it deservedly receives green-eyed glances from Flanders.

SWITZERLAND

Franches-Montagnes
Abbaye de St Bon Chien 11%
Jura
www.brasseriebfm.ch

Locally born vintner Jérôme Rebetez started Brasserie des Franches-Montagnes (aka BFM) in Saignelégier in 1997 and may fairly be credited for single-handedly putting Switzerland back on the world beer map with his flagship Abbaye de St Bon Chien, named after the brewery's late 'guard cat', a stunning blended, berry-tastic aged sour brown ale matured in wine and spirit barrels. Released annually in small numbers and with a fervent following among fans of the funk and farmyard aromas, bottles seldom stick around for long.

SPAIN

Masia Agullons
Setembre 5.5%
Catalonia
www.masia-agullons.com

From a rustic ramshackle countryside brewery based in the small, bucolic town of Mediona comes an acerbic autumnal beer rarer than a misplaced pass from Lionel Messi. A Catalan collaboration with the Belgian brewer Cantillon and a distinct drinking diversion from Spain's traditionally straight-laced cerveza culture, farmhouse meets farmyard as an Anglo-American pale ale (Pura), shaped using English malt and Cascade hops, is blended with young, tart Belgian Lambic. Unleashed each September after 12 months in oak and a further year in bottle, Setembre has clean spikes of citrus and sourness with a rough, grainy undertone.

AUSTRALIA

Moo Brew
Barrel-Aged Vintage Stout 8%
Tasmania
www.moobrew.com.au

Head brewer Owen Johnston makes some devilishly tasty beers at a brewery alongside the Museum of Old and New Art (MONA) on the outskirts of Hobart, and serves them in seriously sexy bottles decorated with labels designed by artist John Kelly. French and American medium-toast barrels host a potent, velvet stout for 12 months before the product of the different casks is brought together to create a thick, layered blend of liquorice, molasses, oats and mouth-tightening tannin.

Moon Dog
Perverse Sexual Amalgam 6%
Melbourne
moondogbrewing.com.au

A bikini-clad lady with a cock (as in chicken) as a head adorns this wild plum ale. Wheat, dark Vienna malt and muscovado sugar make up the mash, its tartness is attained from both sour cherry plums and the four ambient yeast strains that come out to play in the bourbon barrels. Moderately sour, musty and mouldy like a Pedro Ximenez sherry with a soft soy sauce finish.

BRAZIL

Falke Bier
Vivre Pour Vivre 4.5%
Minas Gerias,
www.falkebier.com.br

This mould-shattering micro was founded in 2004 by home-brewer Marco 'Falke' Falcano. The serendipitous genesis of this extraordinary sour occurred when pesky Lactobacillus wheedled its way into a batch of Falcano's Belgian Tripel, Monasterium. Rather than throw it away, Falcano left it to mature in his cellar for three years before blending it with juice made from jabuticaba, an indigenous, acerbic purple grape-like fruit. Refermented with fresh yeast, it is a spicy, sour, cherry-coloured, cider-like aperitif laced with clean lactic character.

MY TOP 5
CRAFT BEERS

Riccardo Franzosi
Birrificio Montegiocco
Italy

✸ **Westmalle Tripel**
In the late 1980s, some brave Italian publicans started to sell a different kind of beer, tasteful and interesting, unlike the ones on the market till then. This is one of those beers. When I first tasted it I exclaimed 'Wow!' It was the first, unconscious, step towards a much wider world.

✸ **Birrificio Italiano Tipopils**
This is a classic Pils, very elegant and fresh, where the aroma of hops is exalted yet balanced at the same time. Produced by one of the pioneers of the Italian craft beer scene.

✸ **Drie Fonteinen Schaarbeekse Kriek**
One of the many turning points on my beer journey. This was my acid curve. I couldn't ignore the Kriek par excellence.

✸ **Cantillon Saint Lamvinus**
A wonderful example of Lambic which calls for the use of grapes and barrels, skilfully made by a great master. When drinking this beer, there's a balance between the world of beer and the world of wine.

✸ **Bi-Du Artigian Ale**
I believe this is a really balanced beer. Malt and hops meet each other and match together extremely well, making it easily drinkable, even if its alcoholic strength is not that low.

LAMBIC AND GUEUZE

Among beer connoisseurs, Lambic and Gueuze tend to divide opinion like the letter 'n'.

There are those who regard them as the most quixotic, cultured expression of the brewer's art and then there are others who simply cannot see the attraction of beer that doesn't really taste like beer at all. With its dryness, sourness and acute acidity, Lambic is closer in character to cider and dry sherry, while the method of its production is influenced significantly by viniculture. But it is exclusively made in Belgium and, as everyone knows, Belgium is beer country.

Lambic has been brewed in and around the south-west corner of Brussels for more than 500 years, and more than a dozen producers remain, keeping the enchanting legacy alive and every year, between October and April, brewing in deliberate, defiant denial of modern science.

Lambic is not popular among conical flask-carrying control freaks. You have to be a pretty laid-back brewer to live with Lambic because, once you have brewed the base wheat beer, you must lay it bare to the fickle whimsies of the weather, wild yeast and wood. The only part of the brewing process where humans have control is at the beginning, with the mash, made up of 40% unmalted wheat.

Rather than using fresh hops to a long vigorous boil, Lambic brewers add musty old varieties up to several years old, almost entirely bereft of bitterness yet still in possession of their preservative powers.

After brewing, the wort is then poured into a broad and shallow swimming-pool shaped vessel at the top of the brewhouse called a koelschip (deep enough for a stingray but a sure death trap for a dolphin).

Small vents and windows in the wall are opened to let in the cool night air and wild yeasts and all manner of bacteria from Brussels (and its surrounding suburbs to the southwest) that descend and infect the cooling liquid.

After ambient airborne inoculation, the cooled and rested wort is transferred into wooden tuns, known either as 'pipes' (around 600 litres) or larger 'foudres', which can hold up to 20,000 litres, and the gun of fermentation is then fired.

There are several stages of fermentation, both acidic and alcoholic, performed by myriad microorganisms who, like gentleman in a bar brawl, politely wait until their companions tire before going to work on the wort.

VARIETIES OF LAMBIC

Lambic
Both the generic term for spontaneous beers from this particular part of Belgium and the name given to the base beer. Taken fresh from the tuns or poured in draught in select cafés, it tastes a bit like sherry-soaked socks.

Gueuze
Normally corked and caged in Champagne bottles, Gueuze (pronounced like 'ghost' without the final 't') is a bottle-conditioned blend of young Lambic (aged for between 6 and 12 months) and old (oude) Lambic (aged in oak for up to 3 years) in a ratio of one to two.

A greater proportion of older Lambic brings more Brett and complexity, while Gueuze blended with more young Lambic will be softer in character. Blenders strive for a signature style and a certain consistency of flavour from year to year but every vintage tends to be different – which merely adds to its allure.

Fruit
Kriek (cherry) is made traditionally by steeping Schaerbeek cherries, native to the Brussels area, in Lambic for six months. Cherries are added whole and, during a vigorous secondary fermentation, the stones dissolve to add an almond edge to the tart character.

While no longer as prevalent as it once was, Framboise used raspberries in the same way while there have been various attempts to use other fruits, ranging from blueberries to cranberries, with varying success.

Beware of Lambic fruit beers made with fruit syrup, which are only suitable for those with a tooth sweeter than a monkey in a dress.

Faro
Popular in the 19th century, Faro is Lambic beer sweetened with sugar to make it more palatable to the everyday drinker.

1st stage: First out the blocks are naturally occurring bacteria which, over four weeks, quickly change the chemical complexion of the wort. Like a pacemaker in a race, they set the right tempo before getting tired, dropping out and coming to a halt, hands on knees and panting …

2nd stage: A brisk eager pack of Saccharomyces yeasts then take up the running, producing alcohol and various flavours. For four months, the action is fast and furious, leaving a foaming scene of destruction behind, white froth bellowing out of the bunghole.

3rd stage: As the temperature gets a little warmer, barrel-dwelling, lactic acid-producing Pediococci come out of the woodwork and, over three to four months, turns things sour.

4th stage: Bring out the Bretts. Brettanomyces bruxellensis and Brettanomyces lambicus (the first found more in urban Lambic beers and the second in surrounding districts), embark on a second alcoholic fermentation. Brett slowly hoovers up any extract left over and turns it into alcohol, sour vinegar flavours (acetic acid) and Lambic's extra distinctive dimension, often characterised as horse blanket, but more reminiscent of your grandfather's closet or a pair of sweaty, grass-covered football boots.

The exact influence of the oak, the air and the natural ecosystem of each particular brewery remains unclear. If you ask a Lambic producer for particulars regarding Pediococci and pals, you'll get a raise of the eyebrows and a resigned shrug of the shoulders.

Far left: Oude Beersel bewery.
Left: Cantillon's barrel room in Brussels.
Above: Whole Shaarbeek cherries added to the beer.

CANTILLON

Kriek 100% Lambic Bio

THE ALE APOTHECARY

Bend, Oregon, USA   www.thealeapothecary.com

Technology, ultimately, disappoints. Mainly because we ask too much of it. Science fiction should shoulder the bulk of the blame, for raising our imaginative expectations to a level that real life simply cannot reach.

For years, films and comics have furnished our minds with visions of flying cars yet, as of 2013, some automobiles don't even have a sunroof. Teleportation has not turned out the way we had hoped; lightspeed is still in second gear; and robots, those malevolent masters of the future as foretold by the past, have been enormous underachievers.

Instead of presiding over a dystopian society, as predicted, the mechanical men find themselves performing tasks humans seldom stoop to: working on bottling lines, doing the vacuuming, being laughed at on Japanese television. Robots have let us down. But more importantly, they've let themselves down.

In 2012, Paul Arney had enough of machines and turned his back on technology. After nearly 15 years working for the Deschutes Brewery, where he had happily been pushing the envelope of innovation as far as it could go, he felt a calling from the forests of Central Oregon.

Just outside the town of Bend, in a small clearing in the woods, Arney set up the Ale Apothecary, an oak barrel brewery living in blissful disregard of modern brewing.

The Ale Apothecary's mission is to derive flavours from the process rather than ingredients. 'These days, a brewer can open up a catalogue and order just about anything his or her

heart desires to create a myriad flavours for beers,' Arney says. 'What we aren't doing as much as brewers in the past did is using equipment totally unique to the brewery or location.

'Beer has only been recently industrialised in its production. I am interested in creating truly handmade beer that connects the drinker with the place that the beer originated from and, indeed, the brewer that makes it.'

Handmade may be an oft-used and abused mantra among microbrewers, but few of Arney's brewing peers could honestly claim their approach is more hands-on than Arney's.

Arney is a man who chooses to do things that machines normally do. He welcomes wild yeast, forages for fruit and herbs and encourages nature to stick its nose in where other brewers would not welcome it. All his beers undergo some kind of spontaneous fermentation and every brewing vessel, apart from the copper, is made from wood.

'Brewers used to make virtually all of their equipment and modified their processes continuously as they did so,' he says. 'In today's modern age, this still happens, but it is done with fabricated, mass-produced stainless steel.'

The beer that epitomises Ale Apothecary's approach is Sahati, a Pacific Northwest interpretation of Sahti, thought to be the longest continuously brewed beer style in the world. Five thousand miles from Finland and five hundred years after it was first brewed, Arney brews with an unswerving fidelity to the 16th-century Finnish methods, if not the ingredients.

To make the Finnish kuurna, the rudimentary, rustic trough-like log that acts as a lauter tun in Sahti brewing, Arney

Arney is a man who chooses to do things that machines normally
do. He welcomes wild yeast, forages for fruit and herbs and
encourages nature to stick its nose in where other brewers would
not welcome it. All his beers undergo some kind of spontaneous
fermentation and every brewing vessel, apart from the copper,
is made of wood.

took an axe to a 200-year-old spruce tree that grew down
the hill on the brewery grounds. 'Taking a spruce tree from
the brewery property and turning it into a piece of brewing
equipment identifies who we are as a brewery and states
exactly what we do. It's very symbolic.'

The long, shallow spruce log that Arney carved allows
a more efficient extraction of wort than contemporary lauter
tuns, which are taller and narrower. Crucially, unlike modern
kuurnas made with steel, the tree also infuses the wort with
resin and aromatic oils.

Arney twists on tradition by lining the log with a lattice
of Oregonian spruce branches, rather than using an aspen
tree bed with juniper and berries as Finnish historical ritual
dictates. As well as acting as a natural filter, spruce flavours
the beer reflects the brewery's surroundings.

'There's a connection with the American colonial brewer
and it grows on our brewery property,' he says. 'I also boil the
spruce branches the night prior to brewing. This sterilises
the branches and infuses the spruce essence into the water,
which I then use for sparging the grain in the kuurna.'

Arney follows Finnish methods by starting an infusion
mash the night before brewing. But while the Finns tend to
mash for four hours, Arney's conversion is a lengthier 12
hour process using a variety of base malts including barley,
wheat, rye. 'I try to avoid heavily kilned malt or speciality malts
that might overpower the input of the process,' he says. 'The
extended time in contact with the oak mash tun encourages
other flavour development not attainable with a couple of
hours in stainless steel mash tuns.'

After lautering, Arney boils the wort before adding a
small amount of hops for bitterness or, in the spring, fresh,
herbal spruce tips. The beer leaves the open fermentation
vessels at around 10% and resides in oak barrels for about
six to nine months.

Arney and his wife Staci then bottle each naturally
carbonated beer by hand, corking and caging the beer using
hemp twine rather than metal. After all this, the 75cl bottles
are then rested for six weeks prior to release.

'The driving force behind this beer is to show what
humans can, and will, do for beer,' Arney says.

Above far left: Arney's spruce lauter tun.
Above centre left: The brewery in the woods.
Above centre right: One of Ale Apothecary's wild beers,
  brewed with Brett.
Above far right: Paul Arney.

KEY BEERS

Sahalie 9.3%
La Tache 6%
Spencer 9.3%

DRIE FONTEINEN

Beersel, Belgium www.3fonteinen.be/

Goddes good was the name given to the fermentation process during the Dark Ages. Back then, when possession of a microscope would have you branded a witch and thrown down a well, no one knew of yeast's existence nor how fermentation occurred.

Ale-making alchemy was simply seen as a miracle. It was mysterious, magical manna from heaven, turning humdrum wort into a substance that was safer than water and made life that little bit easier to cope with.

The extent of the Almighty's influence on contemporary Lambic brewing remains unclear, something for the creationists and chemists to quarrel about. But there was one particular divine intervention that Armand Debelder, a legend among Lambic producers, could have done without.

On 16 May 2009, Debelder's warehouse, containing thousands of litres of languidly maturing Lambics, exploded. A dodgy thermostat had failed to turn off a heater, the mercury had risen to more than 140°C/284°F and 5,000 bottles had shattered in the heat.

Worse still, more than 80,000 bottles of Gueuze were ruined: oxidised and unfit for consumption. It bankrupted Debelder and, within months, he had lost the lease on the brewery. It was, Debelder thought, a sign from God – a God that is not always necessarily good.

Bereft of a brewery and a third of his beer, Debelder questioned carrying on. 'It was tough, people didn't accept that I wanted to give up,' he says, glass of Gueuze in one hand, the other hand pushing up his baseball cap and giving his head an exasperated rub. 'People didn't want the tradition to die. I wasn't allowed to [call it a day]. My wife kept telling me I had to keep going.' Thankfully, dogged devotion and blind faith is an integral part of the Lambic culture. It does delayed gratification better than any other beer style and, whether you are creating it or drinking it, patient perseverance pays off.

Debutant drinkers do not always see the light. If, at first, you don't succeed in 'getting' Lambic or Gueuze then try, try again. Keep the faith. 'You have to learn to love these beers,' Debelder says, swirling the Gueuze around in his wine glass. 'When you take your first sip, clean the mouth with the Gueuze and wait a few seconds,' he adds, allowing silence to descend.

'Then take a second sip and truly taste it, roll it around the tongue and completely clear your mind of what you expect beer to taste like. And then take a third sip. If you don't like it, perhaps it's not for you right now,' he says, before adding: 'But, one day, I think it will be …'

Moneymen may find the concept of Lambic and Gueuze hard to swallow. It is, in fairness, a ludicrous idea for a business. An ever-inconsistent beer reliant on an ethereal natural phenomenon, dependent on maverick microflora and then entombed, along with any profits, in wooden tuns for years – it doesn't get filed in the 'fast buck' folder. 'Here, you buy a beer from a brewer,' Debelder says, 'not a banker.'

It was fellow brewers such as Lindemans and Dogfish Head rather than banks that helped Drie Fonteinen after the disaster. 'The kindness of others was overwhelming,' Debelder says. 'People helped me open 80,000 bottles of oxidised beer, pour it into a tank and distil it.'

The oxidised beer was reborn as Armands Spirit, and inspired Debelder to keep going. After all, he had a Lambic legacy to look after. The Drie Fonteinen blending business in Beersel has been in his family since 1953, when his father Gaston bought it, along with an inn, from Jan-Baptist Vanderlinden, whose own father had built it 70 years earlier.

In the early 1960s, Drie Fonteinen (Three Sources) moved to a new site across from the church and became renowned not only for its Gueuze but also as the home of the De Mijol Club, a legendary literary club, firm in the furthering of Flemish culture, whose members came from Belgium's clever-clog cognoscenti, such as Herman Teirlinck, August Vermeylen, Alfred Hegenscheidt, Ernest Claes and Fernand Toussaint van Boelaere.

'In the 1950s, Beersel was home to 14 different blenders and one brewery,' Debelder says. 'Each café had their own signature style and we just sold our beers through our bar and restaurant. It was a great place to be – especially if you liked Gueuze.'

But by the time Debelder had returned from military service and trained as a chef, the general love for Lambic beer was waning amid appetite for lagers and specialist Belgian beers such as Palm. 'Everything became sweeter,' Debelder says, 'things changed.'

He and his younger brother Guido inherited both the restaurant and the blending businesses in 1982. Debelder's time was divided between working as a chef and looking after the Lambics, often alongside Gaston, a reluctant retiree.

In the 1990s, the bar was making more money than the beer. Lambic land was not an easy place to make a living for a blender. Brewers had recognised the potential profit – albeit small; public palates were pining for sweet rather than sour sensations and Gueuze was growing increasingly synonymous with grandads.

'It was very hard,' Debelder says. 'Very few people were doing what we were doing. We thought very seriously about calling time on the beers, but we kept going. There was a concerted campaign to keep Gueuze alive and, again, we weren't really allowed to stop.'

With Lambic gaining cult status, Debelder began selling his beers beyond the bar and restaurant and in 1998 he began brewing Lambics himself, on a 10-hectolitre brewhouse leased from the Palm brewery. 'I didn't set out to change the world,' he says. 'But I didn't want to die regretting that I didn't ever brew my own beers. So I did it.

'My father was very angry with me. He thought I was crazy. When he tasted a Gueuze made with Lambics that I'd brewed, it was the first direct complement he'd ever paid me.

The cellar is a time-warped temple of wort-filled, wooden tuns. It is here where Debelder performs his art, chalking up the dates, tapping the tuns, blending old Lambics with new and bringing different beers together to create Gueuze - the Champagne of beer.

'Until then, I didn't feel like a brewer in my head. I had no formal brewery training but I received guidance from everywhere and everyone. I have a mantra that it can always be better. You never reach the pinnacle with this kind of brewing – that's what is so wonderful about it.'

In 2002, Debelder focused solely on the beer by setting up A-D Bieren, the brewing and blending division of Drie Fonteinen. New stocks of Lambic were sourced, a new bottling line was installed, he bought six dozen 1,000 litre wooden tuns from Pilsner Urquell and a warehouse to put them all in.

He even breathed life back into an old-fashioned interpretation of a kriek brewed with Belgian cherries. 'We use two kinds of cherries – Polish cherries and Schaerbeek cherries that we pick ourselves,' Debelder says. 'They're sweet, sour and wild cherries and they're hard to find.'

But that was all before the disaster in 2009. 'I needed a catastrophe to wake me up and invigorate me,' Debelder says. 'The setback gave me the courage to continue and we're back where we want to be. I've been one part of a historical chain and, crucially, the chain didn't break.'

It has been strengthened too. First, a 28 year-old apprentice called Michael Blancquaert was taken on, invigorating Debelder they way a young Lambic does an old. Then, in 2012, Debelder opened a small Lambic brewery. 'It's small but it's exciting,' he beams.

Drie Fonteinen will continue to, rather aptly given the name, source Lambics from three producers. 'I use Girardin, Boon and Lindemans,' Debelder says, as we walk down into the beer cellar. 'Lindemans has the most Brettanomyces character, Girardin brings the most bitterness and Boon has great balance.'

The cellar is a time-warped temple of wort-filled, wooden tuns. It is here where Debelder performs his art, chalking up the dates, tapping the tuns, blending old Lambics with new and bringing different beers together to create Gueuze – the Champagne of beer.

Blending, he says, is more instinct than exact science. 'When I studied and looked into Brettanomyces and got out microscopes I made my worst Lambics. It's better not to think about it. Too much analysis is a bad thing sometimes. You've just got to let it do what it does.'

While he endeavours to create Drie Fontienen's 'green apple' signature every time, Debelder concedes his is not a quest for consistency. 'Nothing is exact,' he says. 'That is what is so exciting. I am creating new tastes every time and there is no pressure to conform. I do what I want to do. I'm a free man who can brew what I want to brew. Certitude is not fun for me – I like it when anything can happen.'

KEY BEERS

Vintage Gueuze 7%
Oude Kriek 6%
Oude Gueuze 7%
Schaerbeekse Oude Kriek 8%
Armand 4 6%
Framboos 5%

THE BRUERY

Orange County, California www.thebruery.com

Placentia is the kind of town where Valium would settle down. Located south of Los Angeles, the town motto of this anodyne overspill of über-suburbia is 'a pleasant place to live'.

Entirely incongruous to its anodyne environs, within the walls of a warehouse of A.N. Other industrial park in Orange County, the Bruery produces beer that some of the people of Placentia may not think is very 'pleasant' at all.

Since Patrick Rue founded the operation back in 2008, the Bruery has become a favourite micro among Belgian beer buffs, faithful followers of funk and all those interested in the idiosyncratic.

Rue, cherubic, chunky and curly of hair, like a beefed-up Bacchus, followed a well-trodden path to professional brewing. He was a homebrewer throughout his college years, studying law and dragging growlers of unusual ales to house parties while his classmates clinked glasses in wine bars. He emerged from education with a law degree, yet no burning desire to use it.

Rue felt the financial fear of setting up a brewery: but did it anyway. He knew he was arriving late to southern California's craft brewing party, but he was also acutely aware that he was bringing something genuinely new.

While San Diego had become synonymous with in-yer-face IPAs, hoppier than a hare on a hot tin roof, the Bruery eschewed the extreme and the escalating IBU arms race in favour of elegance and the esoteric.

Rue and head brewer Tyler King employ unusual ageing techniques and ingredients and untamed yeast strains, and adopt the kind of laid-back attitude to bacteria that would bring Placentia's housewives out in hives.

Kumquats, grapes, chinese herbs and the solera system, an approach more readily associated with sherry production, have all contributed to the complexity of the Bruery's eclectic range of beers.

'We don't make Pale Ales, IPAs, or really any style that gets much attention,' Rue says. 'We don't make "extreme" beer for the sake of being extreme, but rather we make beers that showcase unique flavours and often involve some distinctive methods of brewing. Very little prevents us from attempting something new and interesting.

'Alcohol ranges from 2.1% to 21% ABV, from dark to light, intense to subtle,' Rue says. 'I like to focus on styles and flavours that are not well represented by other breweries.' The Bruery's beers, unpasteurised and unfiltered, with a heavy emphasis on barrel-ageing, are matured, on average, for six months. 'Time is an important ingredient to our beer. Approximately 40% of our beer is aged for a year or longer in a variety of oak barrels, which is an extraordinarily long time for a commercial brewery,' Rue says.

The Bruery is a broad church, its pews filled with more than 60 brews that are not afraid to stray off the stylistic pathway, all created on a ten-barrel pilot brewery designed to encourage experimentation.

Right: A Bruery worker makes sure there is no repeat of 'Black Tuesday'.

The Bruery is a broad church, its pews filled with more than 60 brews that are not afraid to stray off the stylistic pathway, all created on a ten-barrel pilot brewery designed to encourage experimentation.

A single sitting at the Bruery's tasting room moved from a Berliner Weisse (3%) called Hoggenroth to Smoked Wood, a smouldering bourbon-barrel-aged after-dinner ale via a strong-selling American Red Ale, a gloriously fruity Belgian Tripel and Tart of Darkness, a subtly sour Belgian stout akin to Hercule Stout from Ellezelloise – just more sour and remarkably refreshing in the 26°C/80°F Southern Californian heat.

For its Anniversary Ales, each year's beer was given a name that was the French translation of the relevant anniversary gift – Papier for the first anniversary, Coton for the second, Cuir for the third, and so on – with a percentage of every previous anniversary beer blended into the current release, on the solera system. This has resulted in great complexity and drinkability in the most recent releases, and has given this beer a bit of heritage for a brewery founded only in 2008. At 15.5% ABV and 100% aged in bourbon barrels, the beer has notes of treacle, figs, apricot, vanilla and burnt wood.

The Bruery's most notorious ale is Black Tuesday, a cult beer that was created from a truly calamitous experience when the brewing gods opened an enormous can of whuppass on Patrick and his team of brewers. The 'brewing day from hell' was Tuesday 1 July 2008, just a few months after the Bruery opened. Patrick was brewing an imperial stout when a leaking pump caused mayhem in the mash tun, sending 25,000lbs of hot, gloopy granular beer all over the brewery floor and, unfortunately, Rue. 'Mash and 170°F water is flying everywhere,' Rue wrote on his blog. 'It's a tidal wave of hot s**t, all over my arms, legs, in my boots, and the brewery is a disaster. I'm cussing, running around in frustration and in pain.'

'I already hate this beer. I'm condemning it to bourbon barrels for over a year, and hopefully I'll forgive it at that point,' he wrote. 'We're aiming for a 20% ABV beer, but I'm sure fermentation will stick, just because the beer despises me.'

One online observer offered a name for Rue's liquid nemesis: 'Clearly, you should call it Black Tuesday.' And the legend was born. Now, every year, its release on the last Tuesday in October draws hundreds of dedicated dark beer diehards to the doors of the Bruery and sparks an almighty annual online scramble for the rare 750ml bottles.

Black Tuesday is a massive bourbon-barrel-aged imperial stout with an ABV that orbits 20%, but is adjusted according to the appetite of the yeast. 'We blend many batches of this beer to be as consistent as possible, as each batch behaves just a little differently,' Rue says. 'There are flavours of dark chocolate, coffee, vanilla, coconut and caramel.'

The Bruery's most award-winning effort is Oude Tart, a tongue-contorting Flemish Red, which scooped gold at the World Beer Cup in consecutive years and is brewed to a recipe created by Tyler King, the Bruery's senior director of brewing, whom Rue met at his homebrewing club. It's a striking, sweet-and-sour blend of young and old beer full of yeast-driven funk, tartness and tannin.

'It's one of the more "to style" beers we brew,' Rue admits. 'We barrel-ferment the wort in puncheon barrels with a variety of yeasts and bacteria, and then age it in retired red wine oak barrels for a range of 8 to 20 months.'

Mischief, brewed with American hops and Belgian yeast, is the Bruery's best-selling dry and deceptively drinkable golden ale, while Humulus Lager, an imperial light lager, is the closest Rue comes to infringing his own anti-IPA rules and committing that rare of craft beer crimes: using rice. 'While we promised to never make an IPA, I admit it's one of my favourite styles and this is my way of skirting my own rules,' he says, laughing. 'It's a hybrid of a rice-adjunct robust American lager with the hopping rate of an American IPA. This was one of my homebrew recipes and it's our answer to anyone who visits The Bruery and asks for an IPA.'

Left: Bruery beers benefit from an unusually long maturation process.

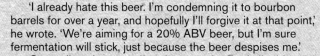

KEY BEERS

Black Tuesday Imperial Stout 19.2 %
Rugbrød 8%
Saison Rue 8.5%
Oude Tart 7.5%
Bruery Melange 3 15.5%
Trade Winds Tripel 8%

* CELLAR

---

* vintage

* limited edition

* special

* mature

* evolving

Wine drinkers have been perfecting the art of delayed gratification for years. In times of austerity, grandiose grape-based giggle juice is considered one of the more reliable cash-creating commodities, with the finest vintages fetching thousands of pounds.

While beer may not be such an attractive investment opportunity, with even the most coveted craft beers rarely reaching more than triple figures, an increasing number of boutique beer lovers are embracing the concept of laying down beer and advancing the art of ageing. After all, true beer drinkers aren't in it for the money. We're better than that.

As brewers continue to stretch strength and styles, venturing into vintage ales and vertical releases, it is becoming increasingly difficult to consider yourself a genuine craft beer connoisseur if you haven't embraced the new world of old beer.

The beers selected for 'Cellar' consist of the strong and the sought-after, rare editions, limited releases, annual vintages and classic brews designed to improve over time; slow-sipping, celebratory scoops certifiably suited for special occasions.

Crafted for moments of quiet contemplation with the closest of companions, they should be plucked out at their prime, dusted down, delicately decanted and treated with the utmost respect and reverence.

Equally, you can swirl them in a snifter as you stare into the smouldering embers of a once roaring fire, your mind pottering around the rag and bone shop of your past, pondering what it's all about.

For every single special cellared beer, we have chosen an ideal and appropriate accompaniment designed to enhance the imbibing experience, be it a piece of music, a cigar, a film, food, poem or novel.

These are, of course, personal recommendations that may not evoke the same experience in you.

So feel free to create some of your own.

THERE ARE BEERS THAT NEED TO BE DRUNK FRESH, AND THERE ARE BEERS THAT ONLY COME INTO THEIR OWN AFTER THEY HAVE BEEN GIVEN TIME TO GATHER THEMSELVES TOGETHER, ADD UP THE SUM OF THEIR PARTS AND PRODUCE SOMETHING MUCH GREATER THAN THE WHOLE.

UK

BrewDog
A B:05 (Belgian imperial stout aged on cacao and coconut) 12.5%
England/Scotland
www.abstrakt.com

No other brewer in Britain polarises opinion quite like the UK's most iconoclastic ale-maker. BrewDog cock a leg on the fire hydrant of conventional brewing, and British craft beer would be a lot blander without them. While their marketing can sometimes be mightier than what emerges from the mash-tun, this tropical take on a dense, slightly sour Belgian stout shows what they can do when not stuffing moonshine into dead squirrels. This is part of their progressive Abstrakt Series, a shrewd stable of one-off experimental bottle-conditioned beers known only by their number and rarer than rocking-horse droppings.

Drink with: *Today Tomorrow: the collected poems of George Bruce 1933-2000*

Fuller Smith & Turner
Vintage Ale 8.5%
London, England
www.fullers.co.uk

A legendary liquid from London's oldest surviving brewer, Vintage Ale was first brewed in 1996 with Golden Pride barley wine as its base. Each year the grist and/or the hopping are tweaked, with different

varieties of malt and hops ensuring a slight variation on previous years. Ignore the Best Before stamp on the bottle, as after just three years Father Time has only begun to coax out the complexity. Age calms down the carbonation, brings down the bitterness and rounds edges. After a decade lying dormant, the 2002 Vintage (Golden Promise malt and Goldings hop), was steeped in smoke, spice and a vinous, port-like body. Make sure you buy three every year – one to try young and then again after five and ten years respectively.

Drink with: Colston Bassett Stilton

Brewer's Reserve Number 4 8.5%
The labyrinthine corridors at Fuller's Griffin brewery in West London have become increasingly cluttered up with oak casks previously filled with Glenmorangie Highland single malt whisky, Courvoisier Cognac and Auchentoshan Lowland single malt. Each has been refilled with a special blend of Golden

Pride and one or more of Fuller's other strong beers, including 1845 and ESB Export, and then stored wherever there's space, for more than a year before being released as part of the limited edition Brewer's Reserve

series. Each is unique and improves with age: yet the fourth edition, matured for more than 16 months in black oak casks that once contained vintage Comte de Lauvia Armagnac, has an exuberance of youth and tannin-texture that bodes well for the future. Rustic and spicy, the sour Brett-bravado should simmer down in the cellar and reveal vanilla, cinnamon and prune flavours.

Drink with: a Punch Churchill 1999 cigar.

Shepherd Neame
2011 Generation Ale 9%
Kent, England
www.shepherdneame.co.uk

It is refreshing to see a legendary regional and England's oldest brewers proved they still had the moves with this 2011 anniversary ale commemorating the fifth generation of the Neame family. Brewer Stuart Main fuses a quintet of Kentish hops with five different malts (pale, crystal, chocolate. amber and brown) before a 12-month maturation at -1°C/30°F. It's a big, strapping boy, with stewed fruit, earthy and full of phenolic, but already mature for its age.

Drink with: Nick Drake's album *Five Leaves Left*

Traquair House
Jacobite Ale 8%
Scotland
www.traquair.co.uk

History buffs who have blown dust from musty tomes reckon Traquair House has been a home since the beginning of the 12th century – making it the oldest inhabited abode in Scotland. There has been a brewery here since at least 1566, when Mary Queen of Scots popped in for a quick pint, while

Bonnie Prince Charlie also had a cheeky sharpener here in 1745. After more than a century in slumber, the brewery was reborn in 1965, and its unlined oak open fermenters, the last in the UK, are still used to create the staunchly Scottish, and sherry-like, signature House ale. This reincarnation of an 18th-century recipe, containing coriander, wraps you up warmly in cloves, figs and mulled wine.

Drink with: Caol Ila 12-year-old single malt whisky

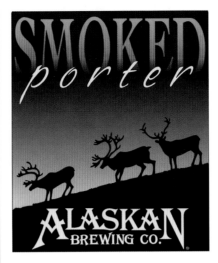

Alaskan Brewing
Smoked Porter 6.5%
Alaska
www.alaskanbeer.com

From the last frontier comes this pioneering new world porter, first brewed 25 years ago and released every November. While resembling a Rauchbier, it is inspired by turn-of-the-century Alaskan ale-makers who malted their own barley and smoked it over indigenous alder wood. Mellowed out by other malts, the smoke is not stifling, like Schlenkerla, and subsides further over time when sherry notes and something of the school satchel set in. Since the earliest records of porter brewing in England suggest that was made with smoky malt, this may be more authentic than most. No surprise that early editions of this classic cellar dweller are fetching high prices.

Drink with: a juicy rack of ribs

Anchor Brewing Company
Old Foghorn 8.2%
California
www.anchorbrewing.com

In 1975, Anchor Brewing owner Fritz Maytag introduced barley wine to American beer drinkers. In a landscape of insipid lagers, it was like bringing a lion to a cat show. Not only did it inspire other American brewers to follow suit, it dispatched a ripple of recognition across the Pond to barley wine's neglectful native land. Old Foghorn is dry-hopped with Cascade: there is a viscous hop oil character on top of the rich toasted malt body and amped-up alcohol in this San Francisco beauty.

Drink with: Milk (2008)

Barley Wine

A brew similar to today's barley wine, aged in wood, vinous in character and with a strength of between 10% and 14%, was originally an 18th-century strong ale that the English landed gentry brewed in small batches in the brewhouses found in the grounds of aristocratic country houses.

Whether the very strong ale the gentry drank out of tiny 5fl oz glasses was referred to as 'barley wine' is unlikely, as it was not until the late 19th century that the term adorned the labels of commercially brewed beers such as the Bass No1 strong ale brewed by Bass, Ratcliff & Gretton, a pale paragon of modern malting techniques.

For a number of brewers in the 1900s, barley wine was used as a synonym for old ale or a slightly superior and strong Burton Ale that was advertised in both America and England as a tonic to be taken for an array of ailments.

Sadly, confusion wasn't one of them and barley wine-style beers continued to be other names such as Stingo or the prefix 'Old' – as in 'Old Tom'. But a stylistic stake was planted in the ground in 1952 when the Sheffield brewer Tennants brewed Gold Label, a 'golden barley wine' with an ABV of 10.6% which quickly became remarkably popular.

Other brewers clambered on the bandwagon and changed the names of their big Burton Ales, Old Ales, and pretty much any other heavyweight beer to 'barley wine'. Encompassing ales that varied in colour from light amber to dark claret, barley wine became a catch-all term for a swath of strong ales.

The general criteria for a 'modern' barley wine include high alcoholic strength, long and vigorous fermentation, lots of hops to balance the sweetness from a big boil with dense grain content, the occasional addition of fermentable sugars, and lengthy maturation. More often than not, barley wines are bottle-conditioned and, as such, extremely well suited for further ripening in the cellar, where sherry-like flavours, fruity ester characteristics and vinous qualities evolve.

English examples include JW Lees' Harvest Ale, Golden Pride from Fuller Smith and Turner and Coniston No 9, voted the 2012 Champion Beer of Britain. Old Tom from Robinsons used to call itself a barley wine but is now known as 'strong ale'. But the late and great Thomas Hardy's Ale is what many drinkers associate with barley wine. Initially brewed as a one-off in 1968 by the now defunct Eldridge Pope brewery in Dorchester, to commemorate the 40th anniversary of the eponymous novelist's death, it disappeared when the Dorchester brewery closed, then was revived by another small Dorset brewer before, sadly, disappearing once more in 2009. (Though at the time of writing there are rumours that it may be resurrected again …)

In the United States, where the style has been embraced with enthusiasm, barley wines tend to be more heavily hopped on the West Coast than they are on the East, where, similar to British versions, a signature sweetness resides.

Anchor Brewery's Old Foghorn, unleashed in 1975, is widely considered the first stateside stab at the style. It was followed by Sierra Nevada's Bigfoot in 1983 and, since then, American brewers tend to showcase the style as a seasonal winter warmer. Samuel Adams' Utopias (25%) is regarded as an 'imperial barley wine', while 'wheat wines' are a recent twist on the style, brewed with a large proportion of wheat.

Avery Brewing
Mephistopheles' Stout 17%
Colorado
www.averybrewing.com

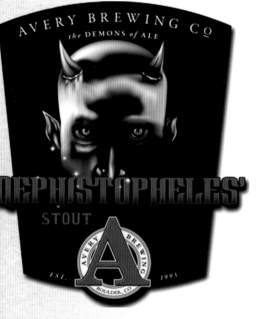

There's a whole load of hops happening here in this big blacker-than-black stout, part of the 'Demons of Ale' series (the others are an oak-aged barley wine called Samaels and a 'Grand Cru' ale called The Beast) from a 20-year-old brewery in Boulder, Colorado. Yet it is the sheer mass of dark malt in the mash that delivers over time, when the fresh hop flavours begin to fade, the dark fruit notes lengthen and the sweetness spreads out.

`Drink with: Dark chocolate`

Boston Beer Company & Bayerische Staatsbraurei
Weihenstephan
Infinium 10%
Massachusetts/Germany
www.samueladams.com

Born of Boston and Bavarian parents, this collaboration between the largest craft brewery in the United States and Germany's oldest brewer sits spiritually somewhere near Champagne. (Geographically, of course, it would sit about 1,800 miles out in the North Atlantic …) Only using ingredients that the German purity laws permits and corked and caged in a 75cl bottle, it's an effervescent affair that froths up the side of the flute. The mouth-filling fruit fizz has a sweet centre with pear, apricot, banana and a lift of fennel at the finish. It took two years to create, but longer to reach its peak.

`Drink with: Top Secret (1984)`

Brooklyn Brewery
Brooklyn Local 2 9%
New York
www.brooklynbrewery.com

Brewmaster Garrett Oliver's corked-and-caged collection of bottle-conditioned 75cl beers, rather cleverly called 'Big Bottles', are ripe for exploration and ageing. While the single hop Saison, Sorachi Ace, is a prime porch-sipper, this beguiling Belgian-style brunette, brewed with wildflower honey made by Big Apple bees and dark sugar from Belgium, is happier after a little hibernation.

`Drink with: Brooklyn Express, You Need a Change of Mind`

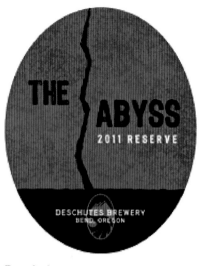

Deschutes
The Abyss 11%
Oregon
www.deschutesbrewery.com

Each year since 2006, the Bend, Oregon-based brewer unleashes this epic opaque imperial stout to enormous acclaim. The latest (2011) saw liquorice and blackstrap molasses melded into a dense mash, spiking the stout's signature sexy characteristics, before the beer was blended with stout aged in bourbon casks, pinot noir barrels and Oregon oak. Cherry bark and vanilla bean soothe, while cellaring adds a further dimension to this voluptuous, viscous vortex of complexity.

`Drink with: Joseph Conrad's Heart of Darkness`

Chocolate Tart with Russian Imperial Stout

Ingredients
- 100g/4oz chocolate, 72% cocoa
- 100g/4oz butter,
- 2 whole eggs, 2 yolks
- 150g/5oz sugar
- 5g/2 oz flour
- 5cc/2fl oz Russian imperial stout

Peter Paul Stil of Eet & Bierlokaal de Molen

Method
Melt the chocolate and the butter in a bowl over gently simmering water. Whisk the eggs, yolks, sugar and beer till creamy, fold the flour through and add the chocolate. Pour into small moulds and bake in a preheated oven for 13 minutes at 170°C/340°F.

The inside should be still soft and slightly fluid. Reheating is easy in a microwave – around 30 seconds should do.

Use a good Russian imperial stout. We usually have some Hel & Verdoemenis or Rasputin on standby, and the small amount needed for the cakes leaves you enough to drink with the cakes.

Hair of the Dog
Adam 10%
Oregon
www.hairofthedog.com

Brilliant brewers of barrel-ageing, big beers and bottle-conditioning, Hair of the Dog, from Portland, Oregon, do a fine line in delayed drinking gratification. Cold-conditioned and inspired by a long-deceased Dortmunder beer style, Adam is only brewed seven times a year and ages extremely elegantly; peaty smoke on the nose, crème brûlée and a touch of toffee apple on the palate.

Drink with: The Book of Genesis. (That's what happens if you don't wait.)

Hoppin' Frog
Oak Aged B.O.R.I.S the Crusher Oatmeal Stout 8.4%
Ohio
www.hoppinfrog.com

Seven years ago and with six GABF medals under his brewing belt, Fred Karm went solo in Ohio after the closure of his previous employers, Thirsty Dog. Given there is a frog on its labels, it is no surprise that a lot of the Akron-based brewery's beers are unashamedly hoppy. His enormous 'Bodacious Oatmeal Russian Imperial Stout', is a boozy blend of molasses, mocha and maple syrup. Like a navy rum in texture, it's oakier and even better when aged in bourbon barrels. Excellent.

Drink with: Eagle Rare 17 bourbon

Kuhnhenn Brewing Company
Raspberry Eisbock 10.6%
Michigan
www.kbrewery.com

While the Kuhnhenn brothers are renowned for their hefeweizen, here they brazenly blow raspberries in the face of the Reinheitsgebot by flagrantly adding fresh fruit into the mix. Sweet, strong and slightly sour with a swirl of dark chocolate, this is very much a beer for dessert – but definitely not a desert beer.

Drink with: Foie gras and brioche

Midnight Sun Brewing
Monk's Mistress 11.5%
Alaska
www.midnightsunbrewing.com

Embodying Alaska's anarchic, out-there air, Midnight Sun have been brewing some big grizzly beers in Anchorage since 1995. This broad-shouldered, Belgian-style dark drop seduces with a swirl of sour cherry, coffee aromas, chocolate, almonds and those fruits, like dates and figs, that keep you regular.

Drink with: Into the Wild (2007)

North Coast
Barrel-aged Old Rasputin Imperial Russian Stout 11.2%
California
www.northcoastbrewing.com

The Northern Californian brewer is widely hailed for its hedonistic, high-gravity ales including this awesome stout, named after the mystic 'mad monk'. In 2006, to mark a decade since the beer's creation, it was put into 12-year-old bourbon barrels for eight months. People liked it, a lot, and so the brewery did it again – but on a bigger scale. It's a terrifically intense, oily effort, tinged with tobacco, dried fruit and dark chocolate.

Drink with: Leo Tolstoy's Anna Karenina

Pelican Pub & Brewery
Storm Watcher's Winterfest 12.7%
Oregon
www.yourlittlebeachtown.com/pelican

The rugged, raw Oregonian coast is stunning, and Pacific Beach, popular with surfers, is particularly breath-taking, with dramatic views of Haystack Rock. The Pelican Brewpub is a lovely place to watch dark thundering clouds roll in. This is warm and weighty, with touches of tobacco, cinnamon and smoke.

Drink with: The Goonies (1985). Haystack Rock stars in the opening scene

Rogue Brewing
Old Crustacean
11.5%
Oregon
www.rogue.com

A riot of resinous, woody aromas waft from this heavily-hopped, boisterous barley wine, born in Newport, Oregon. The 110 IBUs initially hang a little harsh and heavy on the moderately muscular malt substructure, but after a year or so, the astringency and the in-your-face alcohol simmer down to become more measured, more melodious and the beer gets more comfortable in its own body.

Drink with: William Orbit, Adagio for Strings

Shmaltz Brewing Company
Genesis 15:15 13.4%
California/New York
www.shmaltz.com

Oy vey, there's a cacophony of flavours and influences coming together under the kippah of this hedonistic harvest ale, aged for nine months in Sazerac 6-year-old rye whiskey barrels. One of three outrageous efforts released to celebrate Shmaltz Brewing's 15th anniversary, it blends juices from four of the seven sacred species listed in the Torah: figs, dates, grapes and pomegranates, the last harking back to He'Brew, the original beer brewed back in 1996. A bruising, boisterous barley wine with balls so big, it has to carry them around in a wheelbarrow.

Drink with: Jeremy Cowan's Craft Beer Bar Mitzvah

Alaskan Barley Wine & Beer Festival

January: A traditional time of abstinence, a healthy hiatus after all that decadence in December, a month of measured, mature consumption.

Not in Alaska. In a land emptier than an agoraphobic's diary, and at a time when daytime lasts less than six hours and the mercury is well below zero, Alaskans bring out the barley wine. As you would expect from a state where fighting grizzlies and washing moose kill from the back of the pick-up are considered hobbies, Alaskans dig big, brooding barley wines. So, every January, Anchorage plays host to the Alaskan Barley Wine & Beer Festival.

Held on the third weekend in January since 1996 as part of Alaskan Beer Week, it draws more than 70 breweries from Alaska, the Pacific Northwest and beyond, each are bringing their 'A' game. 'A' as in Alcohol.

The gathering brings together some seriously big beers: knee-trembling Belgian tripels go toe-to-toe with strapping strong ales and enormous imperial stouts; heavyweight winter warmers put hairs on body parts where they're frankly not welcome; while around 50 behemoth barley wines leave livers crumpled in the corner, sobbing and shaking.

The festival is staggered (pun very much intended) over two days. The admission price gets you 30 6oz samples, a glass and an ID band so you know who you are at the end of the evening. During the 'Connoisseur Session', which costs a little extra, you get to try extra-special and rare beers and be there when the winners of the barley wine competition are unveiled.

Brasserie Dupont
Avec Les Bons Voeux 9.5%
Tourpes
www.brasserie-dupont.com

This wonderful Walloon farmhouse brewery, which is synonymous with its sensational Saison, by far the best benchmark in terms of style, also shapes some sensational stronger ales at its rustic, red brick brewhouse, which dates to the 1840s. Avec Les Bons Voeux, 'With Best Wishes', was originally brewed in 1970 as a Christmas offering to close friends of the farmhouse. It's a glorious, dark, golden gift. Dry-hopping and lengthy maturation give it cinnamon, pecan pie and a tight, grainy body which fills out over time. A great characterful keeper.

Drink with: *Breakfast at Tiffany's (1961)*

Uinta Brewing Company
Anniversary Ale 10.4%
Utah
www.uintabrewing.com

Ever drunk a barley wine form a Martini glass? I have. I'd highly recommend it within the privacy of your own home. In public, though, it's fighting talk. What the v-shaped vessel lacks in bar brawl acumen, though, it makes up for in looks. This sensual seducer, invites you in and snuggles up next to you on the sofa, plying you with port, coffee, dark chocolate and a nip of navy rum.

Drink with: *Dumb & Dumber (1995)*

CANADA

Les Trois Mousquetaires
Porter Baltique 10%
Quebec
www.LesTroisMousquetaires.ca

If you keep this Quebecois cool and quiet for a couple of years, its raisin and rum-like character and chocolatey charms will become even more beguiling. This is darker than a gravedigger's soul, with a mellifluous roast-malt body. A special edition, aged in bourbon barrels, adds vanilla and smoke to black cherry and espresso.

Drink with: Alexandre Dumas's *The Count of Monte Cristo*

Unibroue
Trois Pistoles 9%
Quebec
www.unibroue.com

A big, muscular, brawling, sprawling double Dubbel ale from Quebec, laced with leather notes and the swirling spicy ester character that unites Unibroue's Belgian-style ales. The beer is a lean and lively when young: ageing fills out the rich fruit, which bolsters the body.

Drink with: *Pink Panther (1963)*

BELGIUM

Achel
Extra Bruin 9.5%
Hamont-Achel
www.achelsekluis.org

One of the littlest of the seven Trappist breweries, hugging the border of the Netherlands. After the German army swiped its coppers during World War I, it ceased brewing until 1998 when it installed new kit in an old dairy. Brother Thomas, a former Westmalle brewer, brought over the yeast strain. Westmalle, however, does not have a big beer to compete with this Christmas cracker – cinnamon, sweet raisin, tobacco and a bit of grassy flavour from the Saaz hop.

Drink with: *The Name of the Rose (1986)*

T'gaverhopke
Den twaalf 12%
West Flanders
www.tgaverhopke.be

A friendly family-run Flemish brewery pushes the Abbey ale envelope with this ambitious dark auburn effort, which becomes more composed the longer you leave it. 'The twelve' is sticky, sweet and syrupy with a sherry finish; there are jaunty little jabs of creamy chocolate and cinnamon in there too. May polarise opinion.

Drink with: Chocolate waffles

Halve Maan
Straffe Hendrick Quadrupel 11%
Bruges
www.halvemaan.be

The 'Half Moon' brewpub, complete with a cracking cobbled courtyard and brewing museum, and dating back to 1856, is the last remaining brewery in Bruges. While it may be a tad touristy, the brewery's flagship Brugse Zot enjoys a strong Belgian following, and this, the strongest of the 'Strong Henri' range unveiled in the 1980s, is a quality quadrupel – deeply dark, intoxicating and intense with an earthy, dry undertow, brewed with several speciality malts.

Drink with: *In Bruges* (2008)

Westvleteren
12 10.2%
Westvleteren
www.sintsixtus.be

Is this the best brewer in the world? Some think so. Hyperbole is heightened by the Trappist halo effect, and scarcity certainly adds to the appeal. But there is no doubt that Westvleteren is up there with the best. The monk-brewers remain unswerving in their reluctance to cut corners or become too commercial at the expense of either quality or, crucially, the quiet contemplation that is at the crux of monastic life. The St Sixtus monks are more involved in the brewing than other Trappist brewers. The brewery at the Westvleteren monastery remains the last to use open fermenters and the beers, neither centrifuged nor filtered, enjoy lengthy conditioning. This barley wine, exuding astonishing elegance after a few years of ageing, certainly warrants its saintly standing. Production is kept at no more than 77,000 gallons a year, all made in a brewery installed in the early 1990s after the St Bernardus brewery lost the licence to brew the Westvleteren beers for commercial sale, which replaced a rather quaint set-up, that dated from the 1920s. The bottles carry no labels, the only identifying mark is the colour of the cap: for the 12, or Abt, it's yellow.

Drink with: Silence

U Medvidku
X-Beer 33 12.8%
Prague
www.umedvidku.cz

Rather incongruously, this petite Prague brewpub brews the biggest bottom-fermented Czech lager, at 33 degrees Plato. Every ounce of fermentable sugar is rigorously rinsed from the sweet mash, then fermented in open squares for a fortnight before a secondary fermentation in 500-litre oak barrels amps up the alcohol even more. X-Beer 33 is not as one-dimensional as one would assume, but creamy and toffee-tinged, with a soft flick of caramel. Left to its own devices, it shapeshifts into something similar to a sweet dessert wine.

Drink with: Crème brûlée

Champagne Beers & Weddings

Deus Les Brut des Flandres 11.5%

Haughty but nice, this slightly sour fruity and effervescent light golden ale is fermented in Belgium by the Bosteels Brewery yet laid down to rest in French Champagne cellars and packaged in a handsome Dom Perignon-style bottle with cork, foil and wire.

There are many reasons to serve beer rather than wine at weddings. Cheaper and lower in alcohol than Champagne, it frees up some cash for more canapés and reduces the chances of embarrassing disco dancing and ill-advised sexual encounters.

There are religious reasons too. If you have read the Bible then you will know there is a really good bit when Jesus, the lead character, is at a wedding and he turns water into wine. It's one of the most famous bits in the whole book.

But the thing is, that never actually happened. Jesus didn't turn water into wine, he turned it into beer. Fact. All the evidence, not to mention some pretty brainy scholars, point to this: grain not grapes grew all over the Middle East when Jesus was alive; and wine was rarely consumed in the region.

Besides, beer has been closely betrothed to the act of matrimony for centuries. Indeed, the very word 'bridal' comes from 'bride ale' – 'ale' here with its ancient secondary meaning of 'feast', though ale was the drink everybody drank at Anglo-Saxon wedding feasts, and sometimes the bride and groom would brew a special strong wedding ale and sell it to the guests.

Even the word 'bride' probably has beery connections: it comes from a word that originally meant 'daughter-in-law' in the ancestor language of English, spoken in Jutland and Southern Sweden nearly 3,000 years ago, which looks to have come itself from a root word meaning 'to brew' and 'to cook, make broth' – the duties of a daughter-in-law in ancient times.

While few brides will brew their own beer today for the celebrations, Champagne beers – referred to as bières de brut – are a natural choice for a wedding. In the past few years, brewers have worked out how to tame the notoriously disobedient Champagne yeast and have begun adopting techniques used by fancy French Champagne houses, such as lengthy maturation, remuage and degorgement. Lambic beers, meanwhile, have similar acidity to sparkling wines, while a classic kriek is another excellent aperitif alternative.

ITALY

Le Baladin
Xyauyù Etichetta Oro (Golden Label) 13.5%
Piozzo
www.birreria.com

Teo Musso is a brewer who does things differently, even by Italy's notoriously esoteric, oft-erratic standards. The breadth of Teo's vision stretches beyond beer, encompassing influences from distilling, winemaking, gastronomy and even the arts – strapping vibrating headphones to his fermentation tanks, Teo adds a whole new dimension to the phrase 'yeast culture'. For this unique 'oxidised' barley wine, Teo turned to the solera ageing process synonymous with sherry. He sporadically allows oxygen into the beer over a period of 30 months. It's an imperfect art, a lot like Lambic, and requires constant tasting and supervision: too much oxygen ends in disaster. Once unshackled from cork and cage, the beer unfolds elegantly, with notes of Amontillado sherry, sweet and sour fruits, maple syrup and tanned leather. Time will crank up the complexity of one of the most interesting beers you will ever drink.

Drink with: *Cinema Paradiso* (1989)

Elav
Progressive Barley Wine 11%
Rimini
www.elavbrewery.com

With the labels referencing a variety of music genres, ranging from techno to reggae, the off-piste antics of this Lombardy-based brewer can appear a touch adolescent. Perhap's that's not too surprising: the brewery only opened in 2010, to supply beer for the owners' two pubs. Within a year, however, production had increased fivefold, as demand boomed. This is a mature, measured barley wine, silky and spicy, and one of the few to showcase Japan's Sorachi Ace hops. It is part of a range named after musical genres.

Drink with: *Pawn hearts* by Van Der Graaf Generator (the original progressive Italian rock group)

Lurisia
Dodici (Twelve)
12%
Mondovi
www.lurisia.it

Joining forces with a spring water bottler, Le Baladin's Teo Musso has created a series of beers made using Lurisia's mineral water, a variety of yeast strains, unusual and indigenous ingredients and oxidisation techniques. This sipper is blended with lapsang souchong tea, with the fuel for the fermentation sourced from both buckwheat and barley. The taste is tart, with smoke and cracked pepper.

Drink with: *La Dolce Vita* (1960)

Montegioco
Demon Hunter 8.5%
Montegioco
www.birrificiomontegioco.com

On the border of Piedmont and Lombardy, brewmaster Riccardo Franzosi has found favour and flavour at the forefront of Italy's epicurean craft brewing scene. Designed for the dinner table, his stable of 18 beers use Italian ingredients ranging from wine barrels to blueberries yet the most exotic ingredient in this classic barley wine is East Kent Golding hops. A perfect post-prandial contemplater, it's a supple swirl of roasted chestnut, treacle and coffee laced with cognac.

Drink with: *The Italian Job* (1969)

AUSTRIA

Handbrauerei Gerhard Forstner
5 Vor Zwölf 13%
Kalsdorf bei Graz
www.forstner-biere.at

This serious sip, with a name that means 'Five before 12', maintains its wood perfectly, hopped with Hallertau and vibrant Cascade, notes of brandy snap, nuts and a slight peppery touch, and stretches its legs all over the snifter. Watch out for the same brewery's smoky 'gammon' ale.

Drink with: *Predator* (1987) Arnold Schwarzenegger was born a few miles away.

NETHERLANDS

Kerkomse
Winterkoninkske Grand Cru 13%
Haspengouw
www.brouwerijkerkom.be/nl

Head brewer Marc Limet hails the hop with unabashed enthusiasm. Bink Blonde is an elegant, aromatic beer to sip in Kerkom's charming courtyard, but when winter comes, within the snug of the brewery bar 'Little Winter King' is the one to go for. Dense, dark with notes of dried leaves, it is seasoned with juniper and other undisclosed herbs and spices to make a roasty fireside companion.

Drink with: *It's a Wonderful Life* (1946)

De Molen
Mout & Mocca 11.6%
Bodegraven
www.brouwerijdemolen.nl

This, ladies and gentleman, is what imperial stouts are all about. It's a quite brilliant bit of black magic brewing, percolated with coffee beans sourced from four ethically aware suppliers. So stunning is this silky-textured satin stout, quite frankly I wouldn't care if they had to force-feed orphans with asbestos to make it. It's enticing, pert and wonderful, with creamy mocha, chocolate, roasted nuts and a hint of smoky oak. A rounded and subtle beer, it is hard to believe it gets better over five years.

Drink with: Jean Luc Godard's *2 or 3 Things I Know About Her* (1967), cinema's most iconic coffee scene

St Christoffel
Christoffel XXV 10.25%
Roermond
www.christoffelbier.nl

If you could judge a beer by its cover, this would be a drinking disaster. The eyesore of the orange ceramic bottle aside, though, this barley wine from a well-loved lager specialist reveals its really rather nice red grape character after having caught forty winks or so. Some chocolate and cherry in there too.

Drink with: Hans Teeuwen *Live in London*

JAPAN

Hakusekikan
Hurricane 15%
Gifu
www.hakusekikan-beer.jp

The best barley wine in Japan may seem to those who don't realise how far brewing has come in the Land of the Rising Sun to be the ale-drinking equivalent of a tallest dwarf competition. But don't let that detract from this warming whirlwind of red wine, fruit cake and liqueur-laden chocolate from a central Japanese brewer that experiments enthusiastically with different strains of yeast, including a wild version used in a sour Lambic. Watch out, too, for the same brewery's Super Vintage, which has a fermentation begun with beer yeast and finished with wine yeast.

Drink with: Haruki Murakami's *What I Talk About When I Talk About Running*

RUSSIA

Baltika/Mikkeller/Jacobsen
Royal Rye Wine 9.5%
St Petersburg
www.carlsberggroup.com

A collaboration with Carlsberg could appear contrary to Mikkeller's maverick mantra but Jacobsen, the Danish giant's small 'house' brewery, named after Carlsberg's founder, Jacob Christian Jacobsen, is imbued with the same experimental verve as its 19th-century namesake. Using a bespoke Baltika yeast strain in St Petersburg, Mikkel Borg Bjergsø of Mikkeller and Jacobsen's Wolfgang David Lindell replaced barley with rye, a popular cereal in Danish (and Russian) cuisine, and added the grapey, catty Nelson Sauvin hops from New Zealand, grape juice and Russian grape leaves, before ageing the resultant brew in oak. At the time of tasting still in its youth, Royal Rye Wine managed all the same to tingle excitingly with notes of tobacco, sherried with wood and beeswax, port and spiced syrup. This is a fine-bodied ruby beer that threatens to be even better as it grows, and about as good an advertisement for collaboration brewing as you're likely to find anywhere on the planet.

Drink with: *Drinking at the Dam* by Smog

CELLARING BEERS

Depending on pasteurisation and packaging, the vast majority of beer consumed has a shelf life of around 6 months and is at its finest when fresh. If you're going to drink a pale ale or a Pilsner, or if you crave a hand-pulled bitter or a Kölsch, then ideally, it's best consumed straight after conditioning.

But which styles best suit cellaring? If you are purchasing beers primarily for maturation, then choose beers that are strong, avoiding anything below around 7 or 8% ABV.

Cellaring contenders should also really be more malt-driven than hop-forward. Father Time plays havoc with hoppy beers, sapping the life out of their flavours and aromas. Aggressively hopped India Pale Ales do not really improve with age, though, if they remain in a refrigerator and are kept cold, they won't get any worse either.

Dark, malty beers with a bit of sweetness are classic candidates, as residual sugars tend to smooth out, mellow and soften over time. They are often a little green in their adolescence; imperial stouts and porters, strong Belgian ales and barley wines all grow into their body over time.

If the words 'bottle-conditioned' are on the beer label then what is inside will evolve with age until you open it. You can thank the yeast for that. While it doesn't ferment the residual sugars ad infinitum, it aids the ageing process and asserts its influence in an array of alluring, interesting ways, fashioning new flavours and creating complexity.

More unpredictable, yet arguably more interesting, are ales spiked with wild yeast and Brettanomyces in the bottle, such as Lambic and Gueuze. These become increasingly quirky and curious with age. Opening aged Lambics and Gueuze, which can rollercoast in drinkability from one month to the next, is like a game of Russian roulette – but that is what is so intriguing about them.

Unsure whether a beer will suit ageing? Then feel the fear and do it anyway. After all, laying down a couple of bottles of stout is not going to break the bank, and trial and error is the best way to understand the ageing process.

HOW LONG SHOULD BEER BE AGED?
How long is a piece of string? Each beer ages differently. There are those who believe Lambics and Gueuze can reach their peak after two decades, while John Keeling, head brewer at Fuller's in West London, reckons his vintage ales stop getting better after ten years.

Orval, however, seems to be at its greatest after 18 months or so. Again, the only way to find out is to drink them at different times. To do this, buy each beer in batches of four or five if you can: one to drink immediately and one every two years or so.

Ensure you note when each was bought and brewed, tie a label to the bottle neck if you can, and then compare and contrast to discover the ideal ageing period for each beer.

Opposite: The temperature of your dimly lit cellar should be constant.

Vertical tastings, in which you taste differing vintages of the same beer in one sitting, can be extremely revealing. Although, if it is strong beer, a vertical tasting can soon become a horizontal one.

CELLAR CONDITIONS
If you don't own a cellar, worry not. A closet, a garage, a cupboard or a spare bedroom (preferably in the middle of the house) all work just as well.

Wherever you lay your beers, however, the temperature needs to be relatively constant. There is no point putting beer in your basement if it blows hot and cold; beers don't like sweltering or shivering below zero. If you can ensure your cellar stays around the 13°C/55°F mark, then your beers will be extremely grateful.

They will also appreciate it if there is no bright light. Like vampires, beers do not favour sunlight, as UV rays decompose the isohumulones in the beer, derived from hops, to create a classic 'skunky' flavour. The lighting conditions of your beer cellar should be similar to those that you might like to make love under: completely dark or dimmed.

Unlike your lovemaking, however, it is better if your basement is not too steamy. Excessive humidity invites a mischief-making black mould which will, without you knowing, ruin the beer. A lack of moistness, meanwhile, will dry out any corked closures and leave beer susceptible to other bacteria in the basement.

I also like to play a bit of music too. It's lonely down there. Maybe some folk music, a bit of Mozart or Marvin Gaye. Imperial porters love Nina Simone while barley wines like nothing better than Elgar. But there is not a single beer in the world that likes modern R'n'B.

HORIZONTAL OR VERTICAL?
Wines are laid down on their side and the debate surrounding whether to do the same for beer has been long-running and impassioned.

Some do not believe it makes a big difference while others reckon horizontal maturation prevents corks from drying out. However, the general consensus among brewers and beer aficionados is to stand beer bottles upright.

It is far more likely that any cork shrinkage will occur due to a lack of humidity outside the bottle, while vertical bottles reduces the surface area of exposed beer, this reducing the effect of oxidization.

What is more, when you pick a vertical bottle to pour, you will not shake up the sediment that has settled on the bottom. And, strangely, it is a fact that some beers stored on their sides will fob violently when opened, while the same beer will stay calm if stored upright.

DE MOLEN

Bodegraven, The Netherlands   www.brouwerijdemolen.nl

Big beers are a big deal, the modern barometer by which craft brewers are considered. But sometimes, big beers can simply be a little too big. All noise and no nuance, lots of loud shouting yet saying nothing.

Like fights in cartoons, random flavours fly out like arms and feet from a whirling, dusty ball of confusion. Causing pandemonium on the palate and often undermined by an adolescent exuberance and aggression, they can be haphazard, lack harmony and exude all the composure of a toddler with a machine gun. As Michael Caine would say: 'They're big men, but they're out of shape.'

De Molen is different. Here, size is not everything. It's what you do with it that counts. A sense of symmetry shapes the high-gravity beers. Big yet not belligerent, there's a restrained and persuasive elegance to them.

The men behind the beers are Menno Olivier and John Brus, two former homebrewers turned pro. Olivier founded 'The Mill' in 2004, having been a gipsy brewer at various small breweries and after spending stints in Belgium and Dutch breweries such as Texelse, De Prael and the De Pelgrim brewpub in Rotterdam.

With some savings and old dairy equipment, he stuck a 500-litre brewery into the red brick base of 'De Arkduif' (Ark's Dove), a 17th-century windmill in the town of Bodegraven. He also fitted in a restaurant in which he could sell his beers and recruited Peter Paul Stil, a chef with whom he had worked at De Pelgrim.

In 2006, John Brus discovered Olivier's beers and they became friends. Brus had been homebrewing, but with no burning desire to brew professionally. 'I was happy doing it as a hobby but I was working in IT,' he said. 'But, after two years, I decided I wanted something else in my life.' With Olivier keen to expand a brewery straining at the seams, Brus invested in the brewery, the restaurant was sold to Stil, money was borrowed from the bank and, by 2011, a new 25 hectolitre brewery was built a few hundred yards from the windmill.

It is still small beer, just 4,000 litres a year, though with room to brew more. 'We want to stay small,' Olivier says. 'We want to control everything ourselves, have fun and stay small.'

With a larger-than-normal lauter tun, the bespoke brewery is geared up to handle high gravity beers when it needs to. 'It was wonderful in the windmill but we craved consistency and this is what we get here,' Brus said. 'I was worried that we wouldn't be able to re-create the signature style but Menno wasn't concerned at all.'

Brewing two dozen beers, De Molen's stylistic scope is vast and varied but it is the dark side, imperial stouts and porters, for which it is renowned. English and German beer styles are amplified yet not distorted and there is an undeniable American influence to its approach. But, unlike the more shouty statements from across the Pond, De Molen's beers smoothly move through the gears, flavours shifting and responding in all the right places.

While much of De Molen's beers are dark, its biggest seller is Vuur & Vlam, a phenomenally fragrant IPA with a name meaning 'Fire & Flames', a Dutch expression that describes being madly in love. It is hopped with Chinook, Cascade, Simcoe and Amarillo, and then dry-hopped with Cascade.

'We love American hops and we use fresh flowers in August and September,' Brus said. 'We like IPAs, imperial stouts and double imperial stouts, but a lot of our beers are very drinkable, very simple. History and styles have been the inspiration and what we always aim at is balance in beers. But it's about flavour, it's all about flavour.'

The duo work wonders with a range of wood, barrel-ageing a lot of their big beers above the brewery. Mooi & Machtig, a rich, rounded barley wine meaning 'Beautiful and Powerful', is laid down in Cognac barrels while two enormous imperial stouts, Hemel & Aarde ('Heaven and Earth') and Rasputin, are introduced to Islay whisky in Caol Ila and Laphroaig casks. Next door, in an old outhouse, is De Molen's 'Brett shed', full of oak barrels teeming with Brettanomyces. 'We're going to create a base beer and blend it with other styles,' Brus said. 'We're making a whiskey with our beer that is six years old, and beers we don't bottle go into making a beer liqueur.'

In 2008, the Dutch craft beer enthusiast society PINT awarded Olivier its 'Zilveren Knuppel', the 'silver bat', given for significant contributions to Dutch beer culture. While there is nothing distinctively Dutch about its beer, De Molen has been a mould-breaking, driving force behind the Netherlands' new-world craft beer scene. 'Dutch beer isn't just copying Belgian beer styles anymore, there are a lot of IPAs, imperial stouts and robust porters and we're in the middle of that,' Brus said. 'Heineken went on the rampage in the 1970s and 1980s, bought up a lot of breweries and shut them down. But now Holland is in a second phase. It's very much a rising star. It's not there yet, but everything is geared towards great things.'

And what of its neighbours? 'Belgium is past its best-before date,' Brus said. 'There were a lot of great brewers and there are a few new ones that are doing very well, but a lot of them are now not as they used to be.'

Each autumn, the cream of Europe's artisan beer-makers descend on De Molen for the epic Borefts Beer Festival, a modern craft beer celebration featuring the likes of Thornbridge, Alvinne, Buxton, Narke and Del Ducato.

'There's a real community among craft brewers. We're not competitors, we are friends fighting the good fight together,' Brus said. 'It's a great gathering of imaginative brewers and we do it because we want to show people that there's more to beer than Leffe and Heineken.'

In 2008, the Dutch craft beer enthusiast society PINT awarded Olivier its 'Zilveren Knuppel', the 'silver bat', given for significant contributions to Dutch beer culture.

Above left: Menno Olivier, brewer.

Far left: The new brewhouse in Bodegraven.

Left: De Molen's 'Dutch Expressions'.

Above: De Molen's original brewery.

KEY BEERS

Hel & Verdoemenis (Hell & Damnation) 10%
Rasputin 10.7%
Vuur & Vlam (Fire & Flames) 6.2 %
Amarillo 9.2%
Bloed, Zweet & Tranen (Blood, Sweat & Tears) 8.1%
Bommen & Granaten (Bombs & Grenades) 15.2%

Just a few of the late, great Michael Jackson's
bottle collection, bequeathed to Meantime Brewing
in London.

Desert Island Dozen

Does your Dad dabble in the dark side? Is your wife into wild fermentation? Are you a closet hophead? Then you're going to dig the 'Desert Island Dozen' beers below, each bespoke beer case designed to make life seem a whole lot better.

STOUTS & PORTERS

1. Harveys Imperial Russian Stout 9% Lewes, East Sussex, England
2. Lion Stout, Lion Brewing 8.8% Columbo, Sri Lanka
3. iStout, 8Wired 10% Marlborough, New Zealand
4. Export Stout 1890, Kernel 7.8% South London, England
5. Profanity Stout, Williams Bros 7% Alloa, Scotland
6. Speedway Stout, Alesmith 12% San Diego, California, USA
7. Chocolate, Marble 5% Manchester, England
8. Beer Geek Breakfast , Mikkeller 7.5% Copenhagen, Denmark
9. Black Mamba Stout, Sainte Helene 4.5% Virton, Belgium
10. Smoked Porter, Alaskan Brewing 6.5% Anchorage, Alaska, USA
11. Mephistopheles' Stout, Avery Brewing 15-17% Boulder, Colorado
12. Mout & Mocca, De Molen 11.6% Bodegraven, Netherlands

INDIA PALE ALES AND PALE ALES

1. Citra, Oakham Brewery 4.5% Peterborough, England
2. Sculpin IPA, Ballast Point Brewing 7% San Diego, California, USA
3. Pliny The Elder, Russian River 8.5% Northern California, USA
4. XX Bitter, De Ranke 6.2% Hainault, Belgium
5. Double Barrel Ale, Firestone Walker 5% California, USA
6. JJJ IPA, Moor Beer 9.5% Somerset, England
7. 90 Minute IPA, Dogfish Head Brewing 9% Delaware, USA
8. Wild Swan, Thornbridge 3.5% Derbyshire, UK
9. Barrel Aged IPA, Epic Brewing 7.25% Auckland, New Zealand
10. Pacific Ale, Stone & Wood Brewing 4.4% Byron Bay, Australia
11. Hommelbier, Van Ecke 7.5% West Flanders, Belgium
12. Raptor IPA, Matuska 6.2% Broumy, Czech Republic

BRETTANOMYCES

1. Orval 6.2% Orval, Belgium
2. Supplication, Russian River 7% California, USA
3. Seizoen Bretta, Logsdon Farmhouse Ales 7.5% Oregon, USA
4. Sour Grapes, Lovibonds 4.6% Henley-upon-Thames, England
5. Cuvee de Tomme, Lost Abbey 5.5% San Diego, California, USA
6. Russian Imperial Stout Wild Brett, Birrificio Toccalmato 12% Parma, Italy
7. Oude Geuze Golden Blend, Drie Fonteinen 6% Beersel, Belgium
8. Kriek Lambic, Cantillon 5% Brussels, Belgium
9. Oude Geuze, Oud Beersel 6% Beersel, Belgium
10. Ora de calabaza, Jolly Pumpkin 8% Michigan. USA
11. Flemish Primitive Surly Bird, De Proef 9% Ghent, Belgium
12. Geuze Black Label 1882, Girardin 5% Flanders, Belgium

LEGENDS

1. Landlord, Timothy Taylor 4.3% Yorkshire, England
2. White Shield, Worthington 5.6% Burton-upon-Trent, England
3. Pilsner Urquell, Plzensky Prazdroj 4.4% Pilsen, Czech Republic
4. Salvator Doppelbock, Paulaner 7.5% Bavaria, Germany
5. Schneider Weiss, Weissbierbrauerei G. Schneider & Sohn 5.4% Bavaria, Germany
6. Steam Beer, Anchor Brewing 4.9% San Francisco, USA
7. Pale Ale, Sierra Nevada Brewing 5.6% California, USA
8. Grand Cru, Rodenbach 6% Flanders, Belgium
9. Helles, Spaten-Fraziskaner 5.2% Munich, Germany
10. Konig Ludwig Dunkel, Kaltenberg 5.1% Bavaria, Germany
11. Gueuze, Cantillon, 5% Brussels, Belgium
12. Blind Pig IPA, Russian River 6.1% California, USA

SUMMER

1. Yankee, Rooster Brewing 4.3% Yorkshire, England
2. Brewer's Gold, Crouch Vale 4.5% Essex, England
3. Tannezipfle, Rothaus 5.1% Black Forest, Germany
4. ViaEmilia, Birrificio del Ducato 5.8% Parma, Italy
5. Kölsch, Muhlen 4.5% Cologne, Germany
6. Saison Cazeau 4.8% Tournai, Belgium
7. Tipopils, Birrificio Italiano 5.2% Parma, Italy
8. Alpine Ale, Alpine Brewing 5.5% San Diego, California
9. Troublette, Caracole, 5% Namur, Belgium
10. Svetlý ležák, Kout Na Sumave 5% Pilsen, Czech Republic
11. Fancy Lawnmower Ale, Saint Arnold 4.8% Texas, USA
12. Taras Boulba, Brasserie de la Senne 4.5% Brussels, Belgium

CHRISTMAS ADVENT CALENDER

1. Aecht Schlenkerla, Brauerei Heller-Trum 5.2% Bamberg, Germany
2. Grand Prestige, Hertog Jan, 10% Arcen, Holland
3. Snoreau, Brasseurs RJ, 7% Quebec, Canada
4. Old Foghorn, Anchor Brewing 8.2% San Francisco. USA
5. Harvest Ale, JW Lees 11.5% Manchester, England
6. Celebrator Doppelbock, Ayinger 6.7% Bavaria, Germany
7. Bourbon Barrel-Aged Bearded Lad, Magic Rock 10.5% Huddersfield, England
8. Cinq Cents, Chimay 8% Wallonia, Belgium
9. Dark Horizon, Nogne O 16% Grimstad, Norway
10. Duchesse de Bourgogne, Verhaeghe 6.2% Flanders, Belgium
11. St. Bernardus Abt 12, St Bernadus 10.5% West Flanders, Belgium
12. Ruination Ten Year Anniversary IPA, Stone Brewing, 10.5% San Diego, USA
13. Stenol Beer, Thisted Brewery 7.8% Jutland, Denmark
14. Panty Peeler, Midnight Sun Brewing 8.5% Alaska, USA
15. Avec Les Bons Voeux, Brasserie Dupont 9.5% Wallonia, Belgium
16. Storm Watcher's Winterfest, Pelican Pub & Brewery 12.7%, Oregon, USA
17. Ola Dubh 16 year-old Harviestoun 8% Clackmannanshire, Scotland
18. Winterkoninske Grand Cru, Kerkomse 13% Limburg, Belgium
19. Demon Hunter, Birrificio Montegioco 8.5% Piedmont, Italy
20. Xyauyù Etichetta Oro (Golden Label) Le Baladin 13.5% Piedmont, Italy
21. 10, Rochefort 11.3% Namur, Belgium
22. Adam, Hair of the Dog 10% Oregon, USA
23. Vintage Ale, Fulller's, Smith & Turner 8.5% London, UK

Christmas Eve Barrel-aged Old Rasputin Imperial Russian Stout, North Coast Brewing, 11.2% California, USA

Christmas Day 12 Westvleteren, St Sixtus Abbey 10.2% Flanders, Belgium

Directory

BEER FESTIVALS

January

Great Alaska Beer & Barley Wine Festival in Anchorage, Alaska, USA
www.auroraproductions.net

National Winter Ale Festival, Manchester, England
www.alefestival.org.uk

February

San Francisco Beer Week in San Francisco, California, USA
www.sfbeerweek.org

Zwickelmania, Oregon, USA
oregonbeer.org/zwickelmania

Bruges Beer Festival, Bruges, Belgium
www.brugsbierfestival.be

Craft Beer Rising, London, England
www.craftbeerrising.co.uk

March

Festival Brasileiro da Cerveja, Blumenau, Brasil
www.festivaldacerveja.com

Barcelona Beer Festival, Barcelona, Spain
www.barcelonabeerfestival.com

Boston beer Week, Boston, MA, USA
bostonbeerweek.org

April

Groningen Bier Festival, Groningen, Netherlands
www.bierfestivalgroningen.nl

Zythos Beer Festival, Leuven, Belgium
www.zbf.be

Helsinki Beer Festival, Helsinki, Finland
www.helsinkibeerfestival.com

Salon de Grande Biere, Toky, Japan
www.craftbeerassociation.jp

May

Copenhagen Beer Celebration, Copenhagen, Denmark
copenhagenbeercelebration.com/blog

Øl festival, Copenhagen, Denmark
www.ale.dk/index.php?id=2872

Weekend of Spontaneous Fermentation, Opstal, Belgium
en.bierpallieters.be

June

SAVOR: An American Craft Beer & Food Experience, New York, USA
www.savorcraftbeer.com/

Mondial de la Biere , Montreal, Canada
www.festivalmondialbiere.qc.ca

Great Japan Beer Festival. Tokyo, Japan
www.craftbeerassociation.jp

July

Toronto Beer Festival, Toronto, Canada
www.beerfestival.ca

Oregon brewers Festival, Portland, Oregon
www.oregonbrewfest.com

Annafest, Farchheim, Germany
bit.ly/ZY4mIB

August

Great British beer Festival, London, England
www.gbbf.org.uk

Brewmasters Craft Beer Festival, Galveston, Texas
www.brewmastersinternationalbeerfestival.com

Beervana, Wellington, New Zealand
www.www.beervana.co.nz

International berlin beer Festival, Berlin, Germany
www.bierfestival-berlin.de

September

Sun in a Glass Festival, Pilsen, Czech Republic
www.slunceveskle.cz

Boreft Beer Festival in Bodegraven, Netherlands
www.brouwerijdemolen.nl/index.php/en/beerfestival.html

Oktoberfest, Munich, Germany
www.oktoberfest.de

October

Indy Man Beer Con, Manchester, England
www.indymanbeercon.co.uk

PINT Bokbierfestival, Amsterdam, Netherlands
www.pint.nl

Stockholm beer & Whisky festival Stockholm Sweden
www.stockholmbeer.se

Great American Beer Festival, Denver, Colorado
www.greatamericanbeerfestival.com

November

Cape Town Festival of Beer, Cape Town, South Africa
www.capetownfestivalofbeer.co.za

Tasmanian Beer Fest, Tasmania, Australia
www.tasmanianbeerfest.com.au

December

Kerstbierfestival, Essen, Belgium
www.kerstbierfestival.be

Phoenix Brew Fest, Phoenix, Arizona
www.phoenixbrewfest.com

BEER BLOGS

Zythophile
An immense and acutely accurate resource from beer historian Martyn Cornell
www.zythophile.wordpress.com

Thinking Drinkers
The official website of award-winning writers and performers Ben McFarland & Tom Sandham
www.thinkingdrinkers.com

Good Beer Blog
Great site courtesy of Alan McLeod
beerblog.genx40.com

Stephen Beaumont's Blogging at World of Beer
Co-author of *World Atlas of Beer*
beaumontdrinks.com

Appellation Beer
Stan Hieronymus: Author of *The Love of Hops* and *Brew Like a Monk*
appellationbeer.com

Shut Up About Barclay Perkins
Comes courtesy of the highly knowledgeable Ron Pattinson
barclayperkins.blogspot.co.uk

Pencil & Spoon
The musings of Mark Dredge, author of *Craft Beer World*
www.pencilandspoon.com

Pete Brown's Beer Blog
Acclaimed author of *Hops & Glory* & *Shakespeare's Local*
petebrown.blogspot.co.uk

Called to The Bar
Barstool scribblings from author Adrian Tierney-Jones
maltworms.blogspot.co.uk

Seen Through a Glass
The blog of leading stateside author Lew Bryson
lewbryson.blogspot.co.uk

Belgian Beer Specialist
Chuck Cook on all things Belgian and beery
belgianbeerspecialist.blogspot.co.uk

Beer Sweden
Solid and stylish Swedish resource
www.beersweden.se

Protz on Beer
The revered Roger Protz . . . on beer
protzonbeer.co.uk

Beer Goddess
The last word on Pacific Northwest beer by Lisa Morrison
www.beergoddess.com

Bier Guide
Conrad Seidl's informative Austrian beer site
www.bier-guide.net

Thirsty Pilgrim
Freelance writer and author Joe Stange is big on beer from Belgium and beyond
www.thirstypilgrim.com/

Beer Scribe
Andy Crouch brings the best from the East Coast (US) beer scene
www.beerscribe.com

Beer Culture
The excellent Evan Rail opines on Czech beer and other stuff too
www.beerculture.org

Knut Albert's Beer Blog
Norwegian blog about beers, bars and travel
www.knutalbert.wordpress.com

Crafty Pint
Awesome beer site all about Australian craft beer
www.craftypint.com

ONLINE BEER RESOURCES

Ratebeer
The largest beer rating website in the world
www.ratebeer.com

Beer Advocate
Rating website and magazine
www.beeradvocate.com

European Beer Guide
Exhaustive online look at European beer scene written by Ron Pattinson
www.europeanbeerguide.net

Campaign for Real Ale
Consumer organisation dedicated to keeping cask conditioned beer alive
www.camra.org.uk

Brewers Association (USA)
The collective voice of America's craft brewing community
www.brewersassociation.org

Canadian Beer News
Canadian craft beer news
www.canadianbeernews.com

American Homebrewers Association
Brewing in your basement, backyard or bedroom? Then this is for you.
www.homebrewersassociation.org

Society of Independent Brewers
Umbrella organisation representing the UK's burgeoning microbrewers
www.siba.co.uk

Germany
Efficient online guide to German beer
www.bierfranken.eu

Micro Birrifici
Comprehensive site for Italy's craft beer scene
www.microbirrifici.org

Australia
www.pint.au.com

Lithuania
Like Lithuanian beer? Then you'll like this.
www.alutis.lt/aludariai

Pint
Netherlands-based consumer group
www.pint.nl

Association des Buveurs D'Orges
Swiss beer site
www.abo-ch.org

European Beer Consumer Union (EBCU)
Promoters of craft beer across more than a dozen European countries.
www.ebcu.org

1 Belgium: Zythos www.zythos.be
2 Czech Republic: Consumer Group SPP www.pratelepiva.cz
3 Italy: Unionbirrai www.unionbirrai.com
4 Norway: Norol www.nor-ale.org
5 Austria: BierIG www.bierig.org
6 Poland: Bractwo Piwni www.bractwopiwne.pl
7 Sweden: SO www.svenskaolframjandet.se
8 Finland: Olutlitto www.olutliitto.fi
9 Denmark: Danske Ølentusiaster www.ale.dk
10 Ireland: Beoir www.beoir.org
11 Netherlands: PINT www.pint.nl
12 Switzerland: Association des Buveurs D'Orges www.abo-ch.org

BEER MAGAZINES

Ale Street News
www.alestreetnews.com

Celebrator
www.celebrator.com

Draft Magazine
www.draftmag.com

Beer
www.camra.org.uk/beer

Northwest Brewing News
www.brewingnews.com/northwest

Beer and Brewer (Australia)
www.beerandbrewer.com

Brewing News
www.brewingnews.com

FURTHER READING

Hieronymus, Stan. *Brew Like A Monk*. Boulder, Colorado, USA. Brewers Publications, 2005.

Webb, Tim. *Good Beer Guide Belgium*. St Albans, Hertfordshire, UK. Campaign for Real Ale, 2009.

Oliver, Garrett. *The Brewmaster's Table: Discovering the Pleasures of Real beer with Real Food*. New York, USA, 2003

Van den Steen, Jef. *Geuze & Kriek: The Secret of Lambic*. Tielt, Belgium. Lannoo Publishers, 2011.

Hales, Steven D (Editor). *Beer & Philosophy: The unexamined beer isn't worth drinking*. Malden, MA, USA. Blackwell Publishing, 2007.

White, Chris. *Yeast: The Practical Guide to Fermentation*. Boulder, Colorado, USA. Brewers Publications, 2010.

Oliver, Garrett (Editor). *The Oxford Companion to Beer*. New York, USA. Oxford University Press, 2012

Webb, Tim & Beaumont, Stephen. *The World Atlas of Beer*. London, UK. Mitchell Beazley, 2012

BUYING BEERS

Beer Merchants
www.beermerchants.com

Beers of Europe
www.beersofeurope.co.uk

Best of British Beer
www.bestofbritishbeer.co.uk

Real Ale Ltd
www.realale.com

The Real Ale Company
www.therealalecompany.co.uk

Beer Ritz
www.beerritz.co.uk

Slurp
www.slurp.co.uk

Beer Hawk
www.beerhawk.co.uk

Index of Beers

Acknowledgements

PICTURE CREDITS

SPECIAL PHOTOGRAPHY

John Carey – Pages 2–3, 4–5, 7, 15, 18, 26–27, 28, 31, 48, 51, 72, 75, 98, 101, 116, 119, 140, 143; centre 152; 158, 161; top 171; 176, 179, 200, 203, 216–217.
(with thanks to Craft Beer Company)

Simon Murrell – Pages 20–21; bottom 30; far right and right 42; top 45; bottom right 54; bottom right 59; inset 76; 95, bottom centre 102; far left 111; left 121; top right 122; top left 128; bottom centre 130; bottom left 133; far left 136; right 137; top centre 145; bottom right 162; bottom 163; top centre 165; centre right 167; top left 181; 187, bottom 188; top & bottom left 190; top left 210.

The publisher wishes to thank the many breweries from around the world that kindly provided the images of their beers, beer labels and brewery facilities reproduced here.

6 Jenny Zarins; 22 Russ Phillips; 23 top right & centre, bottom right Russ Phillips; 24 far left Camilla Stephan og Rasmus Malmstrøm - Kopenhagen Collective; 24 centre, 24 – 25 top & bottom inset, 25 top centre Robert Gale; 25 top right ZUMA Press, Inc/Alamy; 25 bottom centre & right Instinctive PR; 44 inset Incamerastock/ Alamy; 61 top left Nicholas Gill/Alamy; 65 right Imagebroker/Alamy; 67 Nagelestock/ Alamy; 90 left The Art Archive/Alamy & right Mary Evans Picture Library/Alamy; 91 top left M&N/Alamy; 110 left Mary Evans Picture Library/Alamy & right M&N/Alamy; 134-135 inset Arterra Picture Library/Alamy; 135 bottom centre Stephen Roberts Photography/ Alamy; 170-171 inset Camilla Stephan og Rasmus Malmstrøm – Kopenhagen Collective; 197 Adam Slate.

PUBLISHER'S ACKNOWLEDGEMENTS

The publisher would also like to thank the following people who helped in the production of this book:

Beers of Europe, Ales by Mail and Beer Hawk; Brewdog Shoreditch and the Meantime Brewery in Greenwich for welcoming and allowing us to shoot in situ; Sienna Croucher from Brewdog and Alice Gosnell from Meantime Brewing; LSA, Riedel, Spiegelau and Dartington for the loan of glasses for photography; Daisy Christie at Peretti Communications and Victoria Bond at Push PR; Mikkel Borg Bjergsø founder of Mikkeller; Martyn Cornell and Evan Rail.

AUTHOR'S ACKNOWLEDGEMENTS

First and foremost, enormous thanks to every brewery, brewer, bartender, beer writer, blogger and beer lover that has helped put this book together – each giving up their valuable time, advice, expertise. It simply wouldn't have happened without the camaraderie and generous goodwill of the global craft brewing community. So thank you to everyone who helped. You know who you are.

In compiling this book, I am indebted to the following for their help, advice and contributions: Martyn Railton of Euroboozer for his dispatches from Down Under; Paddy Gunningham and Samantha Hopkins for very kindly granting access to the quite incredible bottle collection of the late, great Michael Jackson; Alastair Hook for his encouragement and advice; Laurent Mousson for the Franco-Swiss steers; the incredibly helpful Russ Phillips at www.craftcans.com; Adam 'The Lens' Slate for the Belgian adventure; Stefanie Collins of Beer & Brewer in Australia; Mike Cole in Czech; Japan's Justin Norrie; baby-kissing Shaun O'Sullivan; Sam Houston; Garrett Oliver; the wonderful

British Library – an incredible resource attached to an absurdly overpriced café; James Clay; Cave Direct; the Real Ale Company; Utobeer; Visit Denmark; Visit Flanders; Eurostar; John Humpheys at Shepherd Neame; the guys at Brewdog, Shoreditch; all at Hobo Beer & Co – Cathouse Collins: One Shoe Stu and Hash-house Herb; Google Translate for simultaneously confusing and clarifying communication; and, lest we forget, a very special thank you to the buttons 'C', 'X', 'V' and 'Ctrl' – I love you guys.

Everyone at Jacqui Small Publishing has been an immense help. Enormous gratitude goes to the fabulous Jo Copestick and Jacqui for backing this book from day one; Sian Parkhouse for her patience and gentle 'encouragement'; likewise Lydia Halliday; and a special mention must go to Alexandra Labbe-Thompson whose patience and awesome organisational prowess has been tested more often than was probably necessary. Designer Ashley Western has been fantastic in patiently pulling the words and pictures together while fellow Superhoop, beer historian and phenomenal fount of knowledge Martyn Cornell has been nothing short of incredible in difficult circumstances – if only QPR's strikers had been so 'on the ball'. We'll be back in the big time next year. Probably. Anyway, thanks for all your hard work and help, it's hugely appreciated. It was tricky at times but we all got there in the end.

There are even more of those to thank beyond the world of beer. No one more than Sophie, my wonderful wife to be – your patience, love and laughter got me through the tricky times. Thank you so much for being so lovely – I will make it up to you. I promise. Tom Sandham, the other half of 'Thinking Drinkers', for keeping me sane and juggling all the other bits of the 'business'. You too said this would be painful. It was. Thank God we're not doing another one. Eh? Oh.

My lovely and loving Mum for always being great; Dad & Nicola for your wonderful support, patience and wise words; my brother Barnaby for being the magnificent man that he is. Tom, Hattie, Ned, Esther and Theo Deards for being such incredible friends; Jacques 'Superhoop' Le Bars, Tessa, Alison and Louis; Ania, Mike, Tommy and Alice Gedye; Zosia and Mamusia for the life-saving pierogi and cans of super-strength Polish 'problem solver' and Claire Sandham for her considerable patience.

Now this is finally finished, I'm looking forward to seeing more of the following: Dallat, Sonya, Sophia & Luca; James Wheatley, Fleur, Alexa and Minnie; Eddie & Zoe Gapper; Debbie, Matt & Kit; James Amos, Diane and William; James Shepherd (told you I'd get it done); Catherine, James, Joseph and Thea; Katie, Jack & Loic Simpson; Adela, Toby & Siddi; Sophie & Jamie; Sally Homer and Malachi Bogdanov (erm . . . Hollywood?); Sam, Lee and Bella Baker; Edward and Nikki (I remembered); Sam Deards; Toby Dormer; Tom and Kate Innes and anyone who I have neglected to mention. Drinking more than 500 beers makes a complete mess of one's memory so sincere apologies if I have missed out anyone who I didn't mean to.